D0934324

THE GEOGRAPHY OF INDIA

OF

INDIA

SACRED AND HISTORIC PLACES

UNDERSTANDING INDIA

THE GEOGRAPHY OF INDIA

SACRED AND HISTORIC PLACES

EDITED BY KENNETH PLETCHER, SENIOR EDITOR, GEOGRAPHY AND HISTORY

Britannica®
Educational Publishing

IN ASSOCIATION WITH

ROSEN

Published in 2011 by Britannica Educational Publishing
(a trademark of Encyclopædia Britannica, Inc.)
in association with Rosen Educational Services, LLC
29 East 21st Street, New York, NY 10010.

Distributed exclusively by Rosen Educational Services.
For a listing of additional Britannica Educational Publishing titles, call toll free (800) 237-9932.

First Edition

Britannica Educational Publishing
Michael I. Levy: Executive Editor
J.E. Luebering: Senior Manager
Marilyn L. Barton: Senior Coordinator, Production Control
Steven Bosco: Director, Editorial Technologies
Lisa S. Braucher: Senior Producer and Data Editor
Yvette Charboneau: Senior Copy Editor
Kathy Nakamura: Manager, Media Acquisition
Kenneth Pletcher: Senior Editor, Geography and History

Rosen Educational Services
Alexandra Hanson-Harding: Editor
Nelson Sá: Art Director
Cindy Reiman: Photography Manager
Matthew Cauli: Cover Design, Designer
Introduction by Catherine Vanderhoof

Library of Congress Cataloging-in-Publication Data

The geography of India: sacred and historic places / edited by Kenneth Pletcher.—1st ed.
    p. cm.—(Understanding India)
"In association with Britannica Educational Publishing, Rosen Educational Services."
Includes bibliographical references and index.
ISBN 978-1-61530-142-3 (library binding)
1. India—Geography. 2. Sacred space—India. 3. Historic sites—India. 4. India—History, Local.
I. Pletcher, Kenneth.
DS408.6.G46 2011
915.4—dc22

                                                                            2010008831

Manufactured in the United States of America

On the cover: Houseboat on the Jhelum river, Kashmir, India. *Andrea Pistolesi/Riser/ Getty Images*

On the back cover: The Temple at Khajuraho, India, is a UNESCO World Heritage Site. *© www.istockphoto.com/Keith Molloy*

On pages 21, 44, 64, 94, 114, 139, 161, 181, 198, 230, 260, 290, 323, 341, 357, 359, 364, 366, 368: Thousands gather at Chowpatty Beach in Mumbai to celebrate Ganapati, a festival honouring the elephant-headed god Ganesh. *Sebastian D'Souza/AFP/Getty Images*

CONTENTS

40

47

66

84

104

110

CHAPTER 10: SELECTED NORTHEASTERN INDIAN STATES

214

226

245

268

276

281

214

CHAPTER 10: SELECTED NORTHEASTERN INDIAN STATES

226

245

268

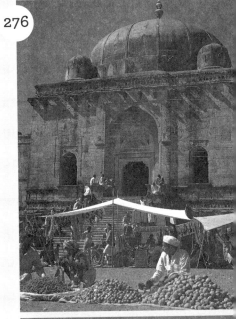

276

281

308

321

331

342

350

352

When many people imagine India, they think of crowded cities full of people, or of arid plains dotted with banyan trees. They might have mental image of crowds of pilgrims immersing themselves in the Ganges River, or the tranquil serenity of the Taj Mahal. India includes all of that and more. This book will explore the many faces of India, from its coastal fishing villages to the highest peaks of the Himalayas.

India is the seventh-largest country in the world by area, encompassing some 1,222,559 square miles (3,166,414 square km). It is roughly triangular in shape, lying primarily within a large peninsula bordered to the west by the Arabian Sea and to the east by the Bay of Bengal. India, along with the neighbouring countries of Bangladesh and Pakistan, is part of a distinct subcontinent, which began colliding with the Asian mainland approximately 50 million years ago. This collision of continental masses formed the Himalayas, the tallest mountain range on Earth, which defines the northern boundary of the Indian subcontinent and effectively isolates it from the rest of Asia. Along this border, India abuts Nepal, Bhutan, and the Tibet Autonomous Region of China). The sixth country bordering India is Myanmar, on India's far eastern edge. India's sovereign territory also includes the union territories of Lakshadweep in the Arabian Sea and the Andaman and Nicobar Islands in the Bay of Bengal.

Within this vast and varied area are a wide diversity of climates and land types. The country's geography is divided into three main geologic regions: the Himalaya ranges in the north; the Indo-Gangetic Plain south of the Himalayas, which extends eastward from northern Pakistan in the west to Assam state in the east; and the peninsular region to the south of the plain, which makes up the majority of the Indian subcontinent. The Indo-Gangetic Plain is formed from an ancient seabed and encompasses the Indus and Ganges river basins with rich soil for farming. On the plain's southwestern edge is found the Thar (or Great Indian) Desert. Peninsular India consists largely of the Deccan uplands in the interior, bordered on the east and west by mountains of the Ghats ranges and, finally, by coastal plains and river deltas along the two coasts.

Almost all of India's area is densely populated, and it is the second-most populous country in the world, after China. Even within the Himalayan range, there are a number of fertile valleys, including the Vale of Kashmir, and only the highest peaks are not habitable. Population patterns within the various areas of the

Street children in Chennai, India, enjoy a day on Marina Beach, one of the longest beaches in the world. Palani Mohan/Edit/Getty Images

country are largely dependent on the availability of water, either from irrigation or rainfall. India provides the world's most classic example of a monsoon climate, meaning that the country has distinct rainy and dry seasons. About three-fourths of India's annual precipitation falls during its wet season, which occurs from June through September. In years when rainfall is plentiful, India enjoys bountiful crop yields. If the monsoons do not bring sufficient rain, however, the nation may experience drought and widespread crop failure.

The amount of rainfall also impacts the types of vegetation found in different sections of the country. About one-quarter of the country is classified as forest, ranging from tropical evergreen and moist deciduous forests to dry deciduous forests and scrubland. Coconut and other varieties of palm trees range along the tropical coasts. Bamboo can be found over much of the country, particularly in the rainy areas. Animal life also ranges from forest-dwelling species such as monkeys, deer, and the Bengal tiger to the lesser pandas, snow leopards, ibex, and wild sheep of the Himalayas. Wild elephants and Indian rhinoceroses are also indigenous to India and are protected in national parks, as are more than 1,200 species of birds including one of the largest breeding colonies of flamingos. Peacocks are also common and are India's official bird.

While relatively young in geological terms, the Indian subcontinent has been the site of some of the oldest and most influential civilizations in human history and is home to several of the world's major religions. It is also home to a significant number of UNESCO World Heritage Sites. One of the best known is the Taj Mahal, the beautiful mausoleum built between 1632 and 1647 by the emperor Shah Jahān to immortalize his beloved wife during the brilliant Muslim Mughal Empire. Many of the other World Heritage Sites date back much earlier, however, and are significant for their importance to Buddhist and Hindu religious heritage as well as for the beauty of their art and architecture. Hinduism dates back in India to at least 1500 BCE. Some of the important sites that honour the Hindu gods include Badrinath, a pilgrimage centre for more than 2,000 years; Elephanta Island, where visitors can enter 8th and 9th century cave temples filled with carvings and sculptures depicting the mythology of the god Shiva; and the temple complex at Khajuraho. Sites important to Buddhism include the Ajanta caves dating from the 1st century BCE to the 7th century CE, which are filled with cave paintings depicting Buddhist legends and divinities, and the town of Bodh Gaya where Gautama Siddhartha attained enlightenment and became the Buddha in the 6th century BCE. Even older are the Bhimbetka rock shelters in Madya Pradesh, with prehistoric cave paintings dating from roughly 10,000 BCE.

Also designated as World Heritage Sites are several wildlife sanctuaries and national parks in India, including the Manas Wildlife Sanctuary, Kaziranga National Park, Keoladeo National Park, Sundarbans National Park, and (designated together) Nanda Devi and Valley of Flowers national parks. In all, India has created 96 national parks and more than 500 wildlife sanctuaries to protect its natural heritage. The first national park in India was Corbett National Park in the foothills of the Himalayas, originally established in 1935 primarily to protect the local tiger population, but also to provide habitat for langurs, sloth bears, mongooses, elephants, and a wide variety of other wildlife. Gir National Park in Gujarat state, on the western coast of India, protects the endangered Asiatic lion and includes a breeding program to repopulate the species. Visitors can go on "Lion Shows" and take guided tours in protected vehicles to see these wild creatures. Elephants are used for transportation in Kanha National Park in Madhya Pradesh state during the monsoon season, and animals from barking deer to langurs can be found there. Jaldapara Wildlife Sanctuary in West Bengal state was established to protect the great Indian rhinoceros. Other wildlife sanctuaries protect wild birds, woodlands, swamps, and other flora and fauna. This book will explore these and many of the other important national parks throughout the various regions of India.

Always a nation of contrasts, India also boasts three of the largest and most densely populated urban areas in the world: Mumbai, Kolkata, and Delhi.

Delhi contains the capital of India and is the most important city of the north-central region. Located in its own national capital territory, it is home to approximately 16 million people. The city is divided into two sections: Old Delhi in the north and New Delhi (the national capital) to the south. Delhi has been an urban centre since at least the first century BCE and was the capital city for many generations of Mughal emperors. It flourished during the period of British rule and also served as the national capital in the later part of that period. The city's neighbourhoods today reflect its history, with narrow winding streets and traditional architecture characterizing Old Delhi and wide avenues and spacious bungalows in the colonial sections. The many flowering trees give people in the hot, dry city shade and beauty. Today, Delhi's economy is based largely on trade, finance, and professional services, as well as on government activities.

Kolkata, formerly known as Calcutta, was the capital of British India from 1772 to 1911, when the capital was moved to Delhi. It is now the largest city in and capital of the West Bengal state in the northeastern part of the country and is one of India's major ports on the Bay of Bengal. With a population slightly smaller than that of Delhi, it is the dominant urban centre of eastern India. Kolkata's climate is subtropical, with high heat and humidity for most of the year and monsoon rains from June to September. Its location along a swampy area near the mouth of the Hugli River has restricted the city's ability to expand, causing a significant housing shortage and overcrowding in many sections of the city. In spite of these circumstances, Kolkata continues to be a major hub of manufacturing as well as trade, although unemployment is high as migrants from even poorer rural areas continue to stream into the city. Kolkata is also important for its rich cultural history and continues as a centre of literature, music, and other artistic pursuits.

Mumbai, formerly Bombay, is the largest city in India by population, with some 12 million inhabitants on an island of about 239 square miles (619 square km) and a regional population of 19 million. In fact, it is one of the largest and most densely populated cities in the world. The city is located on Bombay Island in the Arabian Sea just off the coast of Maharashtra state, of which it is the capital. Mumbai is the economic hub and commercial and financial centre of India as well as an important hub for both air and rail transport. The literacy rate in Mumbai is much higher than that of the country as a whole and the city is home to many educational institutes and colleges. Mumbai's history, like that of all of India, is closely tied to the years of British rule. It was in this city that the Indian National Congress met and in 1942 passed the "Quit India" resolution demanding independence for India from British rule—a goal that was achieved five years later in 1947.

India is divided into 28 states in addition to the Delhi national capital territory and 6 union territories. Punjab province is the homeland of India's Sikh population. Gujarat, which until 1960 was joined together with neighbouring Maharashtra province, has a long history as a trading region. Maharashtra's diverse landscape ranges from the west coast, home of Mumbai, to the high, dry volcanic "traps" in the Western Ghats mountain range. In the south, tiny Goa, on the west coast, was founded by the Portuguese and still has a strong Portuguese influence today. Kerala is famed for its long, beautiful beaches, its renowned Hindu monuments, and its spicy food.

Moving back up north, Uttar Pradesh has been central to the ancient civilization of the Hindus. The great Indian epics of the *Ramayana* and the *Mahabharata* had their origin here. In the foothills of the Himalayas on the east, India's northeastern states include Assam, which is famed for its tea and its beautiful but treacherous landscape. Not only are earthquakes common, but because it is one of the rainiest places in the world (some parts in the east get more than 120 inches [300 mm] a year), flooding can be widespread during the summer monsoon. Another northeastern state, Sikkim, is in a deep basin surrounded on three sides by high mountain walls. One of them, at an elevation of 28,169 feet (8,586 metres) is Kanchenjunga, the third-highest mountain in the world. India is still changing since it was formed as a republic in 1950.

Three states—Chhattisgarh, Jharkhand, and Uttaranchal (since 2007 Uttarakhand) were formed out of other states in 2000.

But the road to independence was not entirely smooth, and it continues to have rough sections today. When the British agreed to leave, British India divided into two nations, India and Pakistan. Pakistan was formed from the primarily Muslim areas of the subcontinent, dividing the former province of Punjab in the northwest between the two countries. The partition also nearly separated the eastern state of Assam from the remainder of India, with Bangladesh (formerly East Pakistan) carved out of the prior province of Bengal. It also led to multiple wars over the region of Kashmir on the far northwestern border and its eventual partition between the two countries as well. The location of Kashmir's northern border with China is also a subject of dispute between those two nations.

Today, India has one of the largest and most highly diversified economies in the world. Its highly educated middle class make India a major centre for technology, trade, and finance and an exporter of skilled labour in high-technology industries and medicine. The cities of Bangalore, Chennai and Hyderabad are among the world's fastest-growing locations for high-tech businesses. However, it is estimated that less than one-fifth of the population is employed in this "organized" sector of the economy. The vast majority of India's workforce is employed in small-scale agriculture, service, commercial, and craft enterprises. On a per capita basis, India remains among the poorest nations.

From its diversity of lands and climates to its people, economy, and cultures, India is a country of contradictions and surprises that is well worth your exploration. Enjoy the journey!

CHAPTER 1

GEOGRAPHIC OVERVIEW

India—officially Republic of India (Hindi: Bharat)—is a country that occupies the greater part of South Asia. It is a constitutional republic consisting of 28 states, each with a substantial degree of control over its own affairs; six less fully empowered union territories; and the Delhi national capital territory, which includes New Delhi, India's capital. With roughly one-sixth of the world's total population, India is the second most populous country, after China, and, in area, it ranks as the seventh-largest country in the world. India's frontier, which is roughly one-third coastline, abuts six countries. It is bounded to the northwest by Pakistan, to the north by Nepal, China, and Bhutan; and to the east by Myanmar (Burma). Bangladesh to the east is surrounded by India to the north, east, and west. The island country of Sri Lanka is situated some 40 miles (65 km) off the southeast coast of India across the Palk Strait and Gulf of Mannar.

The land of India—together with Bangladesh and most of Pakistan—forms a well-defined subcontinent, set off from the rest of Asia by the imposing northern mountain rampart of the Himalayas and by adjoining mountain ranges to the west and east. The most northerly portion of the subcontinent, the Kashmir region, has been in dispute between India and Pakistan since British India was partitioned into the two countries in 1947. Although each country claims sovereignty over Kashmir, for decades the region has been divided administratively between the two; in addition, China administers

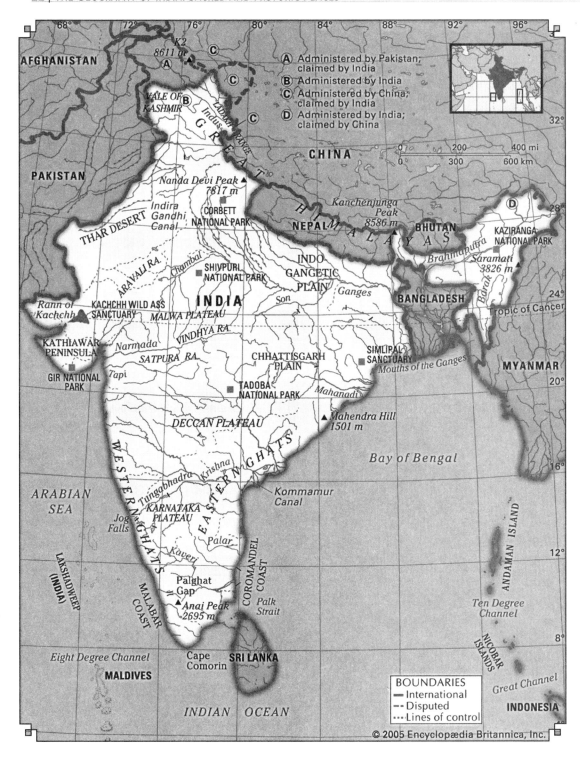

A Administered by Pakistan; claimed by India
B Administered by India
C Administered by China; claimed by India
D Administered by India; claimed by China

BOUNDARIES
— International
-- Disputed
···· Lines of control

© 2005 Encyclopædia Britannica, Inc.

portions of Kashmir territory adjoining its border.

Much of India's territory lies within a large peninsula, surrounded by the Arabian Sea to the west and the Bay of Bengal to the east; Cape Comorin, the southernmost point of the Indian mainland, marks the dividing line between these two bodies of water. Two of India's union territories are composed entirely of islands: Lakshadweep, in the Arabian Sea, and the Andaman and Nicobar Islands, which lie between the Bay of Bengal and the Andaman Sea.

RELIEF

It is now generally accepted that India's geographic position, continental outline, and basic geologic structure resulted from a process of plate tectonics—the shifting of enormous, rigid crustal plates over the Earth's underlying layer of molten material. India's landmass, which forms the northwestern portion of the Indian-Australian Plate, began to drift slowly northward toward the much larger Eurasian Plate several hundred million years ago (after the former broke away from the ancient southern-hemispheric supercontinent known as Gondwana, or Gondwanaland). When the two finally collided (approximately 50 million years ago), the northern edge of the Indian-Australian Plate was thrust under the Eurasian Plate at a low angle. The collision reduced the speed of the oncoming plate, but the underthrusting, or subduction, of the plate has continued into contemporary times.

The effects of the collision and continued subduction are numerous and extremely complicated. An important consequence, however, was the slicing off of crustal rock from the top of the underthrusting plate. These slices were thrown back onto the northern edge of the Indian landmass and came to form much of the Himalayan mountain system. The new mountains—together with vast amounts of sediment eroded from them—were so heavy that the Indian-Australian Plate just south of the range was forced downward, creating a zone of crustal subsidence. Continued rapid erosion of the Himalayas added to the sediment accumulation, which was subsequently carried by mountain streams to fill the subsidence zone and cause it to sink more.

India's present-day relief features have been superimposed on three basic structural units: the Himalayas in the north, the Deccan (plateau region) in the south, and the Indo-Gangetic Plain (lying over the subsidence zone) between the two.

THE HIMALAYAS

The Himalayas (from the Sanskrit words *hima*, "snow," and *alaya*, "abode"), the loftiest mountain system in the world, form the northern limit of India. This great, geologically young mountain arc is about 1,550 miles (2,500 km) long, stretching from the peak of Nanga Parbat (26,660 feet [8,126 metres]) in Pakistan-administered Kashmir to the Namcha Barwa peak in the Tibet Autonomous Region of China. Between these extremes the mountains fall across India, southern Tibet, Nepal, and Bhutan. The width of the system varies between 125 and 250 miles (200 and 400 km).

Within India the Himalayas are divided into three longitudinal belts, called the Outer, Lesser, and Great Himalayas. At each extremity there is a great bend in the system's alignment, from which a number of lower mountain ranges and hills spread out. Those in the west lie wholly within Pakistan and Afghanistan, while those to the east straddle India's border with Myanmar (Burma). North of the Himalayas are the Plateau of Tibet and various Trans-Himalayan ranges, only a small part of which, in the Ladakh region of Jammu and Kashmir state, are within the territorial limits of India.

Because of the continued subduction of the Indian peninsula against the Eurasian Plate, the Himalayas and the associated eastern ranges remain tectonically active. As a result, the mountains are still rising, and earthquakes—often accompanied by landslides—are common. Several since 1900 have been devastating, including one in 1934 in what is now Bihar state that killed more than 10,000 persons. In 2001 another tremor, farther from the mountains, in Gujarat state, was less powerful but caused extensive damage, taking the lives of more than 20,000 people and leaving more than 500,000 homeless. The relatively high frequency and wide distribution of earthquakes likewise have generated controversies about the safety and advisability of several hydroelectric and irrigation projects.

THE OUTER HIMALAYAS (THE SHIWALIK RANGE)

The southernmost of the three mountain belts are the Outer Himalayas, also called the Shiwalik Range. Crests in the Shiwaliks, averaging from 3,000 to 5,000 feet (900 to 1,500 metres) in elevation, seldom exceed 6,500 feet (2,000 metres). The range narrows as it moves east and is hardly discernible beyond the Duars, a plains region in West Bengal state. Interspersed in the Shiwaliks are heavily cultivated flat valleys (*duns*) with a high population density. To the south of the range is the Indo-Gangetic Plain. Weakly indurated, largely deforested, and subject to heavy rain and intense erosion, the Shiwaliks provide much of the sediment transported onto the plain.

THE LESSER HIMALAYAS

To the north of the Shiwaliks and separated from them by a fault zone, the Lesser Himalayas (also called the Lower or Middle Himalayas) rise to heights ranging from 11,900 to 15,100 feet (3,600 to 4,600 metres). Their ancient name is Himachal (Sanskrit: *hima*, "snow," and *acal*, "mountain"). These mountains are composed of both ancient crystalline and geologically young rocks, sometimes in a reversed stratigraphic sequence because of thrust faulting. The Lesser Himalayas are traversed by numerous deep gorges formed by swift-flowing streams (some of them older than the mountains themselves), which are fed by glaciers and snowfields to the north.

THE GREAT HIMALAYAS

The northernmost Great, or Higher, Himalayas (in ancient times, the Himadri), with crests generally above 16,000 feet (4,900 metres) in elevation, are composed of ancient crystalline rocks and old marine sedimentary formations. Between the Great and Lesser Himalayas are several fertile longitudinal vales; in India the largest is the Vale of Kashmir, an ancient lake basin with an area of about 1,700 square miles (4,400 square km). The Great Himalayas, ranging from 30 to 45 miles (50 to 75 km) wide, include some of the world's highest peaks. The highest, Mount Everest (at 29,035 feet [8,850 metres]), is on the China-Nepal border, but India also has many lofty peaks, such as Kanchenjunga (28,169 feet [8,586 metres]) on the border of Nepal and the state of Sikkim and Nanda Devi (25,646 feet [7,817 metres]), Kamet (25,446 feet [7,755 metres]), and Trisul (23,359 feet [7,120]) in Uttaranchal. The Great Himalayas lie mostly above the line of perpetual snow and thus contain most of the Himalayan glaciers.

ASSOCIATED RANGES AND HILLS

In general, the various regional ranges and hills run parallel to the Himalayas'

Barren mountains of Ladakh, Jammu and Kashmir state, India. Courtesy of Iffat Fatima

main axis. These are especially prominent in the northwest, where the Zaskar Range and the Ladakh and Karakoram ranges, all in Jammu and Kashmir state, run to the northeast of the Great Himalayas. Also in Jammu and Kashmir is the Pir Panjal Range, which, extending along the southwest of the Great Himalayas, forms the western and southern flanks of the Vale of Kashmir.

At its eastern extremity, the Himalayas give way to a number of smaller ranges running northeast-southwest—including the heavily forested Patkai Range and the Naga and Mizo hills—which extend along India's borders with Myanmar and the southeastern panhandle of Bangladesh. Within the Naga Hills, the reedy Logtak Lake, in the Manipur River valley, is an important feature. Branching off from these hills to the northwest are the Mikir Hills, and to the west are the Jaintia, Khasi, and Garo hills, which run just north of India's border with Bangladesh. Collectively, the latter group is also designated as the Shillong (Meghalaya) Plateau.

THE INDO-GANGETIC PLAIN

The second great structural component of India, the Indo-Gangetic Plain (also called the North Indian Plain), lies between the Himalayas and the Deccan. The plain occupies the Himalayan foredeep, formerly a seabed but now filled with river-borne alluvium to depths of up to 6,000 feet (1,800 metres). The plain stretches from the Pakistani provinces of Sind and Punjab in the west, where it is watered by the Indus River and its tributaries, eastward to the Brahmaputra River valley in Assam state.

The Ganges (Ganga) River basin (mainly in Uttar Pradesh and Bihar states) forms the central and principal part of this plain. The eastern portion is made up of the combined delta of the Ganges and Brahmaputra rivers, which, though mainly in Bangladesh, also occupies a part of the adjacent Indian state of West Bengal. This deltaic area is characterized by annual flooding attributed to intense monsoon rainfall, an exceedingly gentle gradient, and an enormous discharge that the alluvium-choked rivers cannot contain within their channels. The Indus River basin, extending west from Delhi, forms the western part of the plain; the Indian portion is mainly in the states of Haryana and Punjab.

The overall gradient of the plain is virtually imperceptible, averaging only about 6 inches per mile (95 mm per km) in the Ganges basin and slightly more along the Indus and Brahmaputra. Even so, to those who till its soils, there is an important distinction between *bhangar*—the slightly elevated, terraced land of older alluvium—and *khadar*, the more fertile fresh alluvium on the low-lying floodplain. In general, the ratio of *bhangar* areas to those of *khadar* increases upstream along all major rivers. An exception to the largely monotonous relief is encountered in the southwestern portion of the plain, where there are gullied badlands centring on the Chambal River. That area has long been famous for harbouring violent gangs of criminals called *dacoits*, who find shelter in its many hidden ravines.

The Great Indian, or Thar, Desert, forms an important southern extension of the Indo-Gangetic Plain. It is mostly in India but also extends into Pakistan and is mainly an area of gently undulating terrain, and within it are several areas dominated by shifting sand dunes and numerous isolated hills. The latter provide visible evidence of the fact that the thin surface deposits of the region, partially alluvial and partially wind-borne, are underlain by the much older Indian-Australian Plate, of which the hills are structurally a part.

THE DECCAN

The remainder of India is designated, not altogether accurately, as either the Deccan plateau or peninsular India. It is actually a topographically variegated region that extends well beyond the peninsula—that portion of the country lying between the Arabian Sea and the Bay of Bengal—and includes a substantial area to the north of the Vindhya Range, which has popularly been regarded as the divide between Hindustan (northern India) and the Deccan (from Sanskrit *dakshina*, "south").

Having once constituted a segment of the ancient continent of Gondwana, this land is the oldest and most stable in India. The plateau is mainly between 1,000 and 2,500 feet (300 to 750 metres) above sea level, and its general slope descends toward the east. A number of the hill ranges of the Deccan have been eroded and rejuvenated several times, and only their remaining summits testify to their geologic past. The main peninsular block is composed of gneiss, granite-gneiss, schists, and granites, as well as of more geologically recent basaltic lava flows.

THE WESTERN GHATS

The Western Ghats, also called the Sahyadri, are a north-south chain of mountains or hills that mark the western edge of the Deccan plateau region. They rise abruptly from the coastal plain as an escarpment of variable height, but their eastern slopes are much more gentle. The Western Ghats contain a series of residual plateaus and peaks separated by saddles and passes. The hill station (resort) of Mahabaleshwar, located on a laterite plateau, is one of the highest elevations in the northern half, rising to 4,700 feet (1,430 metres). The chain attains greater heights in the south, where the mountains terminate in several uplifted blocks bordered by steep slopes on all sides. These include the Nilgiri Hills, with their highest peak, Doda Betta (8,652 feet [2,637 metres]); and the Anaimalai, Palni, and Cardamom hills, all three of which radiate from the highest peak in the Western Ghats, Anai Peak (Anai Mudi, 8,842 feet [2,695 metres]). The Western Ghats receive heavy rainfall, and several major rivers—most notably the Krishna (Kistna) and the two holy rivers, the Godavari and the Kaveri (Cauvery)—have their headwaters there.

THE EASTERN GHATS

The Eastern Ghats are a series of discontinuous low ranges running generally northeast-southwest parallel to the coast of the Bay of Bengal. The largest single sector—the remnant of an ancient mountain range that eroded and subsequently rejuvenated—is found in the Dandakaranya region between the Mahanadi and Godavari rivers. This narrow range has a central ridge, the highest peak of which is Arma Konda (5,512 feet [1,680 metres]) in Andhra Pradesh state. The hills become subdued farther southwest, where they are traversed by the Godavari River through a gorge 40 miles (65 km) long. Still farther southwest, beyond the Krishna River, the Eastern Ghats appear as a series of low ranges and hills, including the Erramala, Nallamala, Velikonda, and Palkonda. Southwest of the city of Chennai (Madras), the Eastern Ghats continue as the Javadi and Shevaroy hills, beyond which they merge with the Western Ghats.

INLAND REGIONS

The northernmost portion of the Deccan may be termed the peninsular foreland. This large, ill-defined area lies between the peninsula proper to the south (roughly demarcated by the Vindhya Range) and the Indo-Gangetic Plain and the Great Indian Desert (beyond the Aravali Range) to the north.

The Aravali Range runs southwest-northeast for more than 450 miles (725 km) from a highland node near Ahmedabad, Gujarat, northeast to Delhi. These mountains are composed of ancient rocks and are divided into several parts, in one of which lies Sambhar Salt Lake. Their highest summit is Guru Peak (5,650 feet [1,722 metres]), on Mount Abu. The Aravalis form a divide between the west-flowing streams, draining into the desert or the Rann of Kachchh (Kutch), and the Chambal and its tributaries within the Ganges River catchment area.

Between the Aravalis and the Vindhya Range lies the fertile, basaltic Malwa Plateau. This plateau gradually rises southward toward the so-called Vindhya Range, which is actually a south-facing escarpment deeply eroded by short streams flowing into the valley of the Narmada River below. The escarpment appears from the south as an imposing range of mountains. The Narmada valley forms the western and principal portion of the Narmada-Son trough, a continuous depression running southwest-northeast, mostly at the base of the Vindhya Range, for about 750 miles (1,200 km).

To the east of the peninsular foreland lies the mineral-rich Chota Nagpur Plateau (mostly within Jharkhand, northwestern Orissa, and Chhattisgarh states). This is a region of numerous scarps separating areas of rolling terrain. To the southwest of the Chota Nagpur Plateau is the Chhattisgarh Plain, centred in Chhattisgarh on the upper course of the Mahanadi River.

Most of the inland area south of the peninsular foreland and the Chota Nagpur Plateau is characterized by rolling terrain and generally low relief, within which a number of hill ranges, some of them mesalike formations, run in various directions. Occupying much of the northwestern portion of the peninsula (most of Maharashtra and some bordering areas of Madhya Pradesh, Andhra Pradesh, and Karnataka) is the Deccan lava plateau. The mesa-like features are especially characteristic of this large, fertile area, which is cut across by the Satpura, Ajanta, and Balaghat ranges.

COASTAL AREAS

Most of the coast of India flanks the Eastern and Western Ghats. In the northwest, however, much of coastal Gujarat lies to the northwest of the Western Ghats, extending around the Gulf of Khambhat (Cambay) and into the salt marshes of the Kathiawar and Kachchh (Kutch) peninsulas. These tidal marshes include the Great Rann of Kachchh along the border with Pakistan and the Little Rann of Kachchh between the two peninsulas. Because the level of these marshes rises markedly during the rainy season, the Kachchh Peninsula normally becomes an island for several months each year.

The area farther south, especially the stretch from Daman to Goa (known as the Konkan coast), is indented with rias (flooded valleys) extending inland into narrow riverine plains. These plains are dominated by low-level lateritic plateaus and are marked by alternating headlands and bays, the latter often sheltering crescent-shaped beaches. From Goa south to Cape Comorin (the southernmost tip of India) is the Malabar coastal plain, which was formed by the deposition of sediment along the shoreline. This plain, varying between 15 and 60 miles (25 to 100 km) wide, is characterized by lagoons and brackish, navigable backwater channels.

The predominantly deltaic eastern coastal plain is an area of deep sedimentation. Over most of its length it is considerably wider than the plain on the western coast. The major deltas, from south to north, are of the Kaveri, the Krishna-Godavari, the Mahanadi, and the Ganges-Brahmaputra rivers. The last of these is some 190 miles (300 km) wide, but only about one-third of it lies within India. Traversed by innumerable distributaries, the Ganges delta is an ill-drained region, and the western part within Indian territory has become moribund because of shifts in the channels of the Ganges. Tidal incursions extend far inland, and any small temporary rise in sea level could submerge Kolkata (Calcutta), located about 95 miles (155 km) from the head of the Bay of Bengal. The eastern coastal plain includes several lagoons, the largest of which, Pulicat and Chilika (Chilka) lakes, have resulted from sediment being deposited along the shoreline.

ISLANDS

Several archipelagoes in the Indian Ocean are politically a part of India. The union territory of Lakshadweep is a group of small coral atolls in the Arabian Sea to the west of the Malabar Coast. Far off the eastern coast, separating the Bay of Bengal and the Andaman Sea, lie the considerably larger and hillier chains of the Andaman and Nicobar Islands, also a union territory; the Andamans are closer to Myanmar and the Nicobars closer to Indonesia than to the Indian mainland.

DRAINAGE

More than 70 percent of India's territory drains into the Bay of Bengal via the Ganges-Brahmaputra river system and a number of large and small peninsular rivers. Areas draining into the Arabian Sea, accounting for about 20 percent of the total, lie partially within the Indus drainage basin (in northwestern India) and partially within a completely separate set of drainage basins well to the south (in Gujarat, western Madhya Pradesh, northern Maharashtra, and areas west of the Western Ghats). Most of the remaining area, less than 10 percent of the total, lies in regions of interior drainage, notably in the Great Indian Desert of Rajasthan state (another is in the Aksai Chin, a barren plateau in a portion of Kashmir administered by China but claimed by India). Finally, less than 1 percent of India's area, along the border with Myanmar, drains into the Andaman Sea via tributaries of the Irrawaddy River.

DRAINAGE INTO THE BAY OF BENGAL

The bulk of India's waters draining into the Bay of Bengal come from the extensive Ganges and Brahmaputra river system and its tributaries. This vast combined drainage system alone accounts for about one-third of India's total water discharge.

THE GANGES-BRAHMAPUTRA RIVER SYSTEM

The Ganges (Ganga), considered sacred by the country's Hindu population, is 1,560 miles (2,510 km) long. Although its deltaic portion lies mostly in Bangladesh, the course of the Ganges within India is longer than that of any of the country's other rivers. It has numerous headstreams that are fed by runoff and meltwater from Himalayan glaciers and mountain peaks. The main headwater, the Bhagirathi River, rises at an elevation of about 10,000 feet (3,000 metres) at the foot of the Gangotri Glacier, considered sacred by Hindus.

The Ganges enters the Indo-Gangetic Plain at the city of Haridwar (Hardwar). From Haridwar to Kolkata it is joined by numerous tributaries. Proceeding from west to east, the Ghaghara, Gandak, and Kosi rivers, all of which emerge from the Himalayas, join the Ganges from the north, while the Yamuna and Son are the two most important tributaries from the south. The Yamuna, which also has a Himalayan source (the Yamunotri glacier) and flows roughly parallel to the Ganges throughout its length, receives the flow of several important rivers, including the Chambal, Betwa, and Ken, which originate in India's peninsular foreland. Of the northern tributaries of the Ganges, the Kosi, India's most destructive river (referred to as the "Sorrow of Bihar"), warrants special mention. Because of its large catchment in the Himalayas of Nepal and its gentle gradient once it reaches the plain, the Kosi is unable to discharge the large volume of water it carries at its peak flows, and it frequently floods and changes its course.

The seasonal flows of the Ganges and other rivers fed by meltwaters from the Himalayas vary considerably less than those of the exclusively rain-fed peninsular rivers. This consistency of flow enhances their suitability for irrigation and—where the diversion of water for irrigation is not excessive—for navigation as well.

Although the total length of the Brahmaputra (about 1,800 miles [2,900 km]) exceeds that of the Ganges, only 450 miles (725 km) of its course lies within India. The Brahmaputra, like the Indus, has its source in a trans-Himalayan area about 60 miles (100 km) southeast of Mapam Lake in the Tibet Autonomous Region of China. The river runs east across Tibet for more than half its total length before cutting into India at the northern border of Arunachal Pradesh. It then flows south and west through the state of Assam and south into Bangladesh, where it empties into the vast Ganges-Brahmaputra delta. The narrow Brahmaputra basin in Assam is prone to flooding because of its large catchment areas, parts of which experience exceedingly heavy precipitation.

PENINSULAR RIVERS

The peninsular drainage into the Bay of Bengal includes a number of major rivers, most notably the Mahanadi, Godavari, Krishna, and Kaveri. Except for the Mahanadi, the headwaters of these rivers are in the high-rainfall zones of the Western Ghats, and they traverse the entire width of the plateau (generally from northwest to southeast) before reaching the Bay of Bengal. The Mahanadi has its source at the southern edge of the Chhattisgarh Plain.

India's peninsular rivers have relatively steep gradients and thus rarely give rise to floods of the type that occur in the plains of northern India, despite considerable variations in flow from the dry to wet seasons. The lower courses of a number of these rivers are marked by rapids and gorges, usually as they cross the Eastern Ghats. Because of their steep gradients, rocky underlying terrain, and variable flow regimes, the peninsular rivers are not navigable.

DRAINAGE INTO THE ARABIAN SEA

A substantial part of northwestern India is included in the Indus drainage basin, which India shares with China, Afghanistan, and Pakistan. The Indus and its longest tributary, the Sutlej, both rise in the trans-Himalayan region of Tibet. The Indus initially flows to the northwest between towering mountain ranges and through Jammu and Kashmir state before entering the Pakistani-administered portion of Kashmir. It then travels generally to the southwest through Pakistan until it reaches the Arabian Sea. The Sutlej also flows northwest from its source but enters India farther south, at the border of Himachal Pradesh. From there it travels west into the Indian state of Punjab and eventually enters Pakistan, where it flows into the Indus.

Between the Indus and the Sutlej lie several other major Indus tributaries. The Jhelum, the northernmost of these rivers, flows out of the Pir Panjal Range into the Vale of Kashmir and thence via Baramula Gorge into Pakistani-administered Kashmir. The three others—the Chenab, Ravi, and Beas—originate in the Himalayas within the Indian state of Himachal Pradesh. The Chenab travels across Jammu and Kashmir state before flowing into Pakistan; the Ravi forms a part of the southern boundary between Jammu and Kashmir and Himachal Pradesh states and thereafter a short stretch of the India-Pakistan border prior to entering Pakistan; and the Beas flows entirely within India, joining the Sutlej in the Indian state of Punjab. The area through which the five Indus tributaries flow has traditionally been called the Punjab (from Persian *panj*, "five," and *āb*, "water"). That area currently falls in the Indian state of Punjab (containing the Sutlej and the Beas) and the Pakistani province of Punjab. Despite low rainfall in the Punjab plains, the moderately high runoff from the Himalayas ensures a year-round flow in the Indus and its tributaries, which are extensively utilized for canal irrigation.

Farther to the south, another notable river flowing into the Arabian Sea is the Luni of southern Rajasthan, which in most years has carried enough water to reach the Great Rann of Kachchh in western Gujarat. Also flowing through Gujarat is the Mahi River, as well as the two most important west-flowing rivers of peninsular India—the Narmada (drainage basin 38,200 square miles [98,900 square km]) and Tapi (Tapti; 25,000 square miles [65,000 square km]). The Narmada and its basin are undergoing large-scale multipurpose development. Most of the other peninsular rivers draining into the Arabian Sea have short courses, and those that flow westward from headwaters in the Western Ghats have seasonally torrential flows.

LAKES AND INLAND DRAINAGE

For such a large country, India has few natural lakes. Most of the lakes in the Himalayas were formed when glaciers either dug out a basin or dammed an area with earth and rocks. Wular Lake in Jammu and Kashmir, by contrast, is the result of a tectonic depression. Although its area fluctuates, Wular Lake is the largest natural freshwater lake in India.

Inland drainage in India is mainly ephemeral and almost entirely in the arid and semiarid part of northwestern India, particularly in the Great Indian Desert

Resort house on Wular Lake in the Vale of Kashmir, Jammu and Kashmir state, India. D. Chawda-Keystone

of Rajasthan, where there are several ephemeral salt lakes—most prominently Sambhar Salt Lake, the largest lake in India. These lakes are fed by short, intermittent streams, which experience flash floods during occasional intense rains and become dry and lose their identity once the rains are over. The water in the lakes also evaporates and subsequently leaves a layer of white saline soils, from which a considerable amount of salt is commercially produced. Many of India's largest lakes are reservoirs formed by damming rivers.

SOILS

There is a wide range of soil types in India. As products of natural environmental processes, these can be broadly divided into two groups: in situ soils and transported soils.

IN SITU SOILS

The in situ soils get their distinguishing features from the parent rocks, which are sieved by flowing water, sliding glaciers, and drifting wind and are deposited on landforms such as river valleys and coastal plains. The process of sieving such soils has led to deposition of materials in layers without any marked pedologic horizons, though it has altered the original chemical composition of the in situ soils.

Among the in situ soils are the red-to-yellow (including laterite) and black soils known locally as *regur*. After these the alluvial soil is the third most common type. Also significant are the desert soils of Rajasthan, the saline soils in Gujarat, southern Rajasthan, and some coastal areas, and the mountain soils of the Himalayas. The type of soil is determined by numerous factors, including climate, relief, elevation, and drainage, as well as by the composition of the underlying rock material.

RED-TO-YELLOW SOILS

These soils are encountered over extensive nonalluvial tracts of peninsular India and are made up of such acidic rocks as granite, gneiss, and schist. They develop in areas in which rainfall leaches soluble minerals out of the ground and results in a loss of chemically basic constituents; a corresponding proportional increase in oxidized iron imparts a reddish hue to many such soils. Hence these are commonly described as ferralitic soils. In extreme cases, the concentration of oxides of iron leads to formation of a hard crust, in which case they are described as lateritic (for *later*,

the Latin term meaning "brick") soils. The heavily leached red-to-yellow soils are concentrated in the high-rainfall areas of the Western Ghats, the western Kathiawar Peninsula, eastern Rajasthan, the Eastern Ghats, the Chota Nagpur Plateau, and other upland tracts of northeastern India. Less-leached red-to-yellow soils occur in areas of low rainfall immediately east of the Western Ghats in the dry interior of the Deccan. Red-to-yellow soils are usually infertile, but this problem is partly ameliorated in forested tracts, where humus concentration and the recycling of nutrients help restore fertility in the topsoil.

BLACK SOILS

Among the in situ soils of India, the black soils found in the lava-covered areas are the most conspicuous. These soils are often referred to as *regur* but are popularly known as "black cotton soils," since cotton has been the most common traditional crop in areas where they are found. Black soils are derivatives of trap lava and are spread mostly across interior Gujarat, Maharashtra, Karnataka, and Madhya Pradesh on the Deccan lava plateau and the Malwa Plateau, where there is both moderate rainfall and underlying basaltic rock. Because of their high clay content, black soils develop wide cracks during the dry season, but their iron-rich granular structure makes them resistant to wind and water erosion. They are poor in humus yet highly moisture-retentive, thus responding well to irrigation. These soils are also found on many peripheral tracts where the underlying basalt has been shifted from its original location by fluvial processes. The sifting has only led to an increased concentration of clastic contents.

ALLUVIAL SOILS

Alluvial soils are widespread. They occur throughout the Indo-Gangetic Plain and along the lower courses of virtually all the country's major rivers (especially the deltas along the east coast). The nondeltaic plains along India's coasts are also marked by narrow ribbons of alluvium.

New alluvium found on much of the Indo-Gangetic floodplain is called *khadar* and is extremely fertile and uniform in texture; conversely, the old alluvium on the slightly elevated terraces, termed *bhangar*, carries patches of alkaline efflorescences, called *usar*, rendering some areas infertile. In the Ganges basin, sandy aquifers holding an enormous reserve of groundwater ensure irrigation and help make the plain the most agriculturally productive region of the country.

CLIMATE

India provides the world's most pronounced example of a monsoon climate. The wet and dry seasons of the monsoon system, along with the annual temperature fluctuations, produce three general climatic periods over much of the country: (1) hot, wet weather from about mid-June to the end of September, (2) cool, dry weather from early October to February, and (3) hot, dry weather (though normally with high atmospheric humidity) from about March to mid-June. The actual duration of these periods may vary by several weeks, not only from one part of India to another but also from year to year. Regional differences, which are often considerable, result from a number of internal factors—including elevation, type of relief, and proximity to bodies of water.

THE MONSOONS

A monsoon system is characterized by a seasonal reversal of prevailing wind directions and by alternating wet and dry seasons. In India the wet season, called the southwest monsoon, occurs from about mid-June to early October, when winds from the Indian Ocean carry moisture-laden air across the subcontinent, causing heavy rainfall and often considerable flooding. Usually about three-fourths of the country's total annual precipitation falls during those months. During the driest months (called the retreating monsoon), especially from November through February, this pattern is reversed, as dry air from the Asian interior moves across India toward the ocean. October and March through May, by contrast, are typically periods of desultory breezes with no strong prevailing patterns.

The Southwest Monsoon

Although the winds of the rainy season are called the southwest monsoon, they actually follow two generally distinct branches, one initially flowing eastward from the Arabian Sea and the other northward from the Bay of Bengal. The former begins by lashing the west coast of peninsular India and rising over the adjacent Western Ghats. When crossing these mountains, the air cools (thus losing its moisture-bearing capacity) and deposits rain copiously on the windward side of that highland barrier. Annual precipitation in parts of this region exceeds 100 inches (2,540 mm) and is as high as 245 inches (6,250 mm) at Mahabaleshwar on the crest of the Western Ghats. Conversely, as the winds descend on the leeward side of the Western Ghats, the air's moisture-bearing capacity increases and the resultant rain shadow makes for a belt of semiarid terrain, much of it with less than 25 inches (635 mm) of precipitation per year.

The Bay of Bengal branch of the monsoon sweeps across eastern India and Bangladesh and, in several areas, gives rise to rainfall in much the same way as occurs along the Western Ghats. The effect is particularly pronounced in the Shillong (Meghalaya) Plateau, where at Cherrapunji the average annual rainfall is 450 inches (11,430 mm), one of the heaviest in the world. The Brahmaputra valley to the north also experiences a rain-shadow effect; the problem is mitigated, however, by the adjacent Himalayas, which cause the winds to rise again, thereby establishing a parallel belt of heavy precipitation. Blocked by the Himalayas, the Bay of Bengal branch of the monsoon is diverted westward up the Gangetic Plain, reaching Punjab only in the first week of July.

In the Gangetic Plain the two branches merge into one. By the time they reach the Punjab their moisture is largely spent. The gradual reduction in the amount of rainfall toward the west is evidenced by the decline from 64 inches (1,625 mm) at Kolkata to 26 inches (660 mm) at Delhi and to desert conditions still farther west. Over the northeastern portion of peninsular India, the two branches also intermittently collide, creating weak weather fronts with sufficient rainfall to produce patches of fairly high precipitation (more than 60 inches [1,520 mm]) in the Chota Nagpur Plateau.

Rainfall During the Retreating Monsoon

Much of India experiences infrequent and relatively feeble precipitation during the retreating monsoon. An exception to this rule occurs along the southeastern coast of India and for some distance inland. When the retreating monsoon blows from the northeast across the Bay of Bengal, it picks up a significant amount of moisture, which is subsequently released after moving back onto the peninsula. Thus, from October to December the coast of Tamil Nadu state receives at least half of its roughly 40 inches (1,000 mm) of annual precipitation. This rainy extension of the generally dry retreating monsoon is called the northeast, or winter, monsoon.

Another type of winter precipitation occurs in northern India, which receives weak cyclonic storms originating in the Mediterranean basin. In the Himalayas these storms bring weeks of drizzling rain and cloudiness and are followed by waves of cold temperatures and snowfall. The state of Jammu and Kashmir in particular receives much of its precipitation from these storms.

TROPICAL CYCLONES

Fierce tropical cyclones occur in India during what may be called the premonsoon, early monsoon, or postmonsoon periods. Originating in both the Bay of Bengal and the Arabian Sea, tropical cyclones often attain velocities of more than 100 miles (160 km) per hour and are notorious for causing intense rain and storm tides (surges) as they cross the coast of India. The Andhra Pradesh, Orissa, and West Bengal coasts are especially susceptible to such storms.

IMPORTANCE TO AGRICULTURE

Monsoons play a pivotal role in Indian agriculture, and the substantial year-to-year variability of rainfall, in both timing and quantity, introduces much uncertainty in the country's crop yield. Good years bring bumper crops, but years of poor rain may result in total crop failure over large areas, especially where irrigation is lacking. Large-scale flooding can also cause damage to crops. As a general rule, the higher an area's average annual precipitation, the more dependable its rainfall, but few areas of India have an average precipitation high enough to be free from the possibility of occasional drought and consequent crop failure.

TEMPERATURES

Temperatures in India generally are the warmest in May or June, just prior to the cooling downpours of the southwest monsoon. A secondary maximum often occurs in September or October when precipitation wanes. The temperature range tends to be significantly less along the coastal plains than in interior locations. The range also tends to increase with latitude. Near India's southern extremity the seasonal range is no more than a few degrees; for example, at Thiruvananthapuram (Trivandrum), in Kerala, there is an average fluctuation of just 4.3 °F (2.4 °C) around an annual mean temperature of 81 °F (27 °C). In the northwest, however, the range is much greater, as, for example, at Ambala, in Haryana, where the temperature fluctuates from 56 °F (13 °C) in January to 92 °F (33 °C) in June. Temperatures are also moderated wherever elevations are significant, and many Himalayan resort towns, called hill stations (a legacy of British colonial rule), afford welcome relief from India's sometimes oppressive heat.

PLANT AND ANIMAL LIFE

The great ecological diversity of India is matched by equally varied flora and fauna. However, the flora of India largely reflect the country's distribution of rainfall.

VEGETATION

Tropical broad-leaved evergreen and mixed, partially evergreen forests grow in areas with high precipitation; in successively less rainy areas are found moist and dry deciduous forests, scrub jungle, grassland, and desert vegetation. Coniferous forests are confined to the Himalayas. There are about 17,000 species of flowering plants in the country. The subcontinent's physical isolation, caused by its relief and climatic barriers, has resulted in a considerable number of endemic flora.

Roughly one-fourth of the country is forested. However, beginning in the late 20th century, forest depletion accelerated considerably to make room for more agriculture and urban-industrial development. This has taken its toll on many Indian plant species. About 20 species of higher-order plants are believed to have become extinct, and already some 1,300 species are considered to be endangered.

Tropical evergreen and mixed evergreen-deciduous forests generally occupy areas with more than 80 inches (2,000 mm) of rainfall per year, mainly in upper Assam, the Western Ghats (especially in Kerala), parts of Orissa, and the Andaman and Nicobar Islands. Common trees in these tall multistoried forests include species of *Mesua, Toona ciliata, Hopea*, and *Eugenia*, as well as *gurjun* (*Dipterocarpus turbinatus*), which grows to over 165 feet (50 metres) on the Andaman Islands and in Assam. The mixed evergreen-deciduous forests of Kerala and the Bengal Himalayas have a large variety of commercially valuable hardwood trees, of which *Lagerstroemia lanceolata*, East Indian, or Malabar, *kino* (*Pterocarpus marsupium*), and rosewood (*Dalbergia latifolia*) are well known.

Tropical moist deciduous forests generally occur in areas with 60 to 80 inches (1,500 to 2,000 mm) of rainfall, such as the northern part of the Eastern Ghats, east-central India, and western Karnataka. Dry deciduous forests, which grow in places receiving less than 60 inches (1,500 mm) of precipitation, characterize the subhumid and semiarid regions of Gujarat, Madhya Pradesh, eastern Rajasthan, central Andhra Pradesh, and western Tamil Nadu. Teak, *sal* (*Shorea robusta*), axle-wood (*Anogeissus latifolia*), *tendu*, *ain*, and *Adina cardifolia* are some of the major deciduous species.

Tropical thorn forests occupy areas in various parts of the country, though mainly in the northern Gangetic Plain and southern peninsular India. These forests generally grow in areas with less than 24 inches (600 mm) of rain but are also found in more humid areas, where deciduous forests have been degraded because of unregulated grazing, felling, and shifting agriculture. In those areas, such xerophytic (drought-tolerant) trees as species of acacia (babul and catechu) and *Butea monosperma* predominate.

The important commercial species include teak and *sal*. Teak, the foremost timber species, is largely confined to the peninsula. During the period of British rule, it was used extensively in shipbuilding, and certain forests were therefore reserved as teak plantations. *Sal* is confined to the lower Himalayas, Uttar Pradesh, Bihar, Jharkhand, Chhattisgarh, Assam, and Madhya Pradesh. Other species with commercial uses are sandalwood (*Santalum album*), the fragrant wood that is perhaps the most precious in the world, and rosewood, an evergreen used for carving and furniture.

Many other species are noteworthy, some because of special ecological niches they occupy. Deltaic areas, for example, are fringed with mangrove forests, in which the dominant species—called *sundri* or *sundari* (*Heritiera fomes*), which is not, properly speaking, a mangrove—is characterized by respiratory roots that emerge from the tidal water. Conspicuous features of the tropical landscape are the palms, which are represented in India by some 100 species. Coconut and betel nut (the fruit of which is chewed) are cultivated mainly in coastal Karnataka and Kerala. Among the common, majestic-looking trees found throughout much of India are the mango—a major source of fruit—and two revered *Ficus* species, the pipal (famous as the Bo tree of Buddha) and the banyan. Many types of bamboo (members of the grass family) grow over much of the country, with a concentration in the rainy areas.

Vegetation in the Himalayas can be generally divided into a number of elevation zones. Mixed evergreen-deciduous forests dominate the foothill areas up to a height of 5,000 feet (1,500 metres). Above that level subtropical pine forests make their appearance, followed by the Himalayan moist-temperate forests of oak, fir, deodar (*Cedrus deodara*), and spruce. The highest tree zone, consisting of alpine shrubs, is found up to an elevation of about 15,000 feet (4,500 metres). Rhododendrons are common at 12,000 feet (3,700 metres), above which occasional junipers and alpine meadows are encountered. Zones overlap considerably, and there are wide transitional bands.

ANIMAL LIFE

India forms an important segment of what is known as the Oriental, or Sino-Indian, biogeographic region, which extends eastward from India to include mainland and much of insular Southeast Asia. Its fauna are numerous and quite diverse.

MAMMALS

Mammals of the submontane region include Indian elephants (*Elephas maximus*)—associated from time immemorial with mythology and the splendour of regal pageantry—the great one-horned Indian rhinoceroses, a wide variety of ruminants, and various primates. There

Elephant and rider in the Kabani River near Mysore, Karnataka, India. Gerald Cubitt

are also numerous predators represented by various genera.

Wild herds of elephants can be observed in several areas, particularly in such renowned national parks as Periyar Wildlife Sanctuary, in Kerala, and Bandipur, in Karnataka. The Indian rhinoceros is protected at Kaziranga National Park and Manas Wildlife Sanctuary in Assam.

Examples of ruminants include the wild Indian bison, or gaur (*Bos gaurus*), which inhabits peninsular forests; Indian buffalo; four-horned antelope (*Tetracerus quadricornis*), known locally as *chousingha*; blackbuck (*Antilope cervicapra*), or Indian antelope; antelope known as the *nilgai* (*Boselaphus tragocamelus*), or bluebuck; and Indian wild ass (*Equus hemionus khur*), or *ghorkhar*. There are also several species of deer, such as the rare Kashmir stag (*hangul*), swamp deer (*barasingha*), spotted deer, musk deer, brow-antlered deer (*Cervus eldi eldi*; an endangered species known locally as the *sangai* or *thamin*), and mouse deer.

Among the primates are various monkeys, including rhesus monkeys and gray, or Hanuman, langurs (*Presbytis entellus*), both of which are found in forested areas and near human settlements. The only ape found in India, the hoolock gibbon, is confined to the rainforests of the eastern region. Lion-tailed macaques of the Western Ghats, with halos of hair around their faces, are becoming rare because of poaching.

The country's carnivores include cats, dogs, foxes, jackals, and mongooses. Among the animals of prey, the Asiatic lion—now confined to the Gir Forest National Park, in the Kathiawar Peninsula of Gujarat—is the only extant subspecies of lion found outside of Africa. The majestic Indian, or Bengal, tiger (*Panthera tigris tigris*), the national animal of India, is known for its rich colour, illusive design, and formidable power. Of the five extant tiger subspecies worldwide, the Bengal tiger is the most numerous. Tigers are found in the forests of the Tarai region of northern India, Bihar, and Assam; the Ganges delta in West Bengal; the Eastern Ghats; Madhya Pradesh; and eastern Rajasthan. Once on the verge of extinction, Indian tigers have increased to several thousand, thanks largely to Project Tiger, which has established reserves in various parts of the country. Among other cats are leopards, clouded leopards, and various smaller species.

The Great Himalayas have notable fauna that includes wild sheep and goats, *markhor* (*Capra falconeri*), and ibex. Lesser pandas and snow leopards are also found in the upper reaches of the mountains.

Oxen, buffalo, horses, dromedary camels, sheep, goats, and pigs are common domesticated animals. The cattle breed Brahman, or zebu (*Bos indicus*), a species of ox, is an important draft animal.

BIRDS

India has more than 1,200 species of birds and perhaps 2,000 subspecies, although some migratory species are found in the country only during the winter. This amount of avian life represents roughly one-eighth of the world's species. The major reason for such a high level of diversity is the presence of a wide variety of habitats, from the cold and dry alpine tundra of Ladakh and Sikkim to the steamy, tangled jungles of the Sundarbans and wet, moist forests of the Western Ghats and the northeast. The country's many larger rivers provide deltas and backwaters for aquatic animal life, and many smaller rivers drain internally and end in vast saline lakes that are important breeding grounds for such birds as black-necked cranes (*Grus nigricollis*), barheaded geese (*Anser indicus*), and great crested grebes, as well as various kinds of terns, gulls, plovers, and sandpipers. Herons, storks, ibises, and flamingos are well represented, and many of these birds frequent Keoladeo National Park, near Bharatpur, Rajasthan (designated a UNESCO World Heritage site in 1985). The Rann of Kachchh forms the nesting ground for one of the world's largest breeding colonies of flamingos.

Birds of prey include hawks, vultures, and eagles. Vultures are ubiquitous consumers of carrion. Game birds are represented by pheasants, jungle fowl, partridges, and quails. Peacocks (peafowl) are also common, especially in Gujarat and Rajasthan, where they are kept as pets. Resplendently feathered, the peacock has been adopted as India's national bird.

Other notable birds in India include the Indian crane, commonly known as the *sarus* (*Grus antigone*); a large gray bird with crimson legs, the *sarus* stands as tall as a human. Bustards inhabit India's grasslands. The great Indian bustard (*Choriotis nigriceps*), now confined to central and western India, is an endangered species protected by legislation. Sand grouse, pigeons, doves, parakeets, and cuckoos are found throughout the country. The mainly nonmigratory kingfisher, living close to water bodies, is considered sacred in many areas. Hornbills, barbets, and woodpeckers also are common, as are larks, crows, babblers, and thrushes.

REPTILES, FISH, AND INSECTS

Reptiles are well represented in India. Crocodiles inhabit the country's rivers,
swamps, and lakes. The estuarine crocodile (*Crocodilus porosus*)—once attaining a maximum length of 30 feet (9 metres), though specimens exceeding 20 feet (6 metres) are now rare—usually lives on the fish, birds, and crabs of muddy deltaic regions. The long-snouted gavial, or gharial (*Gavialis gangeticus*), a species similar to the crocodile, is endemic to northern India; it is found in a number of large rivers, including the Ganges and Brahmaputra and their tributaries. Of the nearly 400 species of snakes, one-fifth are poisonous. Kraits and cobras are particularly widespread poisonous species. King cobras often grow to at least 12 feet (3.6 metres) long. The Indian python frequents marshy areas and grasslands. Lizards also are widespread, and turtles are found throughout India, especially along the eastern coast.

Of some 2,000 species of fish in India, about one-fifth live in freshwater. Common edible freshwater fish include catfish and several members of the carp family, notably the mahseer, which grows up to 6.5 feet (2 metres) and 200 pounds (90 kg). Sharks are found in India's coastal waters and sometimes travel inland through major estuaries. Commercially valuable marine species include shrimps, prawns, crabs, lobsters, pearl oysters, and conchs.

Among the commercially valuable insects are silkworms, bees, and the lac insect (*Laccifer lacca*). The latter secretes a sticky, resinous material called lac, from which shellac and a red dye are produced. Many other insects, such as

Gavial (Gavialis gangeticus) of northern India. © Gerry Ellis Nature Photography

various species of mosquitoes, are vectors for disease (e.g., malaria and yellow fever) or for human parasites (e.g., certain flatworms and nematodes).

CONSERVATION

The movement for the protection of forests and wildlife is strong in India. A number of species, including the elephant, rhinoceros, and tiger, have been declared endangered, and numerous others—both large and small—are considered vulnerable or at risk. Legislative measures have declared certain animals protected species, and areas with particularly rich floral diversity have been adopted as biosphere reserves. Virtually no forests are left in private hands. Projects likely to cause ecological damage must be cleared by the national government's Ministry of the Environment and Forests. Despite such measures, the reduced areas of forests, savannas, and grasslands provide little hope that India's population of animals can be restored to what it was at the end of the 19th century.

CHAPTER 2

HUMAN INTERACTIONS WITH INDIA'S ENVIRONMENT

India remains one of the most ethnically diverse countries in the world. Apart from its many religions and sects, India is home to innumerable castes and tribes, as well as to more than a dozen major and hundreds of minor linguistic groups from several language families unrelated to one another. Religious minorities, including Muslims, Christians, Sikhs, Buddhists, and Jains, still account for a significant proportion of the population; collectively, their numbers exceed the populations of all countries except China. Earnest attempts have been made to instill a spirit of nationhood in so varied a population, but tensions between neighbouring groups have remained and at times have resulted in outbreaks of violence. Yet social legislation has done much to alleviate the disabilities previously suffered by Scheduled Castes (formerly "untouchables"), tribal populations, women, and other traditionally disadvantaged segments of society.

SETTLEMENT PATTERNS

Although India is the second most populated country in the world, the bulk of its inhabitants are classified as rural. However, the population distribution is generally high throughout the country; only a tiny fraction of India's surface area is uninhabited.

POPULATION DENSITY

More than half of India's total area is cultivated, with little left fallow in any given year. Most of the area classified as forest—roughly one-fifth of the total—is used for grazing, for gathering firewood and other forest products, for commercial forestry, and, in tribal areas, for shifting cultivation (often in defiance of the law) and hunting. The areas too dry for growing crops without irrigation are largely used for grazing. The higher elevations of the Himalayas are the only places with substantial continuous areas not in use by humans. Although India's population is overwhelmingly rural, the country has three of the largest urban areas in the world—Mumbai (Bombay), Kolkata (Calcutta), and Delhi—and these and other large Indian cities have some of the world's highest population densities.

Most Indians reside in the areas of continuous cultivation, including the towns and cities they encompass. Within such areas, differences in population density are largely a function of water availability (whether directly from rainfall or from irrigation) and soil fertility. Areas receiving more than 60 inches (1,500 mm) of annual rainfall are generally capable of, for example, growing two crops each year, even without irrigation, and thus can support a high population density. More than three-fifths of the total population lives either on the fertile alluvial soils of the Indo-Gangetic Plain and the deltaic regions of the eastern coast or on the mixed alluvial and marine soils along India's western coast. Within those agriculturally productive areas—for example, parts of the eastern Gangetic Plain and of the state of Kerala—densities exceed 2,000 persons per square mile (800 persons per square km).

RURAL SETTLEMENT

Much of India's rural population lives in nucleated villages, which most commonly have a settlement form described as a shapeless agglomerate. Such settlements, though unplanned, are divided by caste into distinct wards and grow outward from a recognizable core area. The dominant and higher castes tend to live in the core area, while the lower artisan and service castes, as well as Muslim groups, generally occupy more peripheral localities. When the centrally located castes increase in population, they either subdivide their existing, often initially large, residential compounds, add second and even third stories on their existing houses (a common expedient in Punjab), leapfrog over lower-caste wards to a new area on the village periphery, or, in rare cases where land is available, found a completely new village.

Within the shapeless agglomerated villages, streets are typically narrow, twisting, and unpaved, often ending in culs-de-sac. There are usually a few open spaces where people gather: adjacent to a temple or mosque, at the main village well, in areas where grain is threshed or where grain and oilseeds are milled, and in front of the homes of the leading families of the village. In such spaces, depending on the size of the village, might be found the *pancayat* (village council) hall, a few shops, a tea stall, a public radio hooked up to a loudspeaker, a small post office, or perhaps a *dharmshala* (a free guest house for travelers). The village school is usually on the edge of the village in order to provide pupils with adequate playing space. Another common feature along the margin of a village is a grove of mango or other trees, which provides shade for people and animals and often contains a large well.

There are many regional variants from the simple agglomerated-villages pattern. Hamlets, each containing only one or a few castes, commonly surround villages in the eastern Gangetic Plain; Scheduled Castes and herding castes are likely to occupy such hamlets. In southern India, especially Tamil Nadu, and in Gujarat, villages have a more planned layout, with streets running north-south and east-west in straight lines. In many tribal areas (or areas that were tribal until relatively recently) the typical village consists of rows of houses along a single street or perhaps two or three parallel streets. In areas of rugged terrain, where relatively level spaces for building are limited, settlements often conform in shape to ridge lines, and few grow to be larger than hamlets. Finally, in

particularly aquatic environments, such as the Gangetic delta and the tidal backwater region of Kerala, agglomerations of even hamlet size are rare; most rural families instead live singly or in clusters of only a few households on their individual plots of owned or rented land.

Most village houses are small, simple one-story mud (*kacha*) structures, housing both people and livestock in one or just a few rooms. Roofs typically are flat and made of mud in dry regions, but in areas with considerable precipitation they generally are sloped for drainage and made of rice straw, other thatching material, or clay tiles. The wetter the region, the greater the pitch of the roof. In some wet regions, especially in tribal areas, bamboo walls are more common than those of mud, and houses often stand on piles above ground level. The houses usually are windowless and contain a minimum of furniture, a storage space for food, water, and implements, a few shelves and pegs for other possessions, a niche in the wall to serve as the household altar, and often a few decorations, such as pictures of gods or film heroes, family photographs, a calendar, or perhaps some memento of a pilgrimage. In one corner of the house or in an exterior court is the earthen hearth on which all meals are cooked. Electricity, running water, and toilet facilities generally are absent. Relatively secluded spots on the edge of the village serve the latter need.

Almost everywhere in India, the dwellings of the more affluent households are larger and usually built of more durable (*pakka*) materials, such as brick or stone. Their roofs are also of sturdier construction, sometimes of corrugated iron, and often rest on sturdy timbers or even steel I beams. Windows, usually barred for security, are common. The number of rooms, the furnishings, and the interior and exterior decor, especially the entrance gate, generally reflect the wealth of the family. There is typically an interior compound where much of the harvest will be stored. Within the compound there may be a private well or even a hand pump, an area for bathing, and a walled latrine enclosure, which is periodically cleaned by the village sweeper. Animal stalls, granaries, and farm equipment are in spaces distinct from those occupied by people.

Nomadic groups may be found in most parts of India. Some are small bands of wandering entertainers, ironworkers, and animal traders who may congregate in communities called *tandas*. A group variously known as the Labhani (Banjari or Vanjari), originally from Rajasthan and related to the Roma (Gypsies) of Europe, roams over large areas of central India

Banjari (Labhani) women in festive dress, near Hyderabad, Andhra Pradesh, India. © John Isaac

and the Deccan, largely as agricultural labourers and construction workers. Many tribal peoples practice similar occupations seasonally. Shepherds, largely of the Gujar caste, practice transhumance in the western Himalayas. In the semi-arid and arid regions where agriculture is either impossible or precarious, herders of cattle, sheep, goats, and camels live in a symbiotic relationship with local or nearby cultivators.

URBAN SETTLEMENT

Although only about one-fourth of India's people live in towns and cities, more than 4,500 places are classified as urban. In general, the proportion is higher in the agriculturally prosperous regions of the northwest, west, and south than in the northeastern rice-growing parts of the country, where the population capacity is limited by generally meagre crop surpluses.

In India large cities long have been growing at faster rates than small cities and towns. The major metropolitan agglomerations have the fastest rates of all, even where, as in Kolkata, there is a high degree of congestion within the central city. Major contributors to urban growth are the burgeoning of the bureaucracy, the increasing commercialization of the agricultural economy, and the spread of factory industry and services.

In many cities dating from the precolonial period, such as Delhi and Agra, the urban core is an exceedingly congested area within an old city wall, portions of

which may still stand. In these "old cities" residential segregation by religion and caste and the layout of streets and open places are, except for scale, not greatly dissimilar from what was described above for shapeless agglomerated villages. In contrast to many Western cities, affluent families commonly occupy houses in the heart of the most congested urban wards. Specialized bazaar streets selling sweets, grain, cloth, metalware, jewelry, books and stationery, and other commodities are characteristic of the old city. In such streets it is common for a single building to be at once a workshop, a retail outlet for what the workshop produces, and the residence for the artisan's family and employees.

Moderately old, highly congested urban cores also characterize many cities that grew up in the wake of British occupation. Of these, Kolkata, Mumbai, and Chennai are the most notable examples. In such cases, however, there are usually a few broad major thoroughfares, some degree of regularity to the street pattern, space reserved for parks, and a central business district, including old government offices, high-rise commercial office buildings, banks, elite shopping establishments, restaurants, hotels, museums, a few churches, and other reminders of the former colonial presence.

Associated with a great many cities are special sections created originally for the needs of the British: largely residential areas known as civil lines, where the families of resident European administrators occupied spacious bungalows, with adjoining outbuildings for their servants, nearby shopping facilities, and a gymkhana (a combined sports and social club); cantonments, where military personnel of all ranks were quartered, together with adjacent parade grounds, polo fields, and firing ranges; and industrial zones, including not only the modern mills but also the adjacent "factory lines," reminiscent of 19th-century company housing in Britain but even more squalid.

In the postindependence period, with the acceleration of urban growth and the consequent need for urban planning, new forms arose. The millions of refugees from Pakistan, for example, led to the establishment of many "model" (i.e., planned) towns on the edges of the existing cities. The subsequent steady influx of job seekers, together with the natural growth of the already settled population, gave rise to many planned residential areas, typically called "colonies," usually consisting of four- or five-story apartment blocks, a small shopping centre, schools, and playgrounds and other recreational spaces. In general, commuting from colonies to jobs in the inner city is by either bus or bicycle.

For poorer immigrants, residence in these urban colonies was not an option. Some could afford to move into slum flats, often sharing space with earlier immigrants from their native villages. Others, however, had no recourse but to find shelter in *bastis* (shantytowns), clusters of anywhere from a few to many hundreds of makeshift dwellings, which are commonly found along the edges of railroad yards and parks, outside the walls of factories, along the banks of rivers, and wherever else the urban authorities might tolerate their presence. Finally, there are the street dwellers, mainly single men in search of temporary employment, who lack even the meagre shelter that the *bastis* afford.

A special type of urban place to which British rule gave rise were the hill stations, such as Shimla (Simla) and Darjiling (Darjeeling). These were erected at elevations high enough to provide cool retreats for the dependents of Europeans stationed in India and, in the summer months, to serve as seasonal capitals of the central or provincial governments. Hotels, guest houses, boarding schools, clubs, and other recreational facilities characterize these settlements. Since independence, affluent Indians have come to depend on the hill stations no less than did the British.

DEMOGRAPHIC TRENDS

A population explosion in India commenced following the great influenza epidemic of 1918–19. In subsequent decades there was a steadily accelerating rate of growth up to the census of 1961, after which the rate leveled off (though it remained high). The total population in 1921 within the present borders of India (i.e., excluding what is now Pakistan and Bangladesh) was 251 million, and in 1947, at the time of independence, it was about 340 million. India's population doubled between 1947 and the 1981 census, and by the 2001 census it had surpassed one billion; the increase between 1991 and 2001 alone—some 185 million—was greater than the total present-day population of all but the world's most populous countries. Although there has been a considerable drop in the birth rate, a much more rapid decline in the death rate has accounted for the rise in the country's rate of population growth. Moreover, the increasing proportion of females attaining and living through their childbearing years continues to inhibit a marked reduction in the birth rate.

The effect of emigration from or immigration to India on the overall growth of population has been negligible throughout modern history. Within India, however, migration from relatively impoverished regions to areas, especially cities, offering some promise of economic betterment has been largely responsible for the differential growth rates from one state or region to another. In general, the larger a city, the greater its proportion of migrants to the total population and the more cosmopolitan its population mix. In Mumbai, for example, more than half of the population speaks languages other than Marathi, the principal language of the state of Maharashtra. The rates of migration to Indian cities severely tax their capacity to cope with the newcomers' needs for housing, safe drinking water, and sanitary facilities, not to mention amenities. The result is that many migrants live in conditions of appalling squalor in *bastis* or, even worse, with no permanent shelter at all.

Refugees constitute another class of migrants. Some date from the 1947 partition of India and many others, especially in Assam and West Bengal, from the violent separation in 1971 of Bangladesh from Pakistan. Still others are internal refugees from the communal violence and other forms of ethnic strife that periodically beset many parts of India.

INDIA'S LAND USE AND ITS ECONOMY

India has one of the largest, most highly diversified economies in the world, but, because of its enormous population, it is—in terms of income and gross national product (GNP) per capita—one of the poorest countries on Earth. Since independence, India has promoted a mixed economic system in which the government, constitutionally defined as "socialist," plays a major role as central planner, regulator, investor, manager, and producer. Starting in 1951, the government based its economic planning on a series of five-year plans influenced by the Soviet model. Initially, the attempt was to boost the domestic savings rate, which more than doubled in the half century following the First Five-Year Plan (1951–55). With the Second Five-Year Plan (1956–61), the focus began to shift to import-substituting industrialization, with an emphasis on capital goods. A broad and diversified industrial base developed.

Following the collapse of the Soviet system in the early 1990s, India adopted a series of free-market reforms that fueled the growth of its middle class, and its highly educated and well-trained workforce made India one of the global centres of the high-technology boom that began in the late 20th century and produced significant annual growth rates. The agricultural sector remains the country's main employer (about half of the workforce), though, with about one-fifth of the gross domestic product (GDP), it is no longer the largest contributor to GDP. Manufacturing remains another solid component of GDP. However, the major growth has been in trade, finance, and other services, which, collectively, are by far the largest component of GDP. Notable has been the establishment of a robust computer software and services industry, located largely in the urban areas of the southern cities of Bangalore (Bengaluru), Chennai (Madras), and Hyderabad. With a large number of Anglophones, India also emerged as a low-cost alternative for U.S. telecommunications companies and other enterprises to establish telephone call centres. India has remained a prime destination for tourists from both Europe and the Americas, and tourism has been a major source of foreign exchange.

Many of the government's decisions are highly political, especially its attempts to invest equitably among the various states of the union. Despite the government's pervasive economic role, large corporate undertakings dominate many spheres of modern economic activity, while tens of millions of generally small agricultural holdings and petty commercial, service, and craft enterprises account for the great bulk of employment. The range of technology runs the gamut from the most traditional to the most sophisticated.

There are few things that India cannot produce, though much of what it does manufacture would not be economically competitive without the protection offered by tariffs on imported goods, which have remained high despite liberalization. In absolute terms and in relation to GDP, foreign trade traditionally has been low. Despite continued government regulation (which has remained strong in many sectors), trade expanded greatly beginning in the 1990s.

Probably no more than one-fifth of India's vast labour force is employed in the so-called "organized" sector of the economy (e.g., mining, plantation agriculture, factory industry, utilities, and modern transportation, commercial, and service enterprises), but that small fraction generates a disproportionate share of GDP, supports most of the middle- and upper-class population, and generates most of the economic growth. It is the organized sector to which most government regulatory activity applies and in which trade unions, chambers of commerce, professional associations, and other institutions of modern capitalist economies play a significant role. Apart from rank-and-file labourers, the organized sector engages most of India's professionals and virtually all of its vast pool of scientists and technicians.

AGRICULTURE, FORESTRY, AND FISHING

Roughly half of all Indians still derive their livelihood directly from agriculture. That proportion has recently been declining from levels that were fairly consistent throughout the 20th century.

AGRICULTURE

The area cultivated, however, has risen steadily and has come to encompass considerably more than half of the country's total area, a proportion matched by few other countries in the world. In the more fertile regions, such as the Indo-Gangetic Plain or the deltas of the eastern coast, the proportion of cultivated to total land often exceeds nine-tenths.

Water availability varies greatly with climate. In all but a small part of the country, the supply of water for agriculture is highly seasonal and depends on the often fickle southwest monsoon. As a result, farmers are able to raise only one crop per year in areas that lack irrigation, and the risk of crop failure is fairly

Milling sugarcane in a small village near Saharanpur, Uttar Pradesh, India. © Robert Frerck/ Odyssey Productions

high in many locales. The prospects and actual development of irrigation also vary greatly from one part of the country to another. They are particularly favourable on the Indo-Gangetic Plain, in part because of the relatively even flow of the rivers issuing from the Himalayas and in part because of the vast reserves of groundwater in the thousands of feet of alluvial deposits underlying the region. In peninsular India, however, surface-water availability relies on the region's highly seasonal rainfall regime, and, in many areas, hard rock formations make it difficult to sink wells and severely curtail access to the groundwater that is present.

For such a predominantly agricultural country as India, resources of cultivable soil and water are of crucial importance. Although India does possess extensive areas of fertile alluvial soils, especially on the Indo-Gangetic Plain, and other substantial areas of relatively productive soils, such as the black (*regur*) soils of the Deccan lava plateau, the red-to-yellow lateritic soils that predominate over most of the remainder of the country are low in fertility. Overall, the per capita availability of cultivable area is low, and less than half of the cultivable land is of high quality. Moreover, many areas have lost much of their fertility because of erosion, alkalinization (caused by excessive irrigation without proper drainage), the subsurface formation of impenetrable hardpans, and protracted cultivation without restoring depleted plant nutrients.

Although the average farm size is only about 5 acres (2 hectares) and is declining, that figure masks the markedly skewed distribution of landholdings. More than half of all farms are less than 3 acres (1.2 hectares) in size, while much of the remainder is controlled by a small number of relatively affluent peasants and landlords. Most cultivators own farms that provide little more than a bare subsistence for their families; given fluctuations in the agricultural market and the fickle nature of the annual monsoon, the farm failure rate often has been quite high, particularly among smallholders. Further, nearly one-third of all agricultural households own no land at all and, along with many sub-marginal landowners, must work for the larger landholders or must supplement their earnings from some subsidiary occupation, often the one traditionally associated with their caste.

Agricultural technology has undergone rapid change in India. Government-sponsored large-scale irrigation canal projects, begun by the British in the mid-19th century, were greatly extended after independence. Emphasis then shifted toward deep wells (called tube wells in India), often privately owned, from which water was raised either by electric or diesel pumps; however, in many places these wells have depleted local groundwater reserves, and efforts have been directed at replenishing aquifers and utilizing rainwater. Tank irrigation, a method by which water is drawn from small reservoirs created along the courses of minor streams, is important in several parts of India, especially the southeast.

Farmers returning from their fields near Yamunanagar, Haryana, India. © Robert Frerck/ Odyssey Productions

The demand for chemical fertilizers also has been steadily increasing, although since the late 1960s the introduction of new, high-yielding hybrid varieties of seeds (HYVs), mainly for wheat and secondarily for rice, has brought about the most dramatic increases in production, especially in Punjab (where their adoption is virtually universal), Haryana, western Uttar Pradesh, and Gujarat. So great has been the success of the so-called Green Revolution that India was able to build up buffer stocks of grain sufficient for the country to weather several years of disastrously bad monsoons with virtually no imports or starvation and even to become, in some years, a modest net food exporter. During the same period, the production of coarse grains and pulses, which were less in demand than rice and wheat, either did not increase significantly or decreased. Hence, the total per capita grain production has been notably less than that suggested by many protagonists of the Green Revolution, and the threat of major food scarcity has not been eliminated.

CROPS

Most Indian farms grow little besides food crops, especially cereal grains, and these account for more than three-fifths of the area under cultivation. Foremost among the grains, in terms of both area sown and total yield, is rice, the crop of choice in almost all areas with more than 40 inches (1,000 mm) of average annual precipitation, as well as in some irrigated areas. Wheat ranks second in both area sown and total yield and, because of the use of HYVs, leads all grains in yield per acre. Wheat is grown mainly on the fertile soils of northern and northwestern India in areas with 15 to 40 inches (380 to 1,000 mm) of average annual precipitation, often with supplementary irrigation. Unlike rice, which is mainly grown during the *kharif* (summer) season, wheat is primarily a *rabi* (cool-season) crop. Other important cereals, in descending order of sown acreage, are sorghum (called jowar in India), pearl millet (*bajra*), corn (maize), and finger millet (*ragi*). All these typically are grown on relatively infertile soils unsuitable for rice or wheat, while corn cultivation is also favoured in hilly and mountainous regions. After cereals, pulses are the most important category of food crop. These ubiquitous leguminous crops—of which the chickpea (gram) is the most important—are the main source of protein for most Indians, for whom the consumption of animal products is an expensive luxury or is proscribed on religious grounds.

Nonstaple food crops, eaten in only small amounts by most Indians, include potatoes, onions, various greens, eggplants, okra, squashes, and other vegetables, as well as such fruits as mangoes, bananas, mandarin oranges, papayas, and melons. Sugarcane is widely cultivated, especially in areas near processing mills. Sugar is also obtained by tapping the trunks of toddy palms (*Caryota urens*), which are abundant in southern India, but much of this syrup is fermented, often illegally, to make an alcoholic beverage. A wide variety of crops—mainly peanuts (groundnuts), coconuts, mustard, cottonseed, and rapeseed—are grown as sources of cooking oil. Others, such as the ubiquitous chilies, turmeric, and ginger, are raised to provide condiments or, in the case of betel leaf (of the pan plant) and betel (areca nut), digestives. Tea is grown, largely for export, on plantations in Assam, West Bengal, Kerala, and Tamil Nadu, while coffee is grown almost exclusively in southern India, mainly in Karnataka. Tobacco is cultivated chiefly in Gujarat and Andhra Pradesh.

Foremost among the commercial industrial crops is cotton. Maharashtra, Gujarat, and Punjab are the principal cotton-growing states. Jute, mainly from West Bengal, Assam, and Bihar, is the second leading natural fibre. Much of it is exported in processed form, largely as burlap. An even coarser fibre is derived from coir, the outer husk of the coconut, the processing of which forms the basis for an important cottage industry in Kerala. Coconuts and oilseeds are also important for the extraction of industrial oils.

LIVESTOCK

Despite the fact that Indians eat little meat, livestock raising plays an important role in the agricultural economy. India has by far the largest bovine population of any country in the world. Cattle and buffalo are used mainly as draft animals but also serve many other purposes—to provide milk, as sources of meat (for those, including Muslims, Christians, and Scheduled Castes, for whom beef eating is not taboo), and as sources of fertilizer, cooking fuel (from dried cow-dung cakes), and leather. Milk yields from Indian cattle and buffaloes are quite low, although milk from buffaloes is somewhat better and richer on average than from cattle. Because cow slaughter is illegal in many states, scarcely any cattle are raised expressly for providing meat, and most of what little beef is consumed comes from animals that die from natural causes. Rather than being slaughtered, cattle that outlive their usefulness may be sent to *goshalas* (homes for aged cattle maintained by contributions from devout Hindus) or allowed to roam as strays. In either case, they compete with humans for scarce vegetal resources.

While many orthodox Indians are vegetarians, others will eat goat, mutton, poultry, eggs, and fish, all of which are produced in modest quantities. Sheep are raised for both wool and meat. Pork is taboo to members of several faiths, including Muslims and most Hindus, but pigs, which serve as village scavengers, are raised and freely eaten by several Scheduled Castes.

FORESTRY

Commercial forestry is not highly developed in India. Nevertheless, the annual cutting of hardwoods is among the highest of any country in the world. Species that are sources of timber, pulp, plywoods, veneers, and matchwood include teak, deodar (a type of cedar), *sal* (*Shorea robusta*), sissoo (*Dalbergia sissoo*), and chir pine (*Pinus roxburghii*). Virtually any woody vegetation is used for firewood, much of it illegally gathered, and substantial amounts go into making charcoal. Minor forest products include bamboo, cane, gum, resins, dyes, tanning agents, lac, and medicinal plants.

The principal areas for commercial forestry, in order of importance, are the Western Ghats, the western Himalayas, and the hill regions of central India. In an effort to counteract forest depletion, the central and state governments have vigorously supported small-scale afforestation projects; these have met with mixed success, both economically and ecologically.

Population growth has, over the centuries, resulted in a continuous diminution of forest land. Most of India's formerly forested area has been converted to agricultural use (though some of that land is no longer productive), and other large areas have been effectively turned into wasteland from either overgrazing or overexploitation for timber and firewood. The problem of obtaining sufficient firewood, mainly for cooking, is particularly acute. In many areas forests have ceased to exist, and the only trees of consequence are found in protected village groves, often planted with mangoes or other fruit trees, where people and animals can seek shade from the fierce summer sun. In some areas, especially the northeast, bamboo thickets provide an important substitute for wood for structural purposes. Official figures on the amount of forested land (roughly one-fifth of India's total area) are virtually meaningless, as much of the area officially classified as forest contains little but scrub. Among the ecological consequences of deforestation in India are the reduced groundwater retentiveness, a concomitant rapid runoff of monsoon rains, a higher incidence of flooding, accelerated erosion and siltation, and an exacerbated problem of water scarcity.

FISHING

Fishing is practiced along the entire length of India's coastline and on virtually all of its many rivers. Production from marine and freshwater fisheries has become roughly equivalent. Because few fishing craft are mechanized, total catches are low, and annual per capita fish consumption is modest. The shift to mechanization and modern processing, however, has been inexorable. Thus, an increasingly large part of the catch now comes from fishing grounds that the small craft of coastal fishing families are unable to reach. The problem is most severe in Kerala, the leading fishing state. Major marine catches include sardine and mackerel; freshwater catches are dominated by carp. Intensive inland aquaculture, for both fish and shrimp (the latter of which has become an important export), has increased significantly.

RESOURCES AND POWER

Although India possesses a wide range of minerals and other natural resources, its per capita endowment of such critical resources as cultivable land, water, timber, and known petroleum reserves is relatively low. Nevertheless, the diversity of resources, especially of minerals, exceeds that of all but a few countries and gives India a distinct advantage in its industrial development.

Domestically supplied minerals form an important underpinning for India's diversified manufacturing industry, as well as a source of modest export revenues. Nationalizing many foreign and domestic enterprises and government initiation and management of others gave the Indian government a predominant role in the mining industry. However, government involvement has been gradually reduced as private investment has grown.

Among mineral resources, iron ore (generally of high quality) and ferroalloys—notably manganese and chromite—are particularly abundant, and all are widely

Fishing boats in the harbour at Panaji, Goa. Gerald Cubitt

distributed over peninsular India. Other exploitable metallic minerals include copper, bauxite (the principal ore of aluminum), zinc, lead, gold, and silver. Among important nonmetallic and non-fuel minerals are limestone, dolomite, rock phosphate, building stones, ceramic clays, mica, gypsum, fluorspar, magnesite, graphite, and diamonds.

Of the many metals produced, iron—mined principally in Madhya Pradesh, Bihar, Goa, Karnataka, and Orissa—ranks first in value. Copper, derived mainly from Rajasthan and Bihar, is a distant second. Gold, zinc and lead (often mined together), the ferroalloys (chiefly manganese and chromite), and bauxite also are important. Noteworthy nonmetallic minerals include limestone, dolomite, rock phosphate, gypsum, building stone, and ceramic clays.

In terms of the value of production, fuel minerals far exceed all others combined. Among the fuels, petroleum ranks first in value, followed by coal (including lignite). India produces only a portion of its petroleum needs but produces a slight exportable surplus of coal. Virtually all of India's petroleum comes from the offshore Bombay High Field and from Gujarat and Assam, while coal comes from some 500 mines, both surface and deep-pit, distributed over a number of states. By far the most important coal-producing region is along the Damodar River, including the Jharia and Raniganj fields in Bihar and West Bengal, which account for about half the nation's output and virtually all the coal of coking quality. Natural gas is

of little importance. Uranium is produced in modest quantities in Bihar.

Among the fossil fuels, India is well endowed with coal and modestly so with lignite. Coal supplies are widespread but are especially abundant and easy to mine in the Chota Nagpur Plateau, which is the principal source area for coking coal. Domestic reserves of petroleum and natural gas, though abundant, do not meet the country's large demand. Petroleum fields are located in eastern Assam (India's oldest production region) and in Gujarat and offshore in the Arabian Sea on an undersea structure known as the Bombay High. Several other onshore and offshore petroleum reserves have been discovered, including sites in Tamil Nadu, Andhra Pradesh, and Arunachal Pradesh.

The country's utilities, overwhelmingly in government hands, are barely able to keep pace with the rapidly rising demand for various types of service. Electricity consumption, for example, increased 16-fold between 1951 and 1980 and more than quadrupled again in the next quarter century. The bulk of all electricity generated is from widely dispersed coal-powered thermal plants; most of the remainder is from hydroelectric plants, built mainly in mountainous regions or along major escarpments; and only a tiny amount comes from a few nuclear installations. Power outages and rationing are frequently necessary in periods of peak demand, since growing demand often outstrips installed capacity in many locales. More than half of all electricity is industrially used. Agricultural use, largely for raising irrigation water from deep wells, exceeds domestic consumption. Rural electrification is increasing rapidly, and the great bulk of all villages are now tied into some distribution grid.

MANUFACTURING

India's manufacturing industry is highly diversified. A substantial majority of all industrial workers are employed in the millions of small-scale handicraft enterprises. These mainly household industries—such as spinning, weaving, pottery making, metalworking, and woodworking—largely serve the local needs of the villages where they are situated.

In terms of total output and value added, however, mechanized factory production predominates. Many factories, especially those manufacturing producers' goods (e.g., basic metals, machinery, fertilizers, and other heavy chemicals), are publicly owned and operated by either the central or the state governments. There

Steel foundry at the Tata truck works, Jamshedpur, Jharkhand, India. © Robert Frerck/ Odyssey Productions

also are thousands of private producers, including a number of large and diversified industrial conglomerates. The steel industry, for example, is one in which a privately owned corporation, the Tata Iron and Steel Company (Tata Steel), at Jamshedpur (production began in 1911), is among the largest and most successful producers. In the Middle East, East Africa, and Southeast Asia, some Indian corporations have established "turnkey operations," which are turned over to local management after a stipulated period. Foreign corporations, however, have been slow to invest in Indian industry because of excessive regulation (subsequently relaxed) and rules limiting foreign ownership of controlling shares.

The long-established textile industries—especially cotton but also jute, wool, silk, and synthetic fibres—account for the greatest share of manufacturing employment. Few large cities are without at least one cotton mill. Jute milling, unlike cotton, is highly concentrated in "Hugliside," the string of cities along the Hugli (Hooghly) River just north of Kolkata. Even more widespread than textile mills are initial processing plants for agricultural and mining products. In general, these are fairly small, seasonal enterprises located close to places of primary production. They include plants for cotton ginning, oil pressing, peanut shelling, sugar refining, drying and cold storage of foodstuffs, and crushing and initial smelting of ores. Consumer goods industries, though widely dispersed, are largely concentrated in large cities. To spread the benefits of development regionally and to alleviate metropolitan congestion, state governments have sponsored numerous industrial parks (or estates), for which entrepreneurs are offered various concessions, including cheap land and reduced taxes. Such programs have been fairly successful.

Among the heavy industries, metallurgical plants, such as iron and steel mills, typically are located close either to raw materials or to coal, depending on the relative mix of materials needed and transportation costs. India is fortunate in having several sites, especially in the Chota Nagpur Plateau, where abundant coal supplies are in close proximity to high-grade iron ore. Within easy reach of the Kolkata market, the Chota Nagpur Plateau has become India's principal area for heavy industry, including many interconnected chemical and engineering enterprises. Production of heavy transportation equipment, such as locomotives and trucks, is also concentrated there.

TRANSPORTATION AND TELECOMMUNICATIONS

At independence, India had a transportation system superior to that of any other large postcolonial region. In the decades that followed, it built steadily on that base, and railroads in particular formed the sinews that initially bound the new nation together. Although railroads have continued to carry the bulk of goods traffic, there has been a steady increase in the relative dependence on roads and motorized transport, and all modes of transport—from human porters and animal traction (India still has millions of bullock carts) to the most modern aircraft—find niches in which they are the preferred and sometimes the sole means for moving people and goods.

RAILWAYS AND ROADS

With some 39,000 miles (62,800 km) of track length, India's rail system, entirely government-owned, is one of the most extensive in the world, while in terms of the distance traveled each year by passengers it is the world's most heavily used system. India's mountain railways were collectively designated a UNESCO World Heritage site in 2008. Railway administration is handled through nine regional subsystems. Routes are mainly broad-gauge (5.5 feet [1.68 metres]) single-track lines, and the remaining metre and narrow-gauge routes are being converted to the broad-gauge standard. There has also been conversion to double-track lines, as well as a shift from steam locomotives to diesel-electric or electric power. Electrified lines have become especially important for urban commuter traffic, and in 1989 South Asia's first subway line began operation in Kolkata. Delhi followed with a new system in the early 21st century.

Although relatively few new rail routes have been built since independence, the length and capacity of the road system and the volume of road traffic by truck, bus, and automobile have all undergone phenomenal expansion. The length of hard-surfaced roads, for example, has increased from only 66,000 to some 950,000 miles (106,000 to 1,530,000 km) since 1947, but this still represented less than half of the national total of all roads. During the same period, the increased volume of road traffic for both passengers and goods was even more dramatic, increasing exponentially. A relatively small number of villages (almost entirely in tribal regions) are still situated more than a few hours' walk from the nearest bus transport. Bus service is largely owned and controlled by state governments, which also build and maintain most hard-surfaced routes. The grid of national highways connects virtually all Indian cities.

WATER AND AIR TRANSPORT

A small number of major ports, led by Mumbai, Kolkata, and Chennai, are centrally managed by the Indian government, while a much larger number of intermediate and minor ports are state-managed. The former handle the great bulk of the country's maritime traffic. Of the country's shipping companies engaged in either overseas or coastal trade, the largest is the publicly owned Shipping Corporation of India. Only about one-third of India's more than 3,100 miles (5,000 km) of navigable inland waterways, including both rivers and a few short stretches of canals, are commercially used, and those no longer carry a significant volume of traffic.

Civil aviation, once entirely in private hands, was nationalized in 1953 into two government-owned companies: Air India, for major international routes from airports at New Delhi, Mumbai, Kolkata, and Chennai; and Indian Airlines, for routes within India and neighbouring countries. The government has tightly restricted access to Indian air routes for foreign carriers, and several small domestic airlines have attempted to service short-haul, low-capacity routes. The networks and volume of traffic are expanding rapidly, and all large and most medium-size cities now have regular air service.

TELECOMMUNICATIONS

The telecommunications sector has traditionally been dominated by the state; even after the liberalization of the 1990s, the government—through several state-owned or operated companies and the Department of Telecommunications—has continued to control the industry. Although telephone service is quite dense in some urban areas, throughout the country as a whole there are relatively few main lines per capita. Many rural towns and villages have no telephone service. Cellular telephone service is available in major urban centres through a number of private vendors. The state dominates television and radio broadcasting through the Ministry of Information and Broadcasting. The number of personal computers—though large in raw numbers—is relatively small given the country's population. Although many individuals have Internet service subscriptions, cybercafes located in most major urban areas provide access for a great proportion of users.

CHAPTER 3

MAJOR PHYSICAL FEATURES OF THE SUBCONTINENT

The Indian subcontinent encompasses some of the Earth's most notable physical features, and three of these are profiled in this chapter. These include the Himalayas, the lofty range that defines the northern limit of the subcontinent; the Ganges, one of the mighty rivers that flows from those mountains; and the Thar (or Great Indian) Desert, which occupies much of northwestern India and southeastern Pakistan.

HIMALAYAS

The Himalayas (Nepali: Himalaya) are the great mountain system of Asia, forming a barrier between the Plateau of Tibet to the north and the alluvial plains of the Indian subcontinent to the south. The Himalayas include the highest mountains in the world, with more than 110 peaks rising to elevations of 24,000 feet (7,300 metres) or more above sea level. One of these peaks is Mount Everest (Tibetan: Chomolungma; Chinese: Qomolangma Feng; Nepali: Sagarmatha), the world's highest, with an elevation of 29,035 feet (8,850 metres). The mountains' high peaks rise into the zone of perpetual snow.

For thousands of years the Himalayas have held a profound significance for the peoples of South Asia, as their literature, mythologies, and religions reflect. Since ancient times the vast glaciated heights have attracted the attention of the pilgrim mountaineers of India, who coined the Sanskrit name Himalaya—from *hima* ("snow") and *alaya* ("abode")—for this great mountain system. In contemporary times the Himalayas have offered the greatest attraction and the greatest challenge to mountaineers throughout the world.

Forming the northern border of the Indian subcontinent and an almost impassable barrier between it and the lands to the north, the ranges are part of a vast mountain belt that stretches halfway around the world from North Africa to the Pacific coast of Southeast Asia. The Himalayas themselves stretch uninterruptedly for about 1,550 miles (2,500 km) from west to east between Nanga Parbat (26,660 feet [8,126 metres]), in the Pakistani-administered portion of the Kashmir region, and Namjagbarwa (Namcha Barwa) Peak (25,445 feet [7,756 metres]), in the Tibet Autonomous Region of China. Between these western and eastern extremities lie the two Himalayan countries of Nepal and Bhutan. The Himalayas are bordered to the northwest by the mountain ranges of the Hindu Kush and the Karakoram and to the north by the high Plateau of Tibet. The width of the Himalayas from south to north varies between 125 and 250 miles (200 and 400 km). Their total area amounts to about 230,000 square miles (595,000 square km).

Though India, Nepal, and Bhutan have sovereignty over most of the Himalayas, Pakistan and China also occupy parts of them. In the disputed Kashmir region, Pakistan has administrative control of some 32,400 square miles (83,900 square km) of the range lying north and west of the "line of control" established between India and Pakistan in 1972. China administers some 14,000 square miles (36,000 square km) in the Ladakh district of Kashmir and has claimed territory at the eastern end of the Himalayas within the Indian state of Arunachal Pradesh. These disputes accentuate the boundary problems faced by India and its neighbours in the Himalayan region.

PHYSICAL FEATURES

The most characteristic features of the Himalayas are their soaring heights, steep-sided jagged peaks, valley and alpine glaciers often of stupendous size, topography deeply cut by erosion, seemingly unfathomable river gorges, complex geologic structure, and series of elevational belts (or zones) that display different ecological associations of flora, fauna, and climate. Viewed from the south, the Himalayas appear as a gigantic crescent with the main axis rising above the snow line, where snowfields, alpine glaciers, and avalanches all feed lower-valley glaciers that in turn constitute the sources of most of the Himalayan rivers. The greater part of the Himalayas, however, lies below the snow line. The mountain-building process that created the range is still active. As the bedrock is lifted, considerable stream erosion and gigantic landslides occur.

Machhapuchhare, a peak in the Great Himalaya Range, north-central Nepal. © Digital Vision/Getty Images

The Himalayan ranges can be grouped into four parallel longitudinal mountain belts of varying width, each having distinct physiographic features and its own geologic history. They are designated, from south to north, as the Outer, or Sub-, Himalayas (also called the Siwalik Range); the Lesser, or Lower, Himalayas; the Great Himalaya Range (Great Himalayas); and the Tethys, or Tibetan, Himalayas. Farther north lie the Trans-Himalayas in Tibet proper. From west to east the Himalayas are divided broadly into three mountainous regions: western, central, and eastern.

GEOLOGIC HISTORY

Over the past 65 million years, powerful global plate-tectonic forces have moved the Earth's crust to form the band of Eurasian mountain ranges—including the Himalayas—that stretch from the Alps to the mountains of Southeast Asia.

During the Jurassic Period (about 200 to 145 million years ago), a deep crustal downwarp—the Tethys Ocean—bordered the entire southern fringe of Eurasia, then excluding the Arabian Peninsula and the Indian subcontinent. About 180 million years ago, the old supercontinent of Gondwana (or Gondwanaland) began to break up. One of Gondwana's fragments, the lithospheric plate that included the Indian subcontinent, pursued a northward collision course toward the Eurasian Plate during the ensuing 130 million years. This Indian-Australian Plate gradually confined the Tethys trench within a giant pincer between itself and the Eurasian Plate. As the Tethys trench narrowed, increasing compressive forces bent the layers of rock beneath it and created interlacing faults in its marine sediments. Masses of granites and basalts intruded from the depth of the mantle into this weakened sedimentary crust. About 50 million years ago, the Indian subcontinent finally collided with Eurasia. The plate containing India was sheared downward, or subducted, beneath the Tethys trench at an ever-increasing pitch.

During the next 30 million years, shallow parts of the Tethys Ocean gradually drained as its sea bottom was pushed up by the plunging Indian-Australian Plate; this formed the Plateau of Tibet. On the plateau's southern edge, marginal mountains—the Trans-Himalayan ranges of today—became the region's first major watershed and rose high enough to become a climatic barrier. As heavier rains fell on the steepening southern slopes, the major southern rivers eroded northward toward the headwaters with increasing force along old transverse faults and captured the streams flowing onto the plateau, thus laying the foundation for today's drainage patterns. To the south the northern reaches of the Arabian Sea and the Bay of Bengal rapidly filled with debris carried down by the ancestral Indus, Ganges (Ganga), and Brahmaputra rivers. The extensive erosion and deposition continue even now as these rivers carry immense quantities of material every day.

Finally, some 20 million years ago, during the early Miocene Epoch, the tempo of the crunching union between the two plates increased sharply, and Himalayan mountain building began in earnest. As the Indian subcontinental plate continued to plunge beneath the former Tethys trench, the topmost layers of old Gondwana metamorphic rocks peeled back over themselves for a long horizontal distance to the south, forming nappes. Wave after wave of nappes thrust southward over the Indian landmass for as far as 60 miles (about 100 km). Each new nappe consisted of Gondwana rocks older than the last. In time these nappes became folded, contracting the former trench by some 250 to 500 horizontal miles (400 to 800 km). All the while, downcutting rivers matched the rate of uplift, carrying vast amounts of eroded material from the rising Himalayas to the plains where it was dumped by the Indus, Ganges, and Brahmaputra rivers. The weight of this sediment created depressions, which in turn could hold more sediment. In some places the alluvium beneath the Gangetic Plain now exceeds 25,000 feet (7,600 metres) in depth.

Probably only within the past 600,000

years, during the Pleistocene Epoch (roughly 2,600,000 to 11,700 years ago), did the Himalayas become the highest mountains on Earth. If strong horizontal thrusting characterized the Miocene and the succeeding Pliocene Epoch (about 23 to 2.6 million years ago), intense uplift epitomized the Pleistocene. Along the core zone of the northernmost nappes—and just beyond—crystalline rocks containing new gneiss and granite intrusions emerged to produce the staggering crests seen today. On a few peaks, such as Mount Everest, the crystalline rocks carried old fossil-bearing Tethys sediments from the north piggyback to the summits.

Once the Great Himalayas had risen high enough, they became a climatic barrier: the marginal mountains to the north were deprived of rain and became as parched as the Plateau of Tibet. In contrast, on the wet southern flanks the rivers surged with such erosive energy that they forced the crest line to migrate slowly northward. Simultaneously, the great transverse rivers breaching the Himalayas continued their downcutting in pace with the uplift. Changes in the landscape, however, compelled all but these major rivers to reroute their lower courses because, as the northern crests rose, so also did the southern edge of the extensive nappes. The formations of the Siwalik Series were overthrust and folded, and in between the Lesser Himalayas downwarped to shape the midlands. Now barred from flowing due south, most minor rivers ran east or west through structural weaknesses in the midlands

until they could break through the new southern barrier or join a major torrent.

In some valleys, such as the Vale of Kashmir and the Kathmandu Valley of Nepal, lakes formed temporarily and then filled with Pleistocene deposits. After drying up some 200,000 years ago, the Kathmandu Valley rose at least 650 feet (200 metres), an indication of localized uplift within the Lesser Himalayas.

PHYSIOGRAPHY

The Outer Himalayas comprise flat-floored structural valleys and the Siwalik Range, which borders the Himalayan mountain system to the south. Except for small gaps in the east, the Siwaliks run for the entire length of the Himalayas, with a maximum width of 62 miles (100 km) in the northern Indian state of Himachal Pradesh. In general, the 900-foot (275-metre) contour line marks their southern boundary; they rise an additional 2,500 feet (760 metres) to the north. The main Siwalik Range has steeper southern slopes facing the Indian plains and descends gently northward to flat-floored basins, called *duns*. The best-known of these is the Dehra Dun, in southern Uttarakhand state, just north of the border with north-western Uttar Pradesh state.

To the north the Siwalik Range abuts a massive mountainous tract, the Lesser Himalayas. In this range, 50 miles (80 km) in width, mountains rising to 15,000 feet (4,500 metres) and valleys with elevations of 3,000 feet (900 metres) run in varying directions. Neighbouring summits share similar elevations, creating the appearance of a highly dissected plateau. The three principal ranges of the Lesser Himalayas—the Nag Tibba, the Dhaola Dhar, and the Pir Panjal—have branched off from the Great Himalaya Range lying farther north. The Nag Tibba, the most easterly of the three ranges, is some 26,800 feet (8,200 metres) high near its eastern end, in Nepal, and forms the watershed between the Ganges and Yamuna rivers in Uttarakhand.

To the west is the picturesque Vale of Kashmir, in Jammu and Kashmir state (the Indian-administered portion of Kashmir). A structural basin (i.e., an elliptical basin in which the rock strata are inclined toward a central point), the vale forms an important section of the Lesser Himalayas. It extends from southeast to northwest for 100 miles (160 km), with a width of 50 miles (80 km), and has an average elevation of 5,100 feet (1,600 metres). The basin is traversed by the meandering Jhelum River, which runs through Wular Lake, a large freshwater lake in Jammu and Kashmir.

The backbone of the entire mountain system is the Great Himalaya Range, rising into the zone of perpetual snow. The range reaches its maximum height in Nepal; among its peaks are 10 of the 13 highest in the world, each of which exceeds 26,250 feet (8,000 metres) in elevation. From west to east those peaks are Nanga Parbat, Dhaulagiri 1, Annapurna 1, Manaslu 1, Xixabangma (Gosainthan), Cho Oyu, Mount Everest, Lhotse, Makalu 1, and Kanchenjunga 1.

The range trends northwest-southeast from Jammu and Kashmir to Sikkim, an old Himalayan kingdom that is now a state of India. East of Sikkim it runs east-west for another 260 miles (420 km) through Bhutan and the eastern part of Arunachal Pradesh as far as the peak of Kangto (23,260 feet [7,090 metres]) and finally bends northeast, terminating at Namcha Barwa.

There is no sharp boundary between the Great Himalayas and the ranges, plateaus, and basins lying to the north of the Great Himalayas, generally grouped together under the names of the Tethys, or Tibetan, Himalayas and the Trans-Himalayas, which extend far northward into Tibet. In Kashmir and in the Indian state of Himachal Pradesh, the Tethys are at their widest, forming the Spiti Basin and the Zaskar Range.

DRAINAGE

The Himalayas are drained by 19 major rivers, of which the Indus and the Brahmaputra are the largest, each having catchment basins in the mountains of about 100,000 square miles (260,000 square km) in extent. Of the other rivers, five belong to the Indus system—the Jhelum, the Chenab, the Ravi, the Beas, and the Sutlej—with a total catchment area of about 51,000 square miles (132,000 square km); nine belong to the Ganges system—the Ganges, Yamuna, Ramganga, Kali (Kali Gandak), Karnali, Rapti, Gandak, Baghmati, and Kosi rivers—draining another 84,000 square miles (218,000 square km) in the mountains; and three belong to the Brahmaputra system—the Tista, the Raidak, and the Manas—draining another 71,000 square miles (184,000 square km) in the Himalayas.

The major Himalayan rivers rise north of the mountain ranges and flow through deep gorges that generally reflect some geologic structural control, such as a fault line. The rivers of the Indus system as a rule follow northwesterly courses, whereas those of the Ganges-Brahmaputra systems generally take easterly courses while flowing through the mountain region.

To the north of India, the Karakoram Range, with the Hindu Kush range on the west and the Ladakh Range on the east, forms the great water divide, shutting off the Indus system from the rivers of Central Asia. The counterpart of this divide on the east is formed by the Kailas Range and its eastward continuation, the Nyainqêntanglha (Nyenchen Tangla) Mountains, which prevent the Brahmaputra from draining the area to the north. South of this divide, the Brahmaputra flows to the east for about 900 miles (1,450 km) before cutting across the Great Himalaya Range in a deep transverse gorge, although many of its Tibetan tributaries flow in an opposite direction, as the Brahmaputra may once have done.

The Great Himalayas, which normally would form the main water divide throughout their entire length, function as such only in limited areas. This situation

exists because the major Himalayan rivers, such as the Indus, the Brahmaputra, the Sutlej, and at least two headwaters of the Ganges—the Alaknanda and the Bhagirathi—are probably older than the mountains they traverse. It is believed that the Himalayas were uplifted so slowly that the old rivers had no difficulty in continuing to flow through their channels and, with the rise of the Himalayas, acquired an even greater momentum, which enabled them to cut their valleys more rapidly. The elevation of the Himalayas and the deepening of the valleys thus proceeded simultaneously. As a result, the mountain ranges emerged with a completely developed river system cut into deep transverse gorges that range in depth from 5,000 to 16,000 feet (1,500 to 5,000 metres) and in width from 6 to 30 miles (10 to 50 km). The earlier origin of the drainage system explains the peculiarity that the major rivers drain not only the southern slopes of the Great Himalayas but, to a large extent, its northern slopes as well, the water divide being north of the crest line.

The role of the Great Himalaya Range as a watershed, nevertheless, can be seen between the Sutlej and Indus valleys for 360 miles (580 km); the drainage of the northern slopes is carried by the north-flowing Zaskar and Dras rivers, which drain into the Indus. Glaciers also play an important role in draining the higher elevations and in feeding the Himalayan rivers. Several glaciers occur in Uttarakhand, of which the largest, the Gangotri, is 20 miles (32 km) long and is one of the sources of the Ganges. The Khumbu Glacier drains the Everest region in Nepal and is one of the most popular routes for the ascent of the mountain. The rate of movement of the Himalayan glaciers varies considerably; in the neighbouring Karakoram Range, for example, the Baltoro Glacier moves about 6 feet (2 metres) per day, while others, such as the Khumbu, move only about 1 foot (30 cm) daily. Most of the Himalayan glaciers are in retreat, at least in part because of climate change.

SOILS

The north-facing slopes generally have a fairly thick soil cover, supporting dense forests at lower elevations and grasses higher up. The forest soils are dark brown in colour and silt loam in texture; they are ideally suited for growing fruit trees. The mountain meadow soils are well developed but vary in thickness and in their chemical properties. Some of the wet deep upland soils of this type in the eastern Himalayas—for example, in the Darjiling (Darjeeling) Hills and in the Assam valley—have a high humus content that is good for growing tea. Podzolic soils (infertile acidic forest soils) occur in a belt some 400 miles (640 km) long in the valleys of the Indus and its tributary the Shyok River, to the north of the Great Himalaya Range, and in patches in Himachal Pradesh. Farther east, saline soils occur in the dry high plains of the Ladakh region. Of the soils that are not restricted to any particular area, alluvial soils (deposited by running water) are the most productive, though they occur in limited areas, such as the Vale of Kashmir, the Dehra Dun, and the high terraces flanking the Himalayan valleys. Lithosols, consisting of imperfectly weathered rock fragments that are deficient in humus content, cover many large areas at high altitudes and are the least productive soils.

CLIMATE

The Himalayas, as a great climatic divide affecting large systems of air and water circulation, help determine meteorological conditions in the Indian subcontinent to the south and in the Central Asian highlands to the north. By virtue of its location and stupendous height, the Great Himalaya Range obstructs the passage of cold continental air from the north into India in winter and also forces the southwesterly monsoon (rain-bearing) winds to give up most of their moisture before crossing the range northward. The result is heavy precipitation (both rain and snow) on the Indian side but arid conditions in Tibet. The average annual rainfall on the south slopes varies between 60 inches (1,530 mm) at Shimla, Himachal Pradesh, and Mussoorie, Uttarakhand, in the western Himalayas and 120 inches (3,050 mm) at Darjiling, West Bengal state, in the eastern Himalayas. North of the Great Himalayas, at places such as Skardu, Gilgit, and Leh in the Kashmir portion of the Indus valley, only 3 to 6 inches (75 to 150 mm) of precipitation occur.

Local relief and location determine climatic variation not only in different parts of the Himalayas but even on different slopes of the same range. Because of its favourable location on top of the Mussoorie Range facing the Dehra Dun, the town of Mussoorie, for example, at an elevation of about 6,100 feet (1,900 metres), receives 92 inches (2,335 mm) of precipitation annually, compared with 62 inches (1,575 mm) in the town of Shimla, which lies some 90 miles (145 km) to the northwest behind a series of ridges reaching 6,600 feet (2,000 metres). The eastern Himalayas, which are at a lower latitude than the western Himalayas, are relatively warmer. The average minimum temperature for the month of May, recorded in Darjiling at an elevation of 6,380 feet (1,945 metres), is 52 °F (11 °C). In the same month, at an elevation of 16,500 feet (5,000 metres) in the neighbourhood of Mount Everest, the minimum temperature is about 17 °F (-8 °C); at 19,500 feet (6,000 metres) it falls to -8 °F (-22 °C), the lowest minimum having been -21 °F (-29 °C); during the day, in areas sheltered from strong winds that often blow at more than 100 miles (160 km) per hour, the sun is often pleasantly warm, even at high elevations.

There are two periods of precipitation: the moderate amounts brought by winter storms and the heavier precipitation of summer, with its southwesterly monsoon winds. During winter, low-pressure weather systems advance into the Himalayas from the west and cause heavy snowfall. Within the regions where western disturbances are felt, condensation occurs in upper air levels; as a result, precipitation is much greater over the high mountains. During this season snow accumulates around the Himalayan high peaks, and precipitation is greater in the west than the east. In January, for example, Mussoorie in the west receives almost 3 inches (75 mm), whereas Darjiling to the east receives less than 1 inch (25 mm). By the end of May the meteorological conditions have reversed. Southwesterly monsoon currents channel moist air toward the eastern Himalayas, where the moisture rising over the steep terrain cools and condenses to fall as rain or snow; in June, therefore, Darjiling receives about 24 inches (600 mm) and Mussoorie less than 8 inches (200 mm). The rain and snow cease in September, after which the finest weather in the Himalayas prevails until the beginning of winter in December.

PLANT LIFE

Himalayan vegetation can be broadly classified into four types—tropical, subtropical, temperate, and alpine—each of which prevails in a zone determined mainly by elevation and precipitation. Local differences in relief and climate, as well as exposure to sunlight and wind, cause considerable variation in the species present within each zone. Tropical evergreen rainforest is confined to the humid foothills of the eastern and central Himalayas. The evergreen dipterocarps—a group of timber- and resin-producing

Birch trees in the western Himalayas, Jammu and Kashmir state, northern India. Ardea London

trees—are common; their different species grow on different soils and on hill slopes of varying steepness. *Mesua ferrea* (Ceylon ironwood) is found on porous soils at elevations between 600 and 2,400 feet (180 and 720 metres); bamboos grow on steep slopes; oaks and chestnuts grow on the lithosol, covering sandstones from Arunachal Pradesh westward to central Nepal at elevations from 3,600 to 5,700 feet (1,100 to 1,700 metres). Alder trees are found along the watercourses on the steeper slopes. At higher elevations these species give way to mountain forests in which the typical evergreen is *Pandanus furcatus*, a type of screw pine. Besides these trees, some 4,000 species of flowering plants, of which 20 are palms, are estimated to occur in the eastern Himalayas.

With decreasing precipitation and increasing elevation westward, the rainforests give way to tropical deciduous forests, where the valuable timber tree *sal* is the dominant species; wet sal forests thrive on high plateaus at elevations of 3,000 feet (900 metres), while dry sal forests prevail higher up, at 4,500 feet (1,400 metres). Farther west, steppe forest (i.e., expanse of grassland dotted with trees), steppe, subtropical thorn steppe, and subtropical semidesert vegetation occur successively. Temperate mixed forests extend from about 4,500 to roughly 11,000 feet (1,400 to 3,400 metres) and contain conifers and broad-leaved temperate trees. Evergreen forests of oaks and conifers have their westernmost outpost on the hills above Murree, some 30 miles (50 km) northwest of Rawalpindi, in Pakistan; these forests are typical of the Lesser Himalayas, being conspicuous on the outer slopes of the Pir Panjal, in Jammu and Kashmir state. *Pinus roxburghii* (chir pine) is the dominant species at elevations from 2,700 to 5,400 feet (800 to 1,600 metres). In the inner valleys this species may occur even up to 6,300 feet (1,900 metres). Deodar cedar, a highly valued endemic species, grows mainly in the western part of the range. Stands of this species occur between 6,300 and 9,000 feet (1,900 and 2,700 metres) and tend to grow at still higher elevations in the upper valleys of the Sutlej and Ganges rivers. Of the other conifers, blue pine and spruce first appear between about 7,300 and 10,000 feet (2,200 and 3,000 metres).

The alpine zone begins above the tree line, between elevations of 10,500 and 11,700 feet (3,200 and 3,600 metres), and extends up to about 13,700 feet (4,200 metres) in the western Himalayas and 14,600 feet (4,500 metres) in the eastern Himalayas. In this zone can be found all the wet and moist alpine vegetation. Juniper is widespread, especially on sunny sites, steep and rocky slopes, and drier areas. Rhododendron occurs everywhere but is more abundant in the wetter parts of the eastern Himalayas, where it grows in all sizes from trees to low shrubs. Mosses and lichens grow in shaded areas at lower levels in the alpine zone where the humidity is high; flowering plants are found at high elevations.

ANIMAL LIFE

The fauna of the eastern Himalayas is similar to that of the southern Chinese and Southeast Asian region. Many of these species are primarily found in tropical forests and are only secondarily adapted to the subtropical, mountain, and temperate conditions prevailing at higher elevations and in the drier western areas. The animal life of the western Himalayas, however, has more affinities with that of the Mediterranean, Ethiopian, and Turkmenian regions. The past presence in the region of some African animals, such as giraffes and the hippopotamuses, can be inferred from fossil remains in deposits found in the Siwalik Range. The animal life at elevations above the tree line consists almost exclusively of cold-tolerant endemic species that evolved from the wildlife of·the steppes after the uplift of the Himalayas. Elephants and rhinoceroses are restricted to parts of the forested Tarai region—moist or marshy areas, now largely drained—at the

Himalayan tahr (Hemitragus jemlahicus). Arthur W. Ambler—The National Audubon Society Collection/Photo Researchers

base of the low hills in southern Nepal. Asiatic black bears, clouded leopards, langurs (a long-tailed Asian monkey), and Himalayan goat antelopes (e.g., the tahr) are some of the denizens of the Himalayan forests. The Indian rhinoceros was once abundant throughout the foothill zone of the Himalayas but is now endangered, as is the musk deer; both species are dwindling, and few live, other than those in a handful of reserves set up to protect them. The Kashmir stag, or *hangul*, is near extinction.

In remote sections of the Himalayas, at higher elevations, snow leopards, brown bears, lesser pandas, and Tibetan yaks have limited populations. The yak has been domesticated and is used as a beast of burden in Ladakh. Above the tree line the most numerous animals, however, are diverse types of insects, spiders, and mites, which are the only animal forms that can live as high up as 20,700 feet (6,300 metres).

Fish of the genus *Glyptothorax* live in most of the Himalayan streams, and the Himalayan water shrew inhabits stream banks. Lizards of the genus *Japalura* are widely distributed. *Typhlops*, a genus of blind snake, is common in the eastern Himalayas. The butterflies of the Himalayas are extremely varied and beautiful, especially those in the genus *Troides*.

The bird life is equally rich but is more abundant in the east than in the west. In Nepal alone almost 800 species have been observed. Among some of the common Himalayan birds are different species of magpies (including the black-rumped,

the blue, and the racket-tailed), titmice, choughs (related to the jackdaw), whistling thrushes, and redstarts. A few strong fliers, such as the lammergeier (bearded vulture), the black-eared kite, and the Himalayan griffon (an Old World vulture), also can be seen. Snow partridges and Cornish choughs are found at elevations of 18,600 feet (5,700 metres).

PEOPLE

Of the four principal language families in the Indian subcontinent—Indo-European, Tibeto-Burman, Austroasiatic, and Dravidian—the first two are well represented in the Himalayas. In ancient times, peoples speaking languages from both families mixed in varying proportions in different areas. Their distribution is the result of a long history of penetrations by Central Asian and Iranian groups from the west, Indian peoples from the south, and Asian peoples from the east and north. In Nepal, which constitutes the middle third of the Himalayas, these groups overlapped and intermingled. The penetrations of the lower Himalayas were instrumental to the migrations into and through the river-plain passageways of South Asia. Generally speaking, the Great Himalayas and the Tethys Himalayas are inhabited by Tibetans and peoples speaking other Tibeto-Burman languages, while the Lesser Himalayas are the home of Indo-European language speakers. Among the latter are the Kashmiri people of the Vale of Kashmir and the Gaddi and Gujari,

Settlement in the Kullu Valley, central Himachal Pradesh, India. The Holton Collection/ SuperStock

who live in the hilly areas of the Lesser Himalayas. Traditionally, the Gaddi are a hill people; they possess large flocks of sheep and herds of goats and go down with them from their snowy abode in the Outer Himalayas only in winter, returning again to the highest pastures in June. The Gujari are traditionally a migrating pastoral people who live off their herds of sheep, goats, and a few cattle, for which they seek pasture at various elevations.

The Champa, Ladakhi, Balti, and Dard peoples live to the north of the Great Himalaya Range in the Kashmir Himalayas. The Dard speak Indo-European languages, while the others are Tibeto-Burman speakers. The Champa traditionally lead a nomadic pastoral life in the upper Indus valley. The Ladakhi have settled on terraces and alluvial fans that flank the Indus in the northeastern Kashmir region. The Balti have spread farther down the Indus valley and have adopted Islam.

Other Indo-European speakers are the Kanet in Himachal Pradesh and the Khasi in Uttarakhand. In Himachal Pradesh most people in the districts of Kalpa and Lahul-Spiti are the descendants of migrants from Tibet who speak Tibeto-Burman languages.

In Nepal the Pahari, speaking Indo-European languages, constitute the majority of the population, although large groups of Tibeto-Burman speakers are found throughout the country. They include the Newar, the Tamang, the Gurung, the Magar, the Sherpa and other peoples related to the Bhutia, and the Kirat. The Kirat were the earliest inhabitants of the Kathmandu Valley. The Newar are also one of the earliest groups in Nepal. The Tamang inhabit the high valleys to the northwest, north, and east of Kathmandu Valley. The Gurung live on the southern slopes of the Annapurna massif, pasturing their cattle as high as 12,000 feet (3,700 metres). The Magar inhabit western Nepal but migrate seasonally to other parts of the country. The Sherpa, who live to the south of Mount Everest, are famed mountaineers.

For some 200 years the Sikkim region (now a state in India) and the kingdom of Bhutan have been safety valves for the absorption of the excess population of eastern Nepal. More Sherpa now live in the Darjiling area than in the Mount Everest homeland. At present the Pahari constitute the majority who come from Nepal in both Sikkim and Bhutan. Thus, the people of Sikkim belong to three distinct ethnic groups—the Lepcha, the Bhutia, and the Pahari. Generally speaking, the Nepalese and the Lepcha live in western Bhutan and the Bhutia of Tibetan origin in eastern Bhutan.

Arunachal Pradesh is the homeland of several groups—the Abor or Adi, the Aka, the Apa Tani, the Dafla, the Khampti, the Khowa, the Mishmi, the Momba, the Miri, and the Singpho. Linguistically, they are Tibeto-Burman. Each group has its homeland in a distinct river valley, and all practice shifting cultivation (i.e., they grow crops on a different tract of land each year).

ECONOMY

Economic conditions in the Himalayas partly depend on the limited resources available in different parts of this vast region of varied ecological zones. The principal activity is animal husbandry, but forestry, trade, and tourism are also important.

RESOURCES

The Himalayas abound in economic resources. These include pockets of rich arable land, extensive grasslands and forests, workable mineral deposits, easy-to-harness waterpower, and great natural beauty. The most productive arable lands in the western Himalayas are in the Vale of Kashmir, the Kangra valley, the Sutlej River basin, and the terraces flanking the Ganges and Yamuna rivers in Uttarakhand; these areas produce rice, corn (maize), wheat, and millet. In the central Himalayas in Nepal, two-thirds of the arable land is in the foothills and on the adjacent plains; this land yields most of the total rice production of the country. The region also produces large crops of corn, wheat, potatoes, and sugarcane.

Most of the fruit orchards of the Himalayas lie in the Vale of Kashmir and in the Kullu valley of Himachal Pradesh. Fruits such as apples, peaches, pears, and cherries—for which there is a great demand in the cities of India—are grown extensively. On the shores of Dal Lake in Kashmir, there are rich vineyards that produce grapes used to make wine and brandy. On the hills surrounding the Vale of Kashmir grow walnut and almond trees. Bhutan also has fruit orchards and exports oranges to India.

Tea is grown in plantations mainly on the hills and on the plain at the foot of the mountains in the Darjiling district. Plantations also produce limited amounts of tea in the Kangra valley. Plantations of the spice cardamom are to be found in Sikkim, Bhutan, and the Darjiling Hills. Medicinal herbs are grown on plantations in areas of Uttarakhand.

Transhumance (the seasonal migration of livestock) is widely practiced in the Himalayan pastures. Sheep, goats, and yaks are raised on the rough grazing lands available. During summer they graze on the pastures at higher elevations, but when the weather turns cold, shepherds migrate with their flocks to lower elevations.

The explosive population growth that has occurred in the Himalayas and elsewhere in the Indian subcontinent since the 1940s has placed great stress on the forests in many areas. Deforestation to clear land for planting and to supply firewood, paper, and construction materials has progressed up steeper and higher slopes of the Lesser Himalayas, triggering environmental degradation. Only in Sikkim and Bhutan are large areas still heavily forested.

The Himalayas are rich in minerals, although exploitation is restricted to the more accessible areas. The Kashmir region has the greatest concentration of minerals. Sapphires are found in the Zaskar Mountains, and alluvial gold is recovered in the nearby bed of the Indus River. There are deposits of copper ore in Baltistan, and iron ores are found in the Vale of Kashmir. Ladakh possesses borax and sulfur deposits. Coal seams are found in the Jammu Hills. Bauxite also occurs in Kashmir. Nepal, Bhutan, and Sikkim have extensive deposits of coal, mica, gypsum, and graphite and ores of iron, copper, lead, and zinc.

The Himalayan rivers have a tremendous potential for hydroelectric generation, which has been harnessed intensively in India since the 1950s. A giant multipurpose project is located at Bhakra-Nangal on the Sutlej River in the Outer Himalayas; its reservoir was completed in 1963 and has a storage capacity of some 348 billion cubic feet (10 billion cubic metres) of water and a total installed generating capacity of 1,050 megawatts. Three other Himalayan rivers—the Kosi, the Gandak (Narayani), and the Jaldhaka—have been harnessed by India, which then supplies electric power to Nepal and Bhutan.

Tourism is an increasingly important source of income and employment in parts of the Himalayas, especially Nepal. Increased traffic and tourists' heavy consumption of the region's limited resources have further stressed the environment.

TRANSPORTATION

Trails and footpaths long were the only means of communication in the Himalayas. Although these continue to be important, especially in the more remote locations, road transport now has made the Himalayas accessible from both north and south. In Nepal an east-west highway stretches through the Tarai lowlands, connecting roads that penetrate into many of the country's mountain valleys. The capital, Kathmandu, is connected to Pokhara by a low Himalayan highway, and another highway through Kodari Pass gives Nepal access to Tibet. A highway running from Kathmandu through Hetaunda and Birganj to Birauni connects Nepal to Bihar state and the rest of India. To the northwest in Pakistan, the Karakoram Highway links that country with China. The Hindustan-Tibet road, which passes through Himachal Pradesh, has been considerably improved; this 300-mile- (480-km-) highway runs through Shimla, once the summer capital of India, and crosses the Indo-Tibetan border near Shipki Pass. From Manali in the Kullu valley, a highway now crosses not only the Great Himalayas but also the Zaskar Range and reaches Leh in the upper Indus valley. Leh is also connected to India via Srinagar in the Vale of Kashmir; the road from Srinagar to Leh passes over the 17,730-foot- (5,404-metre-) high Khardung Pass—the first of the high passes on the historic caravan trail to Central Asia from India. Many other new roads have been built since 1950.

From the Indian Punjab the only direct approach to the Vale of Kashmir is by the highway from Jalandhar in Punjab state, India, to Srinagar through Pathankot, Jammu, Udhampur, Banihal, and Khahabal. It crosses the Pir Panjal Range through a tunnel at Banihal. The old road from Rawalpindi, Pak., to Srinagar, capital of Jammu and Kashmir state, has lost its importance since with the closing of the road at the line of control between the sectors of Kashmir administered by India and Pakistan.

The Sikkim Himalayas command the historic Kalimpang-to-Lhasa caravan trade route, which passes through Gangtok. Before the mid-1950s there was only one 30-mile (50-km) motorable highway running between Gangtok and Rangpo, on the Tista River, which then continued southward another 70 miles (110 km) to Shiliguri in West Bengal. Since then, several roads passable by four-wheel-drive vehicles have been built in the southern part of Sikkim, and the highway from Shiliguri has been extended through Lachung, in northern Sikkim, to Tibet.

Only two main railroads, both of narrow gauge, penetrate into the Lesser Himalayas from the plains of India: one in the western Himalayas, between Kalka and Shimla, and the other in the eastern Himalayas, between Shiliguri and Darjiling. Another narrow-gauge line in Nepal runs some 30 miles from Raxaul in Bihar state, India, to Amlekhganj. Two other short railroads run to the Outer Himalayas—one, the railroad of the Kullu Valley, from Pathankot to Jogindarnagar and the other from Haridwar to Dehra Dun.

There are two major airstrips in the Himalayas, one at Kathmandu and the other at Srinagarr; the airport at Kathmandu is served by international as well as regional flights. Besides these, there are also an increasing number of airstrips of local importance in Nepal and other countries in the region that can accommodate small aircraft. Improvements in both air and ground transportation have facilitated the growth of tourism in the Himalayas.

STUDY AND EXPLORATION

The earliest journeys through the Himalayas were undertaken by traders, shepherds, and pilgrims. The pilgrims believed that the harder the journey was, the nearer it brought them to salvation or enlightenment; the traders and shepherds, though, accepted crossing passes as high as 18,000 to 19,000 feet (5,500 to 5,800 metres) as a way of life. For all others, however, the Himalayas constituted a formidable and fearsome barrier.

The first known Himalayan sketch map of some accuracy was drawn up in 1590 by Antonio Monserrate, a Spanish missionary to the court of the Mughal emperor Akbar. In 1733 a French geographer, Jean-Baptiste Bourguignon d'Arville, compiled the first map of Tibet and the Himalayan range based on systematic exploration. In the mid-19th century the Survey of India organized a systematic program to measure correctly the heights of the Himalayan peaks. The Nepal and Uttarakhand peaks were observed and mapped between 1849 and 1855. Nanga Parbat, as well as the peaks of the Karakoram Range to the north, were surveyed between 1855 and 1859. The surveyors did not assign individual names to the innumerable peaks observed but designated them by letters and Roman numerals. Thus, at first Mount Everest was simply labeled as "H"; this had been changed to Peak XV by 1850. In 1865 Peak XV was renamed for Sir George Everest, surveyor general of India from 1830 to 1843. Not until 1852 were the computations sufficiently advanced for it to be realized that Peak XV was higher than any other peak in the world. By 1862 more than 40 peaks with elevations exceeding 18,000 feet (5,500 metres) had been climbed for surveying purposes.

In addition to the surveying expeditions, various scientific studies of the Himalayas were conducted in the 19th century. Between 1848 and 1849 the English botanist Joseph Dalton Hooker made a pioneering study of the plant life of the Sikkim Himalayas. He was followed by numerous others, including (in the early 20th century) the British naturalist Richard W.G. Hingston, who wrote valuable accounts of the natural history of animals living at high elevations in the Himalayas.

Since World War II the Survey of India has prepared some large-scale maps of the Himalayas from aerial photographs. Parts of the Himalayas also have been mapped by German geographers and cartographers, with the help of ground photogrammetry. In addition, satellite reconnaissance has been employed to produce even more accurate and detailed maps. Aerial photographs have been used in conjunction with other scientific observation methods to monitor the effects of climate change on the Himalayan environment—notably the recession of glaciers.

Himalayan mountaineering began in the 1880s with the Briton W.W. Graham, who claimed to have climbed several peaks in 1883. Though his reports were received with skepticism, they did spark interest in the Himalayas among other European climbers. In the early 20th century the number of mountaineering expeditions increased markedly to the Karakoram Range and to the Kumaun and Sikkim Himalayas. Between World Wars I and II, a certain national preference developed for the various peaks: the Germans concentrated on Nanga Parbat and Kanchenjunga, the Americans on K2 (in the Karakorams), and the British on Mount Everest. Since 1921 there have been several dozen attempts at scaling Everest; about a dozen of them were undertaken before it was first successfully scaled in May 1953 by the New Zealand mountaineer Edmund Hillary and his Sherpa partner Tenzing Norgay. That same year an Austro-German team led by Karl Maria Herrligkoffer reached the summit of Nanga Parbat. As the great peaks were conquered one by one, climbers began to look for greater challenges to test their skills and equipment, attempting to reach the summits by increasingly difficult routes. By the late 20th and early 21st centuries, the annual number of mountaineering expeditions and tourist excursions to the Himalayas had increased so much that in some areas the participants were threatening the delicate environmental balance of the mountains by destroying plant and animal life and by leaving behind a growing quantity of refuse.

GANGES RIVER

The Ganges (Hindi: Ganga) is the great river of the plains of northern India. Although officially as well as popularly called the Ganga in Hindi and in other Indian languages, internationally it is known by its conventional name, the Ganges. From time immemorial it has been the holy river of Hinduism. For most of its course it is a wide and sluggish stream, flowing through one of the most fertile and densely populated regions in the world. Despite its importance, its length of 1,560 miles (2,510 km) is relatively short compared with the other great rivers of Asia or of the world.

Rising in the Himalayas and emptying into the Bay of Bengal, it drains a quarter of the territory of India, while its basin supports hundreds of millions of people. The Gangetic Plain, across which it flows, is the heartland of the region known as Hindustan and has been the cradle of successive civilizations from the Mauryan empire of Ashoka in the 3rd century BCE down to the Mughal Empire, founded in the 16th century.

PHYSICAL FEATURES

For most of its course the Ganges flows through Indian territory, although its large delta in the Bengal area, which it shares with the Brahmaputra River, lies mostly in Bangladesh. The general direction of the river's flow is from northwest to southeast. At its delta the flow is generally southward.

PHYSIOGRAPHY

The Ganges rises in the southern Himalayas on the Indian side of the border with the Tibet Autonomous region of China. Its five headstreams— the Bhagirathi, Alaknanda, Mandakini, Dhauliganga, and Pindar—all rise in the northern mountainous region of Uttarakhand state. Of these, the two main headstreams are the Alaknanda (the longer of the two), which rises about 30 miles (50 km) north of the Himalayan peak of Nanda Devi, and the Bhagirathi, which originates about 10,000 feet (3,000 metres) above sea level in a subglacial meltwater cave at the base of the Himalayan glacier known as Gangotri.

Gangotri itself is a sacred place for Hindu pilgrimage. The true source of the Ganges, however, is considered to be at Gaumukh, about 13 miles (21 km) southeast of Gangotri.

The Alaknanda and Bhagirathi unite at Devaprayag to form the main stream known as the Ganga, which cuts through the Outer (southern) Himalayas to emerge from the mountains at Rishikesh. It then flows onto the plain at Haridwar, another place held sacred by the Hindus.

The volume of the Ganges increases markedly as it receives more tributaries and enters a region of heavier rainfall, and it shows a marked seasonal variation in flow. From April to June the melting Himalayan snows feed the river, while in the rainy season from July to September the rain-bearing monsoons cause floods. During winter the river's flow declines. South of Haridwar, now within the state of Uttar Pradesh, the river receives the principal right-bank tributaries of the Yamuna River, which flows through the Delhi capital region to join the Ganges near Allahabad, and the Tons, which flows north from the Vindhya Range in Madhya Pradesh state and joins the Ganges just below Allahabad. The main left-bank tributaries in Uttar Pradesh are the Ramganga, the Gomati, and the Ghaghara.

The Ganges next enters the state of Bihar, where its main tributaries from the Himalayan region to the north are the Gandak, the Burhi Gandak, the Ghugri, and the Kosi rivers and its most important southern tributary is the Son. The river then skirts the Rajmahal Hills to the south and flows southeast to Farakka, at the apex of the delta. In West Bengal, the last Indian state that the Ganges enters, the Mahananda River joins it from the north. In West Bengal in India, as well as in Bangladesh, the Ganges is locally called the Padma. The westernmost distributaries of the delta are the Bhagirathi and the Hugli (Hooghly) rivers, on the east bank of which stands the huge metropolis of Kolkata (Calcutta). The Hugli itself is joined by two tributaries flowing in from the west, the Damodar and the

Boat traffic on the Buriganga River, Dhaka, Bangl. Hubertus Kanus/SuperStock

Rupnarayan. As the Ganges passes from West Bengal into Bangladesh, a number of distributaries branch off to the south into the river's vast delta. In Bangladesh the Ganges is joined by the mighty Brahmaputra (which is called the Jamuna in Bangladesh) near Goalundo Ghat. The combined stream, there called the Padma, joins with the Meghna River above Chandpur. The waters then flow through the delta region to the Bay of Bengal via innumerable channels, the largest of which is known as the Meghna estuary.

The Ganges-Brahmaputra system has the third-greatest average discharge of the world's rivers, at roughly 1,086,500 cubic feet (30,770 cubic metres) per second; approximately 390,000 cubic feet (11,000 cubic metres) per second is supplied by the Ganges alone. The rivers' combined suspended sediment load of about 1.84 billion tons per year is the world's highest.

Dhaka (Dacca), the capital of Bangladesh, stands on the Buriganga ("Old Ganges"), a tributary of the Dhaleswari. Apart from the Hugli and the Meghna, the other distributary streams that form the Ganges delta are, in West Bengal, the Jalangi River and, in Bangladesh, the Matabhanga, Bhairab, Kabadak, Garai-Madhumati, and Arial Khan rivers.

The Ganges, as well as its tributaries and distributaries, is constantly vulnerable to changes in its course in the delta region. Such changes have occurred in comparatively recent times, especially since 1750. In 1785 the Brahmaputra flowed past the city of Mymensingh; it now flows more than 40 miles (65 km) west of it before joining the Ganges.

The delta, the seaward prolongation of sediment deposits from the Ganges and Brahmaputra river valleys, is about 220 miles (355 km) along the coast and covers an area of about 23,000 square miles (60,000 square km). It is composed of repeated alternations of clays, sands, and marls, with recurring layers of peat, lignite, and beds of what were once forests. The new deposits of the delta, known in Hindi and Urdu as the *khadar*, naturally occur in the vicinity of the present channels. The delta's growth is dominated by tidal processes.

The southern surface of the Ganges delta has been formed by the rapid and comparatively recent deposition of enormous loads of sediment. To the east the seaward side of the delta is being changed at a rapid rate by the formation of new lands, known as *chars*, and new islands. The western coastline of the delta, however, has remained practically unchanged since the 18th century.

The rivers in the West Bengal area are sluggish; little water passes down them to the sea. In the Bangladeshi delta region, the rivers are broad and active, carrying plentiful water and connected by innumerable creeks. During the rains (June to October) the greater part of the region is flooded to a depth of 3 or more feet (at least 1 metre), leaving the villages and homesteads, which are built on artificially raised land, isolated above the floodwaters. Communication between settlements during this season can be accomplished only by boat.

To the seaward side of the delta as a whole, there is a vast stretch of tidal mangrove forests and swampland. The region, called the Sundarbans, is protected by India and Bangladesh for conservation purposes. Each country's portion of the Sundarbans has been designated a UNESCO World Heritage site, India's in 1987 and Bangladesh's in 1997.

In certain parts of the delta there occur layers of peat, composed of the remains of forest vegetation and rice plants. In many natural depressions, known as *bils*, peat, still in the process of formation, has been used as a fertilizer by local farmers, and it also has been dried and used as a domestic and industrial fuel.

Climate and Hydrology

The Ganges basin contains the largest river system on the subcontinent. The water supply depends partly on the rains brought by the southwesterly monsoon winds from July to October, as well as on the flow from melting Himalayan snows in the hot season from April to June. Precipitation in the river basin accompanies the southwest monsoon winds, but it also comes with tropical cyclones that originate in the Bay of Bengal between June and October. Only a small amount of rainfall occurs in December and January. The average annual rainfall varies from 30 inches (760 mm) at the western end of the basin to more than 90 inches (2,290 mm) at the eastern end. (In the upper Gangetic Plain in Uttar Pradesh, rainfall averages about 30–40 inches [760–1,020 mm]; in the Middle Ganges Plain of Bihar, from 40 to 60 inches [1,020 to 1,520 mm]; and in the delta region, between 60 and 100 inches [1,520 to 2,540 mm].) The delta region experiences strong cyclonic storms both before the commencement of the monsoon season, from March to May, and at the end of it, from September to October. Some of these storms result in much loss of life and the destruction of homes, crops, and livestock. One such storm, which occurred in November 1970, was of catastrophic proportions, resulting in deaths of at least 200,000 and possibly as many as 500,000 people; another, in April 1991, killed some 140,000.

Since there is little variation in relief over the entire surface of the Gangetic Plain, the river's rate of flow is slow. Between the Yamuna River at Delhi and the Bay of Bengal, a distance of nearly 1,000 miles (1,600 km), the elevation drops only some 700 feet (210 metres). Altogether the Ganges-Brahmaputra plains extend over an area of 300,000 square miles (800,000 square km). The alluvial mantle of the plain, which in some places is more than 6,000 feet (1,800 metres) thick, is possibly not more than 10,000 years old.

Plant and Animal Life

The Ganges-Yamuna area was once densely forested; historical writings indicate that in the 16th and 17th centuries wild elephants, buffalo, bison, rhinoceroses, lions, and tigers were hunted there. Most of the original natural vegetation has disappeared from the Ganges basin, and the land is now intensely cultivated to meet the needs of an ever-growing population. Large wild animals are few, except for deer, boars, and wildcats and some wolves, jackals, and foxes. Only in the Sundarbans area of the delta are some Bengal tigers, crocodiles, and marsh deer still found. Fish abound in all the rivers, especially in the delta area, where they form an important part of the inhabitants' diet. Many varieties of birds are found, such as mynah birds, parrots, crows, kites, partridges, and fowls. In winter, ducks and snipes migrate south across the high Himalayas, settling in large numbers in water-covered areas. In the Bengal area common fish include featherbacks (Notopteridae family), barbs (Cyprinidae), walking catfish, gouramis (Anabantidae), and milkfish (Chanidae).

PEOPLE

Ethnically, the people of the Ganges basin are of mixed origin. In the west and centre of the basin they were originally descended from an early population—possibly speaking Dravidian or Austroasiatic languages—and were later joined by speakers of Indo-Aryan languages. In historical times, Turks, Mongols, Afghans, Persians, and Arabs came from the west and intermingled with them. To the east

and south, especially in Bengal, peoples speaking Austroasiatic, Indo-Aryan, and Tibeto-Burman languages have joined the population over the centuries. Europeans, arriving still later, did not settle or intermarry to any large extent.

Historically the Gangetic Plain has constituted the heartland of Hindustan and its successive civilizations. The centre of the Mauryan empire of Ashoka was Patna (ancient Pataliputra), on the Ganges in Bihar. The centres of the great Mughal Empire were at Delhi and Agra, in the western Ganges basin. Kannauj on the Ganges, north of Kanpur, was the centre of the feudal empire of Harsha, which covered most of northern India in the middle of the 7th century. During the Muslim era, which began in the 12th century, Muslim rule extended not only over the plain but over all Bengal as well. Dhaka and Murshidabad in the delta region were centres of Muslim power.

The British, having founded Calcutta (Kolkata) on the banks of the Hugli River in the late 17th century, gradually expanded their dominion up the valley of the Ganges, reaching Delhi in the mid-19th century.

A great number of cities have been built on the Gangetic Plain. Among the most notable are Saharanpur, Meerut, Agra (the city of the famous Taj Mahal mausoleum), Mathura (esteemed as the birthplace of the Hindu god Krishna), Aligarh, Kanpur, Bareilly, Lucknow, Allahabad, Varanasi (Benares; the holy city of the Hindus), Patna, Bhagalpur,

Rajshahi, Murshidabad, Kolkata, Haora (Howrah), Dhaka, Khulna, and Barisal.

In the delta, Kolkata and its satellite towns stretch for about 50 miles (80 km) along both banks of the Hugli, forming one of India's most important concentrations of population, commerce, and industry.

The religious importance of the Ganges may exceed that of any other river in the world. It has been revered from the earliest times and today is regarded as the holiest of rivers by Hindus. While places of Hindu pilgrimage, called *tirthas*, are located throughout the subcontinent, those that are situated on the Ganges have particular significance. Among these are the confluence of the Ganges and the Yamuna near Allahabad, where a bathing festival, or *mela*, is held in January and February; during this ceremony hundreds of thousands of pilgrims immerse themselves in the river. Other holy places for immersion are at Varanasi (Benares), or Kashi, and at Haridwar. The Hugli River at Kolkata also is regarded as holy.

Ship laden with cremation ashes to be deposited in the Ganges River, Varanasi, India. © Charles A. Crowell/Black Star

Other places of pilgrimage on the Ganges include Gangotri and the junction of the Alaknanda and Bhagirathi headstreams in the Himalayas. The Hindus cast the ashes of their dead upon the river, believing that this gives the deceased direct passage to heaven, and cremation ghats (temples at the summit of riverside steps) for burning the dead have been built in many places on the banks of the Ganges.

ECONOMY

The Gangetic Plain constitutes the great heartland of Indian population and agriculture, and the Ganges is the region's lifeblood.

IRRIGATION

Use of the Ganges water for irrigation, either when the river is in flood or by means of gravity canals, has been common since ancient times. Such irrigation is described in scriptures and mythological books written more than 2,000 years ago. Megasthenes, a Greek ambassador who was in India, recorded the use of irrigation in the 4th century BCE. Irrigation was highly developed during the period of Muslim rule from the 12th century onward, and the Mughal kings later constructed several canals. The canal system was further extended by the British.

The cultivated area of the Ganges valley in Uttar Pradesh and Bihar benefits from a system of irrigation canals that has increased the production of such cash crops as sugarcane, cotton, and oilseeds. The older canals are mainly in the Ganges-Yamuna Doab (*doab* meaning "land between two rivers"). The Upper Ganga Canal and its branches have a combined length of 5,950 miles (9,575 km); it begins at Hardiwar. The Lower Ganga Canal, extending 5,120 miles (8,240 km) with its branches, begins at Naraura. The Sarda Canal irrigates land near Ayodhya, in Uttar Pradesh. Higher lands at the northern edge of the plain are difficult to irrigate by canal, and groundwater must be pumped to the surface. Large areas in Uttar Pradesh and in Bihar are also irrigated by channels running from hand-dug wells. The Ganges-Kabadak scheme in Bangladesh, largely an irrigation plan, covers parts of the districts of Khulna, Jessore, and Kushtia that lie within the part of the delta where silt and overgrowth choke the slowly flowing rivers. The system of irrigation is based on both gravity canals and electrically powered lifting devices.

NAVIGATION

In ancient times the Ganges and some of its tributaries, especially in the east, were important transportation routes. According to the ancient Greek historian Megasthenes, the Ganges and its main tributaries were being navigated in the 4th century BCE. In the 14th century, inland-river navigation in the Ganges basin was still flourishing. By the 19th century, irrigation-cum-navigation canals formed the main arteries of the water-transport system. The advent of paddle steamers revolutionized inland transport, stimulating the growth of indigo production in Bihar and Bengal. Regular steamer services ran from Kolkata up the Ganges to Allahabad and far beyond, as well as to Agra on the Yamuna and up the Brahmaputra River.

The decline of large-scale water transport began with the construction of railways during the mid-19th century. The increasing withdrawal of water for irrigation also affected navigation. River traffic now is insignificant beyond the middle Ganges basin around Allahabad, mainly consisting of rural rivercraft (including motorboats, sailboats, and rafts).

West Bengal and Bangladesh, however, continue to rely on the waterways to transport jute, tea, grain, and other agricultural and rural products. Principal river ports are Chalna, Khulna, Barisal, Chandpur, Narayanganj, Goalundo Ghat, Sirajganj, Bhairab Bazar, and Fenchuganj in Bangladesh and Kolkata, Goalpara, Dhuburi, and Dibrugarh in India. The partition of British India into India and Pakistan in 1947—with eastern Bengal becoming East Pakistan until in 1971 it declared its independence as Bangladesh—produced far-reaching changes, virtually halting the large trade in tea and jute formerly carried to Kolkata from Assam by inland waterway.

In Bangladesh inland water transport is the responsibility of the Inland Water Transport Authority. In India the Central Inland Water Transport Board formulates policy for inland waterways, while the Inland Waterways Authority develops and maintains an extensive system of national waterways. Approximately 1,000 miles (1,600 km) of waterways in the Ganges basin from Allahabad to Haldia are included in the system.

The Farakka Barrage at the head of the delta, just inside Indian territory in West Bengal, began diverting Ganges waters south into India in 1976. The Indian government argued that hydrological changes had diverted Ganges water from the port of Kolkata over the preceding century and resulted in the deposition of silt and the intrusion of saline seawater. India constructed the dam to ameliorate the condition of Kolkata by flushing away the seawater and raising the water level. The Bangladeshi government maintained that the Farakka Barrage deprived southwestern Bangladesh of a needed source of water. In 1996 both countries signed an agreement resolving the dispute by apportioning the waters of the Ganges between the two countries. Catastrophic floods in Bangladesh in 1987 and 1988—the latter being among the most severe in the country's history—prompted the World Bank to prepare a long-term flood-control plan for the region.

HYDROELECTRIC POWER

The hydroelectric potential of the Ganges and its tributaries has been estimated at

13 million kilowatts, of which about two-fifths lies within India and the rest in Nepal. Some of this potential has been exploited in India with such hydroelectric developments as those along the Chambal and Rihand rivers.

THAR DESERT

The Thar, or Great Indian, Desert is an arid region of rolling sand hills located partly in Rajasthan state, northwestern India, and partly in Punjab and Sindh (Sind) provinces, eastern Pakistan. It covers some 77,000 square miles (200,000 square km) of territory and is bordered by the irrigated Indus River plain to the west, the Aravalli Range to the southeast, the Rann of Kachchh to the south, and the Punjab Plain to the north and northeast. The subtropical desert climate results from persistent high atmospheric pressure and subsidence at this latitude. The prevailing monsoon winds that bring rain to the rest of India in summer tend to bypass the Thar to the east. The name Thar is derived from *t'hul,* the general term for the region's sand ridges.

LAND

The desert sands cover Archean (early Precambrian) gneiss (metamorphic rocks formed more than 2.5 billion years ago), Proterozoic (later Precambrian) sedimentary rocks (about 540 million to 2.5 billion years old), and more recent alluvium (material deposited by rivers). The surface sand is aeolian (wind-deposited) sand that has accumulated over the last 1.8 million years.

The desert presents an undulating surface, with high and low sand dunes separated by sandy plains and low barren hills, or *bhakars,* which rise abruptly from the surrounding plains. The dunes are in continual motion and take on varying shapes and sizes. Older dunes, however, are in a semistabilized or stabilized condition, and many rise to a height of almost 500 feet (150 metres). Several playas (saline lake beds), locally known as *dhands,* are scattered throughout the region.

The soils consist of seven main groups—desert soils, red desertic soils, sierozems (brownish gray soils), the red and yellow soils of the foothills, the saline soils of the depressions, and the lithosols (shallow, weathered soils) and regosols (soft, loose soils) found in the hills. All these soils are predominantly coarse-textured, well-drained, and calcareous (calcium-bearing). A thick accumulation of lime often occurs at varying depths. The soils are generally infertile and, because of severe wind erosion, are overblown with sand.

The amount of annual rainfall in the desert is generally low, ranging from about 4 inches (100 mm) or less in the west to about 20 inches (500 mm) in the east. Precipitation amounts fluctuate widely from year to year. About 90 percent of the total annual rainfall occurs during the season of the southwest monsoon, from July to September. During other seasons the prevailing wind blows from the northeast. May and June are the hottest months of the year, with temperatures rising to 122 °F (50 °C). During January, the coldest month, the mean minimum temperature ranges between 41 and 50 °F (5 and 10 °C), and frost is frequent. Dust storms and dust-raising winds, often blowing with velocities of 87 to 93 miles (140 to 150 km) per hour, are common in May and June.

The desert vegetation is mostly herbaceous or stunted scrub; drought-resistant trees occasionally dot the landscape, especially in the east. On the hills, gum arabic acacia and euphorbia may be found. The *khajri* (or *khejri*) tree (*Prosopis cineraria*) grows throughout the plains.

The thinly populated grasslands support black bucks, chikara (gazelles), and some feathered game, notably francolins (partridges) and quail. Among the migratory birds, sand grouse, ducks, and geese are common. The desert is also the home of the endangered great bustard.

PEOPLE

Most of the desert's inhabitants reside in rural areas and are distributed in varying densities. Both Islam and Hinduism are practiced, and the population is divided into complex economic and social groups. The prevailing languages are Sindhi in the southwest, Lahnda in the northwest, and Rajasthani languages—especially Marwari—in central and eastern portions of the Thar. The ethnic composition of the Thar is diverse. Among the most

prominent groups are the Rajputs, who inhabit the central Thar. Many nomads are engaged in animal husbandry, crafts, or trade. In general, the nomads are symbiotically related to the sedentary population and its economy.

ECONOMY

The grasses form the main natural resources of the desert. They provide nutritive pasturage as well as medicines used locally by the inhabitants. Alkaloids, used for making medicine and oils for making soap are also extracted. There are five major breeds of cattle in the Thar. Among these the Tharparkar breed is the highest milk yielder, and the Kankre breed is good both as a beast of burden and as a milk producer. Sheep are bred for both medium-fine and rough wool. Camels are commonly used for transport as well as for plowing the land and other agricultural purposes. Where water is available, farmers grow crops such as wheat and cotton.

However, water is scarce. Whatever seasonal rain falls is collected in tanks and reservoirs and is used for drinking and domestic purposes. Most groundwater cannot be utilized because it lies deep underground and is often saline. Good aquifers have been detected in the central part of the desert. Apart from wells and tanks, canals are the main sources of water in the desert. The Sukkur Barrage on the Indus River, completed in 1932, irrigates the southern Thar region in Pakistan by means of canals, and the

Gang Canal carries water from the Sutlej River to the northwest. The Indira Gandhi Canal irrigates a vast amount of land in the Indian portion of the Thar. The canal begins at the Harike Barrage—at the confluence of the Sutlej and Beas rivers in the Indian Punjab—and continues in a southwesterly direction for 292 miles (470 km).

Thermal-power-generating plants, fueled by coal and oil, supply power only locally in the large towns. Hydroelectric power is supplied by the Nangal power plant located on the Sutlej River in Punjab.

Roads and railways are few. One railway line serves the southern part of the region. In the Indian part of the desert, a second line goes from Merta Road to Suratgarh via Bikaner, and another connects the towns of Jodhpur and Jaisalmer. In the Pakistani part of the desert, a railway line runs between Bahawalpur and Hyderabad.

The partition of India and Pakistan in 1947 left most of the irrigation canals fed by the rivers of the Indus system in Pakistani territory while a large desert region remained unirrigated on the Indian side of the border. The Indus Water Treaty of 1960 fixed and delimited the rights and obligations of both countries concerning the use of waters of the Indus River system. Under the agreement, waters of the Ravi, Beas, and Sutlej rivers are to be made available to the Indira Gandhi Canal mainly to irrigate portions of the Thar in western Rajasthan.

CHAPTER 4

SPOTLIGHT ON INDIA'S WORLD HERITAGE SITES AND OTHER NOTABLE LOCATIONS

India's natural and cultural landscape is remarkable for its diversity and great antiquity. In addition to many spectacular scenic areas, the country contains many of the world's oldest and most recognizable cultural treasures. India has an extensive list of UNESCO World Heritage sites, including both cultural and natural features. Most prominent among these is the renowned Taj Mahal in Agra, one of the world's best-known architectural masterpieces.

AGRA AND THE TAJ MAHAL

The historic city of Agra, in west-central Uttar Pradesh state, north-central India, is renowned not only for the Taj Mahal but also for its many examples of Mughal architecture. Below is a survey of the city itself, followed by a discussion of its famous mausoleum.

THE CITY

Agra lies on the Yamuna (Jumna) River about 125 miles (200 km) southeast of Delhi. Founded by Sultan Sikandar

Lodī in the early 16th century, it was the Mughal capital during some periods of their empire. In the late 18th century the city fell successively to the Jats, the Marathas, the Mughals, the ruler of Gwalior, and, finally, the British in 1803. It was the capital of Agra (later North-Western) province from 1833 to 1868 and was one of the main centres of the Indian Mutiny (1857–58).

Notable among the city's many architectural masterpieces (other than the Taj Mahal), is the Agra (or Red) Fort (16th century), named for its massive red sandstone walls, which was built by the Mughal emperor Akbar. It contains the Pearl Mosque (Moti Masjid; 17th century), constructed of white marble, and a palace, the Jahangiri Mahal. The fort was designated a UNESCO World Heritage site in 1983.

The Jāmiʿ Masjid, or Great Mosque, and the elegant Itimad al-Dawlah tomb (1628), of white marble, are located near the Taj Mahal. To the northwest, at Sikandra, is the tomb of Akbar.

Agra is a major road and rail junction and a commercial and industrial centre known for its leather goods, cut stone, and handwoven carpets. Tourism is a major factor in the city's economy. The city is the seat of Dr. B.R. Ambedkar University (formerly Agra University), founded in 1927. The suburbs of Agra contain the state psychiatric hospital and Dayalbagh, a colony of the Radha Soami Satsang religious sect (founded in the city in 1861).

Many religious and cultural festivals are held in Agra. Janamashtami commemorates the birthday of Lord Krishna. The annual Taj Mahotsav, a 10-day arts, crafts, and music carnival, usually in February, is held in Shilpagram, a crafts village close to the Taj Mahal.

The region around Agra consists almost entirely of a level plain, with hills in the extreme southwest. The region is watered by the Yamuna River and the Agra Canal. Millet, barley, wheat, and cotton are among the crops grown. The deserted Mughal city of Fatehpur Sikri is about 25 miles (40 km) southwest of Agra city. Pop. (2001) city, 1,275,134; urban agglom., 1,331,339.

TAJ MAHAL

The Taj Mahal (or Tadj Mahall) mausoleum complex is situated on the southern bank of the Yamuna River. In its harmonious proportions and its fluid incorporation of decorative elements, the Taj Mahal is distinguished as the finest example of Mughal architecture, a blend of Indian, Persian, and Islamic styles. One of the most beautiful structural compositions in the world, the Taj Mahal was designated a UNESCO World Heritage site in 1983.

HISTORY OF CONSTRUCTION

It was built by the Mughal emperor Shah Jahān (reigned 1628–58) to immortalize his wife Mumtāz Maḥal ("Chosen One of the Palace"). The name Taj Mahal is a derivation of her name. She died in childbirth in 1631, after having been the emperor's inseparable companion since their marriage in 1612. The plans for the complex have been attributed to various architects of the period, though the chief architect was probably Ustad Aḥmad Lahawrī, an Indian of Persian descent. The five principal elements of the complex—main gateway, garden, mosque, *jawab* (literally "answer"; a building mirroring the mosque), and mausoleum (including its four minarets)—were conceived and designed as a unified entity according to the tenets of Mughal building practice, which allowed no subsequent addition or alteration. Building commenced about 1632. More than 20,000 workers were employed from India, Persia, the Ottoman Empire, and Europe to complete the mausoleum itself by about 1638–39; the adjunct buildings were finished by 1643, and decoration work continued until at least 1647. In total, construction of the 42-acre (17-hectare) complex spanned 22 years.

A tradition relates that Shah Jahān originally intended to build another mausoleum across the river to house his own remains, and the two structures were to be connected by a bridge. He was deposed by his son Aurangzeb, however, and imprisoned for the rest of his life in Agra Fort, on the right bank of the Yamuna River 1 mile (1.6 km) west of the Taj Mahal.

ARCHITECTURE

Resting in the middle of a wide plinth 23 feet (7 metres) high, the mausoleum proper is of white marble that reflects hues according to the intensity of sunlight or moonlight. It has four nearly identical facades, each with a wide central arch rising to 108 feet (33 metres) and chamfered (slanted) corners incorporating smaller arches. The majestic central dome, which reaches a height of 240 feet (73 metres) at the tip of its finial, is surrounded by four lesser domes. The acoustics inside the main dome cause the single note of a flute to reverberate five times. The interior of the mausoleum is organized around an octagonal marble chamber ornamented with low-relief carvings and semiprecious stones (*pietra dura*); therein are the cenotaphs of Mumtāz Maḥal and Shah Jahān. These false tombs are enclosed by a finely wrought filigree marble screen. Beneath the tombs, at garden level, lie the true sarcophagi. Standing gracefully apart from the central building, at each of the four corners of the square plinth, are elegant minarets.

Flanking the mausoleum near the northwestern and northeastern edges of the garden, respectively, are two symmetrically identical buildings—the mosque, which faces east, and its *jawab*, which faces west and provides aesthetic balance. Built of red Sikri sandstone with marble-necked domes and architraves, they contrast in both colour and texture with the mausoleum's white marble.

The garden is set out along classical Mughal lines—a square quartered by long watercourses (pools)—with walking paths, fountains, and ornamental trees. Enclosed by the walls and structures of the complex, it provides a striking approach to the mausoleum, which can be seen reflected in the garden's central pools.

The southern end of the complex is graced by a wide red sandstone gateway with a recessed central arch two stories high. White marble paneling around the arch is inlaid with black Qur'ānic lettering and floral designs. The main arch is flanked by two pairs of smaller arches. Crowning the northern and southern facades of the gateway are matching rows of white *chattris* (*chhattris*; cupola-like structures), 11 to each facade, accompanied by thin ornamental minarets that rise to some 98 feet (30 metres). At the four corners of the structure are octagonal towers capped with larger *chattris*.

Two notable decorative features are repeated throughout the complex: *pietra dura* and Arabic calligraphy. As embodied in the Mughal craft, *pietra dura* (Italian: "hard stone") incorporates the inlay of semiprecious stones of various colours, including lapis lazuli, jade, crystal, turquoise, and amethyst, in highly formalized and intertwining geometric and floral designs. The colours serve to moderate the dazzling expanse of the white Makrana marble. Under the direction of Amānat Khan al-Shīrāzī, Qur'ānic verses were inscribed across numerous sections of the Taj Mahal in calligraphy, central to Islamic artistic tradition. One of the inscriptions in the sandstone gateway is known as Daybreak (89:28–30) and invites the faithful to enter paradise. Calligraphy also encircles the soaring arched entrances to the mausoleum proper. To ensure a uniform appearance from the vantage point of the terrace, the lettering increases in size according to its relative height and distance from the viewer.

ENVIRONMENTAL AND CULTURAL ISSUES

Over the centuries the Taj Mahal has been subject to neglect and decay. A major restoration was carried out at the beginning of the 20th century under the direction of Lord Curzon, then the British viceroy of India. More recently, air pollution caused by emissions from foundries and other nearby factories and exhaust from motor vehicles has damaged the mausoleum, notably its marble facade. A number of steps have been taken to reduce the threat to the monument, among them the closing of some foundries and the installation of pollution-control equipment at others, the creation of a parkland buffer zone around the complex, and the banning of nearby vehicular traffic. Night viewing of the Taj Mahal was banned from 1984 to 2004, because it was feared that the monument would be a target of Sikh militants. A restoration and research program for the Taj Mahal was initiated in 1998. Progress in improving environmental conditions around the monument, however, has been slow.

The Taj Mahal has increasingly come to be seen as an Indian cultural symbol. Some Hindu nationalist groups have attempted to diminish the importance of the Muslim influence in accounting for the origins and design of the Taj Mahal.

OTHER CULTURAL SITES

India's great treasure of cultural assets dates to the earliest days of humanity and the beginnings of civilization on Earth. The following is a selection of some of the best known of these places.

AJANTA CAVES

The Ajanta Caves constitute a complex of Buddhist rock-cut cave temples and monasteries, located near Ajanta village, north-central Maharashtra state, western India; they are celebrated for their wall paintings. The temples are hollowed out of granite cliffs on the inner side of a 70-foot (20-metre) ravine in the Wagurna River valley, 65 miles (105 km) northeast of Aurangabad, at a site of great scenic beauty.

The group of some 30 caves was excavated between the 1st century BCE and the 7th century CE and consists of two types, *caitya*s ("sanctuaries") and *vihara*s ("monasteries"). Although the sculpture, particularly the rich ornamentation of the *caitya* pillars, is noteworthy, it is the fresco-type paintings that are the chief interest of Ajanta. These paintings depict colourful Buddhist legends and divinities with an exuberance and vitality that is unsurpassed in Indian art. The caves were designated a UNESCO World Heritage site in 1983.

BADRINATH

The village of Badrinath and its renowned Hindu shrine are located in eastern Uttarakhand state, northern India. Situated in the Himalayas along a headstream of the Ganges (Ganga) River, it lies at an elevation of about 10,000 feet (3,000 metres) and is uninhabited in winter. The village's site is located along the twin mountain ranges of Nar and Narayan on the left bank of Alakananda River. Badrinath gets its name from *badri*, a type of wild berry that once grew there in profusion. Badrinath is the home of a temple that contains a shrine of Badrinatha (one of the many names of Vishnu) and has been a well-known pilgrimage centre for more than 2,000 years. The temple is believed to have been built by Adi Shankaracharya, a philosopher-saint of the 8th century. Badrinath Peak (23,420 feet [7,138 metres]) is 17 miles (27 km) west. Other sights at Badrinath include Tapt Kund, a hot spring on the bank of the Alakananda; Brahma Kapal, a platform used for rituals; Sheshnetra, a boulder that is believed to contain an imprint of Sesha Nag, the legendary serpent; Charan Paduka, which, according to legend, holds the footprints of Lord Vishnu; and Neelkanth, the snowy peak that towers over Badrinath and is known as the "Garhwal Queen."

BHIMBETKA ROCK SHELTERS

The Bhimbetka rock shelters constitute a series of natural rock shelters situated

Ajanta Caves in north-central Maharashtra state, India. Art Resource, New York

in the foothills of the Vindhya Range, some 28 miles (45 km) south of Bhopal, in the central Indian state of Madhya Pradesh. Discovered in 1957, the complex consists of some 700 shelters and is one of the largest repositories of prehistoric art in India. The shelters were designated a UNESCO World Heritage site in 2003. The complex is surrounded by the Ratapani Wildlife Sanctuary.

The Bhimbetka region is riddled with massively sculpted rock formations. On the Bhimbetka hill site alone—where the bulk of the archaeological research has been concentrated since 1971—243 shelters have been investigated, of which 133 of them contain rock paintings. In addition to the cave paintings, archaeologists have unearthed large numbers of artifacts in the caves and the thick teak forests and fields around Bhimbetka, the oldest of which are Acheulian stone tool assemblages.

The paintings, which display great vitality and narrative skill, are categorized into different prehistoric periods. The oldest are dated to the Upper Paleolithic Period and consist of large linear representations of rhinoceroses and bears. Paintings from Mesolithic times are smaller and, in addition to animals, portray human activities. Drawings from the Chalcolithic (early Bronze) Age showcase early humans' conceptions of agriculture. Finally, the decorative paintings dating to early historic times depict religious motifs, including tree gods and magical sky chariots.

The caves provide a rare glimpse at a sequence of cultural development that traces early nomadic hunter-gatherers to settled cultivators to individuals expressing their spirituality. It has been observed that the present-day cultural traditions of agrarian peoples inhabiting the villages surrounding Bhimbetka resemble those represented in the paintings.

BODH GAYA

The historic town of Bodh Gaya (also spelled Buddh Gaya) is in central Bihar state, northeastern India. It is situated west of the Phalgu River, a tributary of the Ganges (Ganga) River. One of the holiest of Buddhist sites, it was there, under the sacred pipal, or Bo tree, that Gautama Buddha (Prince Siddhartha) attained enlightenment and became the Buddha. A simple shrine was built by the emperor Ashoka (3rd century BCE) to mark the spot, and this was later enclosed by a stone railing (1st century BCE), part of which still remains. The uprights have representations of the Vedic gods Indra and Surya, and the railing medallions are carved with imaginary beasts. The shrine was replaced in the Kushan period (2nd century CE) by the present Mahabodhi temple (designated a UNESCO World Heritage site in 2002), which was itself refurbished in the Pala-Sena period (750–1200), heavily restored by the British archaeologist Sir Alexander Cunningham in the second half of the 19th century, and finally restored by Myanmar (Burmese) Buddhists in 1882.

The temple's central tower stands 180 feet (54 metres) above the ground. A museum contains various Buddhist relics. Bodh Gaya is the site of Magadh University (1962). Pop. (2001) 30,857.

ELEPHANTA ISLAND

Elephanta Island (Hindi: Gharapuri ["Fortress City"]) is an island located in Mumbai (Bombay) Harbour of the Arabian Sea, about 6 miles (10 km) east of Mumbai and 2 miles (3 km) west of the mainland coast of Maharashtra state, western India. Elephanta Island has an area of 4 to 6 square miles (10 to 16 square km), varying with the tide. In the early 16th century Portuguese navigators named the island Ilha Elefante ("Elephant Island") in reference to a large stone elephant that was found there; the statue was later moved to Victoria Gardens (now called Jijamata Udyan), Mumbai. The island's Hindi name, Gharapuri, derives from a small village at its southern end.

Elephanta's famous 8th- and 9th-century cave temples were designated UNESCO World Heritage sites in 1987. Atop a large hill, they occupy some 54,800 square feet (5,000 square metres). The main temple is a long hall stretching 90 feet (27 metres); carved into the rock on the walls and ceiling of the cave are rows of columns and crossbeams. The plan of the temple is such that important points are laid out in the form of a mandala. A series of sculptured panels lining the walls of the cave portray images from Indian mythology, the most celebrated of which is the 20-foot- (6-metre-) high Trimurti, a three-headed bust of Shiva in the roles of destroyer, preserver, and creator emerging from a mountain. Other sculptures depict Shiva crushing Ravana with his toe, the marriage of Shiva and Parvati, Shiva bringing the Ganges (Ganga) River to earth by letting it flow through his hair, and Shiva as the embodiment of cosmic energy, dancing to drums. A linga (Hindu symbol of Shiva) is housed in a sanctuary at the western end of the temple.

When the island was ceded to the Portuguese by the kings of Ahmadabad in the 16th century, it ceased to be a place of worship, and the caves and sculptures were damaged by Portuguese soldiers. In the 1970s the temples were restored and preserved, and the island became a popular tourist site.

ELLORA CAVES

The Ellora Caves (also spelled Elura) are a series of 34 magnificent rock-cut temples in northwest-central Maharashtra state, western India. They are located near the village of Ellora, 19 miles (30 km) northwest of Aurangabad and 50 miles (80 km) southwest of the Ajanta Caves. Spread over a distance of 1.2 miles (2 km), the temples were cut from basaltic cliffs and have elaborate facades and interior walls. The Ellora complex was designated a UNESCO World Heritage site in 1983.

The 12 Buddhist caves (in the south) date from about 200 BCE to 600 CE, the

17 Hindu temples (in the centre) date from about 500 to 900 CE, and the 5 Jaina temples (in the north) date from about 800 to 1000. The Hindu caves are the most dramatic in design, and the Buddhist caves contain the simplest ornamentation. Ellora served as a group of monasteries (*viharas*) and temples (*caityas*); some of the caves include sleeping cells that were carved for itinerant monks.

The most remarkable of the cave temples is Kailasa (Kailasanatha; cave 16), named for the mountain in the Kailas Range of the Himalayas where the Hindu god Shiva resides. Unlike other temples at the site, which were first delved horizontally into the rock face, the Kailasa complex was excavated downward from a basaltic slope and is therefore largely exposed to sunlight. Construction of the temple in the 8th century, beginning in the reign of Krishna I (*c.* 756–773), involved the removal of 150,000 to 200,000 tons of solid rock. The complex measures some 164 feet (50 metres) long, 108 feet (33 metres) wide, and 100 feet (30 metres) high and has four levels, or stories. It contains elaborately carved monoliths and halls with stairs, doorways, windows, and numerous fixed sculptures. One of its better-known decorations is a scene of Vishnu transformed into a man-lion and battling a demon. Just beyond the entrance, in the main courtyard, is a monument to Shiva's bull Nandi. Along the walls of the temple, at the second-story level, are life-size sculptures of elephants and other animals. Among the depictions within the halls is that of the 10-headed demon king Ravana shaking Kailasa Mountain in a show of strength. Erotic and voluptuous representations of Hindu divinities and mythological figures also grace the temple. Some features have been damaged or destroyed over the centuries, such as a rock-hewn footbridge that once joined two upper-story thresholds.

The Vishvakarma cave (cave 10) has carvings of Hindu and Buddhist figures as well as a lively scene of dancing dwarfs. Notable among the Jaina temples is cave 32, which includes fine carvings of lotus flowers and other elaborate ornaments. Each year the caves attract large crowds of religious pilgrims and tourists. The annual Ellora Festival of Classical Dance and Music is held there in the third week of March.

FATEHPUR SIKRI

The historic town of Fatehpur Sikri is located in southwestern Uttar Pradesh state, northern India. The town, lying about 23 miles (37 km) west of Agra, was founded in 1569 by the great Mughal emperor Akbar. In that year Akbar had visited the Muslim hermit Chishti, who was residing in the village of Sikri. Chishti correctly foretold that Akbar's wish for an heir would be gratified with the birth of a son; the child was born in Sikri that very year, and he would later rule as the emperor Jahāngīr. The grateful Akbar decided that the site of Sikri was auspicious and made it his capital. He personally directed the building of the Jāmi' Masjid (Great Mosque; 1571), which stretches some 540 feet (165 metres) in length and contains an ornate tomb for Chishti. The mosque's southern entrance, the colossal gateway Buland Darwaza (Victory Gate; 1575), is one of India's greatest architectural works. This monumental gateway is constructed out of red sandstone and is attractively carved. Fatehpur Sikri contains other early Mughal structures, exhibiting both Muslim and Hindu architectural influences. They include the palace of Akbar's wife (Jodha Bai), a private audience hall, and houses. The Mughal capital was moved to Delhi in 1586 because of Fatehpur Sikri's inadequate water supply. Now maintained as a historic site, Fatehpur Sikri was designated a UNESCO World Heritage site in 1986. Pop. (2001) 28,804.

KHAJURAHO

The historic town of Khajuraho (also spelled Khajraho; ancient Kharjuravahaka) is located in northern Madhya Pradesh state, central India. It is a famous tourist and archaeological site known for its sculptured temples dedicated to Jaina patriarchs and to the Hindu deities Shiva and Vishnu.

Khajuraho, or Kharjuravahaka, was one of the capitals of the kings of the Chandela, who from the 9th to the 11th century CE developed a large realm,

Vishnu with his consort Lakshmi, from the temple dedicated to Parshvanatha in the eastern temple complex, c. 950–970 CE, at Khajuraho, Madhya Pradesh, India. © Anthony Cassidy

Jejakabhukti (Jijhoti), which at its height included almost all of what is now Madhya Pradesh state, centred in what is now Bundelkhand. The original capital extended over 8 square miles (21 square km) and contained about 85 temples, built by successive rulers from about 950 to

1050. In the late 11th century the Chandela, in a period of chaos and decline, moved to hill forts elsewhere. Khajraho continued its religious importance until the 14th century but was afterward largely forgotten; its remoteness probably saved it from the desecration that the Muslim, or Mughal, conquerors generally inflicted on Hindu monuments. In 1838 a British army captain, T.S. Burt, came upon information that led him to the rediscovery of the complex of temples in the jungle in Khajuraho.

Of the area's 85 original temples, 22 are still reasonably well preserved. With a few exceptions they are constructed of hard river sandstone. Both internally and externally the temples are richly carved with excellent sculptures that are frequently sensual and, in a few instances, sexually explicit. The temples are divided into three complexes, of which the western is the largest and best known, containing the magnificent Shaivite temple Kandariya Mahadeva (c. 1000), a 102-foot- (31-metre-) high agglomeration of porches and turrets culminating in a spire. The monuments at Khajuraho were designated a UNESCO World Heritage site in 1986.

Modern Khajuraho is a small village. Tourism is the leading economic factor. An airport connects Khajuraho with several cities in India. The town's name derives from the prevalence of *khajur*, or date palms, in the area. Pop. (2001) 19,286.

KONARAK

The historic village of Konarak (also spelled Konarka, Konark, or Kanarak) is located in east-central Orissa state, eastern India, on the Bay of Bengal coast. It is famous for its 13th-century Surya Deula (or Surya Deul), popularly known as the Sun Temple.

The name Konarak is derived from the Sanskrit words *kona* ("corner") and *arka* ("sun"), a reference to the temple, which was dedicated to the Hindu sun god Surya. It was designed to represent his chariot, with 12 huge carved stone wheels and 7 stone horses around its base. The Surya Deula is about 100 feet (30 metres) high and would have surpassed 200 feet (60 metres) in height at its completion. The exterior is covered with sculptured decorations, many depicting erotic scenes.

The village and the temple are associated with the legend of Samba, the son of the Hindu deity Krishna, who was cured of leprosy by the sun god's blessings. Evidence suggests that the temple was built by Narasimha I (reigned 1238–64) about 1250. It represents the culmination of the Orissan school of temple architecture. Formerly called the Black Pagoda because of the many shipwrecks that occurred off the coast, the temple was used as a navigation landmark by European mariners sailing to Calcutta (now Kolkata). From the 15th to the 17th

Detail of Kandariya Mahadeva temple, Khajuraho, Madhya Pradesh, India. Frederick M. Asher

centuries, the temple was sacked various times by Muslim armies. By the 19th century, much of the temple had been weathered and ruined. Under British rule, sections of the temple complex were restored, but much of it remained in ruins. The complex was designated a UNESCO World Heritage site in 1984.

About 6 miles (10 km) from the village is Ramchandi Temple on Ramchandi beach, on the bank of the Kushabhadra River, which empties into the Bay of Bengal. In general, the beaches at Konarak and beyond are famous for their festivals.

MAMALLAPURAM

The historic town of Mamallapuram (also called Mahabalipuram or Seven Pagodas) is located in northeastern Tamil Nadu state, southeastern India. It lies along the Bay of Bengal 37 miles (60 km) south of Chennai (Madras). The town's religious centre was founded by a 7th-century-CE Hindu Pallava king, Narasimhavarman, also known as Mamalla, for whom the town was named. Ancient Chinese, Persian, and Roman coins found at Mamallapuram point to its earlier existence as a seaport. It contains many surviving 7th- and 8th-century Pallava temples and monuments, chief of which are the sculptured rock relief popularly known as Arjuna's Penance or Descent of the Ganges, a series of sculptured cave temples, and a Shaiva temple on the seashore. The town's five *rathas*, or monolithic temples, are the remnants of seven temples, for which the town was known as Seven

Pagodas. The entire assemblage collectively was designated a UNESCO World Heritage site in 1984. Mamallapuram is a resort and tourist centre. It contains a college offering instruction in architecture and temple sculpture.

RED FORT

The historic Mughal Red Fort (also called Lal Qal'ah; also spelled Lal Kila or Lal Qila) is a prominent landmark in Old Delhi, India. It was built by Shah Jahān in the mid-17th century and remains a major tourist attraction. The fort was designated a UNESCO World Heritage site in 2007.

The fort's massive red sandstone walls, which stand 75 feet (23 metres) high, enclose a complex of palaces and entertainment halls, projecting balconies, baths and indoor canals, and geometrical gardens, as well as an ornate mosque. Among the most famous structures of the complex are the Hall of Public Audience (Diwan-i-Am), which has 60 red sandstone pillars supporting a flat roof, and the Hall of Private Audience (Diwan-i-Khas), which is smaller, with a pavilion of white marble.

An earlier red fort had been built in Old Delhi in the 11th century by the Tomara king Anangapala. The Quṭb Mosque now stands on the site.

SANCHI

The historic site of Sanchi in west-central Madhya Pradesh state, central India, is located just west of the Betwa River. On a flat-topped sandstone hill that rises some 300 feet (90 metres) above the surrounding country stands India's best-preserved group of Buddhist monuments, collectively designated a UNESCO World Heritage site in 1989. The most noteworthy of the structures is the Great Stupa (stupa No. 1), discovered in 1818. It was probably begun by the emperor Ashoka in the mid-3rd century BCE and later enlarged. Solid throughout, it is enclosed by a massive stone railing pierced by four gateways, which are adorned with elaborate carvings (known as Sanchi sculpture) depicting the life of the Buddha. The stupa itself consists of a base bearing a hemispherical dome (*anda*) symbolizing the dome of heaven enclosing the Earth; it is surmounted by a squared rail unit (*harmika*) representing the world mountain, from which rises a mast (*yashti*) symbolizing the cosmic axis. The mast bears umbrellas (*chatras*) that represent the various heavens (*devaloka*). Other remains at the site include several smaller stupas, an assembly hall (*chaitya*), an Ashokan pillar with inscriptions, and several monasteries (4th–11th century CE). A number of relic caskets (containers holding various remains of the Buddha) and more than 400 epigraphical records have also been discovered.

VIJAYANAGAR

The great ruined city of Vijayanagar (Sanskrit: "City of Victory") lies in southern India. Vijayanagar is also the name of the empire ruled first from that city and later from Penukonda (in Anantapur district, Andhra Pradesh) between 1336 and about 1614. The site of the city, on the Tungabhadra River, is now partly occupied by the village of Hampi in eastern Karnataka state.

The city and its first dynasty were founded in 1336 by five sons of Sangama, of whom Harihara and Bukka became the city's first kings. In time Vijayanagar became the greatest empire of southern India. By serving as a barrier against invasion by the Muslim sultanates of the north, it fostered the reconstruction of Hindu life and administration after the disorders and disunities of the 12th and 13th centuries. Contact with the Muslims (who were not personally disliked) stimulated new thought and creative productivity. Sanskrit was encouraged as a unifying force, and regional literatures thrived. Behind its frontiers the country flourished in unexampled peace and prosperity.

The first dynasty, the Sangama, lasted until about 1485, when—at a time of pressure from the Bahmanī sultan and the raja of Orissa—Narasimha of the Saluva family usurped power. By 1503 the Saluva dynasty had been supplanted by the Tuluva dynasty. The outstanding Tuluva king was Krishna Deva Raya. During his reign (1509–29) the land between the Tungabhadra and Krishna rivers (the Raichur *doab*) was acquired (1512), the Orissa Hindus were subdued by the capture of Udayagiri (1514) and other towns, and severe defeats were inflicted on the

Bijapur sultan (1520). Krishna Deva's successors, however, allowed their enemies to unite against them. In 1565 Rama Raya, the chief minister of Vijayanagar, led the empire into the fatal battle at Talikota, in which its army was routed by the combined forces of the Muslim states of Bijapur, Ahmadnagar, and Golconda and the city of Vijayanagar was destroyed. Tirumala, brother of Rama Raya, then seized control of the empire and founded the Aravidu dynasty, which established a new capital at Penukonda and kept the empire intact for a time. Internal dissensions and the intrigues of the sultans of Bijapur and Golconda, however, led to the final collapse of the empire about 1614.

NATURAL SITES

Although India is best known for its high population density, the country also has many places of great natural beauty, and many of these are important tourist destinations. Notable are the numerous national parks and preserves and wildlife sanctuaries, many of which are World Heritage sites.

CORBETT NATIONAL PARK

Corbett National Park is a hilly natural area in Uttarakhand state, northern India. It extends over an area of 201 square miles (521 square km). Established as Hailey National Park in 1935, it was first renamed Ramganga in 1954 and then Corbett in 1957 in memory of Jim Corbett, a well-known British sportsman and writer. Located in the foothills of the Himalayas about 36 miles (50 km) northwest of Ramnagar, the park consists mainly of the broad Patlidoon Valley, through which the Ramganga River flows in a westerly direction. The forest cover includes species of sal (*Shorea*), teak, oak, silver fir, spruce, cypress, and birch. The park was established mainly for the protection of the tiger; it is there that India's Project Tiger was established in 1973 to provide havens for tigers in the national parks. Langurs, sloth bears, Indian gray mongooses, jungle cats, elephants, wild boars, barking deer, nilgai (Indian antelope), black kile, shikras, Indian whitebacked vultures, black partridges, red jungle fowl, and peafowl are also found in the park. It has roads for elephant rides and *machans*, or observation posts. A reed forest was planted to afford natural cover for the animals, and a large man-made lake on the western side of the park is used for sport fishing.

GIR NATIONAL PARK

Gir National Park is a large natural area in Gujarat state, west-central India. It is located about 37 miles (60 km) south-southwest of Junagadh in a hilly region of dry scrubland and has an area of about 500 square miles (1,295 square km). Vegetation consists of teak with an admixture of deciduous trees, including sal (*Shorea robusta*), dhak (*Butea frondosa*), and thorn forests.

The Gir Forests Reserve, created in 1913 to protect the largest of the surviving groups of Asiatic lions, was accorded sanctuary status in 1965. Several hundred Asiatic lions have been bred in the sanctuary since it was established. "Lion shows" consisting of guided tours in protected vehicles are held regularly for visitors. Other fauna include leopards, wild pigs, spotted deer, nilgai (a type of antelope), four-horned antelope, and chinkaras (a type of gazelle). A large central water hole contains a few crocodiles. The park also has a small temple dedicated to Krishna near the Tulsi-Shyam Springs.

HAZARIBAG WILDLIFE SANCTUARY

Hazaribag (or Hazaribagh) Wildlife Sanctuary is a protected natural area in north-central Jharkhand state, northeastern India. The sanctuary is situated on a hilly plateau at an average elevation of 2,000 feet (600 metres), about 55 miles (90 km) north of Ranchi, the state capital. Established in 1955, it covers an area of 71 square miles (184 square km). Its hills are covered by a dense forest of sal (*Shorea robusta*) that provide habitat for tigers, leopards, sloth bears, black bears, several varieties of deer, wild pigs, hyenas, and many species of birds, including peafowl, red jungle fowl, and green pigeons. Observation towers connected by all-weather roads facilitate wildlife viewing; several salt licks have also been constructed.

JALDAPARA WILDLIFE SANCTUARY

Jaldapara Wildlife Sanctuary is a natural refuge for wildlife in West Bengal state, northeastern India. The preserve was established in 1941 mainly for the protection of the great Indian rhinoceros (*Rhinoceros unicornis*). It extends over an area of 84 square miles (217 square km) in the northern part of the state, near the Bhutan border, and is composed of forested flatlands dissected by the Torsa River and its tributaries. The forest cover consists mainly of scattered teak and tall grass. Also within the sanctuary are swamp deer, leopards, sambars, hog deer, barking deer, wild pigs, jungle fowl, peafowl, quail, and an occasional elephant or tiger. There are riding elephants available in the preserve.

KANHA NATIONAL PARK

Kanha National Park is located in Madhya Pradesh state, central India. The park extends over 122 square miles (316 square km) of the central highlands at an elevation of about 2,000 to 3,000 feet (600 to 900 metres). Originally established as the Banjar Valley Sanctuary in 1935, it became a national park in 1955 and was enlarged in 1964. Rolling, sometimes rugged hills that tend to be flat-topped enclose on three sides a large meadowlike grassland. Although there are occasional patches of bamboo, dense bush, or tall grass high on the slopes and on the hilltops, much of the park consists of dry deciduous woodlands. Fauna includes langurs, wild dogs, tigers, leopards, wild pigs, barking deer, chitals, sambars, swamp deer, gaur, quail, red and gray jungle fowl, and peafowl. The park can be reached by road from Nagpur, Jabalpur, and Mandla. There are observation towers, or *machans*, and elephants are used for transport in the park, especially when motorable tracks become impassable during the summer monsoon rains.

KAZIRANGA NATIONAL PARK

Kaziranga National Park is a scenic natural area in north-central Assam state, northeastern India. It is situated on the south bank of the Brahmaputra River, about 60 miles (100 km) west of Jorhat on the main road to Guwahati.

First established in 1908 as a reserved forest, it subsequently was designated a game (1916) and wildlife (1950) sanctuary before becoming a national park in 1974. Kaziranga was designated a UNESCO World Heritage site in 1985. The park has an area of some 165 square miles (430 square km) and lies between the Brahmaputra River and the Karbi (Mikir) Hills. Much of the park is marshland interspersed with large pools fringed with reeds, patches of elephant grass, scattered trees, and thickets. Wildlife includes the world's largest population of great Indian one-horned rhinoceroses (*Rhinoceros unicornis*), tigers, leopards, panthers,

bears, elephants, wild pigs, hog deer, swamp deer, buffalo, and pelicans, storks, and other waterfowl. Seasonal flooding regularly inundates much of the park and kills numerous animals; the land near the river is also subject to erosion. These events have been major factors for a gradual decrease in animal populations over the years.

Guest houses perched above the main road at Kohra, near the southern

Ferry in Kaziranga National Park, Assam, India.
© *Suraj N. Sharma/Dinodia Photo Library*

boundary, give a panoramic view of the Himalayas on the rare occasions when the sky is clear. There are several low watchtowers, and elephant rides are available for viewing wildlife in the swampland.

KEOLADEO GHANA NATIONAL PARK

Keoladeo Ghana National Park (also called Bharatpur National Park) is situated in eastern Rajasthan state, northwestern India, just south of the city of Bharatpur. It was founded in the late 19th century as a hunting preserve by Suraj Mal, the maharaja of Bharatpur princely state, and was given the status of a bird sanctuary in 1956. Declared a national park in 1982 it was renamed Keoladeo for its ancient temple dedicated to the Hindu god, Shiva. Woodlands, swamps, and wet grasslands cover a large part of the park, which has an area of 11 square miles (29 square km).

Keoladeo is home to more than 370 species of permanent and migratory birds. During the annual migratory period (August to February), birds from throughout the world can be found in the park. Winter visitors there include waterfowl from Afghanistan, Turkmenistan, China, and Siberia, including species such as gadwalls, shovellers, common teals, tufted ducks, pintails, white spoonbills, Asian open-billed storks, Oriental ibises, and the rare Siberian crane. The park is also home to a range of mammals and reptiles, including pythons, deer, sambars, black bucks, jackals, monitor

lizards, and fishing cats. It was designated a UNESCO World Heritage site in 1985.

MANAS WILDLIFE SANCTUARY

Manas Wildlife Sanctuary (also called Kamrup Sanctuary) is a large natural area in western Assam state, eastern India. It is situated at the foot of the Himalayas on the eastern bank of the Manas River, 92 miles (153 km) west of Guwahati. Established in 1928, it has an area of some 200 square miles (520 square km) and lies in a dense, mixed semievergreen, evergreen, and wet-deciduous forest region. The southern part of the preserve is grassland. Wildlife includes great Indian rhinoceroses, elephants, bison, deer, tigers, golden langurs, black bears, and wild pigs. A tiger reserve was established there in 1973. The sanctuary was designated a UNESCO World Heritage site in 1985.

MUDUMALAI WILDLIFE SANCTUARY

Mudumalai Wildlife Sanctuary is located in western Tamil Nadu state, southern India. Established in 1940, it has an area of 124 square miles (322 square km) and is located about 35 miles (56 km) north of Udhagamandalam on the main road to Mysore. The sanctuary is composed of hills and valleys with several perennial streams and swamps. The thick jungle growth of teak, rosewood, laurel, and bamboo provides cover for the elephants, gaurs (Indian bison), tigers, black leopards, sloth bears, hyenas, jackals, wild pigs, pythons, gray jungle fowl, spur fowl, and golden eagles found in the preserve. It has a network of fair-weather tracks and observation towers overlooking salt licks and water holes; riding elephants are available for transport.

PERIYAR WILDLIFE SANCTUARY

Periyar Wildlife Sanctuary is a large wildlife preserve in south-central Kerala state, southern India. The sanctuary is noted for herds of Asian elephants, sometimes having 50 members. In addition, bonnet monkeys, nilgai (Indian antelope), langurs, porcupines, sloth bears, tigers, leopards, barking deer, gray jungle fowl, kingfishers, great Indian hornbills, and southern grackles are found in the preserve. Extending over an area of 297 square miles (770 square km), the sanctuary encompasses Periyar Lake, formed in the early 1900s by impounding the Periyar River, and is located near the border between Kerala and Tamil Nadu states, about 73 miles (118 km) south of Ernakulam and 170 miles (274 km) northeast of Thiruvananthapuram. At an elevation of about 4,600 feet (1,600 metres), the hilly topography has produced a lakeshore varied by numerous creeks, bays, and promontories. The vegetal cover is tropical evergreen and deciduous, with patches of dense forest including jackfruit, teak, and kokam (tropical evergreen [*Garcinia indica*]) trees that produce a dark purple, plumlike fruit).

Most of the grassland is now planted with eucalyptus.

SARISKA NATIONAL PARK

Sariska National Park is a wildlife preserve in eastern Rajasthan state, northwestern India. It has an area of 190 square miles (492 square km). It was established in 1955 in Sariska Forest as a wildlife sanctuary and was declared a national park in 1979. Acacia forests cover the arid lower slopes of the hills and the deep, narrow valleys; male bamboo (*Dendrocalamus strictus*), the culms (stems) of which form nearly solid, impenetrable thickets, grows along the streams. Wildlife includes tigers, leopards, wild pigs, nilgai (Indian antelope), chital, porcupines, peafowl, partridges, and thrushes. Kankwari Fort, a Shiva temple of the 12th century, and a 10th-century Neelkanth (Shiva) temple are of archaeological interest. There are good roads within the park and observation towers at Bandi Pul and Kalighati.

SHIVPURI NATIONAL PARK

Shivpuri National Park is located in northern Madhya Pradesh state, central India. It has an area of 61 square miles (158 square km). Originally the private game preserve of the rulers of the former princely state of Gwalior, the park was established as Madhya Bharat National Park in 1955. It received its present name in 1959. Located about 70 miles (110 km) south of Gwalior on the main road between

Mumbai (Bombay) and Agra, it consists of hills and valleys in the Vindhya Range. The park's vegetation includes mixed forests of sal (*Shorea robusta*), teak, and khair (*Acacia catechu*), interspersed with grassland. Tigers, leopards, langurs, jackals, mouse deer, wild pigs, four-horned antelope, jungle fowl, quail, and bustards inhabit the park. Tigers can be photographed from protected areas. Lake Sakhya, or Chandpatha, a man-made lake with a circumference of 7 miles (11 km), offers canoeing and picnic sites.

SUNDARBANS

The Sundarbans (formerly Sunderbunds) is a vast tract of forest and saltwater swamp forming the lower part of the Padma River (Ganges [Ganga] River) delta, extending roughly 160 miles (260 km) along the Bay of Bengal from the Hugli River estuary in India (west) to the western segment of the Meghna River estuary in Bangladesh (east). The tract reaches inland for about 50 miles (80 km) at its broadest point. A network of estuaries, tidal rivers, and creeks intersected by numerous channels, it encloses flat, marshy islands covered with dense forests.

The name Sundarbans is perhaps derived from the term meaning "forest of *sundari*," a reference to the large mangrove trees that are most plentiful in the area. The forest passes into a mangrove swamp along the coast, with many wild animals and crocodile-infested estuaries in its southern region. The area has long had the status of a forest reserve; it also is one of the last preserves of the Bengal tiger (*Panthera tigris tigris*). In 1997 the mangrove forest of the Sundarbans was designated a UNESCO World Heritage site.

TADOBA NATIONAL PARK

Tadoba National Park is situated in eastern Maharashtra state, western India. Extending over an area of 45 square miles (117 square km), the park consists of dense forests of sal (*Shorea robusta*), *margosa*, *mahua*, and mango, interspersed with lakes and plains; stretches of bamboo thickets are found around Tadoba Lake. It was established as a wildlife sanctuary in 1935 and declared a national park in 1955. The park is part of the Tadoba-Andhari Tiger reserve, which was created in 1995. The park has tigers, leopards, *chital*, jackals, gaurs (Indian bison), mouse deer, sambars, antelope, sloth bears, and crocodiles. A network of roads and observation towers facilitates wildlife viewing. Chandrapur, the nearest city, is about 28 miles (45 km) south of the park.

CHAPTER 5

THE MAJOR CITIES OF NORTHERN AND NORTHWESTERN INDIA

The northern and northwestern region of India is home to many of the country's most ancient and historically significant cities. The largest and most important among these is Delhi, which includes New Delhi, the national capital.

DELHI

The capital city and national capital territory of Delhi is located in north-central India. The city actually consists of two "cities": Old Delhi, in the north, and New Delhi, in the south. One of India's largest urban agglomerations, Delhi sits astride (but primarily on the west bank of) the Yamuna River, a tributary of the Ganges (Ganga) River, about 100 miles (160 km) south of the Himalayas. The national capital territory embraces the city of Delhi and its metropolitan region, as well as the surrounding rural areas. To the east, the territory is bounded by the state of Uttar Pradesh, and to the north, west, and south, it is bounded by the state of Haryana.

Delhi is of great historical significance as an important commercial, transport, and cultural hub, as well as the political centre of India. According to legend, the city was named for Raja Dhilu, a king who reigned in the region in the 1st century BCE. The names by which the city has been known—including Delhi,

The tomb of Humāyūn, Delhi, India, c. 1564 CE. P. Chandra

Dehli, Dilli, and Dhilli, among others—likely are corruptions of his name. The city became the capital of British India in 1911, and it remained the capital after the country achieved independence in 1947. Area national capital territory, 573 square miles (1,483 square km); Old Delhi, 360 square miles (932 square km); New Delhi, 169 square miles (438 square km). Pop. (2001) Old Delhi city, 9,879,172; New Delhi city, 302,363; urban agglom., 12,877,470; (2008 est.) national capital territory, 17,076,000.

Landscape

Delhi has been the centre of a succession of mighty empires and powerful kingdoms. Numerous ruins scattered throughout the territory offer a constant reminder of the area's history. Popular lore holds that the city changed its locality a total of seven times between 3000 BCE and the 17th century CE, although some authorities, who take smaller towns and strongholds into account, claim it changed its site as many as 15 times.

City Site

All of the earlier locations of Delhi fall within a triangular area of about 70 square miles (180 square km), commonly called the Delhi Triangle. Two sides of the triangle are articulated by the rocky hills of the Aravalli Range—one to the south of the city, the other on its western edge, where it is known as the Delhi Ridge. The third side of the triangle is formed by the shifting channel of the Yamuna River.

Between the river and the hills lie broad alluvial plains; the elevation of the territory ranges from about 700 to 1,000 feet (200 to 300 metres).

The ridges and hillsides of the national capital territory abound in thorny trees, such as acacias, as well as seasonal herbaceous species. The sissoo (shisham; *Dalbergia sissoo*) tree, which yields a dark brown and durable timber, is commonly found in the plains. Riverine vegetation, consisting of weeds and grass, occurs on the banks of the Yamuna. New Delhi is known for its flowering shade trees, such as the neem (*Azadirachta indica*; a drought-resistant tree with a pale yellow fruit), jaman (*Syzygium cumini*; a tree with an edible grapelike fruit), mango, pipal (*Ficus religiosa*; a fig tree), and sissoo. It also is known for its flowering plants, which include a large number of multicoloured seasonals: chrysanthemums, phlox, violas, and verbenas.

The animal life of the national capital territory, like its plant life, is quite diverse. Among carnivorous animals are leopards, hyenas, foxes, wolves, and jackals, which inhabit the ravine lands and hilly ridges. Wild boars are sometimes spotted along the banks of the Yamuna. Monkeys are found in the city, especially around some of the temples and historical ruins. Birdlife is profuse; year-round species include pigeons, sparrows, kites, parrots, partridges, bush quail, and, on the ridges, peafowl. The lakes around the city attract seasonal species. Fish are plentiful in the Yamuna, and an occasional crocodile also may be found there.

CLIMATE

The climate of Delhi is characterized by extreme dryness, with intensely hot summers. It is associated with a general prevalence of continental air, which moves in from the west or northwest, except during the season of the monsoon, when an easterly to southeasterly influx of oceanic air brings rain and increased humidity. The summer season lasts from mid-March to the end of June, with maximum temperatures typically reaching about 100 °F (about 37 °C) and minimum temperatures falling into the high 70s F (about 25 °C); it is characterized by frequent thunderstorms and squalls, especially in April and May. The monsoon season normally begins in July and continues until the end of September. It is during these months that Delhi receives the bulk of its rainfall—roughly 23 inches (600 mm), or nearly three-fourths of the annual average. October and November constitute a transition period from monsoon to winter conditions. The dry winter season extends from late November to mid-March. The coldest month is January, with high temperatures in the low 70s F (about 21 °C) and low temperatures in the mid-40s F (about 7 °C).

CITY LAYOUT

The city plan of Delhi is a mixture of old and new road patterns. The street network of Old Delhi reflects the defense needs of an earlier era, with a few transverse streets leading from one major gate to another. Occasionally a street from a subsidiary gate leads directly to the main axes, but most Old Delhi streets tend to be irregular in direction, length, and width. Narrow and winding paths, culs-de-sac, alleys, and byways form an intricate matrix that renders much of Old Delhi accessible only to pedestrian traffic. Conversely, the Civil Lines (residential areas originally built by the British for senior officers) in the north and New Delhi in the south embody an element of relative openness, characterized by green grass, trees, and a sense of order.

When the decision was made in 1911 to transfer the capital of British India from Calcutta (now Kolkata) to Delhi, a planning committee was formed, and a site 3 miles (5 km) south of the existing city of Delhi, around Raisina Hill, was chosen for the new administrative centre. A well-drained, healthy area between the Delhi Ridge and the Yamuna River, it provided ample room for expansion. Raisina Hill, commanding a view of the entire area, stood about 50 feet (15 metres) above the plain, but the top 20 feet (6 metres) were blasted off to make a level plateau for the major government buildings and to fill in depressions. With this low acropolis as the focus, the plan for New Delhi was laid out.

The New Delhi plan was characterized by wide avenues, with trees in double rows on either side, that connected various points of interest and provided vistas of the surrounding area. The most prominent feature of the plan, aside from its diagonal road pattern, was the Rajpath, a broad central avenue that in present-day New Delhi stretches westward from the National Stadium, through the All India War Memorial arch (popularly called the India Gate), to the Central Secretariat buildings and the Presidential House (Rashtrapati Bhavan). This is the main east-west axis; it divides New Delhi into two parts, with a large shopping and business district, Connaught Place, in the north and extensive residential areas in the south.

Land Use

The pattern of land use in Delhi was influenced considerably by the implementation (albeit partial) of the Delhi Development Authority's 20-year (1962–81) master plan. Broadly, public and semipublic land use was concentrated in the Central Secretariat area of New Delhi and in the Old Secretariat area in the Civil Lines, with subsidiary centres developing in the Indraprastha Estate (an office complex) in the east and in Ramakrishnapuram (an office-cum-residence complex) in the south. A large number of small manufacturing establishments have entrenched themselves in almost every part of Old Delhi, but the main industrial areas have gravitated toward Najafgarh Road in the west and the large planned Okhla Industrial Estate in the south. Land for commercial use is found mainly in the Chandni Chowk and Khari Baoli areas, both in the north; in the Sadar Bazar of Old Delhi; in the Ajmal Khan Road area of Karol Bagh in western

Delhi; around Connaught Place in New Delhi; and in the areas of Lajpat Nagar and Srojini Nagar in the south. A number of district and local shopping centres have developed in other localities.

Traditional Regions

There is a clear distinction in Delhi between areas where local influences are foremost and areas where colonial and cosmopolitan aesthetics predominate. In Old Delhi, gates or doorways open onto one-, two-, or three-story residences and courtyards or onto *katra* (one-room tenements facing a courtyard or other enclosure that has access to the street only by a single opening or gate). The prevalence of courtyards has helped to cultivate a strong sense of *mohalla* ("neighbourhood") in the area. Also typical of Old Delhi are urban village enclaves, such as Kotla Mubarakpur, where houses and streets retain their rural character. The Civil Lines area is characterized by old one-story bungalows inhabited by those in the upper-income bracket. In New Delhi, the government housing areas are grouped by income. Significant parts of the city are densely packed with substandard, often dilapidated housing, inhabited mostly by construction workers, sweepers, factory labourers, and other low-income groups.

People

In the demographic history of Delhi, a turning point was the year 1947, when thousands of Hindu and Sikh refugees from predominantly Muslim Pakistan entered the city in the wake of India's independence. Since that time the population has grown steadily, with an ongoing heavy flow of immigrants, most arriving from other Indian states or from adjacent countries.

Immigrant (or other foreign) communities often are found in the newer housing developments. Chanakyapuri (more commonly known as the Diplomatic Enclave), for instance, is the site of many foreign embassies. Concentrations of specific ethnic communities have formed in such areas as Chittaranjan Park and Karol Bagh; the former is a predominantly Bengali subdivision and the latter largely a Punjabi one. Such areas have been diversifying since the late 20th century, however.

The religious composition of Delhi's population is also varied. The great majority of the residents are Hindu. Adherents of Islam constitute the largest minority, followed by smaller numbers of Sikhs, Jains, Christians, and Buddhists.

ECONOMY

The service sector is the most important part of Delhi's economy, and it is the city's largest employer. Manufacturing has remained significant, after a surge in the 1980s. Agriculture once contributed significantly to the economy of the national capital territory, but now it is of little importance.

The bulk of Delhi's working population is engaged in trade, finance, public administration, professional services, and various community, personal, and social services. Indeed, for many centuries Old Delhi has been a dominant trading and commercial centre in northern India. Since the 1990s New Delhi has emerged as an important node in the international corporate and financial network.

MANUFACTURING

Mechanized industry arrived in Delhi early in the 20th century and focused on cotton ginning, spinning, and weaving; flour grinding and packaging; and sugarcane and oil pressing. More recently, electronics and engineering goods, automobile parts, precision instruments, machinery, and electrical appliances have moved to the centre of the city's manufacturing activities, although the production of apparel, sports-related products, and leather goods is also important.

Delhi long has been renowned for its handmade artistic works, such as ivory carvings and paintings, engravings, sculpture of various sorts, miniature paintings, jewelry, gold and silver brocades and embroidery, and metalwork. Such items remain a small but significant segment of Delhi's manufacturing sector.

FINANCE AND OTHER SERVICES

Delhi's position as the national capital and as a major industrial city has supported its function as a banking, wholesale-trade, and distribution centre. The city is the headquarters of the

Reserve Bank of India and of the regional offices of the State Bank of India and other banking institutions. Many foreign banks offering both retail and corporate services also have branches in the city. Delhi is a divisional headquarters for the insurance business and is the home of the Delhi Stock Exchange. The city has long acted as a major distribution centre for much of northern India, with a large proportion of the trade conducted from within the Old Delhi area, where most of the markets are concentrated. In addition to its financial and trade services, Delhi hosts a thriving tourism industry, which has grown rapidly since the late 20th century.

TRANSPORTATION

The geographic position of Delhi on the great plain of India, where the Deccan plateau and the Thar Desert approach the Himalayas to produce a narrow corridor, ensures that all land routes from northwestern India to the eastern plain must pass through it, thus making it a pivotal centre in the subcontinent's transportation network. A number of national highways converge on Delhi, and several railway lines also meet there, linking the city with all parts of the country. Delhi is an important air terminus in northern India for both international and domestic services. Indira Gandhi International Airport, located in the southwestern part of the city, handles international flights. One of its terminals, which was once known as the Palam Airport, lies about 2 miles (3 km) from the international facility and is a hub of the domestic airway system.

The traffic-circulation pattern of Delhi was originally designed for a smaller population, and, with Delhi's explosive growth, the system quickly became overburdened. Improvements to the road system—such as adding overpasses and underpasses and widening major thoroughfares—have alleviated the worst traffic congestion, but the sheer volume of traffic—which includes slow-moving vehicles such as bullock carts, pedicabs, and bicycles—makes road travel in Delhi difficult. Although they are improving, mass-transportation facilities remain inadequate, with the principal means of public transport consisting of an ever-increasing fleet of buses. Long-distance commuting within the city is facilitated by chartered buses during rush hours, as well as by a rapid transit system, the first phase of which was completed in November 2006. Several bridges built in the late 20th and early 21st centuries have helped to ease the flow of traffic over the Yamuna River.

ADMINISTRATION AND SOCIETY

Delhi was a British province headed by a chief commissioner until 1947, when India attained its independence. It became a centrally administered state in 1952, but in 1956 its status was changed to that of a union territory under the central government. A unified corporation for both urban and rural areas was established in 1958, and Delhi was designated the national capital territory in 1991.

GOVERNMENT

A lieutenant governor, appointed by the president of India, is the chief administrator of the national capital territory; the lieutenant governor is assisted by a chief minister, who also is appointed. Nested in different layers of administrative and planning regions, Delhi consists of both the urban agglomeration and more than 200 villages distributed mostly across the Delhi and Mehrauli *tehsils* (subdistricts) of the territory. At the macro level, Delhi is part of the National Capital Region (NCR), a planning region carved out in 1971 by the Town and Country Planning Organisation to guide future growth around Delhi. The NCR comprises not only Delhi but also the bordering *tehsils* in the states of Haryana, Uttar Pradesh, and Rajasthan.

At the micro level is the national capital territory itself, which consists of three administrative bodies known locally as statutory towns—the Municipal Corporation of Delhi (MCD), the New Delhi Municipal Council (NDMC), and the Cantonment Board—that are in some ways distinguished by function and in other ways by the geographic area over which they have authority. The MCD, which is an elected body, performs municipal and discretionary welfare functions, a foremost focus of which has been the elimination of substandard housing (either through destruction or improvement). The NDMC, which is an appointed body, is essentially responsible for New Delhi and its adjoining areas. The Cantonment Board consists of both elected members and appointed ex officio members; among its principal responsibilities are water and public-utilities management, public health and sanitation, birth and death registration, and elementary education.

MUNICIPAL SERVICES

Delhi's water and electricity are provided by various public and private companies. The Delhi Jal Board distributes treated drinkable water. Electricity is supplied largely by local coal-burning thermal stations, although several gas-fired plants, built in the national capital territory in the early 21st century, also generate a significant amount of power. A portion of Delhi's energy is tapped from sources outside the national capital territory.

The jurisdiction of the Delhi Fire Service extends over both the urban and rural areas of the national capital territory. The Delhi Police force is headed by a commissioner who oversees the operation of several districts, each of which is administered by a superintendent of police. Scattered across these districts are well over 100 police stations, which are responsible for regular patrol in their respective areas.

HEALTH

Overall health standards in Delhi exceed the national average, but the accessibility of health care facilities varies widely. Much of the city's health care is provided by a large number of allopathic and homeopathic clinics, as well as by dispensaries of various indigenous medical treatments (most of which are based on herbs and minerals). Hospitals in Delhi are numerous; many of the larger facilities are administered by the national government or by the national capital territory.

EDUCATION

The growth of the school system in the national capital territory generally has kept pace with the expansion of the city's population. Primary-level education is nearly universal, and a large proportion of students also attend secondary school. The national boards for secondary education are located in Delhi.

There are many institutions of higher education in the national capital territory, the most prominent of which include the Jamia Millia Islamia (1920); the University of Delhi (1922), which has many affiliated colleges and research institutions; and Jawaharlal Nehru University (1969). Among the major colleges for professional and other studies are the All India Institute of Medical Sciences (1956), the National School of Drama (1959), the Indian Institute of Technology (1959), and the Indian Institute of Mass Communications (1965). One of the largest distance-learning universities in India, Indira Gandhi National Open University (1985), is also located in Delhi. In addition to these major institutions, an array of vocational schools offer a wide variety of courses.

CULTURAL LIFE

Delhi's cultural life exhibits a unique blend of the traditional and cosmopolitan styles. The city is dotted with numerous museums, historic forts and monuments, libraries, auditoriums, botanical gardens, and places of worship. Complementing such traditional institutions are the ever-changing urban commercial and leisure centres, with their privately held contemporary art galleries, cinema multiplexes, bowling alleys and other sports venues, and restaurants serving a variety of Indian and international cuisines.

Also reflecting Delhi's cultural and stylistic diversity are its numerous fairs and festivals. These include an annual film festival as well as many sorts of trade and book fairs. The various religious groups in Delhi contribute to an ongoing succession of religious festivals and celebrations.

ARCHITECTURE

A varied history has left behind a rich architectural heritage in Delhi. The oldest buildings in the city belong to the early Muslim period; they are not homogenous in construction or in ornamentation, however. The influence of Hindu Rajput craftsmen is visible in the naturalistic motifs, the serpentine tendrils, and even the curves of the alphabets

THE MAJOR CITIES OF NORTHERN AND NORTHWESTERN INDIA | 123

of Qur'ānic inscriptions. Some artists, poets, and architects from Central Asia brought with them the Seljuq (Turkish) tradition of architecture, characterized by a lotus-bud fringe on the underside of arches, ornamental reliefs, and bricks laid endwise and lengthwise in alternating courses in the masonry face.

By the time of the Khaljīs (1290–1320), a specific method and idiom, called the Pashtun style, had been established in Islamic architecture. Among the typical features of this style are red sandstone surfaces with white marble inlays, arches in the shape of a pointed horseshoe, windows fitted with perforated screens, and intricate and abundant decoration with arabesques and inspirational texts. Examples of early Pashtun architecture in Delhi include the Quwat-ul-Islam mosque; the Qutb Minar, which, with its surrounding monuments, has been designated a UNESCO World Heritage site; the tomb of Iltutmish; and the Ala'i Gate. Later Pashtun styles are represented by the tombs of the Sayyid (1414–51) and Lodī kings (1451–1526); these tombs exhibit either a low octagonal shape or a higher square edifice, the facade of which is broken by a horizontal decorative band and a series of panels that suggest a much larger structure.

The first important piece of Mughal architecture in Delhi was Humāyūn's tomb, which was the precursor of the Taj Mahal (in Agra). It introduced high arches and double domes to Indian architecture. Some of the finest representatives of later Mughal architecture are found within the Red Fort (Lal Qila). The fort's massive red sandstone walls, which stand 75 feet (23 metres) high, enclose a complex of palaces and entertainment halls, projecting balconies, baths and indoor canals, and geometrical gardens, as well as an ornate mosque. Among the most famous structures of the complex are the Hall of Public Audience (Diwan-i-Am), which has 60 red sandstone pillars supporting a flat roof, and the smaller Hall of Private Audience (Diwan-i-Khas), with a pavilion of white marble. The Jama Masjid is a fine example of a true Mughal mosque, in part because it has minarets, where its precursors did not. Both Humāyūn's tomb and the Red Fort complex are UNESCO World Heritage sites.

The architectural styles of the British period combined British colonial and Mughal elements. Structures ranged from the grand—as represented by the Presidential House (Rashtrapati Bhavan) and the Parliament and Secretariat buildings—to the utilitarian, as seen in the bungalows and institutional buildings. Since independence India has aimed to develop its own architectural language in a synthesis between Western and local styles. In Delhi examples of such architecture can be seen in the Supreme Court building, the Vigyan Bhavan (a conference centre), the Crafts Museum, offices of the various ministries, and the institutional buildings near Connaught Place. Since the late 20th century, a number of Indian and foreign architects have added buildings to the city's landscape that may be considered postmodern (mixing

many elements of diverse origin) in style. Notable among these are the National Institute of Immunology, the headquarters of the Life Insurance Corporation of India, the building of the Embassy of Belgium, and the Indian Bahā'ī Temple.

CULTURAL INSTITUTIONS

Delhi is home to a number of important museums and busy cultural centres. The National Museum of India, the National Gallery of Modern Arts, and the Indira Gandhi National Centre for the Arts are all dedicated to the preservation, documentation, and dissemination of the country's artistic heritage. The Crafts Museum showcases Indian carving, metalwork, painting, and other crafts; the institution regularly hosts events at which local craftspeople demonstrate their art and sell their wares. The Siri Fort Auditorium is an important centre for major cultural events. The Pragati Maidan, a world-class trade and cultural centre, is another prominent landmark where events and exhibitions of international scale are held throughout the year. Dilli Haat is a popular bazaar that offers a diverse range of handicrafts and cuisines from the various states.

Aside from its museums, auditoriums, and other cultural centres, Delhi is a city of gardens and fountains, among the most notable of which are the Roshan Ara Gardens and the meticulously planned Mughal Gardens. Many park and garden areas have grown up around historical monuments, such as the Lodī Gardens (around the Lodī Tombs) and the Firoz Shah Kotla Grounds (around Ashoka's Pillar). Along the Yamuna riverfront, memorials set in flowering gardens have been built for various 20th-century national leaders. Among these are Raj Ghat (honouring Mahatma Gandhi), Shanti Vana (honouring Jawaharlal Nehru), and Vijay Ghat (honouring Lal Bahadur Shastri).

SPORTS AND RECREATION

The national capital territory has well-developed sporting facilities, including a number of stadiums that were built when Delhi hosted the Asian Games in 1982. Several sports complexes are located within the city, while world-class golf courses are situated on its periphery. Among the major outdoor natural recreation areas are the Delhi Ridge and the Yamuna riverfront.

MEDIA AND PUBLISHING

Delhi is an important centre for publishing, the press, and other mass communications. Doordarshan, the country's national television network, and All India Radio are both headquartered there. Major daily newspapers issued from Delhi include *The Times of India* and the *Hindustan Times*.

Detail of the Qutb Minar, Old Delhi, India. Frederick M. Asher

History

The earliest reference to a settlement in the Delhi area is found in the *Mahabharata,* an epic narrative about two groups of warring cousins, the Pandavas and the Kauravas, both descendants of the prince Bharata. According to the narrative, a city called Indraprastha ("City of the God Indra"), built about 1400 BCE, was the capital of the Pandavas. Although nothing remains of Indraprastha, legend holds it to have been a thriving city. The first reference to the place-name Delhi seems to have been made in the 1st century BCE, when Raja Dhilu built a city near the site of the future Qutb Minar tower (in present-day southwestern Delhi) and named it for himself.

The next notable city to emerge in the area now known as the Delhi Triangle was Anangpur (Anandpur), established as a royal resort in about 1020 CE by Anangapala of the Tomara dynasty. Anangapala later moved Anangpur some 6 miles (10 km) westward to a walled citadel called Lal Kot. The Tomara kings occupied Lal Kot for about a century. In 1164 Prithviraj III (Rai Pithora) extended the citadel by building massive ramparts around it; the city then became known as Qila Rai Pithora. In the late 12th century Prithviraj III was defeated, and the city passed into Muslim hands. Qutb al-Dīn Aybak, builder of the famous tower Qutb Minar (completed in the early 13th century), made Lal Kot the seat of his empire.

The Khaljī dynasty came to power in the Delhi area in the last decade of the 13th century. During the reign of the Khaljīs, the suburbs were ravaged by Mongol plunderers. As a defense against subsequent attacks by the Mongols, 'Alā' al-Dīn Khaljī (reigned 1296–1316) built a new circular fortified city at Siri, a short distance northeast of the Qutb Minar, that was designated as the Khaljī capital. Siri was the first completely new city to be built by the Muslim conquerors in India.

The region passed into the hands of the Tughluq dynasty in 1321. A new capital was built by Ghiyāth al-Dīn Tughluq (1320–25) at Tughlakabad, but it had to be abandoned in favour of the old site near the Qutb Minar because of a scarcity of water. Ghiyāth's successor, Muḥammad ibn Tughluq, extended the city farther northeast and built new fortifications around it. He then suddenly moved the capital to Deogiri (which he renamed Daulatabad), in the Deccan plateau to the south, in order to supervise territories that he had recently annexed there. Muḥammad ibn Tughluq's successor, Fīrūz Shah Tughluq, abandoned the Daulatabad site and in 1354 moved his capital farther north, near the ancient site of Indraprastha. The capital he founded, Firuzabad, was situated in what is now the Firoz Shah Kotla area of contemporary Delhi.

After the invasion and sack of the Delhi area by Timur (Tamerlane) at the end of the 14th century, the Sayyid (c. 1414–51) and the Lodī (1451–1526) dynasties, which followed the Tughluqs, confined themselves within the precincts of Firuzabad. Bābur, the first Mughal ruler, arrived in 1526 and made his base at Agra to the southeast (in what is now the state of Uttar Pradesh). His son Humāyūn ascended the throne in 1530 and in 1533 founded a new city, Din Panah, on the bank of the Yamuna River. Shēr Shah, who overthrew Humāyūn in 1540, razed Din Panah to the ground and built his new capital, the Sher Shahi, now known as Purana Qila fort, in southeastern Delhi.

The next two Mughal emperors, Akbar (reigned 1556–1605) and Jahāngīr (reigned 1605–27), preferred to rule India from Agra. In 1639, however, Shah Jahān, Akbar's grandson, instructed his engineers, architects, and astrologers to choose a location with a mild climate somewhere between Agra and Lahore (now in Pakistan). The choice was on the western bank of the Yamuna, just north of Purana Qila. Shah Jahān started the construction of the new capital, focusing on his fort, Urdu-i-Mualla, today called Lal Qila, or the Red Fort. The structure was completed in eight years, and on April 19, 1648, Shah Jahān entered his fort and his new capital, Shajahanabad, from its riverfront gate. Shahjahanabad today is Old Delhi. The greater part of Old Delhi is still confined within the space of Shah Jahān's walls, and several gates built during his rule—the Kashmiri Gate, the Delhi Gate, the Turkman Gate, and the Ajmeri Gate—still stand.

With the fall of the Mughal Empire during the mid-18th century, Delhi faced raids by the Marathas (a people of peninsular India), invasion by Nāder Shah of Persia, and a brief spell of Maratha rule before the British arrived in 1803. Under British rule the city flourished—except during the Indian Mutiny in 1857, when the mutineers seized the city for several months, after which British power was restored and Mughal rule ended. In 1911 the British determined to shift the capital of India from Calcutta (Kolkata) to Delhi, and a three-member committee was formed to plan the construction of the new administrative centre. The key architect on the committee was Sir Edwin Lutyens; it was he who gave shape to the city. The British moved to the partially built New Delhi in 1912, and construction was completed in 1931.

Since India's independence in 1947, Delhi has become a major metropolitan area; it has spread north and south along the Yamuna River, spilled onto the river's east bank, stretched over the Delhi Ridge to the west, and extended beyond the boundaries of the national capital territory into adjacent states. Initially, the city's growth was attributable to the enormous influx of Hindu refugees from Pakistan following its partition from India (also in 1947). Since the early 1950s, however, Delhi has absorbed immigrants from throughout India at an astounding rate. New Delhi, once adjacent to Delhi, is now part of the larger city, as are the seats (or their remains) of the former empires. Between ancient mausoleums and forts have sprouted high-rise towers, commercial complexes, and other features of the contemporary city.

This rapid development has not been without cost. In a pattern familiar to many postcolonial megalopolises, the deluge of job-seeking immigrants has placed a colossal strain on the city's infrastructure and on the ingenuity of city planners to provide sufficient electricity, sanitation, and clean water for the population. Especially problematic—in a city in which the population more than doubled in the final two decades of the 20th century—has been the large number of residents who have continued to live in substandard makeshift urban dwellings called *jhuggi-jhompri*. Lacking the most basic services, such housing has ultimately burdened city planners and administrators with the difficult task of integrating a tremendous population of *jhuggi-jhompri* residents into a city whose infrastructure barely accommodates already-existing households.

Also since the mid-20th century, traffic congestion in Delhi has become a serious impediment to mobility and, ultimately, to the city's development. This situation has contributed greatly to Delhi's already-hazardous level of air pollution. Although antipollution measures undertaken since the 1980s have improved the city's air quality considerably, congestion has continued to be a significant problem.

OTHER IMPORTANT NORTHERN AND NORTHWESTERN INDIAN CITIES

Although Delhi dominates northern India, the region is also home to many other large and historic cities. These range from Lucknow in the heart of the Gangetic Plain to Srinagar deep in the mountainous Kashmir region of the far northwest. The nine cities selected are presented below in alphabetical order.

ALLAHABAD

The city of Allahabad is situated at the confluence of the Ganges (Ganga) and Yamuna (Jumna) rivers in southern Uttar Pradesh state, northern India. It stands on the site of ancient Prayag, a holy city that was comparable in fame to Varanasi (Benares) and Haridwar. Prayag's importance in the ancient Buddhist period of Indian history is attested by the inscriptions on the Pillar of Ashoka. The pillar still stands inside the gateway to the old Allahabad fort, which is situated strategically at the confluence of the two rivers. The site's religious importance persists; each year a festival takes place at the rivers' confluence, and every 12th year a much larger festival, Kumbh Mela, is attended by millions of Hindus.

The present city of Allahabad was founded in 1583 by the Mughal emperor Akbar, who named it al-Ilahābād ("City of God"). It became a provincial capital in the Mughal Empire, and from 1599 to 1604 it was the headquarters of the rebellious prince Salim (later the emperor Jahangir). Outside Allahabad fort is the tomb built for Jahangir's rebellious son, Khusru. With the Mughal decline, Allahabad changed hands many times before being ceded to the British in 1801.

The city was the scene of a great massacre during the 1857–58 Indian Mutiny against British rule. From 1904 to 1949 the city was the capital of the United Provinces (now Uttar Pradesh). It was a centre of the Indian independence movement and was the home of the Nehru family, whose estate is now a museum.

Primarily an administrative and educational centre, Allahabad has some industry (food processing and manufacturing) and is a marketplace for agricultural products. The administrative and professional sector and the military cantonment are located north of the city proper. The city is a major road and rail centre and is served by a nearby airport. The University of Allahabad (1887) has a number of affiliated colleges, and there is an aviation training centre. The city has several museums. Allahabad has a Government House dating from the British period, Anglican and Roman Catholic cathedrals, and the Jāmiʻ Masjid, or Great Mosque. The surrounding area lies entirely on the Ganges Plain. Rice, barley, wheat, and chickpeas are among the region's chief crops. Pop. (2001) 975,393.

AMRITSAR

The city of Amritsar lies in northern Punjab state, northwestern India, about 15 miles (25 km) east of the border with Pakistan. It is the largest and most important city in Punjab and is a major commercial, cultural, and transportation centre. It is also the centre of Sikhism and the site of the Sikhs' principal place of worship—the Harimandir, or Golden Temple.

Amritsar was founded in 1577 by Ram Das, fourth Guru of the Sikhs, on a site granted by the Mughal emperor Akbar. Ram Das ordered the excavation of the sacred tank, or pool, called Amrita Saras ("Pool of Nectar"), from which the city's name is derived. A temple was erected on an island in the tank's centre by Arjun, the fifth Guru of the Sikhs. During the reign of Maharaja Ranjit Singh (1801–39), the upper part of the temple was decorated with a gold-foil-covered copper dome, and since then the building has been known as the Harimandir. Amritsar became the centre of the Sikh faith, and, as the centre of growing Sikh power, the city experienced a corresponding increase in trade. It was annexed to British India in 1849.

A short distance away from the Golden Temple is a spacious park, Jallianwalla Bagh, where on April 13, 1919, British colonial government troops fired on a crowd of unarmed Indian protesters, killing 379 of them and wounding many more. The site of the Amritsar Massacre, as this incident is now called, is a national monument. Another violent political clash took place in Amritsar in 1984, when troops of the Indian army attacked hundreds of Sikh separatists who had taken up positions in, and heavily fortified, the Golden Temple. Conflicting reports indicated that between 450 and 1,200 persons were killed before the Sikh extremists were evicted from the temple.

Amritsar is a centre for the textile and chemical industries and also engages

in food milling and processing, silk weaving, tanning, canning, and the manufacture of machinery. The city lies on the main highway from Delhi to Lahore, Pak., and is a major rail hub. An airport is nearby. Amritsar is home to Guru Nanak Dev University, which was founded in 1969 as the leading educational centre of the Sikhs. Medical, dental, arts, and technical colleges are also located in Amritsar, and Khalsa College (1899) lies just outside the city. In the newer, northern section of the city is the Ram Bagh, a large, well-maintained park that contains the summer palace of Ranjit Singh. Pop. (2001) 966,862.

AYODHYA

The town of Ayodhya (also called Oudh or Awadh) is located in south-central Uttar Pradesh state, northern India, on the Ghaghara River near Faizabad. An ancient town, it is regarded as one of the seven sacred cities of the Hindus, revered because of its association in the great Indian epic poem *Ramayana* with the birth of Rama and with the rule of his father, Dasharatha. According to this source, the town was prosperous and well-fortified and had a large population.

In traditional history, Ayodhya was the early capital of the kingdom of Koshala, though in Buddhist times (6th–5th century BCE) Shravasti became the kingdom's chief city. Scholars generally agree that Ayodhya is identical with the town of Saketa, where the Buddha is said to have resided for a time. Its later importance as a Buddhist centre can be gauged from the statement of the Chinese Buddhist monk Faxian in the 5th century CE that there were 100 monasteries there. There were also a number of other monuments, including a stupa (shrine) reputed to have been founded by the Mauryan emperor Ashoka (3rd century BCE).

The Kanauj kingdom arose in Ayodhya, then called Oudh, during the 11th and 12th centuries CE. The region was later included in the Delhi sultanate, the Jaunpur kingdom, and, in the 16th century, the Mughal Empire. Oudh gained a measure of independence early in the 18th century but became subordinate to the British East India Company in 1764. In 1856 it was annexed by the British; the annexation and subsequent loss of rights by the hereditary land revenue receivers provided one of the causes of the Indian Mutiny in 1857. Oudh was joined with the Agra Presidency in 1877 to form the North-Western Provinces and later the United Provinces of Agra and Oudh, now Uttar Pradesh state.

Despite the town's great age, there are few surviving monuments of any antiquity. The Babri Masjid ("Mosque of Bābur") was built in the early 16th century

Headquarters of the Organization for the Management of the Sikh Temples at Amritsar, Punjab, India. Milt and Joan Mann/CameraMann International

by the Mughal emperor Bābur on a site traditionally identified as Rama's birthplace and as the location of an ancient Hindu temple, the Ram Janmabhoomi. Because of its significance to both Hindus and Muslims, the site was often a matter of contention. In 1990 riots in northern India followed the storming of the mosque by militant Hindus intent on erecting a temple on the site; the ensuing crisis brought down the Indian government. Two years later, on Dec. 6, 1992, the three-story mosque was demolished in a few hours by a crowd of Hindu fundamentalists. It was estimated that more than 1,000 people died in the rioting that swept through India following the mosque's destruction.

The numerous Vaishnava shrines and bathing ghats are of no great age. Close to the modern town are several mounds marking the site of ancient Ayodhya that have not yet been adequately explored by archaeologists. Pop. (2001) 49,417.

GWALIOR

Gwalior, in northern Madhya Pradesh state, central India, is located about 75 miles (120 km) south of Agra. It is on a major national highway and is a railway junction. It is a cultural, industrial, and political centre and takes its name from the historic rock fortress that forms the centre of the city. Gwalior has been referred to as Gopa Parvat, Gopachal Durg, Gopagiri, and Gopadiri, all which mean "Cowherd's Hill." Pop. (2001) 827,026.

HISTORY

The area in which Gwalior is situated was the core of the former Gwalior princely state. That state was once the domain of the Sindhia family, a Maratha dynasty that controlled much of northwestern India during the second half of the 18th century. The foundations of the Gwalior state were laid by Ranoji Sindhia about 1745, and the state reached its greatest extent under Sindhia Mahadaji (reigned 1761–94). Mahadaji was the ruler of a vast territory that included parts of central India and Hindustan proper (northern India), while his officers exacted tribute from the principal Rajput rulers, including those of Jaipur and Jodhpur. Under Mahadaji's grandnephew, Daulat Rao, the Gwalior state lost considerable territory to the British in 1803 and 1818 after losing wars to them. The state came completely under British domination in the 1840s. During the Indian Mutiny of 1857–58, the Sindhia ruler of Gwalior remained loyal to the British, but his army joined the mutineers and temporarily occupied Gwalior city before being defeated.

Gwalior was constituted a municipality in 1887, and the princely state of Gwalior was absorbed by independent India in 1948. At the time of its incorporation, it had an area of about 26,000 square miles (68,000 square km) and comprised almost all of what is now northern Madhya Pradesh state; the Gwalior state extended from the Chambal River southward to the

Vindhya mountain range. The area was merged with Madhya Pradesh in 1956.

THE CONTEMPORARY CITY

The old city of Gwalior centres on the walled fortress, one of the most famous in India, that is situated atop a cliffed plateau nearly 2 miles (3 km) long that rises a sheer 300 feet (90 metres) from the plain. The fort was first mentioned in a temple inscription about 525 CE. Of strategic importance in guarding the main route from the plains of northern India, it was in the hands of Hindu rulers until 1232 and then changed hands several times between Muslim and Hindu rulers until 1751; thereafter it remained a Maratha stronghold, although it was captured by the British in 1780, 1843, and 1858. It was evacuated by the British in 1886 in exchange for the imposition of British rule over the city of Jhansi. The fortress contains several tanks (reservoirs), six palaces, six temples, a mosque, and several other buildings. The Teli-ka-Mandir (11th century), the Gujari Mahal (c. 1500), and the surviving atrium of the Great Sas-Bahu Temple (1093) are outstanding examples of Hindu architecture within the fort. Just below the fort's walls are 15th-century rock-cut Jaina statues that are nearly 60 feet (18 metres) high.

The city of Lashkar lies 4 miles (6 km) south of the fortress. Founded in 1810 as a military camp, it later served as capital of the princely state of Gwalior. The city of Lashkar contains many palaces and the cenotaph of the rani of Jhansi. Nearby at Anti stands the tomb of the Mughal scholar Abū al-Faḍl ʿAllāmī. To the east of the fort is the area of Morar, which was a British cantonment.

Gwalior is an important commercial and industrial centre that is engaged in the distribution of agricultural produce, cloth fabrics, building stone, and iron ore. The city's major industries include the manufacture of footwear, pottery, biscuits (cookies), cigarettes, textiles, carpets, plastics, rayon, glass, and matches; cotton, flour, sugar, and oilseed milling; and stone carving.

Other places of interest in Gwalior include a zoological garden, several museums, a central technical institute, and an industrial research laboratory. Gwalior is the seat of Jiwaji University (founded 1964) with several affiliated colleges in the city, including science, medical, and education schools. Nearby is the 16th-century tomb of the Indian singer Tansen. The city is still a music centre, with its own distinctive style and tradition.

Gwalior's surrounding region consists of a rich alluvial plain, irrigated by canal networks from the Harsi, Tigra, and Kaketo dams. Wheat, sorghum, rice, and pulses are the chief crops grown, and sandstone is quarried.

JAIPUR

The city of Jaipur is the capital of Rajasthan state, northwestern India. It is a popular tourist destination and a commercial trade centre with major road, rail, and air connections. A walled town surrounded (except to the south) by hills, the city was founded in 1727 by Maharaja Sawai Jai Singh to replace Amber (now Amer) as the capital of the princely state of Jaipur (founded by the Rajputs in the 12th century CE). Known for its beauty, the city is unique in its straight-line planning; its buildings are predominantly rose-coloured, and it is sometimes called the "pink city." The chief buildings are the City Palace, part of which is home to the royal family of Jaipur; Jantar Mantar, an 18th-century open-air observatory; Hawa Mahal (Hall of Winds); Ram Bagh palace; and Nahargarh, the Tiger Fort. Other public buildings include a museum and a library. Jaipur is the seat of the University of Rajasthan, founded in 1947. Jaipur has a mixed Hindu-Muslim population. The city was the site of numerous bombing attacks in the early 21st century, with mosques and Hindu temples being targets.

Industries include engineering and metalworking, hand-loom weaving, distilling, and the manufacture of glass, hosiery, carpets, blankets, shoes, and drugs. Jaipur's famous arts and crafts include the making of jewelry, enamel, metalwork, and printed cloths, as well as stone, marble, and ivory carving.

The city is surrounded by fertile alluvial plains to the east and south and hill chains and desert areas to the north and west. Pearl millet, barley, chickpeas, pulses, and cotton are the chief crops grown in this region. Iron ore, beryllium, mica, feldspar, marble, copper, and garnet deposits are worked. Pop. (2001) city, 2,322,575.

JODHPUR

The city of Jodhpur is located in central Rajasthan state, northwestern India. It was founded in 1459 by Rao Jodha, a Rajput (one of the warrior rulers of the historical region of Rajputana), and served as the capital of the former princely state of Jodhpur. Parts of the city are surrounded by an 18th-century wall. The fort, which contains the palace and a historical museum, is built on an isolated rock eminence that dominates the city. The 4th-century ruins of Mandor, the ancient capital of Marwar, lie immediately to the north.

Jodhpur, the largest princely state in the former Rajputana Agency, consisted of the present district of Jodhpur as well as Nagaur, Pali, Jalor, and Barmer districts. It was founded about 1212, reached the zenith of its power under the ruler Rao Maldeo (1532–69), and gave allegiance to the Mughals after the invasion of the Mughal emperor Akbar in 1561. The Mughal emperor Aurangzeb invaded and plundered Marwar in 1679, ordering the conversion of its inhabitants to Islam. The princely states of Jodhpur, Jaipur, and Udaipur formed an alliance, however, and prevented control by the Muslims. The Jodhpur and Jaipur princes then regained the privilege of marriage with the Udaipur family (which they had forfeited when allying with the Mughals) on condition that children of Udaipur

The fort overlooking Jodhpur, Rajasthan, India. Kaypix—Shostal

princesses be first in succession. Quarrels resulting from this stipulation, however, finally led to the establishment of the supremacy of the Marathas, a Hindu warrior caste. In 1818 Jodhpur came under British paramountcy. It joined the state of Rajasthan in 1949.

The city is a major road and rail junction and a trade centre for agricultural crops, wool, cattle, salt, and hides. It has engineering and railway workshops and manufactures cotton textiles, brass and iron utensils, bicycles, ink, and polo equipment. Jodhpur is famous for its handicraft products, which include ivory goods, glass bangles, cutlery, dyed cloth, lacquerwork, felt and leather products, marble stonework, and carpets. Jodhpur, the second-largest city of Rajasthan, is the seat of the Rajasthan state high court. The city is the site of an air force college and airfield, the University of Jodhpur (established 1962), and a medical college affiliated with the University of Rajasthan.

Jodhpur's surrounding region chiefly consists of a sterile tract covered with high sand hills, sometimes referred to as Marwar (derived from *maru-war* ["region of death"] because of the area's harsh desert conditions). Its north and northwest areas form part of the Great Indian (Thar) Desert. Pearl millet, pulses such as beans, grain sorghum, oilseeds, mung (the edible seeds of an Asian bean), and corn (maize) are the chief crops; some cotton and wheat are produced. Lignite, iron ore, tungsten, garnet, glass-sand, and gypsum deposits are worked. There are also several poultry farms, and sheep, cattle, and camels are bred there. Pop. (2001) city, 851,051.

Kanpur

Kanpur (formerly Cawnpore) is in south-central Uttar Pradesh state, northern India. It lies southwest of Lucknow, on the Ganges (Ganga) River. Kanpur was only a village when it and the surrounding territory were acquired in 1801 by the British, who made it one of their frontier stations. In 1857, during the Indian Mutiny, the British troops in the town were massacred by native forces. The survivors are said to have been thrown into a well, where a memorial has since been built.

The largest city of Uttar Pradesh and one of the largest in India, Kanpur has an area of more than 100 square miles (260 square km). It is an important road and rail hub and a major commercial and industrial centre. The city proper lies northwest of the cantonment; most of its industry is still farther northwest. The urban area also includes three railway colonies and Armapur, a suburb. There is a military airfield nearby. Kanpur has a university; colleges of medicine, law, and education; the Indian Institute of Technology; and a government

experimental farm. Notable buildings include a sacred Hindu glass temple and Kamla Retreat, a rest house on a small lake. There are several museums.

The surrounding region is a fertile stretch of alluvial plain between the Ganges and Yamuna rivers. It is watered by tributaries of the two rivers and by the Lower Ganges Canal. Crops include wheat, chickpeas, grain sorghum, and barley. There are mango and mahua (*Madhuca latifolia*, a medium to large deciduous tree that produces oilseeds) groves and a *dhak* (*Butea frondosa*) forest. Bithur, a ruined town, is a Hindu holy place; the region contains many small temples built between the 6th and 9th centuries. Pop. (2001) 2,551,337.

Lucknow

The city of Lucknow is the capital of Uttar Pradesh state, northern India. It is located on the Gomati River at the junction of numerous roads and rail lines. The city is a marketplace for agricultural products (mangoes, melons, and various grains are grown locally), and its industries include food processing, manufacturing, handicrafts, and railroad shops.

Lucknow became important in 1528, when it was captured by Bābur, the first Mughal ruler of India. Under Akbar, his grandson, the city became part of Oudh province. Āṣaf al-Dawlah, who became nawab of Oudh (now Ayodhya) in 1775, transferred his capital from Faizabad to Lucknow. When the Indian Mutiny broke out in 1857, Sir Henry Lawrence, the

British commissioner, and the European inhabitants of Lucknow were besieged for several months until rescued by British troops. The British then abandoned the city until the following year, when they regained control over India.

Lucknow contains notable examples of architecture. The Great Imāmbāṛā (1784) is a single-storied structure where Shīʿite Muslims assemble during the month of Muḥarram. The Rumi Darwaza, or Turkish Gate, was modeled (1784) after the Sublime Porte (Bab-i Hümayun) in Istanbul. The best-preserved monument is the Residency (1800), the scene of the defense by British troops during the Indian Mutiny. A memorial commemorating the Indians who died during the uprising was erected in 1957.

Among Lucknow's educational institutions are the University of Lucknow (1921), a music academy, an institute of Muslim theology, the Central Drug Research Institute (1951), an arts-and-crafts college, and a state museum. The city also has a botanical and a national zoological garden. Pop. (2001) 2,185,927.

SRINAGAR

Srinagar is the summer capital of Jammu and Kashmir state (Jammu is the winter

Nishat gardens, Srinagar, Jammu and Kashmir, India. Frederick M. Asher

capital), northern India, in the Kashmir region of the Indian subcontinent. It lies along the banks of the Jhelum River at an elevation of 5,200 feet (1,600 metres) in the Vale of Kashmir.

Situated amid clear lakes and lofty, forested mountains, Srinagar has long had a considerable tourist economy. Along its course through the city, the Jhelum River is spanned by several wooden bridges, and numerous adjacent canals and waterways abound with *shikara*, the gondolas of Kashmir. Srinagar is well known for its many mosques and temples; the Hazratbal Mosque contains a hair that reportedly belonged to the Prophet Muhammad, and the Jāmi' Masjid (Congregational Mosque), built in the 15th century, is said to be the largest mosque in Kashmir. Dal Lake, with its "floating gardens," is a well-known

attraction, as are the nearby Shalimar and Nishat gardens.

Srinagar's industries include carpet and silk mills, silverware and copperware manufacture, leatherworking, and wood carving. The University of Kashmir (1948) is in the city, as is the Sher-e-Kashmir University of Agricultural Sciences and Technology Kashmir (1982). Regular flights connect Srinagar with Delhi and Amritsar. Not far from Srinagar is the town of Gulmarg, the "Meadow of Flowers," at an elevation of about 8,500 feet (2,600 metres). It affords magnificent views of the Vale of Kashmir and of Nanga Parbat, which at 26,660 feet (8,126 metres) is one of the highest peaks in the Himalayas. The Vale of Kashmir contains the area's most fertile agricultural land and is one of the most densely populated parts of the Kashmir region. Pop. (2001) 898,440.

CHAPTER 6

THE MAJOR CITIES OF NORTHEASTERN INDIA

Northeastern India encompasses the densely populated eastern portion of the Gangetic Plain and lowlands of West Bengal state, the latter containing Kolkata (Calcutta), India's third-largest conurbation.

KOLKATA

The great city of Kolkata (Bengali: Kalikata; formerly Calcutta) is the capital of West Bengal state and the former capital (1772–1911) of British India. It is one of India's largest cities and one of its major ports. The city is centred on the east bank of the Hugli (Hooghly) River, once the main channel of the Ganges (Ganga) River, about 96 miles (154 km) upstream from the head of the Bay of Bengal; there the port city developed as a point of transshipment from water to land and from river to sea. A city of commerce, transport, and manufacture, Kolkata is the dominant urban centre of eastern India.The city's former name, Calcutta, is an Anglicized version of the Bengali name Kalikata. According to some, Kalikata is derived from the Bengali word Kalikshetra, meaning "Ground of (the goddess) Kali." Some say the city's name derives from the location of its original settlement on the bank of a canal (*khal*). A third opinion traces it to the Bengali words for "lime" (calcium oxide; *kali*) and "burnt shell" (*kata*),

Victoria Memorial Hall in Kolkata (Calcutta), India. Photos.com/Jupiterimages.

since the area was noted for the manufacture of shell lime. In 2001 the government of West Bengal officially changed the name of the city to Kolkata. Area city, 40 square miles (104 square km); urban agglomeration, 533 square miles (1,380 square km). Pop. (2001) city, 4,580,546; urban agglomeration, 13,205,697.

CHARACTER OF THE CITY

Fashioned by the colonial British in the manner of a grand European capital—yet now set in one of the poorest and most overpopulated regions of India—Kolkata has grown into a city of sharp contrasts and contradictions. Kolkata has had to assimilate strong European influences and overcome the limitations of its colonial legacy in order to find its own unique identity. In the process it created an amalgam of East and West that found its expression in the life and works of the 19th-century Bengali elite and its most noteworthy figure, the poet and mystic Rabindranath Tagore.

This large and vibrant Indian city thrives amid seemingly insurmountable economic, social, and political problems. Its citizens exhibit a great joie de vivre that is demonstrated in a penchant for art and culture and a high level of intellectual vitality and political awareness. Crowds throng to Kolkata's book fairs, art exhibitions, and concerts, and there is a lively trading of polemics on walls, which has led to Kolkata being dubbed the "city of posters."

Yet for all of Kolkata's vitality, many of the city's residents live in some of the worst conditions, far removed from the cultural milieu. The city's energy nevertheless penetrates even to the poorest areas, as a large number of Kolkatans sincerely support the efforts of those who minister to the underprivileged. In short, Kolkata remains an enigma to many Indians as well as to foreigners. It continues to puzzle newcomers and to arouse an abiding nostalgia in the minds of those who have lived there.

LANDSCAPE

The location of the city appears to have been originally selected partly because of its easily defensible position and partly because of its favourable trading location. The low, swampy, hot, and humid riverbank otherwise has little to recommend it.

CITY SITE

Kolkata's maximum elevation is about 30 feet (9 metres) above sea level. Eastward from the river the land slopes away to marshes and swamplands. Similar topography on the west bank of the river has confined the metropolitan area largely to a strip 3 to 5 miles (5 to 8 km) wide on either bank of the river. Reclamation of the Salt Lake area on the northeastern fringe of the city, however, demonstrated that the spatial expansion of the city is feasible, and further reclamation projects have been undertaken to the east, south, and west of the central area.

Suburbs of Kolkata include Howrah (on the west bank), Baranagar to the north, South Dum Dum to the northeast, Behala to the south, and Garden Reach in the southwest. The whole urban complex is held together by close socioeconomic ties.

HOUSING

The city has an acute housing shortage. Of the persons living in institutional shelters in the Kolkata metropolitan area, more than two-thirds live in the city itself. About three-fourths of the housing units in the city are used for dwelling purposes only. There are hundreds of urban settlements called *bastis*, where about one-third of the city's population lives. A *basti* (also spelled *busti* or *bustee*) is officially defined as "a collection of huts standing on a plot of land of at least one-sixth of an acre." There also are *bastis* built on less than one-sixth of an acre (one-fifteenth of a hectare). The majority of *basti* dwellings are tiny, unventilated, single-story rooms, often dilapidated. They have few sanitary facilities, and there is very little open space. The government has sponsored *basti* improvement and resettlement programs.

CLIMATE

Kolkata has a subtropical climate with a seasonal regime of monsoons (rain-bearing winds). It is warm year-round, with average high temperatures ranging from about 80 °F (27 °C) in December and January to nearly 100 °F (38 °C) in April and May. The average annual rainfall is about 64 inches (1,625 mm). Most of this falls from June to September, the period of the monsoon. These months are very humid and sometimes sultry. During October and November the rainfall dwindles. The winter months, from about the end of November to the end of February, are pleasant and rainless; fogs and mists occasionally reduce visibility in the early morning hours at this season, as also do thick blankets of smog in the evenings. The atmospheric pollution has greatly increased since the early 1950s. Factories, motor vehicles, and thermal-generating stations, which burn coal, are primary causes of this pollution, but monsoon winds act as cleansing agents by bringing in fresh air masses and also hastening the removal of water pollution.

ARCHITECTURE

In contemporary Kolkata the skyline is broken in some areas by skyscrapers and tall multistory blocks. The cityscape has changed rapidly. The Chowringhee area in central Kolkata, once a row of palatial houses, has been given up to offices, hotels, and shops. In northern and central Kolkata, buildings are still mainly two or three stories high. In southern and south-central Kolkata, multistoried apartment buildings have become more common.

Western influence is dominant in many of Kolkata's architectural monuments, though Indian influences also are apparent. The Raj Bhavan (the state governor's residence) is an imitation of Kedleston Hall in Derbyshire, Eng.; the High Court resembles the Cloth Hall at Ypres, Belg.; the Town Hall is in Grecian style with a Doric-Hellenic portico; St. Paul's Cathedral is of Indo-Gothic-style architecture; the Writers' Building is of Gothic-style architecture with statuary on top; the Indian Museum is in an Italian style; and the General Post Office, with its majestic dome, has Corinthian columns. The beautiful column of the Sahid Minar (Ochterlony Monument) is 165 feet (50 metres) high—its base is Egyptian, its column Syrian, and its cupola in the Turkish style. Victoria Memorial Hall represents an attempt to combine classical Western influence with Mughal architecture; the Nakhoda Mosque is modeled on the tomb of the Mughal emperor Akbar at Sikandra; the Birla Planetarium is based on the stupa (Buddhist reliquary) at Sanchi. The Ramakrishna Mission Institute of Culture, the most important example of postindependence construction, follows the style of ancient Hindu palace architecture in northwestern India.

CITY LAYOUT

The most striking aspect of the layout of Kolkata is its rectangular, north-south orientation. With the exception of the central areas where Europeans formerly lived, the city has grown haphazardly. This haphazard development is most noticeable in the fringe areas around the central core formed by the city of Kolkata and the suburb of Howrah. The bulk of the city's administrative and commercial activity is concentrated in the Barabazar district, a small area north of the Maidan (the park containing Fort William and many of the city's cultural and recreational facilities). The layout has encouraged the development of a pattern of daily commuting that has overburdened Kolkata's transportation system, utilities, and other municipal facilities.

Kolkata's system of streets and roads reflects the city's historical development. An express highway, Kazi Nazrul Islam Avenue, stretches from Kolkata to Dum Dum, though most local streets are narrow. The main roads form a grid pattern primarily in the old European sector, but elsewhere road planning has a random character. Part of the reason for this has been the difficulty of providing enough river crossings; it is for the same reason that most streets and highways run from north to south. Nullahs (watercourses) and canals that require bridging also have been important factors in influencing the road pattern.

PEOPLE

More than four-fifths of the population is Hindu. Muslims and Christians constitute the largest minorities, but there are some Sikhs, Jains, and Buddhists. The dominant language is Bengali, but Urdu, Oriya, Tamil, Punjabi, and other languages also are spoken. Kolkata is a cosmopolitan city: other than Indians, groups present include a variety of peoples from elsewhere in Asia (notably Bangladeshis and Chinese), Europeans, North Americans, and Australians. Kolkata was segregated under British rule, the Europeans living in the city centre and Indians living to the north and south. The pattern of segregation has continued in the modern city, although the distribution is now based on religious, linguistic, educational, and economic criteria. Shantytowns and low-income residential areas, however, exist side-by-side with more affluent areas.

The density of population is extremely high, and overcrowding has reached virtually intolerable proportions in many sections of the city. Kolkata experienced a high rate of population growth for more than a century, and events such as the partitioning of Bengal in 1947 and warfare in Bangladesh in the early 1970s precipitated massive population influxes. Large refugee colonies also have sprung up in the northern and southern suburbs. In addition, a great number of migrants from other states—mostly from neighbouring Bihar and Orissa and eastern

Uttar Pradesh—have come to Kolkata in search of employment.

ECONOMY

Kolkata's position as one of India's pre-eminent economic centres is rooted in its manufacturing industries, its financial and trade activities, and its role as a major port; it is also a major centre for printing, publishing, and newspaper circulation, as well as for recreation and entertainment. Among the products of Kolkata's hinterland have been coal, iron, manganese, mica, petroleum, tea, and jute. Unemployment, however, has been a continuing and growing problem since the 1950s.

MANUFACTURING

Kolkata is the centre of India's large jute-processing industry. The jute industry was established in the 1870s, and mills now extend north and south of the city centre on both banks of the Hugli River. Engineering constitutes the city's other major industry. In addition, city factories produce and distribute a variety of consumer goods—notably foodstuffs, beverages, tobacco, and textiles—other light manufactures, and chemicals. Kolkata's industries have been in a general decline since Indian independence in 1947. Major factors contributing to this decline have been the loss of the eastern part of Bengal at independence, an overall decline in Kolkata's industrial productivity, and the lack of industrial diversification in the city.

FINANCE, TRADE, AND OTHER SERVICES

The Kolkata stock exchange plays an important part in the organized financial market of the country. Foreign banks also have a significant business base in Kolkata, although the city's importance as an international banking centre has declined. In addition, coal mines, jute mills, and large-scale engineering industries are controlled from offices in the city. State and national chambers of commerce are based in Kolkata as well.

The mercantile nature of the city's economy is reflected in the fact that about two-fifths of the workers are employed in trade and commerce. Other important occupations include public-sector service in government departments, financial institutions, and medical and educational institutions. Private-sector services include the stock exchange, medical and educational services, legal services, accountancy and credit firms, and various utility services.

TRANSPORTATION

The condition of the surfaced roads in the city is poor, although the traffic load is heavy. The mass transit system features numerous trams and buses, some under government management and others run by private companies. In 1986 the first section of a subway system—the first in India—was opened in the city. By the early 21st century it was the primary means of commuting within the city, with almost two million commuters using it every day.

The connection between Kolkata and its hinterland to the west depends upon several bridges over the Hugli—those linked to Howrah and, farther north, the bridges at Bally and Naihati. The main Howrah bridge, Rabindra Setu, carries multiple lanes of vehicular traffic and is one of the most heavily used bridges in the world. Two additional bridges between Kolkata and Howrah, Vidyasagar Setu and Nivedita Setu, have eased traffic on the main bridge.

The Grand Trunk Road, a national highway, is one of the oldest road routes in India. It runs through Howrah to Pakistan and is the main route connecting the city with northern India. National highways also connect Kolkata with the west coast of India, the northern part of West Bengal, and the frontier with Bangladesh.

Two railway terminals—Howrah on the west bank and Sealdah on the east—serve the railway networks running north and south as well as those running east and west. Kolkata's major air terminal, at Dum Dum, handles international and domestic flights.

The Kolkata port lost its position as India's preeminent cargo handler in the 1960s, but it and the port of Haldia (about 40 miles [65 km] downstream) still account for a large portion of the country's foreign exchange. The decline in traffic occurred partly because of problems encountered in dredging silt from the river and partly because of labour difficulties. Transport, storage, wholesaling, and retailing requirements for exports and imports are concentrated in Kolkata and Howrah.

ADMINISTRATION AND SOCIETY

Two levels of governance are found in Kolkata: that of the city proper, which is the responsibility of the Kolkata Municipal Corporation, and, because Kolkata is the capital of West Bengal, that of the state government.

GOVERNMENT

The Kolkata Municipal Corporation's council is composed of one elected representative from each of the city's wards. The council members annually elect a mayor, a deputy mayor, and a number of committees to conduct the activities of the corporation. A commissioner, the executive head of the corporation, is responsible to its elected membership. The city is also a part of the Kolkata Metropolitan District, an entity created to oversee planning and development on a regional basis. This district includes a large rural hinterland around the urban centres.

The governor of West Bengal resides in the city in the historic Raj Bhavan. The state Legislative Assembly is located in the city, as is the Secretariat, housed in the Writers' Building, with the state ministries in charge of various departments. The Kolkata High Court, exercising original jurisdiction over the city and appellate jurisdiction over West Bengal, is also located there. A number of national government institutions—including the National Library, the Indian Museum, and the Geological Survey of India—are in the city as well.

MUNICIPAL SERVICES

Filtered water is supplied from the main waterworks located outside the city at Palta, as well as from some 200 major wells and 3,000 smaller ones. The Farakka Barrage (dam) on the Ganges, 240 miles (386 km) upriver from Kolkata, ensures a generally saline-free water supply for the city, but because existing water supplies are inadequate, salinity continues to be a problem during the dry months. In addition, unfiltered water, supplied daily for watering the city streets and for the fire brigade, is used by many residents for their daily needs. This circumstance was largely responsible for the former prevalence of cholera during the summer months, but chlorination of unfiltered water and cholera inoculation have reduced considerably the occurrence of the disease.

Municipal Kolkata has several hundred miles of sewers and surface drains, but much of the city remains unsupplied with sewers. Accumulation of silt has narrowed many sewer channels. The system of removing garbage and of garbage dumping is also unsatisfactory.

Kolkata is supplied with electricity by a variety of sources. There is still a gap, however, between generating capacity and potential demand, and temporary power interruptions occur on occasion.

Administration of the Kolkata police force is vested in the city's commissioner of police, as is direction of the suburban police force. The city is divided into a number of police precincts. The fire brigade has its headquarters in central Kolkata.

HEALTH

Hundreds of hospitals, private clinics, free dispensaries run by the Kolkata Municipal Corporation and charitable trusts, and state-operated polyclinics serve the Kolkata region. The number of doctors per 1,000 persons is greater in Kolkata than in most parts of the country, but their distribution is uneven; since the city is a medical centre for the northeastern region of India, its health-care facilities are always overcrowded. The Order of the Missionaries of Charity, an organization founded (1948) by Mother Teresa (recipient of the Nobel Peace Prize of 1979), cares for the blind, the elderly, the dying, and people afflicted with leprosy in the poorest sections of the city. There are several medical colleges, in addition to other medical research centres.

EDUCATION

Education has long been a mark of higher social status in Kolkata. The city has been a centre of learning since the resurgence in Indian education that began in Bengal in the early 19th century. The first

English-style school, the Hindu College (later called Presidency College), was founded in 1817.

Primary education is supervised by the government of West Bengal and is free in schools run by the municipal corporation. A large number of children, however, attend recognized schools that are under private management. Most secondary schools are under the supervision of the state, but some are accredited through the national government.

Kolkata has three major universities: the University of Calcutta, Jadavpur University, and Rabindra Bharati University. The University of Calcutta, founded in 1857, has more than 150 affiliated colleges. Besides these colleges, university colleges of arts (humanities), commerce, law, medicine, science, and technology specialize in postgraduate teaching and research. Jadavpur University (1955) has faculties in the arts (humanities), science, and engineering. Although the university has a small number of colleges affiliated with it, its main focus is on graduate and postgraduate instruction on a single campus. Rabindra Bharati University (1962), founded in honour of Rabindranath Tagore, specializes in humanities and the fine arts (dance, drama, and music).

Research institutions include the Indian Statistical Institute, the Indian Association for the Cultivation of Science, the Bose Institute (natural science), and the All-India Institute of Hygiene and Public Health, which is a constituent college of the University of Calcutta.

CULTURAL LIFE

Kolkata is perhaps the most important cultural centre of India. The city is the birthplace of modern Indian literary and artistic thought and of Indian nationalism, and its citizens have made great efforts to preserve Indian culture and civilization. The blending of Eastern and Western cultural influences over the centuries has stimulated the creation of numerous and diverse organizations that contribute to Kolkata's cultural life. In addition to the universities, these include the Asiatic Society of Bengal, the Bengal Literary Society (Bangiya Sahitya Parishad), the Ramakrishna Mission Institute of Culture, the Academy of Fine Arts, the Birla Academy of Art and Culture, and the Maha Bodhi Society.

MUSEUMS AND LIBRARIES

Greater Kolkata has more than 30 museums, which cover a wide variety of fields. The Indian Museum, founded in 1814, is the oldest in India; the archaeology and numismatic sections contain valuable collections. The exhibits at Victoria Memorial Hall trace Britain's relations with India. The Asutosh Museum of Indian Art in the University of Calcutta has exhibits of the folk art of Bengal among its collections. Science City, a large science museum and entertainment complex, was among the first of its kind in Asia. Valuable library collections are to be found in the Asiatic Society of Bengal, the Bengal Literary Society, and the University of Calcutta; the

National Library is the largest in India and contains a fine collection of rare books and manuscripts.

The Arts

Kolkatans have long been active in literary and artistic pursuits. The city saw the dawn of the mid-19th-century literary movement that sparked a cultural renaissance throughout India. The best exponent of this movement was Rabindranath Tagore, winner of the Nobel Prize for Literature of 1913, whose remarkable creativity in poetry, music, drama, and painting continues to enrich the cultural life of the city. Kolkata remains at the vanguard of artistic movements in the country, and several artists' societies present annual shows.

Kolkata is also a centre of traditional and contemporary music and dance. In 1934 Tagore inaugurated the first All-Bengal Music Conference in Kolkata. Since then, a number of classical Indian music conferences have been held every year. The home of many classical dancers, Kolkata was the location of Uday Shankar's experiments at adapting Western theatrical techniques to traditional dance forms. The school of dance, music, and drama founded by him has been in the city since 1965.

Professional drama got its start in Kolkata in the 1870s with the founding of the National Theatre (later replaced by the Minerva Theatre). Modern dramatic forms were pioneered in the city by such playwrights as Girish Chandra Ghosh and Dirabandhu Mitra. Kolkata is still an important centre of professional and amateur theatre and of experimental drama. The city also has been a pioneering centre of motion-picture production in India. The avant-garde film directors Satyajit Ray and Mrinal Sen have achieved international acclaim. There are scores of cinemas in the city, which regularly show films in English, Bengali, and Hindi.

Recreation

More than 200 parks, squares, and open spaces are maintained by the Kolkata Municipal Corporation. There is, however, very little open space in the overcrowded parts of the city. The Maidan, about 1,000 acres (400 hectares) in area, is the best-known open space; the major football (soccer), cricket, and hockey fields are located there. Adjacent to the Maidan is one of the oldest cricket fields in the world, Ranji Stadium, in the Eden Gardens; Netaji Stadium, for indoor events, is also in the vicinity. The Salt Lake Stadium, built to the east of the city, can seat 100,000 spectators. There are racecourses and golf courses within the city, and rowing at the Lake Club and the Bengal Rowing Club is popular. The Zoological Gardens are spread over an area of some 40 acres (16 hectares). The Indian Botanic Gardens in Howrah, on the west bank, contain thousands of species of plants.

History

The name Kalikata was mentioned in the rent-roll of the Mughal emperor

Akbar (reigned 1556–1605) and also in the *Manasa-mangal* of the Bengali poet Bipradas (1495). The history of Kolkata as a British settlement, known to the British as Calcutta, dates from the establishment of a trading post there by Job Charnock, an agent of the English East India Company, in 1690.

THE EARLY PERIOD

Charnock had previously had disputes with officials of the Mughal Empire at the river port of Hugli (Hooghly) and had been obliged to leave, after which he attempted unsuccessfully to establish himself at other places down the river. When the Mughal officials, not wishing to lose what they had gained from the English company's commerce, permitted Charnock to return once more, he chose Calcutta as the seat of his operations. The site was apparently carefully selected, being protected by the Hugli (Hooghly) River on the west, a creek to the north, and salt lakes to the east. Rival Dutch, French, and other European settlements were higher up the river on the west bank, so that access from the sea was not threatened, as it was at the port of Hugli. The river at this point was also wide and deep; the only disadvantage was that the marshes to the east and swamps within the area made the spot unhealthy. Moreover, before the coming of the English, three local villages—Sutanati, Kalikata, and Gobindapore, which were later to become parts of Calcutta—had been chosen as places to settle by Indian merchants who had migrated from the silted-up port of

Satgaon, farther upstream. The presence of these merchants may have been to some extent responsible for Charnock's choice of the site.

By 1696, when a rebellion broke out in the nearby district of Burdwan, the Mughal provincial administration had become friendly to the growing settlement. The servants of the company, who asked for permission to fortify their trading post, or factory, were given permission in general terms to defend themselves. The rebels were easily crushed by the Mughal government, but the settlers' defensive structure of brick and mud remained and came to be known as Fort William. In 1698 the English obtained letters patent that granted them the privilege of purchasing the zamindari right (the right of revenue collection; in effect, the ownership) of the three villages. This area around Fort William—Calcutta—became the seat of the British province known as the Bengal Presidency.

GROWTH OF THE CITY

In 1717 the Mughal emperor Farrukh-Siyar granted the East India Company freedom of trade in return for a yearly payment of 3,000 rupees; this arrangement gave a great impetus to the growth of Calcutta. A large number of Indian merchants flocked to the city. The servants of the company, under the company's flag, carried on a duty-free private trade. When the Marathas from the southwest began incursions against the Mughals in the western districts of Bengal in 1742, the

English obtained permission from 'Alī Vardī Khan, the nawab (ruler) of Bengal, to dig an entrenchment in the northern and eastern part of the town to form a moat on the land side. This came to be known as the Maratha Ditch. Although it was not completed to the southern end of the settlement, it marked the city's eastern boundary.

In 1756 the nawab's successor, Sirāj al-Dawlah, captured the fort and sacked the town. A number of Europeans were imprisoned in a small lockup popularly known as the Black Hole of Calcutta, and many died. Calcutta was recaptured in January 1757 by Robert Clive, one of the founders of British power in India, and by the British admiral Charles Watson. The nawab was defeated shortly afterward at Plassey (June 1757), after which British rule in Bengal was assured. Gobindapore was cleared of its forests, and the new Fort William was built on its present site, overlooking the Hugli at Calcutta, where it became the symbol of British military ascendancy.

CAPITAL OF BRITISH INDIA

Calcutta did not become the capital of British India until 1772, when the first governor-general, Warren Hastings, transferred all important offices to the city from Murshidabad, the provincial Mughal capital. In 1773 Bombay (now Mumbai) and Madras (now Chennai) became subordinate to the government at Fort William. A supreme court administering English law began to exercise original jurisdiction over the city as far as the Maratha Ditch (now Acharya Prafulla Chandra and Jagadish Chandra Bose roads).

In 1706 the population of Calcutta was roughly between 10,000 and 12,000. It increased to nearly 120,000 by 1752 and to 180,000 by 1821. The White (British) Town was built on ground that had been raised and drained. There were so many palaces in the British sector of the city that it was named the "city of palaces." Outside the British town were built the mansions of the newly rich, as well as clusters of huts. The names of different quarters of the city—such as Kumartuli (the potters' district) and Sankaripara (the conch-shell workers' district)—still indicate the various occupational castes of the people who became residents of the growing metropolis. Two distinct areas—one British, one Indian—came to coexist in Calcutta.

Calcutta at that time was described as a pestilential town. There were few good roads. In 1814 the Lottery Committee was constituted to finance public improvement by means of lotteries, and between 1814 and 1836 it took some effective measures to improve conditions. The municipal corporation was established in 1841. Cyclones in 1864, 1867, and 1870, however, devastated the poorer, low-lying areas.

By successive stages, as British power extended over the subcontinent, the whole of northern India became a hinterland for the port of Calcutta. The abolition of inland customs duties in 1835 created an open market, and the construction of railways (beginning in 1854) further quickened the development of business and industry. It was at this time that the Grand Trunk Road from Calcutta to Peshawar (now in Pakistan) was completed. British mercantile, banking, and insurance interests flourished. The Indian sector of Calcutta also became a busy hub of commerce and was thronged with people from throughout India and many other parts of Asia. Calcutta became the intellectual centre of the subcontinent.

Pre-Independence Troubles

The turn of the 20th century marked the beginning of a troublesome period for

Map of Calcutta (c. 1900), from the 10th edition of Encyclopædia Britannica.

Calcutta. Lord Curzon, viceroy of India, partitioned Bengal in 1905, making Dacca (now Dhaka, Bangl.) the capital of eastern Bengal and Assam. Insistent agitation led to the annulment of this partition in 1911, but at that time the capital of British India was removed from Calcutta to Delhi, where the government could enjoy relative calm.

Meanwhile, as Calcutta's population grew larger, social problems also became more insistent, as did demands for home rule for India. Communal riots occurred in 1926, and, when the nationalist leader Mohandas Gandhi called for noncompliance with unjust laws, riots occurred in 1930. In World War II, Japanese air raids upon the Calcutta docks caused damage and loss of life. The most serious communal riots of all took place in 1946, when the partition of British India became imminent and tensions between Muslims and Hindus reached their height.

CAPITAL OF WEST BENGAL

In 1947 the partition of Bengal between newly independent India and Pakistan constituted a serious setback for Calcutta, which became the capital of West Bengal only, losing the trade of a part of its former hinterland. At the same time, millions of refugees from the eastern portion of Bengal—which had become East Pakistan (now Bangladesh)—flocked to Calcutta, aggravating social problems and increasing overcrowding, which had already assumed serious proportions. Economic stagnation in the mid-1960s

further increased the instability of the city's social and political life and fueled a flight of capital from the city. The management of many companies was assumed by the state government.

In the 1980s, large-scale public works programs and centralized regional planning contributed to the improvement of economic and social conditions in the city. Beginning in the 1990s, large-scale manufacturing companies were mostly replaced with small-scale assembly, commercial, and other service-sector business firms. However, militant trade unions slowed the introduction of new technology and deterred entrepreneurial activity and investment. In addition, despite the construction of a subway system—a welcome addition to the existing mass transit system—a rapid increase in the number of privately owned vehicles produced severe traffic congestion. The city was dealt a major blow in September 2000, when parts of it were inundated by floodwaters. The flooding left hundreds of people dead and tens of thousands homeless.

In 2001 the city's name was officially changed from Calcutta to Kolkata. Although Kolkata is not as economically dynamic as some of the other major Indian cities, it continues to be a cultural, artistic, literary, and intellectual centre.

OTHER IMPORTANT NORTHEASTERN INDIAN CITIES

Outside of the Kolkata urban region, there is a considerable contrast in northeastern India between the densely populated Gangetic Plain and the much more sparsely settled hill areas of the far northeastern states. Patna, on the plain northwest of Kolkata, is some 10 times larger than Shillong, the largest city in the northeast.

DARJILING

Darjiling (also spelled Darjeeling; Tibetan: Dorje-ling) is located in extreme northern West Bengal state, northeastern India, about 305 miles (490 km) north of Kolkata (Calcutta). The city is situated on a long, narrow mountain ridge of the Sikkim Himalayas that descends abruptly to the bed of the Great Rangit River.

Darjiling lies at an elevation of about 7,000 feet (2,100 metres). On a clear day the city affords a magnificent view of Kanchenjunga (28,169 feet [8,586 metres]), and Mount Everest can be seen from a nearby viewing point. The name of the city means "Place of the Thunderbolt." Darjiling is a noted hill resort, and the city's economy is based

Workers picking tea leaves near Darjiling, West Bengal, India. Gerald Cubitt

largely on tourism; the peak periods for visitors are April to June and September to November. The city has major road, rail, and air connections with Kolkata.

Darjiling was ceded by the raja of Sikkim to the British in 1835 and was developed as a sanatorium for British troops. It was constituted a municipality in 1850. The Chaurastha ("Four Roads") district encompasses the Mall, where the roads converge; it is the city's main shopping centre and the most attractive promenade. Observatory Hill, Darjiling's highest point (7,137 feet [2,175 metres]), is crowned by Mahakal Temple, which is sacred to both Hindus and Buddhists. Birch Hill contains a natural park and the Himalayan Mountaineering Institute. The Lloyd Botanic Gardens, well-known for their varieties of Himalayan flora, were laid out in 1865. Besides these attractions, Darjiling has a zoo, a natural history museum, and a racecourse. It is well-known for its residential schools, and there are several colleges affiliated with the University of North Bengal (founded 1962) in and around the city.

The area in which Darjiling is situated receives plentiful rainfall and has a wide range of climates, from tropical to subalpine, owing to its varying elevations. Local coniferous and oak forests yield valuable timber. The local rural economy is based primarily on tea, which is plantation-grown up to elevations of 6,000 feet (1,800 metres). Other crops are rice, corn (maize), cardamom, and wheat. Pop. (2001) 107,197.

GANGTOK

The town of Gangtok is the capital of Sikkim state, northeastern India. It lies at an elevation of 5,600 feet (1,700 metres), and its name means "Top of the Hill." The town rises over slopes extensively terraced in corn (maize). It was the governmental seat of the kingdom of Sikkim until the monarchy was abolished (1975) and Sikkim was annexed by India (1976).

Gangtok's population includes Nepalese, Tibetans, Lepchas, and Indians. The town serves as a market centre for corn, rice, pulses, and oranges. It was an important point on the India-Tibet trade route via Nathu Pass (Nathu-la), 13 miles (21 km) northeast, until the border with Tibet was closed in 1962. The pass was reopened for trade, however, in 2006. From Gangtok the North Sikkim Highway (1962) reaches the Tibetan border areas via Lachung and Lachen, and the National Highway runs southwest to India.

Gangtok's townscape is marked by the former royal palace and chapel, two monasteries, the open-air Lall Market, the Namgyal Institute of Tibetology (1958; a centre for research in Mahayana Buddhism, including a library and a museum), and the Cottage Industries Institute (1957). The noted Buddhist monastery of Rumtek is 5 miles (8 km) southwest, and the royal cremation ground is at nearby Lukshiyama. Also nearby is the Do-drul Chorten (Do-drul Stupa), built by Tibetan Buddhists in the 1940s; its gold-topped

Market in Gangtok, Sikkim. Gerald Cubitt

stupa (commemorative monument) is encircled by 108 prayer wheels. Gangtok has government-maintained nurseries for cardamom—an important export from the state—and subtropical fruits, and there is an experimental agricultural station at Tadong, to the south. The town's Deorali Orchid Sanctuary houses some 200 species of orchids found in Sikkim. Pop. (2001) 29,354.

GUWAHATI

Guwahati (formerly Gauhati), in western Assam state, northeastern India, lies along the Brahmaputra River and is picturesquely situated with an amphitheatre of wooded hills to the south. The city was the capital of the Hindu kingdom of Kamarupa (under the name of Pragjyotisa) about 400 CE. In the 17th century it repeatedly changed hands between the Muslims and the Ahoms (a Tai-speaking people who had migrated from Yunnan province, China, and ruled much of Assam from the 13th century CE) until it became the seat of the Ahom governor of Lower Assam in 1681; in 1786 the Ahom raja made it his capital. The Myanmar (Burmese) held Guwahati from 1816 until 1826, when it became the British capital of Assam. The capital was moved 67 miles (108 km) south to Shillong in 1874.

Guwahati is an important river port and Assam's principal commercial centre. It has an oil refinery and a state farm, and its industries include tea processing, milling of agricultural products, and soap manufacturing. Gauhati University (founded 1948), Earle Law College, the state high court, the state museum, several scientific museums, and a zoological garden are located there. Several Hindu pilgrimage centres and temple ruins are nearby. Guwahati is served by an airport and a rail line. Pop. (2001) 809,895.

PATNA

The city of Patna (ancient Pataliputra) is the capital of Bihar state, northern India. It lies about 290 miles (470 km) northwest of Kolkata (Calcutta). Patna is one of the oldest cities in India. During the Mughal period it was known as Azimabad.

Patna is a riverside city that extends along the south bank of the Ganges (Ganga) River for about 12 miles (19 km). West of the old city lies the section called Bankipur, and farther southwest is a spacious new capital area with wide roads, shady avenues, and new buildings. Prominent among Patna's modern structures are the Government House, the Assembly Chambers, the Oriental Library, a medical college, and an engineering college. Patna's historic monuments include the mosque of Ḥusayn Shah of Bengal (1499); the Sikh Temple associated with the 10th Guru, Govinda Singh; and the granary at Bankipur (1786), popularly called the Golghar. The city also has the University of Patna (1917) and the Patna Museum.

The ancient city of Pataliputra was founded in the 5th century BCE by Ajatashatru, king of Magadha (South Bihar). His son Udaya (Udayin) made it the capital of Magadha, which it remained until the 1st century BCE. The second Magadha dynasty, the Maurya, ruled in the 3rd and early 2nd centuries BCE until the city was sacked in 185 by Indo-Greeks. The Shunga dynasty then began, ruling until about 73 BCE. Pataliputra remained a centre of learning and in the 4th century CE became the Gupta capital. It declined and was deserted by the 7th century. The city was refounded as Patna by an Afghan ruler in 1541 and again rose to prosperity under the Mughal Empire. It passed to the British in 1765. Extensive archaeological excavations have been made in the vicinity. Pop. (2001) 1,366,444; urban agglom., 1,697,976.

SHILLONG

Shillong (formerly Yeddo or Lewduh), the capital of Meghalaya state, northeastern

Morning mist and frosty hillsides south of Shillong, Meghalaya, India. Gerald Cubitt

India, is located on the Shillong Plateau at an elevation of 4,990 feet (1,520 metres). The city first became prominent in 1864, when it succeeded Cherrapunji as the district headquarters. In 1874 it was made the capital of the new province of Assam. An earthquake destroyed the city in 1897, necessitating its complete rebuilding. The North East Frontier Agency's headquarters were in Shillong until that region became the union territory of Arunachal Pradesh in 1972. In that year Shillong became the capital of Meghalaya, which had been newly created out of territory that was formerly within the state of Assam.

Shillong is one of the largest cities in northeastern India. It is an important trade centre for agricultural products and has research stations focusing on dairy farm, fruit, and silk production. It also has the Pasteur Institute and Medical Research Institute and two hospitals. The Barpani hydroelectric station lies a few miles to the north. Traffic congestion is a problem in the city.

Khasi people have long lived in the Shillong region. Large-scale migrations to Shillong took place following the partition of India in 1947. The immigrants were mostly from the portion of Assam that became part of East Pakistan (now Bangladesh). Pop. (2001) city, 132,867; urban agglom., 267,662.

TAMLUK

The town of Tamluk (ancient Tamralipti; also called Tamralipta; Pali: Tamalitti) is located in southern West Bengal state, northeastern India, just south of the Rupnarayan River. Archaeological excavations have revealed a sequence of occupation going back to a period in which stone axes and crude pottery were in use, with continuous settlement from about the 3rd century BCE. Jaina sources identify Tamralipti as the capital of the kingdom of Vanga. It was long known as a port. According to the *Mahavamsa*, an epic history of Sri Lanka, it was the departure point of Prince Vijaya's expedition to colonize Sri Lanka (c. 500 BCE) and for the Buddhist missionary expedition dispatched by the Mauryan emperor Ashoka to Sri Lanka 250 years later. Tamralipti was also the port for trade with Southeast Asia. The Chinese pilgrim Faxian visited the city in the 5th century CE, and Xuanzang visited it in the 7th century. Xuanzang reported that there were 10 Buddhist monasteries and an Ashokan pillar there, and he referred to Tamralipti as a thriving port for export of indigo, silk, and copper (Sanskrit: *tamra*), from which it derived its name. In ancient times it was near the sea. With the advance of the Ganges (Ganga) delta, the town is now about 60 miles (97 km) inland and about 20 miles (32 km) from the port of Haldia on the Hugli (Hooghly) River.

A centre for boat traffic on the river, it is an agricultural distribution centre and has chemical factories and general engineering works. A Buddhist temple survives, now dedicated to the Hindu goddess Kali. A number of terra-cotta figurines were found at the site, most of which are kept in a small museum. Tamluk became a municipality in 1864. Pop. (2001) 45,830.

VARANASI

The historic city of Varanasi (also called Benares, Banaras, or Kashi) is in southeastern Uttar Pradesh state, northern India. Situated on the left bank of the Ganges (Ganga) River, it is one of the seven sacred cities of the Hindus. Pop. (2001) city, 1,091,918; urban agglom., 1,203,961.

HISTORY

Varanasi is one of the oldest continuously inhabited cities in the world. Its early history is that of the first Aryan settlement in the middle Ganges valley. By the 2nd millennium BCE, Varanasi was a seat of Aryan religion and philosophy and was also a commercial and industrial centre famous for its muslin and silk fabrics, perfumes, ivory works, and sculpture. Varanasi was the capital of the kingdom of Kashi during the time of the Buddha (6th century BCE), who gave his first sermon nearby at Sarnath. The city remained a centre of religious, educational, and artistic activities as attested by the celebrated Chinese Buddhist pilgrim Xuanzang, who visited it in about 635 CE and said that the city extended for about 3 miles (5 km) along the western bank of the Ganges.

Varanasi subsequently declined during three centuries of Muslim occupation, beginning in 1194. Many of the city's Hindu temples were destroyed during the period of Muslim rule, and learned scholars fled to other parts of the country. The Mughal emperor Akbar in the 16th century brought some relief to the city's religious and cultural activities. There was another setback during the reign of the Mughal emperor Aurangzeb in the late 17th century, but later the Marathas sponsored a new revival. Varanasi became an independent kingdom in the 18th century, and under subsequent British rule it remained a commercial and religious centre.

In 1910 the British made Varanasi a new Indian state, with Ramnagar (on the opposite bank) as headquarters but with no jurisdiction over the city of Varanasi. In 1949, after Indian independence, the Varanasi state became part of the state of Uttar Pradesh.

THE CONTEMPORARY CITY

Varanasi has the finest river frontage in India, with miles of ghats, or steps, for religious bathing; an array of shrines, temples, and palaces rises tier on tier from the water's edge. The inner streets of the city are narrow, winding, and impassable for motor traffic; the newer outer suburbs are more spacious and are laid out more systematically. The sacred city is bounded by a road known as Panchakosi; every devout Hindu hopes to walk this road and visit the city once in a lifetime and, if possible, to die there in old age. More than a million pilgrims each year.

Among the city's numerous temples, the most venerated are those of

Vishvanatha, dedicated to Shiva; that of Sankatmochana, dedicated to the monkey-god Hanuman; and that of the fierce goddess Durga. The Durga Temple is famous for the swarms of monkeys that inhabit the large trees near it. The Great Mosque of Aurangzeb is another prominent religious building. Two of the more important modern temples are those of Tulasi Manas and the Vishvanatha on the campus of the Banaras Hindu University. The city has hundreds of other temples. At Sarnath, a few miles north of Varanasi, there are ruins of ancient Buddhist monasteries and temples as well as temples built by the Maha Bodhi Society and by the Chinese, Burmese, and Tibetan Buddhists.

Varanasi has been a city of Hindu learning through the ages. There are innumerable schools and countless Brahman pandits (learned scholars), who are responsible for the continuation of traditional learning. There are three universities, including the large and important Banaras Hindu University (1915), and more than a dozen colleges and high schools.

The city is a centre of arts and crafts and of music and dance. Varanasi is famous for its production of silks and brocades with gold and silver threadwork. A renowned carpet-weaving centre is at Bhadoi. Wooden toys, bangles made of glass, ivory work, and brass ware are also produced in Varanasi.

The city is host to numerous religious festivals. Mahashivaratri, the great night of Shiva, is celebrated by a procession from the Mahamrityunjaya Temple to the Kashi Vishvanath Temple. The Ganga festival in November or December is dedicated to the goddess of the Ganges River, considered sacred by all Hindus. Thousands of lamps are placed on the ghats and set afloat on the river. The festival of Bharat Milap in October or November commemorates the reunion of Lord Rama with his younger brother Bharat after 14 years of exile. A five-day festival of *dhrupad* (classical Indian vocal style) in March attracts renowned artists from all over India to the city's Tulsi Ghat along the river.

An airport lies about 12 miles (20 km) from the city centre. Varanasi is also a major railway junction and is connected by highways to other major cities.

CHAPTER 7

THE MAJOR CITIES OF CENTRAL INDIA

Central India generally corresponds to the northern portion of peninsular India. Its major city, Mumbai (Bombay), in the west on the Arabian Sea coast, is India's largest urban agglomeration and one of the world's most populous cities.

MUMBAI

Mumbai (formerly Bombay) is the capital of Maharashtra state, southwestern India, and is the country's financial and commercial centre and principal port on the Arabian Sea. Located on an island just off Maharashtra's coast, Mumbai is one of the largest and most densely populated cities in the world. It was built on a site of ancient settlement, and it took its name from the local goddess Mumba—a form of Parvati, the consort of Shiva, one of the principal deities of Hinduism—whose temple once stood in what is now the southeastern section of the city.

Mumbai has long been the centre of India's cotton textile industry, but its manufacturing industries are now well diversified, and its commercial and financial institutions are strong and vigorous. It suffers, however, from some of the perennial problems of many large, expanding industrial cities: air and water pollution, widespread areas of substandard housing, and overcrowding. The last problem is exacerbated by the physical limits of the city's island location. Area

Gateway of India, located on the waterfront in southern Mumbai, India. Jupiterimages Corporation

about 239 square miles (619 square km). Pop. (2001) city, 11,978,450; urban agglom., 16,434,386.

LANDSCAPE

CITY SITE

The city of Mumbai occupies a peninsular site on Bombay Island, a landmass originally composed of seven islets lying off the Konkan coast of western India; since the 17th century the islets have been joined through drainage and reclamation projects, as well as through the construction of causeways and breakwaters to form Bombay Island. East of the island are the sheltered waters of Mumbai Harbour. Bombay Island consists of a low-lying plain, about one-fourth of which lies below sea level; the plain is flanked on the east and west by two parallel ridges of low hills. Colaba Point, the headland formed on the extreme south by the longer of these ridges, protects Mumbai Harbour from the open sea. The western ridge terminates at Malabar Hill, which, rising 180 feet (55 metres) above sea level, is one of the highest points in Mumbai. Between Colaba Point and Malabar Hill lies the shallow expanse of Back Bay. On a slightly raised strip of land between the head of Back Bay and the harbour is an area called the Fort, the site of the 17th-century British fortifications (little of which remains standing) within and around which the city grew; the area is now occupied chiefly by public and commercial offices. From Back Bay the land stretches northward to the central plain. The extreme northern segment of Mumbai is occupied by a large salt marsh.

The old city covered about 26 square miles (67 square km), stretching from Colaba Point on the southern tip of Bombay Island to the areas known as Mahim and Sion on its northern coast. In 1950 Mumbai expanded northward, embracing the large island of Salsette, which was joined to Bombay Island by a causeway. By 1957 a number of suburban municipal boroughs and some neighbouring villages on Salsette were incorporated into Greater Mumbai— the metropolitan region surrounding Bombay Island and the city itself. Since then Greater Mumbai has continued to expand. During the early 1970s, in an effort to relieve congestion, Salsette Island was linked to the mainland by a bridge across Thana Creek, the headwaters of Mumbai Harbour.

The natural beauty of Mumbai is unsurpassed by that of most other cities in the region. The entrance into Mumbai Harbour from the sea discloses a magnificent panorama framed by the Western Ghats (mountains) on the mainland. The wide harbour, studded with islands and dotted with the white sails of innumerable small craft, affords secure shelter to ships, particularly when storms lash the coast. The largest of the harbour's islands is Elephanta, which is famous for its 8th- and 9th-century cave temples.

Typical trees in the city include coconut palms, mango trees, and tamarinds, as well as banyan trees. Salsette Island was once the haunt of wild animals such as tigers, leopards, jackals, and deer, but those are no longer found there. Animal life now consists of cows, oxen, sheep, goats, and other domestic species. Birdlife includes vultures, pigeons, cranes, and ducks.

CLIMATE

The climate of Mumbai is warm and humid. There are four seasons. Cool weather prevails from December to February and hot weather from March to May. The rainy season, brought by monsoon winds from the southwest, lasts from June to September and is followed by the postmonsoon season, lasting through October and November, when the weather is again hot. Mean monthly temperatures vary from 91 °F (33 °C) in May to 67 °F (19 °C) in January. Annual rainfall is about 70 inches (1,800 mm), with an average of 24 inches (600 mm) occurring in July alone.

CITY LAYOUT

The older part of Mumbai is much built-up and devoid of vegetation, but the more affluent areas, such as Malabar Hill, contain some greenery; there are also a number of open playgrounds and parks. In the course of urbanization, some residential sections of Mumbai have fallen into a state of serious disrepair, while in other areas clusters of makeshift houses (often illegal "squatter" settlements) have arisen to accommodate the city's expanding population. Moreover, an alarming amount of air and water pollution has been generated by Mumbai's many factories, by the growing volume of vehicular traffic, and by the nearby oil refineries.

The financial district is located in the southern part of the city, in the Fort area. Farther south (around Colaba) and to the west along the Back Bay coast and on Malabar Hill are residential neighbourhoods. To the north of the Fort is the principal business district, which gradually merges into a commercial-residential area. Most of the older factories are located in this part of the city. Still farther north are more residential areas, and beyond them are recently developed industrial zones as well as some squatter districts and other areas of overcrowded and poorly maintained housing.

Housing is largely privately owned, though there is some public housing built by the government through publicly funded corporations or by private cooperatives with public funds. Mumbai is very crowded, and housing is scarce for anyone who is not wealthy. (For this reason, commercial and industrial enterprises have found it increasingly difficult to attract mid-level professional, technical, or managerial staff.) In an attempt to stem the ongoing immigration of unskilled labour that has increased the city's indigent and homeless population, city planners have encouraged enterprises to locate across Mumbai Harbour and have banned the development and expansion of industrial units inside the city; their efforts, however, have been largely unsuccessful.

Mumbai's architecture is a mixture of florid Gothic Revival styles—characteristic of the United States and Britain in the 18th and 19th centuries—and contemporary designs. The older administrative and commercial buildings are intermingled with skyscrapers and multi-storied concrete-block buildings.

PEOPLE

Mumbai's growth since the 1940s has been steady if not phenomenal. At the turn of the 20th century its population was some 850,000; by 1950 it had more than doubled; and over the next 50 years it increased nearly 10-fold to exceed 16 million. The city's birth rate is much lower than that of the country as a whole because of family-planning programs. The high overall growth rate is largely attributable to the influx of people in search of employment. Because of the

Haji Ali Dargah, a 15th-century tomb and mosque, Mumbai, India. Jupiterimages Corporation

limited physical expanse of the city, the growth in Mumbai's population has been accompanied by an astounding increase in population density. By the start of the 21st century the city had reached an average of some 68,500 persons per square mile (26,500 per square km). Settlement is especially dense in much of the city's older section; the wealthy areas near Back Bay are less heavily populated.

The city is truly cosmopolitan, and representatives of almost every religion and region of the world can be found there. Almost half the population is Hindu. Significant religious minorities include Muslims, Christians, Buddhists, Jains, Sikhs, Zoroastrians, and Jews. Almost every Indian language and many foreign languages are spoken in Mumbai. Marathi, the state language, is the dominant Indian language, followed by Gujarati, Hindi, and Bengali (Bangla). Other languages include Pashto, Arabic, Chinese, English, and Urdu.

ECONOMY

Mumbai is the economic hub and commercial and financial centre of India. Its economic composition in some respects mirrors India's unique mosaic of prosperity and technological achievement vis-à-vis impoverishment and underdevelopment. While Mumbai contains the Indian Atomic Energy Commission's establishment, with its nuclear reactors and plutonium separators, many areas of the city continue to rely on traditional biogenic sources of fuel and energy (such as cow dung).

MANUFACTURING

Although cotton textile manufacturing, through which Mumbai prospered in the 19th century, remains important, it has lost much ground to newer industries, especially since the late 20th century. Production of metals, chemicals, automobiles, and electronics along with a host of ancillary industries are now among the city's major enterprises. Other manufacturing activities, such as food processing, papermaking, printing, and publishing, also are significant sources of income and employment.

FINANCE AND OTHER SERVICES

The Reserve Bank of India, the country's central bank, is located in Mumbai. A number of other commercial banks, a government-owned life insurance corporation, and various long-term investment financial institutions also are based in the city. All these institutions have attracted major financial and business services to Mumbai.

The Bombay Stock Exchange is the country's leading stock and share market. Although a number of economic hubs sprang up around the country since independence and reduced the exchange's pre-independence stature, it remains the preeminent centre in volume of financial and other business transacted and serves as a barometer of the country's economy.

TRANSPORTATION

Mumbai is connected by a network of roads to the rest of India. It is the railhead for the Western and Central railways, and trains from the city carry goods and passengers to all parts of the country. Chhatrapati Shivaji International Airport is an important point of entry for many international flights, and nearby Santa Cruz Airport accommodates domestic traffic. Mumbai handles some three-fifths of India's international flights and nearly two-fifths of its domestic flights. The facilities provided by the city's harbour make Mumbai India's principal western port. Although other major ports have sprung up on the west coast—Kandla, in the state of Gujarat, to the north; Marmagao, in the state of Goa, to the south; and Kochi (Cochin), in the state of Kerala, farther south—Mumbai still handles a significant portion of India's maritime trade. Suburban electric train systems provide the main public transportation, conveying hundreds of thousands of commuters within the metropolitan region daily. There also is a municipally owned bus fleet.

ADMINISTRATION AND SOCIETY

As the capital of Maharashtra state, the city is an integral political division of the state government, the headquarters of which are called the Mantralaya. The state administers Mumbai's police force and has administrative control over certain city departments. The central Indian government controls communication and transportation infrastructure, including the postal service, the railways, the port, and the airport. Mumbai is the headquarters of India's western naval fleet and the base for the Indian flagship, INS *Mumbai*.

GOVERNMENT

The government of the city is vested in the fully autonomous Municipal Corporation of Greater Mumbai (MCGM). Its legislative body is elected on adult franchise every four years and functions through its various standing committees. The chief executive, who is appointed every three years by the state government, is the municipal commissioner. The mayor is annually elected by the MCGM; the mayor presides over corporation meetings and enjoys the highest honour in the city but has no real administrative authority.

MUNICIPAL SERVICES

The manifold functions of the city government include the provision or maintenance of medical services, education, water supply, fire services, garbage disposal, markets, gardens, and engineering projects such as drainage development and the improvement of roads and street lighting. The MCGM operates the transport system inside the city and the supply of electricity as public utilities. After obtaining electric energy from a grid system supplied by publicly and privately owned agencies, the MCGM ensures that it is distributed throughout the city. The water supply, also maintained by the municipality, comes largely from Tansa Lake, in the adjoining Thane district of Maharashtra, and secondarily from Vaitarna, Tulsi, and Vehar lakes in Mumbai.

HEALTH

Mumbai has more than 100 hospitals, including those run by federal, state, or city authorities and a number of specialized institutions treating tuberculosis, cancer, and heart disease. In addition, there are a number of prominent private hospitals. Also located in Mumbai is the Haffkine Institute, a leading bacteriologic research centre specializing in tropical diseases.

EDUCATION

Mumbai's literacy rate is much higher than that of the country as a whole. Primary education is free and compulsory; it is the responsibility of the MCGM. Secondary education is provided by public and private schools supervised by the state government. There also are public and private polytechnic institutes and institutions offering students a variety of degree and diploma courses in mechanical, electrical, and chemical engineering. The Indian Institute of Technology, operated by the central government, is located

in the city. The University of Mumbai, established in 1857, has more than 100 constituent colleges and more than two dozen teaching departments. Several colleges in the state of Goa are affiliated with the university.

CULTURAL LIFE

Mumbai's cultural life reflects its ethnically diverse population. The city has a number of museums, libraries, literary organizations, art galleries, theatres, and other cultural institutions. The Chhatrapati Shivaji Maharaj Vastu Sangrahalaya (formerly the Prince of Wales Museum of Western India), housed in a building that is a British architectural mixture of Hindu and Muslim styles, contains three main sections: art, archaeology, and natural history. Nearby is the Jehangir Art Gallery, Mumbai's first permanent art gallery and a centre for cultural and educational activities. Western and Indian music concerts, festivals, and dance productions are held throughout the year in the city's many cultural and entertainment facilities. Mumbai also is the centre of the enormous Indian film industry, known as Bollywood.

Krishnagiri Forest, a national park in the north of metropolitan Mumbai, is a pleasant vacation resort located near the Kanheri Caves, site of an ancient Buddhist university; the more than 100 caves contain gigantic Buddhist sculptures dating from the 2nd to the 9th century BCE. There are several public gardens, including the Jijamata Udyan, which houses Mumbai's zoo in the city proper; the Baptista Garden, located on a water reservoir, also in the centre of the city; and the Pherozshah Mehta Gardens and the Kamala Nehru Park, both on Malabar Hill.

Sports enjoy a broad following in Mumbai. Cricket matches, which are popular throughout India, are played at the Cricket Club of India. Athletic and cycling track events attract many enthusiasts. Juhu Beach is a popular area for bathing and swimming.

Mumbai is an important centre for the Indian printing industry and has a vigorous press. Daily newspapers are printed in English, Marathi, Hindi, Gujarati, Urdu, and other languages. Several monthlies, biweeklies, and weeklies also are published in the city. The regional station of All-India Radio is centred in Mumbai. Television services for the city began in 1972.

HISTORY

The Koli, an aboriginal tribe of fishermen, were the earliest known inhabitants of present-day Mumbai, though Paleolithic stone implements found at Kandivli, in Greater Mumbai, indicate that the area has been inhabited by humans for hundreds of thousands of years. The city was a centre of maritime trade with Persia and Egypt in 1000 BCE. It was part of Ashoka's empire in the 3rd century BCE, and in the 2nd century CE it was known as Heptanesia to Ptolemy, the ancient Egyptian astronomer and geographer of Greek descent. The city was ruled in the 6th to 8th centuries by the Chalukyas, who left their mark on Elephanta Island (Gharapuri). The Walkeswar Temple at Malabar Point was probably built during the rule of Shilahara chiefs from the Konkan coast (9th–13th century). Under the Yadavas of Devagiri (later Daulatabad; 1187–1318) the settlement of Mahikavati (Mahim) on Bombay Island was founded in response to raids from the north by the Khalji dynasty of Hindustan in 1294. Descendants of these settlers are found in contemporary Mumbai, and most of the place-names on the island date from this era. In 1348 the island was conquered by invading Muslim forces and became part of the kingdom of Gujarat.

A Portuguese attempt to conquer Mahim failed in 1507, but in 1534 Sultan Bahādur Shah, the ruler of Gujarat, ceded the island to the Portuguese. In 1661 it came under British control as part of the marriage settlement between King Charles II and Catherine of Braganza, sister of the king of Portugal. The crown ceded it to the East India Company in 1668.

In the beginning, compared with Calcutta (Kolkata) and Madras (Chennai), Bombay—as it was called by the British—was not a great asset to the company but merely helped it keep a toehold on the west coast. On the mainland the Mughals in the north, the Marathas (under the venerated leader Chhatrapati Shivaji) in the area surrounding and stretching eastward from Bombay, and the territorial princes in Gujarat to the northwest were more powerful. Even British naval power was no match for the Mughals, Marathas, Portuguese, and Dutch, all of whom had interests in the region. By the turn of the 19th century, however, external events helped stimulate the growth of the city. The decay of Mughal power in Delhi, the Mughal-Maratha rivalries, and the instability in Gujarat drove artisans and merchants to the islands for refuge, and Bombay began to grow. With the destruction of Maratha power, trade and communications to the mainland were established and those to Europe were extended, and Bombay began to prosper.

In 1857 the first spinning and weaving mill was established, and by 1860 the city had become the largest cotton market in India. The American Civil War (1861–65) and the resulting cutoff of cotton supplies to Britain caused a great trade boom in Bombay. But, with the end of the Civil War, cotton prices crashed and the bubble burst. By that time, though, the hinterland had been opened, and Bombay had become a strong centre of import trade. The opening in 1869 of the Suez Canal, which greatly facilitated trade with Britain and continental Europe, also contributed to Bombay's prosperity.

Yet as the population increased, unkempt, overcrowded, and unsanitary conditions became more widespread. Plague, for example, broke out in 1896. In response to these problems, the City Improvement Trust was established to open new localities for settlement and to erect dwellings for the artisan classes. An ambitious scheme for the construction of a seawall in Back Bay to reclaim an area of 1,300 acres (525 hectares) of land was proposed in 1918, but it was not finished until the completion of Netaji Subhas Chandra Bose Road (Marine Drive) from Nariman Point to Malabar Point—the first two-way highway of its kind in India—after World War II (1939–45). In the postwar years the development of residential quarters in suburban areas was begun, and the administration of Bombay city through a municipal corporation was extended to the suburbs of Greater Bombay.

Under the British, the city had served as the capital of Bombay Presidency (province), and during the late 19th and early 20th centuries it was a centre of both Indian national and South Asian regional political activity. In 1885 the first session of the Indian National Congress (a focus of both pro-Indian and anti-British sentiment until independence) was held in the city, where subsequently, at its 1942 session, the Congress passed the "Quit India" resolution, which demanded complete independence for India—finally achieved in 1947. From 1956 until 1960 Bombay was the scene of intense Maratha protests against the two-language (Marathi-Gujarati) makeup of Bombay state (of which Bombay remained the capital), a legacy of British imperialism. These protests led to the state's partition into the modern states of Gujarat and Maharashtra in 1960. The city of Bombay was made the capital of Maharashtra that year, and in the mid-1990s it changed its name to Mumbai, the Marathi name for the city. In the early 21st century

Mumbai experienced a number of terrorist attacks. Among the most notable of these were the bombing of a train in July 2006 and the simultaneous siege of several sites in the city in late November 2008; nearly 200 lives were lost in each of the two incidents.

OTHER IMPORTANT CENTRAL INDIAN CITIES

In addition to Mumbai, two other major central Indian cities—Ahmadabad and Surat—are located in the western lowland plain adjacent to the Arabian Sea. The remainder of the region's most important urban centres lie on the great upland region of the northern Deccan.

AHMADABAD

The city of Ahmadabad (also spelled Ahmedabad) lies in eastern Gujarat state, west-central India, along the Sabarmati River about 275 miles (440 km) north of Mumbai (Bombay). It is situated in a strategic location at the junction of the main roads leading to Mumbai and central India, the Kathiawar Peninsula, and the Rajasthan border. The city is also a major junction on the Western Railway, with lines running to Mumbai, Delhi, and the Kathiawar Peninsula. Pop. (2001) city, 3,520,085; urban agglom., 4,518,240.

HISTORY

The city was founded in 1411 by the Muslim ruler of Gujarat, Sultan Ahmad Shah, next to the older Hindu town of Asawal. Ahmadabad grew larger and wealthier for a century, but dynastic decay and anarchy eventually brought about a decline, and the city was captured in 1572 by the Mughal emperor Akbar. Its renewed eminence under the Mughals ceased with the death of Aurangzeb in 1707. Ahmadabad's further decline was arrested by the British annexation of Gujarat in 1818. The city's first cotton mills were opened in 1859–61, and Ahmadabad grew to become one of the most populous cities and largest inland industrial centres in India. The city became the temporary capital of Gujarat state in 1960, but the state administration was moved to Gandhinagar in 1970. In 2001 the city was rocked by a massive earthquake that destroyed hundreds of homes and several historic buildings; up to 20,000 people were killed.

THE CONTEMPORARY CITY

The old city lies east of the Sabarmati River, while newer sections lie along the west bank. An interesting local feature is the division of the old city centre into *pols*, or self-contained blocks of houses that shelter several thousand people each. Some *pols* are virtually small townships, crossed by a street with gates at either end.

Ahmadabad's dynastic history has made it a meeting place of the Hindu, Muslim, and Jaina architectural traditions. Ahmad Shah and his successors ordered the dismantling and adaptation

Window on the Sidi Sayyid Mosque, Ahmadabad, Gujarat state, India. Frederick M. Asher

of Hindu temples in order to build mosques. This gave many of Ahmadabad's mosques and tombs a Hindu flavour in their form and decoration. The dense "forest" of 260 richly carved columns within the Jāmi' Masjid (Great Mosque), which was completed in 1423, recalls the hall of a Hindu temple. At the mosque's entrance is the domed tomb of Aḥmad Shah (1441), and on the road leading to it is the Tin Darwaza (c. 1425), a triumphal triple-arch gateway through which the sultan was borne to worship. Just to the west of the sultan's tomb is Bhadra Fort (1411), also built by Aḥmad Shah. The fort

is best known for the Bhadrakali Temple inside, dedicated to the Hindu goddess Bhadra. Among the city's many other Muslim buildings are the Rani (Queen) Sipri mosque and tomb (c. 1505); the Sidi Sayyid Mosque (1510–15), with minutely pierced arch-screens; and the exuberantly rich Rani Rupmati Mosque (1515). Just northeast of the city centre are the distinctive Dada Hari (1501) and Mata Bhavani *wavs* (step wells), which are used for religious purposes.

There are also several Jain temples in the city. The Hathi Singh Temple (1848) is perhaps the most visited. It is made of white marble and has 24 Jain Tirthankaras sculpted on the building. Jain bird sanctuaries are also common in Ahmadabad.

Ahmadabad's ancient architectural remains contrast sharply with the modern mills and factories in the newer parts of the city. The cotton-milling industry is one of the largest in India. Other industries produce pharmaceuticals, computer software, chemicals, vegetable oil, flour, soap, matches, glass, tobacco, hosiery, and carpets. The city's handicrafts include brocades, lace, copper and brass ware, jewelry, and wood carving. Services also have become significant.

Ahmadabad is the home of Gujarat University (1949), the Lalbhai Dalpatbhai Institute for Indological Research, and the Mill Owners' Association Headquarters (1951–54). The Calico Museum houses a collection of spun and handwoven cloth, brocades, and other textiles, as well as a display of rare tapestries, costumes, and looms; the Shreyas Folk Museum exhibits arts and crafts of Gujarat; and the Utensils Museum displays nutcrackers, knives, cooking vessels, and various other culinary items.

Major Hindu festivals celebrated in Ahmadabad are Makar Sankranti (January 14), a kite festival; Navratri (October or November), a nine-day display of music and folk dances (notably the *garaba*) dedicated to the goddess Durga; and Rath Yatra (June or July), when massive chariots carrying the statues of Krishna, Balram, and Subhadra are led from the Jagannath temple through the city.

Southeast of the city is Lake Kankaria, which offers promenades, boating, a hill garden, and a museum designed by the architect Le Corbusier. Sabarmati, a suburb west of the Sabarmati River, became well known as the seat of Mohandas K. Gandhi's ashram, or religious retreat. Chief crops grown in the surrounding area are cotton, millet, wheat, and pulses.

BHOPAL

Bhopal, the capital of Madhya Pradesh state, central India, is situated in the fertile plain of the Malwa Plateau. Lying just north of the Vindhya Range, along the slopes of a sandstone ridge, it is a major rail junction and has an airport.

HISTORY

Bhopal was formerly a part of the Bhopal princely state, which was founded in 1723 by Dōst Moḥammad Khan, an Afghan adventurer, and was the second-largest Muslim principality of the British Empire. In its struggles with the Marathas, Bhopal was friendly to the British and concluded a treaty with them at the outbreak of the Pindari War in 1817. The Bhopal Agency, created in 1818, was a subdivision of the British Central India Agency and comprised the former princely states of Bhopal, Rajgarh, Narsinghgarh, and several others. The headquarters was at Sehore.

Bhopal was constituted a municipality in 1903. At India's independence in 1947, Bhopal remained a separate province until 1949, when it acceded to India.

In 1952 the nawab's absolute rule was abolished, and a chief commissioner's state was established. It merged with Madhya Pradesh in 1956, and Bhopal replaced Nagpur as the state capital.

In December 1984 Bhopal was the site of the worst industrial accident in history, when about 45 tons of the dangerous gas methyl isocyanate escaped from an insecticide plant that was owned by the Indian subsidiary of the American firm Union Carbide Corporation. The gas drifted over the densely populated neighbourhoods around the plant, killing thousands of people immediately and creating a panic as tens of thousands of others attempted to flee the city. The final death toll was estimated to be between 15,000 and 20,000, and some half million survivors suffered respiratory problems, eye irritation or blindness, and other maladies resulting from exposure to the toxic gas. Soil and water contamination due to the accident was blamed for chronic health problems of the area's inhabitants. Investigations later established that substandard operating and safety procedures at the understaffed plant had led to the catastrophe.

THE CONTEMPORARY CITY

Bhopal is known as the "city of lakes"; its name is a derivation of Bhoj Tal ("Bhoj's Lake"), a lake constructed by Bhoj, a Hindu raja, in the 11th century. Today, that lake is the Upper Bhopal Lake (Bada Talab), which is connected to the Lower Bhopal Lake (Chhota Talab) by an aqueduct. The lakes supply drinking water and are used for recreation. Around the lakes are several palaces and a fort dating from about 1728. Bhopal has several mosques, including the 19th-century Taj al-Masjid, the largest mosque in India. A three-day religious pilgrimage is held at the mosque annually, which attracts Muslim pilgrims from all parts of India. Other significant attractions in and around Bhopal include Fatehgarh Fort; Lakshminarayan Temple; Bharat Bhawan, a multipurpose arts centre; the Museum of Man, an open-air exhibit of replicas of different Indian tribal dwellings; and Van Vihar National Park, a zoological park.

Bhopal has several hospitals and a musical academy and is the seat of Bhopal University (founded 1970), which has several affiliated colleges in the city. Industries in the city include cotton and flour milling, cloth weaving and painting, and the manufacture of transformers, switch gears, traction motors, and other heavy electrical equipment, as well as matches, sealing wax, and sporting goods. Pop. (2001) 1,437,354.

INDORE

Indore (also spelled Indur) lies in western Madhya Pradesh state, central India. The city is a major trunk road and rail junction and is located on the Saraswati and Khan rivers, which are tributaries of the Shipra River.

Indore was founded in 1715 as a trade market on the Narmada River valley route by local landowners, who erected

Indreshwar Temple (1741), from which the name Indore is derived. It became the capital of the former Indore princely state of the Maratha Holkars, and it was the headquarters of the British Central India Agency and the summer capital of Madhya Bharat (1948–56). Krishnapura *chhatris* (cenotaphs) situated on the bank of the Khan River are dedicated to the Holkar rulers of the city.

The largest city in the state, Indore is the chief collecting and distributing centre for western Madhya Pradesh as well as a commercial and industrial centre. Major industries include the manufacture of textiles, tile, cement, chemicals, tents, furniture, and sporting goods; grain milling; and metalworking. There are auto and cycle workshops and engineering works. Such traditional industries as pottery making and hand-loom weaving continue.

Indore is the seat of Devi Ahilya University (founded in 1964 as the University of Indore), with numerous constituent and affiliated colleges in the city, including Holkar Science College and Indore Christian College. Indore also has a number of Ayurvedic and allopathic hospitals and training institutes, the Atomic Centre for Advanced Technology, and the Indian Institute of Management.

Places of cultural interest in the city include Indreshwar and Harsiddhi temples; Bada Ganapati Temple, with a 26-foot (8-metre) replica of Lord Ganesh, the Hindu elephant god; the Kanch Mandir, a Jain temple built of glass inlays and mirrors; the Lal Bagh Palace, constructed during the Holkar dynasty; and Rajwada, a seven-story Holkar palace. Mahatma Gandhi Hall (built in 1904 and originally named King Edward Hall) has an impressive clock tower. The Indore, or Central, Museum houses a fine collection of Paramar sculptures. Well-known Indian painters Narayan Shridhar Bendre and Muqbool Fida Husain attended the Vishnu Deolalikar Art School in Indore, one of the oldest art schools in the country. Indore is also a centre of Hindustani classical music.

Nehru Park, the oldest park in the city, has a swimming pool, library, and recreation centre. Just outside Indore city is Gomatgiri, a major pilgrimage site with a cluster of 24 marble temples and a 21-foot (6-metre) statue of Lord Gomateshwar, a replica of the Bahubali statue of Shravanbelagola. Also nearby is Patalpani, a hilly area with a 250-foot (76-metre) waterfall. Pop. (2001) 1,474,968.

JABALPUR

Jabalpur (also spelled Jubbulpore), in central Madhya Pradesh state, central India, lies just north of the Narmada River in a rocky basin surrounded by low hills that are dotted with lakes and temples. On one of the hills stands the Madan Mahal, an old Gond castle built about 1100 CE by King Madan Singh. Garha, just west, was the chief city of the four independent Gond kingdoms that arose in the 14th century. Jabalpur was selected as the Maratha headquarters in 1781, and it later became the British commission headquarters of Saugor (now Sagar) and

Narmada territories. It was constituted a municipality in 1864.

One of the largest cities in the state, Jabalpur is located at a major road and rail junction. The city is a military headquarters, containing the central gun-carriage factory, an ordnance factory, and an ammunition depot. Its major industries include food processing, sawmilling, and varied manufactures. The city has the state high court and several public and private institutions of higher education, notably Jawaharlal Nehru Agricultural University (1964). Jabalpur has long been a centre of literary, cultural, social, and political activities, and it has produced many writers, publishers and printers in English, Hindi, and Urdu.

The surrounding region includes the Haveli, an extremely fertile wheat-growing area at the western end of the Narmada River valley. Rice, grain sorghum, chickpeas, and oilseeds are other important crops. Iron ore, limestone, bauxite, clay, fireclay, steatite, feldspar, manganese, and ochre deposits are extensively worked. Buddhist, Hindu, and Jaina ruins are found throughout the region. The Narmada River runs 11 miles (18 km) south-southwest of town. After forming the Dhuandhar waterfall, the river passes through the Marble Rocks, a major tourist destination. Pop. (2001) city, 932,484; urban agglom., 1,098,000.

NAGPUR

The city of Nagpur, in northeastern Maharashtra state, western India, lies along the Nag River and is situated almost at the geographic centre of India. The present city was founded in the early 18th century by Bakht Buland, a Gond raja. It became the capital of the Bhonsles of the Maratha confederacy but in 1817 came under British influence. In 1853 the city lapsed into British control and in 1861 became the capital of the Central Provinces. The advent of the Great Indian Peninsula Railway in 1867 spurred its development as a trade centre. After Indian independence, Nagpur was briefly the capital of Madhya Pradesh state—until 1956, when what is now Maharashtra state was created.

The growing of cotton in the region at about the time of the construction of the railway led to the establishment of a large textile mill and signaled the development of the city as an important industrial centre. Since that time Nagpur's industrial complex has diversified considerably. In the 1970s the city expanded to absorb the nearby town of Kamptee, with its factories that produce ferromanganese products, transport equipment, and other metal goods. Situated at the junction of road, rail, and air routes from Mumbai (Bombay) to Kolkata (Calcutta) and from Chennai (Madras) to Delhi, Nagpur has developed a flourishing trade sector.

Nagpur is dominated by the British fort built on the twin hills of Sitabuldi, in the centre of the city. An educational and cultural centre, Nagpur has a large museum specializing in local exhibits and is the site of the University of Nagpur (1923), which has numerous affiliated colleges in the city. The surrounding region is an undulating plateau rising northward to the Satpura Range. In the northeast are the Ramtek Hills, site of a temple at the town of Ramtek that draws many pilgrims to its sacred annual festivals. A memorial monument for the poet Kalidasa and Sanskrit University are also in the Ramtek Hills. Interspersing the hills are two major rivers—the Wardha (west) and the Wainganga (east)—that are both tributaries of the Godavari. The region is important agriculturally. Grain sorghum and cotton are major crops.

The region is especially known for its oranges, which are shipped all over India. Extensive coal and manganese deposits support growing industry. Pop. (2001) 2,052,066.

NASHIK

Nashik (also spelled Nasik), in northwestern Maharashtra state, western India, lies along the Godavari River and is situated along major road and rail routes at a point about 110 miles (180 km) northeast of Mumbai (Bombay).

Ghats along the Godavari River in Nashik, Maharashtra, India. © Ann & Bury Peerless Slide Resources & Picture Library

It is an important religious centre and attracts thousands of pilgrims annually because of the sanctity of the Godavari River and because of the legend that Rama, the hero of the *Ramayana* epic, lived there for a time with his wife Sita and his brother Lakshmana.

The main part of the city lies on the right (south) bank of the river; Panchavati, a quarter on the left bank, has several temples. The city's riverbanks are lined with ghats (stepped bathing places). Nashik is the site of the Pandu (Buddhist) and Chamar (Jaina) cave temples dating to the 1st century CE. Of its many Hindu temples, Kala Ram and Gora Ram are among the holiest. Tryambakeshvar, a village and the site of a Shaivite Jyotirlinga temple 14 miles (22 km) from Nashik, is the most important of the pilgrim sites.

By the second half of the 20th century, the city had become industrialized; silk and cotton weaving and sugar and oil processing are important. Ozar is a suburban township. Nashik has several colleges affiliated with the University of Pune. The area in which Nashik is situated is drained by the Girna and Godavari rivers, which flow through open, fertile valleys. The chief crops grown in the region are wheat, millet, and peanuts (groundnuts). Sugar is an important irrigated cash crop. The region is also known for its viticulture. Regional industries consist primarily of sugar and oil processing and cotton spinning and weaving. A military-aircraft factory is nearby. Pop. (2001) city, 1,077,236.

PUNE

Pune (also called Poona) is a major city of west-central Maharashtra state, western India, located at the junction of the Mula and Mutha rivers. Called "Queen of the Deccan," it is the cultural capital of the Maratha peoples. The city first gained importance as the capital of the Bhonsle Marathas in the 17th century. It was temporarily captured by the Mughals but again served as the official Maratha capital from 1714 until its fall to the British in 1817. It was the seasonal capital of the Bombay Presidency and is now a popular tourist resort, offering cool weather, historic and religious monuments, museums, parks, hotels, and cultural attractions.

Pune has long been a major educational and cultural centre; former prime minister Jawaharlal Nehru referred to it as the "Oxford and Cambridge of India." The city houses some 30 constituent and affiliated colleges of the University of Pune (1948); the Bhandarkar Oriental Research Institute (1917) is renowned for research and instruction in the Sanskrit and Prakrit languages and has more than 20,000 ancient manuscripts. Pune is also the headquarters of the southern command of the Indian army, with the Khadakwasla Academy located nearby.

A sprawling complex of industrial suburbs has developed around the city. Large factories producing a wide variety of products are distributed along the roads radiating from Pune to Mumbai

(Bombay), Ahmadnagar, Solapur, and Satara. The old city is largely residential and commercial and is served by large-scale commuter transport. In 1961 the Panshet Dam collapsed, washing away a substantial part of the old town.

The region surrounding Pune includes the Sahyadri Hills, the Balaghat Range (north), and the Mahadeo Hills (south), which enclose the northern Bhima River valley. Chief crops are grain sorghum, pearl millet, sugarcane, and rice. Most of the important religious, historical, and tourist attractions of the region are located in the Sahyadri Hills. Some of the famous hill forts of the Marathas, such as Sinhgad, are now resorts. The important religious centres include Bhimashankar, site of a Jyotirlinga shrine; Dehu, birthplace of the Marathi poet-saint Tukaram; Alandi, home of Jnaneshvara (Jnanadeva), author of a well-known commentary on the *Bhagavadgita*, a Hindu scripture; and Karli, site of famous Buddhist caves. Nearby are Meherazad and Meherabad, sites associated with Meher Baba. Pop. (2001) city, 2,538,473; urban agglom., 3,760,636.

SURAT

The city of Surat, in southeastern Gujarat state, west-central India, lies near the mouth of the Tapti River at the Gulf of Khambhat (Cambay). It is believed to have been founded by a Brahman named Gopi, who built the Gopi Tank (water reservoir) in 1516 and named the area Surajpur or Suryapur. Surat became the name of the city in 1520. It was plundered by Muslims in the 12th and 15th centuries. In 1514 the Portuguese traveler Duarte Barbosa described Surat as a leading port. It was burned by the Portuguese (1512 and 1530) and conquered by the Mughals (1573) and was twice sacked by the Maratha king Shivaji (17th century). Surat thereafter became the emporium of India, exporting cloth and gold. Its major industries were textile manufacture and shipbuilding. The British established their first Indian factory (trading post) at Surat (1612). The city gradually declined throughout the 18th century. The British and Dutch both claimed control, but in 1800 its administration passed to the British. By the mid-19th century Surat was a stagnant city of 80,000 inhabitants. It prospered again with the opening of India's railways. The ancient art of manufacturing fine muslin was revived, and Surat's cottons, silks, brocades, and objects of gold and silver became famous. The city houses other industries and has several educational institutions. It is served by highways and the Western Railway. The surrounding area is intensively cultivated; chief crops include cotton, millet, pulses, and rice. Pop. (2001) city, 2,433,835; urban agglom., 2,811,614.

VADODARA

Vadodara (also called Baroda) is a city of east-central Gujarat state, west-central

India. It is located on the Vishvamitra River, southeast of Ahmadabad. The earliest record of the city is in a grant or charter of 812 CE that mentions it as Vadapadraka, a hamlet attached to the town of Ankottaka. In the 10th century Vadapadraka displaced Ankottaka as the urban centre. It seems also to have been known as Chandanavati, named for Raja Chandan of the Dor Rajputs, who wrested it from the Jainas. The city underwent periodic renamings: Varavati, Vatpatraka, Baroda, and, in 1971, Vadodara.

The history of Vadodara falls into a Hindu period (until 1297); a period under the Muslim Delhi sultanate (1297–c. 1401); an independent Gujarat sultanate, during which the nucleus of the present city was built (c. 1401–c. 1573); a Mughal Empire period (c. 1573–1734); and a Maratha period, during which it became the capital of the powerful Gaekwar dynasty (1734–1947). In 1802 the British established a residency in the city to conduct relations between the East India Company and the Gaekwars; later the company was also responsible for British relations with all the states of Gujarat and the Kathiawar Peninsula.

The long history of Vadodara is reflected in its many palaces, gates, parks, and avenues. It houses the Maharaja Sayajirao University of Baroda (1949) and other educational and cultural institutions, including several museums. The Baroda Museum and Picture Gallery, founded by the Maharaja Gaekwar of Baroda in 1894, formally opened in 1921. The museum displays European paintings, including portraits by British painters George Romney and Sir Joshua Reynolds and by Dutch painter Sir Peter Lely. The museum also contains Hindu illustrations, sculpture, folk art, and ethnography.

Among the city's varied products are cotton textiles and homespun cloth, chemicals, matches, machinery, and furniture. Vadodara is a rail and highway junction and has an airfield. Vadodara's surrounding region extends from the Narmada River (south) to the Mahi River (north). It corresponds roughly to the capital division of the former princely state of Baroda (the Gaekwar dominions). Cash crops are cotton, tobacco, and castor beans. Wheat, pulses, corn (maize), rice, and garden crops are grown for local use and export. Pop. (2001) city, 1,306,227; urban agglom., 1,491,045.

CHAPTER 8

THE MAJOR CITIES OF SOUTHERN INDIA

The southern portion of peninsular India is demarcated roughly along a line running in an east-west direction south of the Mumbai-Pune urban complex. No one single city dominates southern India, contrary to the case in the three regions to the north, but Chennai, on the Bay of Bengal, is its largest metropolis.

CHENNAI

Chennai (formerly Madras), the capital of Tamil Nadu state, southern India, is on the Coromandel Coast of the Bay of Bengal. Known as the "Gateway to South India," the city is a major administrative and cultural centre. Pop. (2001) city, 4,343,645; urban agglom., 6,560,242.

HISTORY

Armenian and Portuguese traders were living in the San Thome area of what is now present-day Chennai before the arrival of the British in 1639. Madras was the shortened name of the fishing village Madraspatnam, where the British East India Company built a fort and factory (trading post) in 1639–40. At that time, the weaving of cotton fabrics was a local industry, and the English invited the weavers and native merchants to settle near the fort. By 1652 the factory of Fort St. George was recognized as a presidency (an

administrative unit governed by a president), and between 1668 and 1749 the company expanded its control. About 1801, by which time the last of the local rulers had been shorn of his powers, the English had become masters of southern India, and Madras had become their administrative and commercial capital. The government of Tamil Nadu officially changed the name of the city to Chennai in 1996.

THE CONTEMPORARY CITY

Madras developed without a plan from its 17th-century core, formed by Fort St. George and the Indian quarters. To the north and northwest are the industrial areas; the main residential areas are to the west and south, where a number of modern high-rise apartment buildings have been constructed, and the old villages are in the centre. The most distinctive buildings in the city are the seven large temples in the Dravidian style, situated in the city sections of George Town, Mylapore, and Triplicane. The Chepauk Palace (the former residence of the nawab [Mughal ruler] of Karnataka) and the University Senate House, both in the Deccan Muslim style, and the Victoria Technical Institute and the High Court buildings, both in the Indo-Saracenic style, are generally considered the most attractive buildings of the British period.

Chennai and its suburbs have more than 600 Hindu temples. The oldest is the Parthasarathi Temple built in the 8th century by Pallava kings. The Kapaleeswarar Temple (16th century) is dedicated to the Hindu god Shiva. Other places of worship within the city include Luz Church (1547–82), one of the oldest churches in Chennai; St. Mary's Church (1678–80), the first British church in India; the San Thome Basilica (1898), built over the tomb of the apostle St. Thomas; and Wallajah Mosque (1795), built by the nawab of Karnataka. The Armenian Church of the Holy Virgin Mary (1772), in the George Town section of Chennai, surrounds a courtyard cemetery with Armenian tombstones dating from the mid-17th century. The international headquarters of the Theosophical Society is situated in gardens between the Adyar River and the coast. Of particular interest there is a banyan tree dating from about 1600.

Since the late 1990s, software development and electronics manufacturing have made up the bulk of Chennai's economy. Numerous technology parks, where many foreign companies have offices, are found throughout the city. Other major industries include the manufacture of automobiles, rubber, fertilizer, leather, iron ore, and cotton textiles. Wheat, machinery, iron and steel, and raw cotton are imported. There is an oil refinery

Kapaleeswarar, a Hindu temple, in Mylapore, Chennai, Tamil Nadu, India. Jupiterimages Corporation

in Chennai. Services, especially finance and tourism, are also significant. Hotels, luxury resorts, restaurants, marinas, and parks line Marina Beach, the coastline abutting Chennai city.

Chennai has numerous educational institutions. Professional education can be obtained in the state medical and veterinary sciences colleges, the colleges of engineering and technology, the College of Carnatic Music, the College of Arts and Crafts, and the teacher-training colleges. The city is the site of the University of Madras (1857), which has several advanced centres of research. The Indian Institute of Technology, the Central Leather Research Institute, and the Regional Laboratories of the Council of Scientific and Industrial Research are other noteworthy scientific institutions. The M.S. Swaminathan Research Foundation focuses on agricultural development in Chennai and Tamil Nadu.

Since the 1980s Chennai has emerged as one of the leading medical centres of the country. This was a result of the proliferation of private specialty hospitals, especially those which provide treatment for cardiac and eye ailments. Among the leading medical facilities in the city are the Apollo Hospital, the Madras Medical Mission's Institute of Cardiovascular Diseases, the Sri Ramachandra University Hospital, the Heart Institute of Chennai, and the Shankara Nethralaya ("Temple of the Eye"), an eye hospital.

Cultural institutions in Chennai include the Madras Music Academy, devoted to the encouragement of Carnatic music—the music of Karnataka, the historical region between the southern Coromandel Coast of the Bay of Bengal and the Deccan plateau. The Kalakshetra is a centre of dance and music, and the Rasika Ranjini Sabha, in Mylapore, encourages the theatrical arts. The city has training centres for *kuchipudi* and *bharata natyam* (Indian classical dance forms). Kalakshetra and Sri Krishna Gana Sabha, a cultural institution, both host annual dance festivals. The suburban town of Kodambakkam, with its numerous film studios, is described as the Hollywood of southern India. Three theatres—the Children's Theatre, the Annamalai Manram, and the Museum Theatre—are popular. The Chennai Government Museum has exhibitions on the history and physical aspects of Tamil Nadu. There is a small collection of East India Company antiquities in the Fort Museum (within Fort St. George) and a collection of paintings in the National Art Gallery.

Squash, cricket, tennis, and hockey are popular sports in Chennai and its surrounding region. The Madras Cricket Club (1848), located behind the Chepauk Palace, is host to major national sports tournaments. The city has many other clubs and associations including motor sports, chess, and equestrian events. Rowing and yachting have a small but loyal following at the Madras Boat Club (1867) and the Royal Madras Yacht Club (1911). Guindy National Park is a wildlife sanctuary situated in the

Mamallapuram shore temple, Chennai, Tamil Nadu, India. Jupiterimages Corporation

heart of the city. Other places for recreation in and around Chennai are the Chennai Crocodile Bank, Pulicat Lake (a large saltwater lagoon), a bird sanctuary, and a zoological park.

Chennai is well connected by road, rail, air, and sea. It has an international airport and seaport. Within the city a network of bus services and auto-rickshaws are common modes of transport. The historic town of Mamallapuram with its shore temple, about 37 miles (60 km) south of Chennai, is a popular tourist destination.

OTHER IMPORTANT SOUTHERN INDIAN CITIES

Two other southern Indian cities—Bangalore and Hyderabad, both in the Deccan uplands—have populations comparable to that of Chennai; and, like Chennai, they have become centres of the country's high-technology industry. Another notable urbanized area is along the Malabar Coast of the Arabian Sea in Kerala state, from Kozhikode southeastward to Thiruvananthapuram.

BANGALORE

The city of Bangalore (official name Bengaluru; also spelled Bengalooru) is the capital (since 1830) of Karnataka state, southern India. It lies at an elevation of 3,113 feet (949 metres) above sea level atop an east-west ridge in the Karnataka Plateau in the southeastern part of the state, at a cultural meeting point of the Kannada-, Telugu-, and Tamil-speaking peoples.

The city consists of the closely built old town, together with a number of modern suburbs laid out in a gridiron pattern to the north and south, with many parks and wide streets. A sprawl of military cantonments lies to the east. The city's nucleus was a settlement around a mud fort, built in 1537 by a local chief, Kempe Gowda, and constructed of stone in 1761. Bangalore was the headquarters of the British administration from 1831 to 1881, when the raja was restored, but Britain retained an administrative and military presence until Indian independence in 1947. The city officially changed its name to Bengaluru in 2006.

Prominent buildings include the legislative building Vidhana Saudha (1956) and the High Court building, Attara Kacheri (1967), which are situated across from one another. Also of note are the maharaja of Mysore's palace, the Mysore Government Museum (1866), and Tippu Sultan's fort and palace. Notable local scenic spots are the Lal Bagh (a botanic garden laid out in the 18th century),

Cubbon Park (a garden with a lake, aquarium, and library), Hesaraghatta Lake, Chamaraja Lake Reservoir, and Nandi (Nandidrug) Hill Station, a summer resort 38 miles (61 km) north, which is the site of two temples to the god Shiva.

Bangalore has pleasant summers and mild winters. Summer temperatures average in the low to mid-90s F (about 34 °C), while winter temperatures rarely drop below 60 °F (16 °C). The city receives about 36 inches (914 mm) of annual rainfall, which has been inadequate as a water supply for its increasing population and industry. Most of the city's water comes from the Kaveri (Cauvery) River. The city government has undertaken projects to develop more reservoir lakes in the city and to reuse water.

Aircraft, railway-coach, and machine-tool installations in the city are run by the federal government, and the state owns plants manufacturing electrical and telephone equipment, porcelain, and soap. Privately owned entities produce pharmaceuticals, textiles (silk), radio parts, glassware, leather and footwear, agricultural implements, paper, and watches. Granite exports are sustained by the large number of quarries in and around the city. Sandalwood products and *agarbattis* (incense sticks) are also manufactured in Bangalore.

From the late 20th century the city became a centre of high-technology industry, and a number of large multinational technology corporations opened offices there. In addition, major domestic firms such as Infosys and Wipro established headquarters in the city. In 1998 an information technology park opened in Whitefield, about 10 miles (16 km) from Bangalore. As a self-contained city with hundreds of technology, software, and telecommunications companies, the park is known as the Silicon Valley of India.

Situated at the focus of southern India's road system, Bangalore lies on the Varanasi-Kanniyakumari National Highway, is connected by major roads with Mumbai and Chennai (Bombay and Madras), and is linked to Kerala state via Mysore, through the Nilgiri Hills and Palghat Gap. It is also a junction for the Southern Railway's broad-gauge line (from Chennai) with an extensive metre-gauge system to the north and west. Hindustan Airport, 5 miles (8 km) east, has flights to Mumbai, Chennai, Mangalore, and Colombo (Sri Lanka). The city has a fairly extensive bus network, and taxis and rickshaws are easily accessible.

Bangalore University (succeeding a branch of the University of Mysore, founded 1916) was opened in 1964, as was the University of Agricultural Sciences. The city also has several evening colleges and a public library and is the site of the Indian Institute of Science (1909), the Raman Research Institute (1943), the National Aeronautical Research Laboratory (1960), and a division of the National Power Research Institute (1960). Private universities proliferated in the early 21st century. Bangalore is also a centre for publishing (newspapers and periodicals) and is the headquarters of the regional radio broadcasting station.

The surrounding region is drained by the Arkavati and Kanva rivers, which are tributaries of the Kaveri River. Millet and oilseeds are the main crops, and cattle and sheep are grazed. Pop. (2001) city, 4,301,326; urban agglom., 5,701,456.

BIDAR

Bidar, in northeastern Karnataka state, southern India, is situated 2,300 feet (700 metres) above sea level and 68 miles (109 km) northwest of Hyderabad. The city contains some of the finest examples of Muslim architecture in the Deccan.

Bidar was important under the medieval Hindu dynasties. It was captured in 1324 by the Muslim prince Muḥammad ibn Tughluq, who became the sultan of Delhi the following year. In 1347 the Deccan region broke away from the sultanate's control under the leadership of the Bahmanis, whose ruler Aḥmad Shah Bahmanī moved the site of his capital from Gulbarga to Bidar about 1425. He rebuilt and extended the fort that still dominates the city's layout. Bidar became an independent sultanate in 1531 under the Barīd Shāhī dynasty. The city was annexed by the sultanate of Bijapur in 1619–20 but was captured by the Mughal viceroy Aurangzeb in 1657 and formally annexed to the Mughal Empire in 1686. Upon that empire's breakup, Bidar fell to the nizam of Hyderabad in 1724. When

Hyderabad state was partitioned in 1956, Bidar was transferred to Mysore (now Karnataka) state.

The fortress that Aḥmad Shah Bahmanī rebuilt about 1428 at Bidar has a triple moat and walls built of red laterite. Within the fortress complex is the Rangin Mahal ("Painted Palace"), so called because of its elaborate decoration with coloured tiles; the Takht Mahal, or throne room; and several other palaces. Elsewhere in Bidar are the Jami Masjid ("Great Mosque") and the Sola Khamba ("Sixteen-Pillar") mosque; these are typical Bahmanī buildings without minarets or prominent domes. Another notable Bahmanī monument is the great madrasa, an Islamic college, that was built in 1472–81 and is now a massive ruin. East of the town are the domed tombs of eight Bahmanī kings, while to the west lies the royal necropolis of the Barīd sultans.

Since the 14th century, Bidar has been noted for its production of Bidri ware—metal articles damascened (ornamented with wavy lines) in floral and geometric designs with silver wire. Several colleges in the city, including schools of law and commerce, are affiliated with Gulbarga University, which was established in 1980. Bidar is reached by northward branches of the Hyderabad-Mumbai road and railway.

The surrounding lowland area is drained by the Karanja River and produces millet, wheat, and oilseeds. Kalyani, about 40 miles (65 km) west of Bidar, was the capital of the second Chalukya dynasty (10th–12th century). Pop. (2001) 172,877.

HYDERABAD

Hyderabad is the capital of Andhra Pradesh state, south-central India. It is also Andhra Pradesh's largest and most populous city and is the major urban centre for all of south-central interior India.

Hyderabad is located on the Musi River in the heart of the Deccan plateau. The city site is relatively level to the gently rolling terrain, at an elevation of about 1,600 feet (500 metres). The climate is warm to hot and monsoonal (i.e., marked by wet and dry periods), with moderate annual precipitation. Most rain falls during the wet monsoon months of June to October. Pop. (2001) city, 3,637,483; urban agglom., 5,742,036.

HISTORY

Hyderabad was founded by the Quṭb Shāhi sultans of Golconda, under whom the kingdom of Golconda attained a position of importance second only to that of the Mughal Empire in the north. The old fortress town of Golconda had proved inadequate as the kingdom's capital, and so about 1591 Muḥammad Qulī Quṭb Shāhi, the fifth of the Quṭb Shāhis, built a new city called Hyderabad on the east bank of the Musi River, a few miles from old Golconda. The Charminar, a grand architectural composition in Indo-Saracenic style with open arches and four minarets, is regarded as the supreme achievement of the Quṭb Shāhī period. It formed the centrepiece around which the city was planned. The Mecca Mosque, which was built later, can accommodate 10,000 people. The mosque was the site of a bombing attack in 2007 that killed several Muslims and injured many others. The incident aggravated Muslim-Hindu tensions in the city, which has experienced periodic outbreaks of violence over the years.

Hyderabad was known for its beauty and affluence, but this glory lasted only as long as the Quṭb Shāhīs, for the Mughals conquered Hyderabad in 1685. The Mughal occupation was accompanied by plunder and destruction and was followed by the intervention of European powers in Indian affairs. In 1724 Āṣaf Jāh Nizam al-Mulk, the Mughal viceroy in the Deccan, declared independence. This Deccan kingdom, with Hyderabad as its capital, came to be known as Hyderabad. The Āṣaf Jāhīs, during the 19th century, started to rebuild, expanding to the north of the old city across the Musi. Farther north, Secunderabad grew as a British cantonment, connected to Hyderabad by a bund (embankment) 1 mile (1.6 km) long on the Husain Sagar Lake. The bund now serves as a promenade and is the pride of the city. Many new structures, reflecting a beautiful blend of Hindu and Muslim styles, have been added along it.

Under the nizams the Hindu and Muslim populations lived in amity, although immediately after Indian independence in 1947 a fanatical Muslim faction, the Raẓākārs, fomented tensions in the state and in the city. The Indian government intervened, and eventually the state of Hyderabad was acceded to India. In 1956 the state was split up; its Telugu-speaking areas were combined with the erstwhile Andhra state to form the state of Andhra Pradesh with Hyderabad as the capital.

THE CONTEMPORARY CITY

Hyderabad has become a centre of trade and commerce. Cigarettes and textiles are manufactured, and service activities have been expanded. The city has good transport facilities. There are rail and air services to Delhi, Kolkata, Mumbai, Chennai, and Bangalore (Bengaluru), as well as to historical sites including the Ajanta and Ellora caves, both of which were designated UNESCO World Heritage sites in 1983. Taxis, auto-rickshaws, cycle rickshaws, private vehicles, and suburban bus and rail services provide local transport.

Initially, Hyderabad was the location of two colleges of the University of Madras. In 1918, however, the nizam established Osmania University, and it is now one of the best universities in India. The University of Hyderabad was established in 1974. An agricultural university and a number of advanced research and training institutes are also located there, as are several nongovernmental institutions, notably the American Studies Research

Centre and the German Institute of Oriental Research.

The city has many public and private cultural organizations, such as state-sponsored dramatic, literary, and fine arts academies. The public auditorium, Ravindra Bharati, provides a venue for dance and music festivals, and the Salar Jung museum has a unique collection of rare pieces, including jade, jewelry, paintings, and furniture.

The public gardens provide the main recreational facilities. Many parks and the large parade grounds in Secunderabad offer space for play and relaxation. The zoological gardens and the university's botanical gardens are popular picnic spots. Hyderabad is reputed for its football (soccer) and cricket. There is also a racecourse.

KOCHI

Kochi (formerly Cochin) is a major port on the Arabian Sea, west-central Kerala state, southwestern India. Also the name of a former princely state, "Kochi" is sometimes used to refer to a cluster of islands and towns, including Ernakulam, Mattancheri, Fort Cochin, Willingdon Island, Vypin Island, and Gundu Island. The urban agglomeration includes the localities of Trikkakara, Eloor, Kalamassery, and Trippunithura.

Kochi was an insignificant fishing village until, in the 14th century, the backwaters of the Arabian Sea and the streams descending from the Ghats caused the separation of the village from the mainland, turning the landlocked harbour into one of the safest ports on India's southwestern coast. The port assumed a new strategic importance and began to experience commercial prosperity.

When the Portuguese penetrated the Indian Ocean in the late 15th century and reached India's southwestern coast, the Portuguese navigator Pedro Álvares Cabral founded the first European settlement on Indian soil at Kochi in 1500. Vasco da Gama, discoverer of the sea route to India (1498), established the first Portuguese factory (trading station) there in 1502, and the Portuguese viceroy Afonso de Albuquerque built the first European fort in India there in 1503. The city remained a Portuguese possession until it was conquered by the Dutch in 1663. Much Portuguese architecture still exists in the city.

Under Dutch rule (1663–1795) Kochi had its greatest prosperity. Through its harbour were shipped pepper, cardamom, and other spices and drugs as well as coir, coconut, and copra. All the city's ethnic and religious groups, including its Hindu majority and the Muslim, Syrian Christian, and Jewish minorities, shared in the city's prosperity.

British rule over Kochi lasted from 1795 until 1947, when India became independent. At the beginning of the 20th century a modern port with dry docks and ship repair yards was constructed, and Willingdon Island (connecting Fort Cochin with Ernakulam and other townships by a rail bridge and road) was built from the dredgings of the harbour's inner channels. After India's independence, Kochi became the major training centre for the Indian Navy.

A system of inland waterways running parallel to the coast provides Kochi with cheap transportation, encouraging trade. The deepwater harbour is open year-round, even in the monsoon season, and is served by a railway that connects it with Ernakulam. An international airport, about 17 miles (28 km) northeast of central Kochi, offers flights to major Indian cities including Mumbai (Bombay), Delhi, Bangalore (Bengaluru), and Chennai (Madras), as well as to many international destinations.

Kochi, set among picturesque lagoons and backwaters, attracts a considerable tourist trade. At Fort Cochin is St. Francis Church, built by the Portuguese in 1510 and reputedly the first European church on Indian soil. It was for a time the burial place of Vasco da Gama before his remains were taken to Portugal. Other churches as well as Hindu temples, mosques, and the historic synagogue at Mattancheri all stand in the area. The Jewish community in Kochi was the oldest in India, claiming to date from the 4th century CE. Almost all of its several thousand members had emigrated to Israel by the late 20th century, however. Pop. (2001) city, 595,575; urban agglom., 1,355,972.

KOZHIKODE

The city of Kozhikode (also called Calicut) is in northern Kerala state, southwestern India. It is situated on the Malabar Coast, 414 miles (666 km) west-southwest of Chennai (Madras) by rail. Once a famous cotton-weaving centre, it is remembered as the place of origin of calico, to which it gave its name (i.e., Calicut). The place was an early focus for Arab traders, who first settled there in the 7th century. Vasco da Gama, the Portuguese discoverer of the sea route to India, reached Kozhikode in 1498. The Portuguese built a fortified trading post there in 1511, but it was abandoned in 1525.

An English expedition visited Kozhikode in 1615, but not until 1664 did the British East India Company found a trading post there. The French followed in 1698 and the Danes in 1752. Hyder Ali, the 18th-century Indian ruler and military commander of Mysore (now Karnataka state), captured the town in 1765 and destroyed it. In 1790 the British occupied Kozhikode, and it passed into their hands by treaty in 1792, when the inhabitants returned and rebuilt the city.

Kozhikode's port is virtually closed during the summer monsoon season, and ships must lie 3 miles (5 km) offshore at other times of the year. Besides coconut products, the city exports pepper, ginger, coffee, tea, and other crops. Its industries include sawmills, tile making, coffee curing, and hosiery works. Kozhikode is the seat of the University of Calicut (1968), which includes colleges of arts and sciences, medical and teacher-training colleges, and a marine research institute. Pop. (2001) city, 436,556; urban agglom., 880,247.

MADURAI

Madurai (formerly Madura) is in south-central Tamil Nadu state, southeastern India, bounded on the west by Kerala state. It is the second largest, and probably the oldest, city in the state. Located on the Vaigai River and enclosed by the Anai, Naga, and Pasu (Elephant, Snake, and Cow) hills, the compact old city was the site of the Pandya (4th–11th century CE) capital and is centred on Minaksi-Sundareshvara Temple. The temple, Tirumala Nayak palace, Teppakulam tank (an earthen embankment reservoir), and a 1,000-pillared hall were rebuilt in the Vijayanagar period (16th–17th century) after the total destruction of the city in 1310. The city walls were removed by the British in 1837 to enable the city to expand, and administrative and residential quarters formed north of the river.

Large-scale industry has developed in the suburbs. Predominant are cotton spinning and weaving and the manufacture of transport equipment, tobacco, and sugar. Small-scale hand-loom weaving of silks and cottons, which have made Madurai famous throughout history, remains important. In the early years CE, Madurai was also well known for its Tamil *shangam* (literary society), and a new *shangam* was established in 1901. The city is the seat of Madurai-Kamaraj University (1966).

Lying southeast of the Eastern Ghats, the surrounding region occupies part of the plain of South India and contains several mountain spurs, including the Palni and Sirumalai hills (north), the Cardamom Hills (west), and the Varushanad and Andipatti hills (south). Between these hills in the west lies the high Kambam Valley. Eastward, the plains drop to 300 feet (90 metres) above sea level but contain isolated hills. The chief river, the Vaigai, flows northeast through the Kambam Valley and east across the centre of the state.

The ancient history of the region is associated with the Pandya kings. Later it was conquered by Chola, Vijayanagar, Muslim, Maratha, and British rulers. In the 1940s it became known as the centre of the civil disobedience movement and remained an important seat of political leadership.

The region has never been self-sufficient in rice, despite the completion of the Periyar (1895) and Vaigai (1960) irrigation works. Its chief cash crops are peanuts (groundnuts), cotton, sugarcane, coffee, cardamom, potatoes, and pears. Pop. (2001) city, 928,869.

MANGALORE

Mangalore (also spelled Mangaluru), in southwestern Karnataka state, southern India, is a port on the Arabian Sea. Lying on the backwaters formed by the Netravati and Gurpur rivers, it has long been a roadstead along the Malabar Coast. Engaged in Persian Gulf trade in the 14th century, Mangalore was occupied by the Portuguese in the mid-16th century. Under the Mysore sultans (1763) it became a strategic shipbuilding base, which was ceded to the British in 1799 after numerous sieges.

The city, heavily dotted with coconut plantations, has a deceptively rural appearance. It is a busy transshipment centre; ships must anchor 3 miles (5 km) offshore because of sandbars, but a deepwater port has been developed for the shipment of mineral ores. Cashew nuts, coffee, and sandalwood are brought from the Mysore and Coorg regions; rice, areca nuts, coir yarn (coconut fibre), fish, and cardamom are local products. In the 19th century the German Basel Mission introduced cotton weaving and tile manufacture, and Mangalore remains an important producer of roofing tiles. Other industries include boatbuilding, coffee curing, pottery manufacture, and the making of brick kilns. The suburb of Ullal produces hosiery and coir yarn. Mangalore maintains a large bazaar near its coastal landing place.

The city is served by both public and private thermal power stations, an airport, and a national highway and is the terminus of the west-coast branch of the Southern Railway. Mangalore is the seat of a Roman Catholic bishopric and a Lutheran mission. It also is an educational centre and is home to St. Aloysius College (founded by Jesuits in 1880), St. Agnes College, and St. Ann's College, all of which are affiliated with the University of Mangalore. The Konkani language is associated with the city, and a large percentage of its inhabitants are Christian. Pop. (2001) city, 399,565; urban agglom., 539,387.

MYSORE

Mysore (also spelled Mysuru) is in south-central Karnataka state, southern India. It lies northwest of Chamundi Hill and midway between the Kaveri (Cauvery) and Kabbani rivers on the undulating Deccan Plateau at an elevation of 2,525 feet (770 metres). The land surrounding the city is characterized by rain-filled shallow depressions (tanks). The site was mentioned in the epic *Mahabharata* as Mahishmati (Mahismati); it was known as Purigere in the Mauryan era (3rd century BCE) and later became Mahishapura. It was the administrative capital of the princely state of Mysore from 1799 to 1831 and remains the second largest city (after Bangalore [Bengaluru]) of Karnataka state.

An important manufacturing and trading centre, Mysore has textile (cotton and silk), rice, and oil mills, sandalwood-oil and chemical factories, and tanneries. The suburb of Belagula, to the northwest, produces chrome dyes and chemical fertilizer. The city's industries are powered by the hydroelectric station near Sivasamudram Island to the east. Mysore's cottage industries include cotton weaving, tobacco and coffee processing, and the making of *bidis* (cigarettes). The area is known for its artwork in ivory, metal, and wood, and the market

Farmers plowing a field near Mysore, southern Karnataka. Christina Gascoigne/Robert Harding Picture Library

near the railway station serves as a collection centre for local farm products. The city has an airport, lies at the junction of two northern railway lines, and is a major intersection on India's principal western road system.

An ancient fort, rebuilt along European lines in the 18th century, stands in the centre of Mysore. The fort area comprises the Maharaja's Palace (1897) with its ivory and gold throne, Curzon Park, the Silver Jubilee Clock Tower (1927), Gandhi Square, and two statues of maharajas. To the west, near Gordon Park, are the former British residency (1805), the noted Oriental Library, university buildings, and public offices. Jaganmohan Palace and Lalitha Mahal are other notable buildings. The University of Mysore was founded in 1916; other educational facilities include Maharaja's College, Maharani's College for Women, and affiliated colleges of medicine, law, engineering, and teacher training. There are also several institutions for the advancement of Kannada culture.

Pilgrims frequent Chamundi Hill (about 3,490 feet [1,064 metres]), with its monolith of Nandi, the sacred bull of Shiva; the summit affords an excellent view of the Nilgiri Hills to the south. Krishnaraja Lake, a large reservoir with a dam, lies 12 miles (19 km) northwest of Mysore at the Kaveri River. Spreading below the dam are the terraced Vrindavan Gardens with their cascades and fountains, which are flood-lit at night. Somnathpur, to the east, has a temple built (1268) under the Hoysala dynasty. Bandipur Sanctuary, part of the Venugopal Wildlife Park (1941), is usually approached from Mysore; it is noted for herds of gaur (Indian bison) and spotted deer, has a network of roads for observation, and adjoins Mudumalai Wildlife Sanctuary in Tamil Nadu state. The area in which Mysore is situated is drained by the Kaveri River and its tributaries. Cotton is grown on large tracts of black soil, and rice, millet, and oilseed are exported. Pop. (2001) 755,379.

THANJAVUR

Thanjavur (formerly Tanjore), in eastern Tamil Nadu state, southeastern India, lies in the Kaveri (Cauvery) River delta, about 30 miles (50 km) east of Tiruchchirappalli. An early capital of the Chola empire from the 9th to the 11th century, it was important during the Vijayanagar, Maratha, and British periods. It is now a tourist centre. Attractions include the Brihadishvara Chola temple, which was designated a UNESCO World Heritage site in 1987 (expanded in 2004 by naming two other nearby Chola temples); a Vijayanagar fort; the palace of Sarfoji, a Maratha prince; and Sarasvati Mahal Library, known for its large collection of manuscripts dating from the 16th to the 19th century. The city is also known for a distinctive painting style—in which such materials as gold foil, lace, and semi-precious stones are used to embellish the painting—and for a style of embossed metal plates. Industries include cotton mills, traditional hand-loom weaving, and the manufacture of *vinas* (south Indian stringed instruments). The city is the seat of Tamil University (1981) and has several other colleges.

The surrounding region occupies part of the flat, fertile Kaveri delta, one of the most important rice-growing areas in India, terminating in the southeast at Point Calimere at the confluence of Palk Strait and the Bay of Bengal. The delta is traversed by innumerable channels of the Kaveri, linked by irrigation canals, some of them used for at least 10 centuries. Sugarcane and peanuts (groundnuts) are grown in addition to rice; grain processing is a significant industry. Pop. (2001) city, 215,314.

Nataraja statue at the Brihadishvara Chola temple, Thanjavur, Tamil Nadu, India.
Frederick M. Asher

THIRUVANANTHAPURAM

Thiruvananthapuram (formerly known as Trivandrum), the capital of Kerala state, southwestern India, is situated on a coastal plain with isolated hills. The community became prominent under Raja Martanda Varma, who made it the capital of his kingdom of Travancore in 1745. The city's former name, Trivandrum, was given by the British and is a contraction of Thiruvananthapuram, its ancient name that was adopted again in the early 21st century. It is the site of the University of Kerala (1937) and its affiliated colleges and technical schools. It also has a museum, zoological gardens, an observatory, and an art gallery. A large fort contains several palaces and a Vaishnava temple (a temple dedicated to Vishnu), which is a noted pilgrimage centre. Thiruvananthapuram's industries include mineral processing, sugar milling, textiles, and handicrafts. Rice and coconut cultivation and coastal fishing are economically important. It is a rail terminus and road hub and has an airport and a harbour. Pop. (2001) city, 744,983; urban agglom., 889,635.

CHAPTER 9

SELECTED NORTHERN AND NORTHWESTERN INDIAN STATES

The northern and northwestern region of India constitutes the cradle of civilization on the subcontinent and also the heart of Hindustan, the traditional homeland of Hindus. Three among its states are featured below: Punjab, which occupies a portion of the historic Punjab Plain that is now shared by India and Pakistan; Rajasthan, the largest state in India in terms of area; and Uttar Pradesh, India's most populous state.

PUNJAB

The Indian state of Punjab is located in the northwestern part of the subcontinent. It is bounded by the Indian states of Jammu and Kashmir to the north, Himachal Pradesh to the northeast, Haryana to the south and southeast, and Rajasthan to the southwest and by the country of Pakistan to the west. Punjab in its present form came into existence on Nov. 1, 1966, when most of its predominantly Hindi-speaking areas were separated to form the new state of Haryana. The city of Chandigarh, within the Chandigarh union territory, is the joint capital of Punjab and Haryana. Area 19,445 square miles (50,362 square km). Pop. (2008 est.) 26,591,000.

LAND

The word Punjab is a compound of two Persian words, *panj* ("five") and *āb* ("water"), thus signifying the land of five waters, or rivers (the Beas, Chenab, Jhelum, Ravi, and Sutlej). The word's origin can perhaps be traced to *panca nada*, Sanskrit for "five rivers" and the name of a region mentioned in the ancient epic the *Mahabharata*. As applied to the present Indian state of Punjab, however, it is a misnomer; since the partition of India in 1947, only two of these rivers, the Sutlej and the Beas, lie within Punjab's territory, while the Ravi flows only along part of its western border.

RELIEF, DRAINAGE, AND SOILS

Punjab spans three physiographic regions, the smallest being the Siwalik Range in the northeast, where elevations reach about 3,000 feet (900 metres). Farther south, the narrow, undulating foothill region is dissected by closely spaced seasonal torrents, locally known as *chos*, several of which terminate in the plain below without joining any stream. To the south and west of the foothills lies the broad flat tract, with low-lying floodplains separated by slightly elevated uplands. This region, with its fertile alluvial soils, slopes gently from an elevation of about 900 feet (275 metres) in the northeast to about 550 feet (170 metres) in the southwest. The southwestern part of the plains, formerly strewn with sand dunes, has mostly been levelled off with the expansion of irrigation projects.

CLIMATE

Punjab has an inland subtropical location, and its climate is continental, being semiarid to subhumid. Summers are very hot. In June, the warmest month, daily temperatures in Ludhiana usually reach about 100 °F (upper 30s C) from a low in the upper 70s F (mid-20s C). In January, the coolest month, daily temperatures normally rise from the mid-40s (about 7 °C) into the mid-60s F (upper 10s C). Annual rainfall is highest in the Siwalik Range, which may receive more than 45 inches (1,150 mm), and lowest in the southwest, which may receive less than 12 inches (300 mm); statewide average annual precipitation is roughly 16 inches (400 mm). Most of the annual rainfall occurs from July to September, the months of the southwest monsoon. Winter rains from the western cyclones, occurring from December to March, account for less than one-fourth of the total rainfall.

PLANT AND ANIMAL LIFE

With the growth of human settlement over the centuries, Punjab has been cleared of most of its forest cover. Over large parts of the Siwalik Range, bush vegetation has succeeded trees as a result of extensive deforestation. There have been attempts at reforestation on the hillsides, and eucalyptus trees have been planted along major roads.

Natural habitats for wildlife are severely limited because of intense competition from agriculture. Even so, many types of rodents (such as mice, rats, squirrels, and gerbils), bats, birds, and snakes, as well as some species of monkeys, have adapted to the farming environment. Larger mammals, including jackals, leopards, wild boar, various types of deer, civets, and pangolins (scaly anteaters), among others, are found in the Siwaliks.

PEOPLE

The people of Punjab are mainly descendants of the so-called Aryan tribes that entered India from the northwest during the 2nd millennium BCE, as well as the pre-Aryan population, probably Dravidians (speakers of Dravidian languages), who had a highly developed civilization. Relics of this civilization have been unearthed at Rupnagar (Ropar).

POPULATION COMPOSITION

Successive waves of invaders—Greeks, Parthians, Kushans, and Hephthalites (Hunas)—added to the diversity of earlier social, or caste, groups (*jatis*). Later, invaders under the banner of Islam forced several vanquished groups (such as the Jat peasant caste and the Rajput class of landowners) to convert to the Muslim faith, although many conversions were voluntary under the influence of Ṣūfī saints.

Today, however, the majority religion of Punjab is Sikhism, which originated from the teachings of Nanak, the first Sikh Guru. Hindus make up the largest minority, but there also is a significant population of Muslims. There are small communities of Christians and Jains in some areas. More than one-fourth of Punjab's population consists of Hindus and Sikhs who officially belong to the Scheduled Castes (formerly "untouchables"), which occupy a relatively low position within the traditional Indian caste system.

Punjabi is the official state language. Along with Hindi, it is the most widely spoken. However, many people also speak English and Urdu.

SETTLEMENT PATTERNS

About one-third of Punjab's population lives in cities and towns. Its major cities are Ludhiana in the central region, Amritsar in the northwest, Jalandhar in north-central Punjab, Patiala in the southeast, and Bathinda in the south-central part of the state. Muslims reside mostly in and around the southwest-central city of Maler Kotla, which was once the centre of a princely state ruled by a Muslim nawab (provincial governor).

ECONOMY

Punjab has a reasonably diversified economy based on agriculture, manufacturing, and services. It also has a well-developed transportation network.

AGRICULTURE

Some two-fifths of Punjab's population is engaged in the agricultural sector, which accounts for a significant segment of the state's gross product. Punjab produces an important portion of India's food grain and contributes a major share of the wheat and rice stock held by the Central Pool (a national repository system of surplus food grain). Much of the state's

agricultural progress and productivity is attributable to the so-called Green Revolution, an international movement launched in the 1960s that introduced not only new agricultural technologies but also high-yielding varieties of wheat and rice.

Aside from wheat and rice, corn (maize), barley, and pearl millet are important cereal products of Punjab. Although the yield of pulses (legumes) has declined since the late 20th century, there has been a rapid increase in the commercial production of fruit, especially

Communal well in Hoshiarpur, Punjab, India. Shostal Associates

citrus, mangoes, and guavas. Other major crops include cotton, sugarcane, oilseeds, chickpeas, peanuts (groundnuts), and vegetables.

With almost the entire cultivated area receiving irrigation, Punjab is among India's most widely irrigated states. Government-owned canals and wells are the main sources of irrigation; canals are most common in southern and southwestern Punjab, while wells are more typical of the north and the northeast. The Bhakra Dam project in neighbouring Himachal Pradesh provides much of Punjab's supply of irrigation water.

RESOURCES AND POWER

Lacking fossil fuels, Punjab draws its energy primarily from thermal plants fired with imported coal. However, a significant amount of power is provided by hydroelectric plants and, to a lesser extent, by solar power stations. In the early 21st century, the demand for electricity in Punjab continued to exceed the supply.

MANUFACTURING

The manufacturing sector (including construction) has expanded notably since

Buses at a rail crossing near Amritsar, Punjab. © Robert Holmes

the late 20th century. Industries with the largest number of workers include those producing silk, wool, and other textiles; processed foods and beverages; metal products and machinery; transport equipment; and furniture. Other important manufactures include leather goods, chemicals, rubber and plastics, and hosiery.

SERVICES

Punjab's services sector includes trade, transportation and storage, financial services, real estate, public administration, and other services. The sector has grown rapidly since the late 20th century. By the early 21st century it had become the largest component of Punjab's economy.

TRANSPORTATION

Punjab has one of the best-developed road networks in the country. All-weather paved roads extend to most villages, and the state is crossed by a number of national highways. Punjab also is well served by the Northern Railway—part of the national railway system. There is an international airport in Amritsar, and regular domestic service is available in Chandigarh and Ludhiana. Several other airports offer cargo service.

GOVERNMENT AND SOCIETY

The structure of Punjab's government, like that of most other states of India, is determined by the national constitution of 1950.

CONSTITUTIONAL FRAMEWORK

The state is led by a governor, who is appointed by the president of India. The governor is aided and advised by a Council of Ministers, which is led by a chief minister and responsible to the unicameral Legislative Assembly (Vidhan Sabha).

At the head of the judiciary is the High Court, which is located in Chandigarh and is shared with the state of Haryana. Appeals from the High Court are directed to the Supreme Court of India. Below the High Court are district-level courts.

The state is divided into more than a dozen districts, which are grouped into several revenue divisions. Each district is headed by a deputy commissioner. The districts are parceled further into a number of *tehsils*, or subdivisions. Lower administrative and revenue units include circles, blocks, and villages, as well as police districts and police stations.

HEALTH AND WELFARE

Punjab enjoys better health conditions than most states in India. Hospitals attached to medical colleges, district- and *tehsil*-level medical facilities, health care centres in rural areas, and numerous dispensaries constitute a widespread health care network.

Numerous social services are provided by government and voluntary organizations. The government provides pensions for the elderly and operates a network of employment exchanges to assist the unemployed. The state also has schemes to aid those from traditionally disadvantaged social groups through scholarships, employment services, and assorted loans and grants for business activities.

EDUCATION

In addition to the government, private organizations have played a significant role in the extension of education at the primary, secondary, and tertiary levels throughout the state. Education is compulsory and free for pupils aged 6 to 11. Secondary education is also free in state schools. Broadcasting has been especially important in the dissemination of vocational and cultural education throughout the state.

Punjab has several state universities, including Punjabi University (1962) in Patiala, Guru Nanak Dev University (1969) in Amritsar, Panjab University (1956) in Chandigarh, Punjab Agricultural University (1962) in Ludhiana, Punjab Technical University (1997) in Jalandhar, and Baba Farid University of Health Sciences (1998) in Faridkot. In addition, there are more than 200 specialized colleges and technical institutions.

CULTURAL LIFE

Ballads of love and war, fairs and festivals, dancing, music, and Punjabi literature are among the characteristic expressions of the state's cultural life. The origins of Punjabi literature trace to the mystical and religious verse of the 13th-century Ṣūfī (mystic) Shaikh Farīd and to the 15th–16th-century founder of the Sikh faith, Guru Nanak; these figures were the first to use Punjabi extensively as a medium of poetic expression. The works of Ṣūfī poet Waris Shah greatly enriched Punjabi literature in the second half of the 18th century. In the 20th and early 21st centuries, contemporary Punjabi literature found some of its greatest exponents in poet and author Bhai Vir Singh and the poets Puran Singh, Dhani Ram Chatrik, Mohan Singh "Mahir," and Shiv Kumar Batalvi; renowned novelists have included Jaswant Singh Kanwal, Gurdial Singh, Giani Gurdit Singh, and Sohan Singh Shital, among others. Kulwant Singh Virk is one of the best-known writers of short stories in Punjabi.

Punjab holds numerous religious and seasonal festivals, such as Dussehra, a Hindu festival celebrating the victory of Prince Rama over the demon king Ravana, as recounted in the epic *Ramayana*; Diwali, a festival of lights celebrated by both Hindus and Sikhs; and Baisakhi, which for Hindus is a new year's festival and for Sikhs is both an agricultural festival and a celebration of the birth of the community's Khalsa order. There also are numerous anniversary celebrations in honour of the Gurus (the 10 historical leaders of Sikhism) and various saints. Dancing is a typical feature of such festivities, with *bhangra, jhumar,* and *sammi* among the most popular genres. *Giddha*, a native Punjabi tradition, is a humorous song-and-dance genre performed by women. In addition to Sikh religious music, semiclassical Mughal forms, such as the *khyal* dance and the *ṭhumrī, ghazal,* and *qawwālī* vocal performance genres, continue to be popular.

The state's outstanding architectural monument is the Harimandir (Golden Temple) at Amritsar, which blends Indian and Muslim styles. Its chief motifs, such as the dome and the geometric design, are repeated in most of the Sikh places of worship. The Harimandir is rich in gold filigree work, panels with floral designs, and marble facings inlaid with coloured stones. Other important buildings include the Martyr's Memorial at Jallianwalla Bagh (a park in Amritsar), the Hindu Temple of Durgiana (also in Amritsar), the so-called Moorish Mosque in Kapurthala (patterned after a Moroccan model), and the old forts of Bathinda and Bahadurgarh.

HISTORY

The foundations of the present Punjab were laid by Banda Singh Bahadur, a hermit who became a military leader and, with his fighting band of Sikhs, temporarily liberated the eastern part of the province from Mughal rule in 1709–10. Banda Singh's defeat and execution in 1716 were followed by a prolonged struggle between the Sikhs on one side and the Mughals and Afghans on the other. By 1764–65 the Sikhs had established their dominance in the area. Ranjit Singh (1780–1839) subsequently built up the Punjab region into a powerful Sikh kingdom and attached to it the adjacent provinces of Multan, Kashmir, and Peshawar (all of which are now fully or partially administered by Pakistan).

In 1849 the Punjab kingdom fell to the troops of the British East India Company and subsequently became a province under British rule. By the late 19th century, however, the Indian nationalist movement took hold in the province. One of the most significant events associated with the movement was the 1919 Massacre of Amritsar, which resulted from an order given by British general Reginald Edward Harry Dyer to fire on a group of some 10,000 Indians who had convened to protest new antisubversion regulations enacted by the British administration; nearly 400 died, and about 1,200 were injured in the conflict. When India gained its independence in 1947, the British province of Punjab was split between the new sovereign states of India and Pakistan, and the smaller, eastern portion became part of India.

After independence, the history of the Indian Punjab was dominated by Sikh agitation for a separate Punjabi-speaking state, led by Tara Singh and later by his political successor, Sant Fateh Singh. In November 1956, however, rather than being divided along linguistic lines, the Indian state of Punjab was enlarged through incorporation of the Patiala and East Punjab States Union (PEPSU), an amalgamation of the preindependence princely territories of Patiala, Jind, Nabha, Faridkot, Kapurthala, Kalsia, Malerkotla (Maler Kotla), and Nalagarh. Political and administrative leadership for the enlarged Punjab was provided by Sardar Partap Singh Kairon, chief minister of the state from 1956 to 1964. The call for a separate Indian state containing the predominantly Punjabi-speaking areas intensified in the wake of Punjab's expansion. Eventually, the government of India met the demand. On Nov. 1, 1966, Punjab was divided on the basis of language into the mostly Hindi-speaking state of Haryana and the new, primarily Punjabi-speaking state of Punjab; meanwhile, the northernmost districts were transferred to Himachal Pradesh, and the newly constructed city of Chandigarh and its immediate surroundings became a separate union territory. Though not a part of either state, the city of Chandigarh was retained as the joint administrative headquarters, or capital, of both Haryana and Punjab.

Although Sikhs had won the use of Punjabi within the state, by the 1980s militant factions of the Shiromani Akali Dal ("Leading Akali Party") and the All India Sikh Students' Federation were demanding the establishment of an autonomous Sikh homeland, or Khalistan ("Land of the Pure," a term introduced as early as 1946 by Tara Singh). In order to attain their goal, these groups began to use terrorism, including the indiscriminate killing of Punjabi Hindus and even those Sikhs who opposed the creation of Khalistan. In June 1984, in an effort to dislodge Sikh militants fortified in the Harimandir (the Sikhs' holiest shrine), the Indian army carried out an attack. The Sikh leader Jarnail Singh Bhindranwale and most of his armed followers were killed, as were at least 100 Indian soldiers. In retaliation, Prime Minister Indira Gandhi was assassinated at her Delhi home by two of her Sikh bodyguards, which in turn led to violence against Sikhs in Delhi and elsewhere. A climate of violence and disorder persisted in Punjab through the 1980s, but by the early 1990s the state had returned to relative stability.

RAJASTHAN

The northwestern Indian state of Rajasthan is bounded to the north and northeast by the states of Punjab and Haryana, to the east and southeast by the states of Uttar Pradesh and Madhya Pradesh, to the southwest by the state of Gujarat, and to the west and northwest by Pakistan. The capital city is Jaipur, in the east-central part of the state. Area 132,139 square miles (342,239 square km). Pop. (2008 est.) 64,641,000.

LAND

Rajasthan, meaning "The Abode of the Rajas," was formerly called Rajputana, "The Country of the Rajputs" (sons of rajas [princes]). Before 1947, when India achieved independence from British rule, it comprised some two dozen princely states and chieftainships, the small British-administered province of Ajmer-Merwara, and a few pockets of territory outside the main boundaries. After 1947 the princely states and chieftainships were integrated into India in stages, and the state took the name Rajasthan. It assumed its present form on Nov. 1, 1956, when the States Reorganization Act came into force.

Relief

The Aravalli (Aravali) Range forms a line across the state running roughly from Guru Peak (about 5,650 feet [1,722 metres]), near the town of Abu (Mount Abu) in the southwest, to the town of Khetri in the northeast. About three-fifths of the state lies northwest of this line, leaving two-fifths in the southeast. These are the two natural divisions of Rajasthan. The northwestern tract is generally arid and unproductive, although its character shifts gradually from desert in the far west and northwest to comparatively fertile and habitable land toward the east. The area includes the Thar (Great Indian) Desert.

The southeastern area lies at a somewhat higher elevation (330 to 1,150 feet [100 to 350 metres]) than its northwestern counterpart; it also is more fertile and has a more diverse topography. The hilly tract of Mewar lies in the southern region, while a broad plateau stretches across the southeast. In the northeast a rugged badlands region follows the line of the Chambal River. Farther north the country levels out into flat plains that are part of the alluvial basin of the Yamuna River.

Drainage

The Aravallis form Rajasthan's most important watershed. To the east of this range, the Chambal River—the only large and perennial river in the state—and other waterways generally drain toward the northeast. The principal tributary of the Chambal, the Banas, rises in the Aravallis near the great Kumbhalgarh fort and collects all the drainage of the Mewar plateau. Farther north, the Banganga, after rising near Jaipur, flows east toward the Yamuna before disappearing. The Luni is the only significant river west of the Aravallis. It rises near the city of Ajmer in central Rajasthan and flows 200 miles (320 km) west-southwest into the Rann of Kachchh in the state of Gujarat. Northeast of the Luni basin is an area of internal drainage characterized by salt lakes, the largest of which is Sambhar Salt Lake. Farther to the west lies the true Marusthali ("Land of the Dead"), the barren wastelands and areas of sand dunes that form the heart of the Thar Desert.

Soils

In the vast sandy northwestern region, soils are predominantly saline or alkaline. Water is scarce but is found at a depth of

100 to 200 feet (30 to 60 metres). The soil and sand are calcareous (chalky). Nitrates in the soil increase its fertility, and cultivation is often possible where adequate water supplies are made available.

The soils in central Rajasthan are sandy; clay content varies between 3 and 9 percent. In the east, soils vary from sandy loam to loamy sand. In the southeast, they are in general black and deep and are well drained. In the south-central region, the tendency is toward a mixture of red and black soils in the east and a range of red to yellow soils in the west.

CLIMATE

Rajasthan has a wide range of climate varying from extremely arid to humid. The humid zone spans the southeast and east. Except in the hills, the heat during the summer is great everywhere, with temperatures in June—the warmest month—typically rising from the mid-80s F (about 30 °C) to nearly 110 °F (low 40s C) daily. Hot winds and dust storms occur in the summer, especially in the desert tract. In January—the coolest of the winter months—daily maximum temperatures range from the upper 60s to the mid-70s F (low to mid-20s C), while minimum temperatures are generally in the mid-40s F (about 7 °C). The western desert has little rain, averaging about 4 inches (100 mm) annually. In the southeast, however, some areas may receive almost 20 inches (500 mm). Southeastern Rajasthan benefits from both the Arabian Sea and Bay of Bengal branches of the southwest (summer) monsoon winds, which bring the bulk of the annual rainfall.

PLANT AND ANIMAL LIFE

The predominant vegetation of Rajasthan is scrub jungle. Toward the west there are typical arid-zone plants, such as tamarisk (genus *Tamarix*) and false tamarisk (genus *Myricaria*). Trees are scarce, limited mostly to small, scattered forest areas in the Aravallis and in the eastern part of the state. Less than 10 percent of Rajasthan is under forest cover.

A number of notable large mammals are regular residents of Rajasthan. Tigers are found primarily in the Aravallis. Leopards, sloth bears, Indian sambar (dark brown Indian deer), and chital (spotted deer) occur in the hills and forests. Nilgais (bluebucks; large antelope) are also found in parts, and blackbucks are numerous in the plains. Common birds include snipes, quail, partridges, and wild ducks; they occur everywhere except in the desert. The northwest is well known for several species of sandgrouse.

Numerous sanctuaries and wildlife parks have been established in the state. Among the most important of these are the Sariska National Park (established in 1955), near Alwar in the northeast, and the Desert National Park (established in 1980), near Jaisalmer in western Rajasthan.

A tiger on a road near Ranthambhor, eastern Rajasthan, India. G. Ziesler/Bruce Coleman Ltd.

PEOPLE

Most of Rajasthan's population consist of Indians of various social, occupational, and religious backgrounds.

POPULATION COMPOSITION

The Rajputs (various clans of landowning rulers and their descendants), though representing only a small percentage of Rajasthan's residents, are perhaps the most notable section of the population; indeed, the state draws its name from this community. In terms of caste structure, the Brahmans (highest caste) are subdivided into many *gotra*s (lineages), while the Mahajans (trading caste) are subdivided into a bewildering number of groups. In the north and west the Jats (peasant caste) and Gujars (herding caste) are among the largest agricultural communities.

Aboriginal (tribal) peoples constitute more than one-tenth of the population of

Rajasthan. In the eastern part of the state, these groups include the Mina (and the related Meo), most of whom are farmers; the Banjara, who have been known as traveling tradesmen and artisans; and the Gadia Lohar, another historically itinerant tribe, who traditionally have made and repaired agricultural and household implements. The Bhil, one of the oldest communities in India, generally inhabit southern Rajasthan and have a history of possessing great skill in archery. The Grasia and Kathodi also largely live in the south, mostly in the Mewar region. Sahariya communities are found in the southeast, and the Rabari, who traditionally are cattle breeders, live to the west of the Aravallis in west-central Rajasthan.

Hindi is the official language of the state, and to some degree it has overshadowed the local languages of Rajasthan. Much of the state's population, however, continues to speak Rajasthani languages, which comprise a group of Indo-Aryan languages and dialects derived from Dingal, a tongue in which bards once sang of the glories of their masters. The four main Rajasthani language groups are Marwari in western Rajasthan, Jaipuri or Dhundhari in the east and southeast, Malvi in the southeast, and, in the northeast, Mewati, which shades off into Braj Bhasa (a Hindi dialect) toward the border with Uttar Pradesh.

Hinduism, the religion of the vast majority of the population, is generally practiced through the worship of Brahma, Shiva, Shakti, Vishnu, and other gods and goddesses. The town of Nathdwara, in southern Rajasthan, is an important religious centre for the Vallabhacharya school of Krishna worshippers. There are also followers of Arya Samaj, a type of reformed Hinduism that stems from the late 19th century.

Islam, the state's second-largest religious community, expanded in Rajasthan with the conquest of the city of Ajmer and the surrounding area by Muslim invaders in the late 12th century. Khwājah Muʿīn al-Dīn Chishtī, the Muslim missionary and mystic, had his headquarters at Ajmer, and Muslim traders, craftsmen, and soldiers settled there.

Jainism is also important; it has not been the religion of the rulers of Rajasthan but has followers among the trading class and the wealthy section of society. The towns and temples of Mahavirji, Ranakpur, Dhulev, and Karera are the chief centres of Jaina pilgrimage. Another important religious community is formed by the Dadupanthis, the followers of the 16th-century saint Dadu, who preached the equality of all men, strict vegetarianism, total abstinence from intoxicating liquor, and lifelong celibacy. The state's population of Christians and Sikhs is small.

SETTLEMENT PATTERNS

Rajasthan is one of the least densely populated states in India, with roughly three-fourths of its residents living in rural settlements. Traditional rural houses are huts with mud walls and roofs thatched with straw. They have a single door but no windows or ventilators. The houses of more-affluent farmers and artisans in larger villages have more than one room. They are roofed with tiles and have a veranda and large courtyard, whose main door will admit a loaded bull cart. The earthen floors are coated with mud and dung.

The state's urban population has been growing faster than the rural population since the late 20th century. Jaipur is by far the largest city of Rajasthan. Other major urban centres include Jodhpur, Kota, Bikaner, Ajmer, and Udaipur. With the exception of Jodhpur and Bikaner, all lie to the east of the Aravalli Range.

ECONOMY

The state's economy is centred largely on agriculture, although the mining sector is also important. Industry is focused largely on processed raw materials and light manufactures.

AGRICULTURE

The agricultural sector is the mainstay of Rajasthan's economy, employing about two-thirds of the state's working population. Despite scant and scattered rainfall, nearly all types of crops are grown, including pearl millet in the desert area, sorghum around Kota, and mainly corn (maize) around Udaipur.

Wheat and barley are fairly well distributed (except in the desert area), as are pulses (such as peas, beans, and lentils), sugarcane, and oilseeds. Rice is grown in the irrigated areas of both the southeast and the northwest. Cotton and tobacco are important cash crops. Rajasthan has a large livestock population and is a major wool-producing state. It also is a source of camels and draft animals of various breeds.

Rajasthan needs extensive irrigation to be agriculturally productive. The state receives much water from the rivers of Punjab, from the Western Yamuna Canal in Haryana and the Agra Canal in Uttar Pradesh, and from the Sabarmati and Narmada Sagar projects in Gujarat and Madhya Pradesh, respectively. Desert land in northwestern and western Rajasthan is irrigated by the Indira Gandhi Canal (formerly the Rajasthan Canal), which carries water some 400 miles (640 km) from the Beas and Sutlej rivers in Punjab. Rajasthan shares the Bhakra Nangal project with Punjab and Haryana and the Chambal Valley project with Madhya Pradesh; both are used to supply water for irrigation and for drinking purposes.

RESOURCES AND POWER

Rajasthan is an important producer of lead and zinc concentrates, emeralds, and garnets. A major portion of the country's gypsum and silver ore also are produced in Rajasthan. Electricity supplies are obtained mostly from neighbouring states and from the Chambal Valley project. Power is generated primarily from hydroelectric stations and gas-fired thermal plants. The state also draws a portion of its energy from wind farms and from a nuclear power plant at Rawatbhata, near Kota.

MANUFACTURING

Textiles, vegetable oil, wool, minerals, and chemicals are among the major manufactures of Rajasthan. However, handicrafts, such as leather goods, marble work, jewelry, pottery, and embossed brass, have earned much foreign exchange. Kota, which is the industrial capital of the state, has a nylon factory and a precision-instruments factory, as well as plants for the manufacture of calcium carbide, caustic soda, and rayon tire cord. There is a zinc smelter plant near Udaipur.

GOVERNMENT AND SOCIETY

The structure of Rajasthan's government, like that of most other states in India, is determined by the national constitution of 1950.

CONSTITUTIONAL FRAMEWORK

The state's chief executive is the governor, who is appointed by the president of India for a five-year term. The governor has administrative, legislative, financial, and judicial powers. Rajasthan has a unicameral Legislative Assembly (Vidhan Sabha); members are elected by universal adult franchise, although some seats are reserved for representatives of tribal groups and other traditionally disadvantaged communities.

The state is divided into more than 30 districts. In each district the collector, who is also the district magistrate, is the principal representative of the administration. The collector functions in close cooperation with the superintendent of police to maintain law and order in the district and also serves as the principal revenue officer. For administrative purposes, each district is split into a few subdivisions, which are divided into smaller units called *tehsils*, which, in turn, contain a number of villages.

Rajasthan was the first state to experiment at the village level with *panchayat raj* (rule by *panchayat*, or village council), having enacted in 1959 the legislation necessary to implement this bold experiment in democratic decentralization. The system, embracing Gandhian concepts of the importance of traditional village institutions in Indian society, created three levels of local government within the state based on elected village *panchayats*. Villages were grouped into administrative units called community development blocks, each having a *panchayat samiti* (block council) composed of the chairmen of the *panchayats*, appointees, and ex officio members. There were also district-level councils (*zila parishads*), composed of the chairmen of the *panchayat samitis*, along with representatives of special-interest groups (such as women and disadvantaged social classes) and local members of the state and national legislatures. The key level in this organization was the community development block, which was assigned the responsibility of planning and implementing a wide range of community and development programs. *Panchayat raj* initially achieved a considerable measure of success, but, with increasing politicization of the system and conflicting interests with state-level development agencies, the system has become less effective.

HEALTH AND EDUCATION

Rajasthan has many hospitals and dispensaries specializing in allopathic (Western) medicine, as well as numerous institutions offering Ayurvedic (traditional Indian), Unānī (a medicinal system using prescribed herbs and shrubs), and homeopathic treatment. The state participates in the major national health programs to control tuberculosis, various vector-borne diseases, leprosy, iodine deficiency, and blindness.

There are a number of institutions of higher education in Rajasthan. State universities are located in Jaipur, Udaipur, Jodhpur, Bikaner, and Ajmer. Other prominent tertiary institutions include the Open University in Kota and the Birla Institute of Technology and Science in Pilani.

CULTURAL LIFE

Rajasthan has a rich tradition of the arts: oral and written literature, dance, and architecture.

THE ARTS

The most famous song is *Kurja*, which tells the story of a woman who wishes to send a message to her absent husband by a *kurja* (a type of bird), who is promised a priceless reward for his service. In the literary tradition Chand Bardai's epic poem *Prithviraj Raso* (or *Chand Raisa*), the earliest manuscript of which dates to the 12th century, is particularly notable.

The typical dance of Rajasthan is the *ghoomar*, which is performed on festive occasions only by women. Other well-known dances include the *geer*, which is performed by men and women; the *panihari*, a graceful dance for women; and the *kacchi ghori*, in which male dancers ride dummy horses. Performances of *khyal*, a type of dance-drama composed in verse with celebratory, historical, or romantic themes, also is widely popular.

Rajasthan abounds in objects of antiquarian interest. Early Buddhist rock inscriptions and carvings are found in caves in the southeastern district of Jhalawar; the area around Ajmer has a number of Muslim mosques and tombs, the oldest of which dates to the end of the 12th century; and Bikaner, in the northwest, has a spectacular 15th-century Jaina temple. Splendid princely palaces, many elaborately decorated with wall paintings, are scattered throughout the state.

FESTIVALS

Cultural life in Rajasthan is characterized by numerous religious festivals. Among the most popular of these celebrations is the Gangor festival, during which clay images of Mahadevi and Parvati (representing the benevolent aspects of the Hindu mother goddess) are worshipped by women of all castes for 15 days and are then taken out to be immersed in water. Another important festival, held at Pushkar near Ajmer, takes the form of a mixed religious festival and livestock fair; Hindu pilgrims come seeking salvation during the celebration, while farmers from all corners of the state bring their camels and cattle to show and sell. The tomb of the Ṣūfī mystic Khwājah Muʿīn al-Dīn Chishtī at Ajmer is one of the most sacred Muslim shrines in India. Hundreds of thousands of pilgrims, many

Hindu pilgrims gathering at Pushkar, in the Thar Desert, Rajasthan state, India. © Brian A. Vikander/West Light

from foreign countries, visit the shrine on the occasion of the saint's *'urs* (death anniversary).

HISTORY

Archaeological evidence indicates that early humans lived along the banks of the Banas River and its tributaries some 100,000 years ago. The Indus (Harappan) and post-Indus civilizations (3rd–2nd millennium BCE) are traceable at Kalibangan in northern Rajasthan, as well as at Ahar and Gilund, both near the city of Udaipur in the south. Pottery fragments at Kalibangan date to 2700 BCE. The discovery near Bairat (in north-central Rajasthan) of two rock inscriptions from the 3rd century BCE indicate that the area was at that time under the rule of Ashoka, the last great emperor of the Mauryan dynasty of India. The whole or parts of present-day Rajasthan were ruled by Bactrian (Indo-Greek) kings in the 2nd century BCE, the Shaka satraps (Scythians) from the 2nd to the 4th century CE, the Gupta dynasty from the early 4th to the late 6th century, the Hephthalites (Hunas) in the 6th century, and Harsha (Harshavardhana), a Rajput ruler, in the early 7th century.

Several Rajput dynasties arose between the 7th and 11th centuries, including that of the Gurjara-Pratiharas, who kept the Arab invaders of the Sindh area (now in southeastern Pakistan) at bay. Under Bhoja I (or Mihira Bhoja;

836–885), the territory of the Gurjara-Pratiharas stretched from the foothills of the Himalayas southward to the Narmada River and from the lower Ganges (Ganga) River valley westward to Sindh. With the disintegration of this empire by the late 10th century, several rival Rajput clans came to power in Rajasthan. The Guhilas, feudal lords of the Pratiharas, asserted their independence in 940 and established control of the region around Mewar (present-day Udaipur). By the 11th century the Chauhans (Chahamanas), with their capital at Ajmer and later at Delhi, had emerged as the major power in the eastern region. In the following centuries other clans, such as the Kachwahas, Bhattis, and Rathors, succeeded in establishing independent kingdoms in the area.

The second of a series of encounters known as the Battles of Taraori (Tarain), fought near Delhi in 1192, initiated a new period in Rajasthan's history. Muḥammad Ghūrī's victory over a Rajput army under Prithviraja III not only led to the destruction of Rajput power in the Indo-Gangetic plain but also firmly established the Muslim presence in northern India. As Muslim forces pushed south and then west along the traditional routes to the Kathiawar Peninsula (Saurashtra; now part of the state of Gujarat), the Rajput kingdoms of what is now Rajasthan were encircled. The next four centuries saw repeated, though unsuccessful, attempts by the central power based in Delhi to subdue the Rajput states of the region.

The Rajputs, however, despite common historical and cultural traditions, were never able to unite to inflict a decisive defeat on their opponents.

Rajput strength reached its zenith at the beginning of the 16th century under Rana Sanga (Rana Sangram Singh) of Mewar, but he was defeated in a fierce battle by the Mughal invader Bābur, and the brief splendour of a united Rajput polity waned rapidly. It is largely from this period of Rajasthan's history that the romantic view of the Rajput as a valiant warrior is derived.

Toward the end of the 16th century, the Mughal emperor Akbar was able to achieve, through diplomacy and military action, what his predecessors had been unable to accomplish by force alone. Military campaigns were still undertaken by imperial Mughal forces, and Rajput strongholds, such as Ranthambhor and Chittaurgarh (Chitor), were besieged and destroyed (1567–68), but Akbar also entered into a series of alliances with numerous Rajput ruling houses, arranging marriages with Rajput princesses for himself and for his heirs. Akbar's son and successor, Jahāngīr (ruled 1605–27), as well as Jahāngīr's third son and builder of the Taj Mahal, Shah Jahān (ruled 1628–58), were both born of Rajput mothers. Mughal-Rajput marriages continued until the early 18th century, bringing many Rajput states (along with their not insubstantial military resources) into the imperial fold without costly military subjugation. Furthermore, some Rajput rulers, such as Man Singh of Amber (Jaipur) and Jaswant Singh of Marwar (Jodhpur), served with loyalty and distinction in the imperial Mughal forces. Under Akbar, the Rajput states of the region were grouped together under the Suba of Ajmer, an administrative unit of the Mughal Empire.

Rajput palace between Ajmer and Jaipur, Rajasthan, India; built by Man Singh, 16th century.
A.C. Lyon

After the death of the emperor Aurangzeb in 1707, the Rajput state of Bharatpur was developed by a Jat (peasant caste) conqueror, but by 1803 most of the surrounding states paid tribute to the Maratha dynasties of west-central India. Later in the 19th century the British subdued the Marathas and, having established paramountcy in the region, organized the Rajput states into Rajputana province. The government of India was represented in Rajputana by a political officer, with the title of agent to the governor-general, who was also chief commissioner of the small British province of Ajmer-Merwara. Under him were residents and political agents who were accredited to the various states.

It was during this period that the idea of Indian nationalism was born. In Udaipur, Dayananda Sarasvati wrote his *Satyarth Prakash*; intended to restore Hinduism to its pristine purity, the work created a ferment in Rajputana. Important movements of thought also occurred among the Jaina sadhus (holy men) and scholars. Ajmer was the centre of political activity, and nationalist leaders included Arjun Lal Sethi, Manik Lal Varma, Gopal Singh, and Jai Narain Vyas.

After India became independent in 1947, the princely states and chiefships of Rajputana were integrated by stages into a single entity. They were first grouped into small unions, such as the Matsya Union and the Rajasthan Union, which were merged with the remaining Rajput states to create Greater Rajasthan in 1949. When the new constitution of India came into force in 1950, the state of Rajasthan became an integral part of India. The Rajput princes—though retaining a recognition of their original title, some special privileges, and a privy purse—surrendered their political powers to the central government. When the States Reorganization Act was implemented in 1956, Rajasthan acquired the shape that it has today. The privileged status given to rulers of the former princely states was discontinued in 1970.

UTTAR PRADESH

Uttar Pradesh, the most populous state of India, lies in north-central India. It is bordered by the state of Uttarakhand and the country of Nepal to the north, the state of Bihar to the east, the states of Jharkhand and Chhattisgarh to the southeast, the state of Madhya Pradesh to the south, and the states of Rajasthan and Haryana and the national capital territory of Delhi to the west. On Jan. 26, 1950, when India became a republic, the state was given its present name, Uttar Pradesh (literally, "Northern State"). Its capital is Lucknow. Area 93,933 square miles (243,286 square km). Pop. (2008 est.) 190,891,000.

LAND

The state can be divided into two physiographic regions: the central plains of the

Ganges (Ganga) River and its tributaries (part of the Indo-Gangetic Plain) and the southern uplands.

Relief

The vast majority of Uttar Pradesh lies within the Gangetic Plain, which is composed of alluvial deposits brought down from the Himalayas by the Ganges network. Most of this area is a featureless, though fertile, plain varying in elevation from about 1,000 feet (300 metres) in the northwest to about 190 feet (60 metres) in the extreme east. The southern uplands form part of the highly dissected and rugged Vindhya Range, which rises generally toward the southeast. The elevation of this region rarely exceeds 1,000 feet.

Drainage

The state is well drained by a number of rivers originating in either the Himalayas to the north or the Vindhya Range to the south. The Ganges and its main tributaries—the Yamuna, the Ramganga, the Gomati, the Ghaghara, and the Gandak—are fed by the perpetual snows of the Himalayas. The Chambal, the Betwa, and the Ken, originating from the Vindhya Range, drain the southwestern part of the state before joining the Yamuna. The Son, also originating in the Vindhya Range, drains the southeastern part of the state and joins the Ganges beyond the state borders (in Bihar).

Soils

Much of the area of Uttar Pradesh is covered by a deep layer of alluvium spread by the slow-moving rivers of the Ganges system. These extremely fertile alluvial soils range from sandy to clayey loam. The soils in the southern part of the state are generally mixed red and black or red-to-yellow.

Climate

The climate of Uttar Pradesh is the tropical monsoon type, with warm weather year-round. Average high temperatures in Lucknow range from about 70 °F (low 20s C) in January to over 100 °F (38 °C) in May and June. High temperatures of around 120 °F (50 °C) have been recorded at Gonda.

Annual rainfall in the state ranges from 40–80 inches (1,000–2,000 mm) in the east to 24–40 inches (600–1,000 mm) in the west. About 90 percent of the rainfall occurs during the southwest monsoon, lasting from about June to September. With most of the rainfall concentrated during this four-month period, floods are a recurring problem and can cause fatalities and heavy damage to crops and property, particularly in the eastern part of the state. Periodic failure of monsoons results in drought conditions.

Plant and Animal Life

The vegetation of Uttar Pradesh consists mostly of scrub. Forests are generally concentrated in the southern uplands. Animals of the region include tigers, leopards, elephants, wild boars, and crocodiles, as well as pigeons, doves, wild ducks, partridges, peafowls, blue jays, quails, and woodpeckers. Several species, such as lions from the Gangetic Plain, have become extinct. To preserve its wildlife, the state has established several game sanctuaries.

PEOPLE

Uttar Pradesh is the most populous state in India. In the early 21st century it had an overall population density of more than twice the national average. The Gangetic Plain supports the overwhelming majority of the state's population.

POPULATION COMPOSITION

Roughly one-fifth of the state's people belong to groups known as Scheduled Castes (formerly "untouchables"; groups that officially occupy a low position within the caste system). A tiny percentage of the people belong to Scheduled Tribes (a term generally applied to indigenous peoples who fall outside the predominant Indian social hierarchy). The vast majority of the people, including members of all levels of the caste hierarchy, are Hindus. Muslims are the largest religious minority. There also are relatively small groups of Sikhs, Christians, Jains, and Buddhists. Hindi is an official language of the state and the mother tongue of most of the people. Urdu, additionally an official language, is primarily spoken by Muslims. The vernacular Hindustani is widely understood.

SETTLEMENT PATTERNS

The majority of the state's population lives in rural areas. The rural settlements are characterized by compact villages in the western part of the state, groupings of hamlets in the eastern part, and a combination of the two in the central part. A traditional village in Uttar Pradesh is a cluster of mud huts with roofs made of thatch (such as straw) or clay tiles and few amenities of modern living. Villages near the cities, however, are likely to have cement-plastered homes, paved roads, and electricity.

Most urban inhabitants live in cities with populations of more than 100,000. Among the largest cities of Uttar Pradesh are Kanpur, Lucknow, Agra, Varanasi, Meerut, and Allahabad. Kanpur, located in the central portion of the state, is the premier industrial city of Uttar Pradesh. Lucknow, the state capital, is about 30 miles (48 km) northeast of Kanpur. Agra, in the western part of the state, is the site of the Taj Mahal, a mausoleum built by the Mughal emperor Shah Jahan (ruled 1628–58) in memory of his wife; it is the most famous tourist attraction in India. Varanasi, the city most sacred to Hindus, is one of the world's oldest continuously inhabited cities. Meerut, northeast of

Delhi, is an important centre of transportation, trade, and industry. Allahabad (on the site of the ancient holy city of Prayag), located at the confluence of the Ganges and the Yamuna River, is another city sacred to Hindus.

DEMOGRAPHIC TRENDS

The population of Uttar Pradesh continues to grow at a high rate. Because of this high growth rate and a substantial reduction in infant mortality in the 20th century, there has been a significant increase in the proportion of young adults and children. The sex ratio also has improved; in 2001 there were 898 females per 1,000 males, up from 876 per 1,000 in 1991. Toward the end of the 19th century, dire poverty and the promise of better opportunities forced many people of the region to migrate to distant lands, such as South Africa, Mauritius, Fiji, and the West Indies. In more recent years, migration from Uttar Pradesh has been mainly to other parts of India, particularly to large cities such as Kolkata (Calcutta), Mumbai (Bombay), and Delhi.

ECONOMY

Agriculture is the mainstay of the state's economy, although mining (notably of coal) is also important. Industrial activity is focused largely on processing raw materials. The service sector has become more significant, particularly activity associated with tourism.

AGRICULTURE

The chief crops are rice, wheat, and sugarcane. Since the late 1960s, with the introduction of high-yielding varieties of seed for wheat and rice, greater availability of fertilizers, and increased use of irrigation, the state has become a major producer of food grains in the country. Many of its farmers, however, still suffer from two major constraints: small landholdings and insufficient resources to invest in the technology required for improved production. Livestock and dairy farming often provide a supplementary source of income.

RESOURCES AND POWER

Silica, limestone, and coal are found in considerable quantities in Uttar Pradesh. There also are small reserves of gypsum, magnesite, phosphorite, and bauxite. The national government has supported the development of coal fields in the southeastern area around Mirzapur.

The state often suffers from shortages of power. Installed capacity has greatly increased since Indian independence, but the gap between supply and demand remains wide. Power is generated at the Obra-Rihand complex (in southeastern Uttar Pradesh), one of India's biggest thermal stations; at a number of hydroelectric power plants in various parts of the state; and at a nuclear power station in the western district of Bulandshahr (near Delhi).

MANUFACTURING

Textiles and sugar refining, both long-standing industries in Uttar Pradesh, employ an important percentage of the state's total factory labour. Other resource-based industries in Uttar Pradesh produce vegetable oil, jute, and cement. The Indian government established a number of large factories that manufacture heavy equipment, machinery, steel, aircraft, telephone and electronics equipment, and fertilizers. The national government has funded an oil refinery at Mathura. The state government has promoted medium- and small-scale industries.

The state's exports include such products as footwear, leather goods, and sporting gear. Handicrafts constitute a significant portion of exports as well. Carpets from Bhadohi and Mirzapur, for example, are prized worldwide. Among other local specialities are the silks and brocades of Varanasi, ornamental brass ware from Moradabad, *chikan* embroidery from Lucknow, ebony work from Nagina, glassware from Firozabad, and carved woodwork from Saharanpur.

TOURISM

Tourism in the state is of growing economic importance. Many visitors flock to Hindu centres such as Varanasi, Allahabad, Ayodhya, and the Mathura-Vrindavan area; Buddhist centres such as Sarnath, Kasia (site of Kushinagara, where the Buddha died), and Shravasti; and other historic places such as Agra, Lucknow, and Kannauj.

TRANSPORTATION

The state's cities and towns are connected by a vast network of roads, including a number of national highways, and railways. Major cities in Uttar Pradesh are connected by air to Delhi and other large cities of India. The three inland waterways of the Ganges, Yamuna, and Ghaghara rivers also are an integral part of the state's transportation system.

GOVERNMENT AND SOCIETY

The government of Uttar Pradesh, like that of most other states in India, is determined by the national constitution of 1950 and consists of executive, legislative, and judicial branches.

CONSTITUTIONAL FRAMEWORK

The executive branch comprises the governor and the Council of Ministers (headed by a chief minister), which aids and advises the governor. The governor is appointed by the president of India; the governor in turn appoints the chief minister and the other ministers. The Council of Ministers is responsible to the legislature. The legislature consists of two houses: the upper house, the Legislative Council (Vidhan Parishad), which comprises both elected and appointed members; and the lower house, the Legislative Assembly (Vidhan Sabha), whose members are popularly elected. The judiciary includes the High Court, headed by a chief justice, and a subordinate justice system. Below the state level, dozens of district governments are responsible for local administration.

HEALTH AND WELFARE

Health care in the state is provided by a number of hospitals and clinics, as well as by private practitioners of allopathic (Western), homeopathic, Ayurvedic (traditional Hindu), and Unanī (traditional Muslim) medicine. Since independence many national and state welfare programs have provided improved opportunities in education, employment, and political representation to members of the Scheduled Castes and Scheduled Tribes.

EDUCATION

Beginning in the 1950s, both the number of schools in Uttar Pradesh and the number of students enrolled at all levels grew dramatically. In 1951 only about 12 percent of the population was literate; by 2001 the literacy rate had risen to about 57 percent, a figure close to the national rate. Hindi is the medium of instruction at the primary-school level (English is used at some private schools), Hindi and English are required courses for high school students, and English is generally

the medium of instruction at the university level.

The state has more than a dozen universities, hundreds of affiliated colleges, and several medical colleges. Some of the oldest universities in Uttar Pradesh are Aligarh Muslim University (1875), founded by Sir Sayyid Ahmad Khan; Banaras Hindu University (1916), founded by Pandit Madan Mohan Malaviya; and the University of Lucknow (1921). Among the state's many institutes for specialized studies and research are the Indian Institute of Technology at Kanpur (1959), the Indian Institute of Management at Lucknow (1984), the Indian Institute of Information Technology at Allahabad (1999), and several polytechnic schools, engineering institutes, and industrial training institutes.

CULTURAL LIFE

Uttar Pradesh is the springhead of the ancient civilization of the Hindus. Much of India's cultural heritage in literature, the visual and performing arts, and architecture had its origins in the state.

THE ARTS

A substantial portion of the subcontinent's ancient Vedic literature had its origin in the area's many hermitages, as did the great Indian epics the *Ramayana* and the *Mahabharata* (which includes the *Bhagavadgita* [Sanskrit: "Song of the Lord"]). Sculptures and architecture of the Buddhist-Hindu period (*c.* 600 BCE to *c.* 1200 CE) have contributed greatly to the Indian cultural heritage. Since 1947 the emblem of the government of India has been based on the four-lion capital of a pillar (preserved in a museum at Sarnath, near Varanasi) left by the 3rd-century-BCE Mauryan emperor Ashoka.

Architecture, painting, music, and dance all flourished during the Mughal period (16th–18th centuries). Mughal architecture reached its height under the emperor Shah Jahān, who built the spectacular Taj Mahal at Agra. Paintings of the period were generally portraits or illustrations of religious and historic texts. Much of the musical tradition in Uttar Pradesh also was developed during the period. The type of music performed by Tansen and Baiju Bawra, contemporaries of the Mughal emperor Akbar, is still well known in the state and throughout India. The sitar (a stringed instrument of the lute family) and the tabla (consisting of two small drums)—perhaps the two most popular instruments of Indian music—were developed in the region during this period. The *kathak* classical dance style, which originated in the 18th century as a devotional dance in the temples of Vrindavan and Mathura, is the most popular form of classical dance in northern India.

As the birthplace of Hindi, an official language of the state and the country, Uttar Pradesh is an important centre of Hindi literature. Although various

A yakshi (female nature spirit) holding tray and pitcher, red sandstone relief from Mathura, Uttar Pradesh, India, 2nd century CE; in the Archaeological Museum, Mathura. P. Chandra

vernacular forms of the language developed over the centuries, literary Hindi (like Urdu) did not take its present form until the 19th century. Bhartendu Harishchandra (1850–85) of Varanasi was one of the first major writers to use this form of Hindi as a literary medium.

CULTURAL INSTITUTIONS

Among the prominent art museums in Uttar Pradesh are the State Museum at Lucknow; the Archaeological Museum at Mathura; the Sarnath Museum, specializing in Buddhist antiquities; the Bharat Kala Bhavan, a museum of art and archaeology at Varanasi; and the Municipal Museum at Allahabad. Colleges of arts and Hindustani music at Lucknow and the Prayag Sangeet Samiti, a music institute based in Allahabad, have contributed immensely to the development of the fine arts and of classical music in the country. Such organizations as the Nagri Pracharni Sabha, the Hindi Sahitya Sammelan, and the Hindustani Academy have been instrumental in the development of Hindi literature. In addition, the Uttar Pradesh Urdu Academy was set up by the state government for the preservation and enrichment of Urdu literature.

FESTIVALS AND HOLIDAYS

Most of the festivals and holidays in the state are tied to the Hindu calendar. They include Dussehra, celebrating the victory of Rama over Ravana, the symbol of evil on earth; Diwali, a festival of lights devoted to Lakshmi, the goddess of wealth; Shivaratri, a day devoted to the worship of the god Shiva; Holi, a colourful spring festival; and Janmashtami, celebrating the birthday of the god Krishna. Important religious occasions for Muslims in Uttar Pradesh include *mawlids*, birthdays of holy figures; Muḥarram, commemorating the martyrdom of the hero al-Ḥusayn ibn ʿĀli; Ramadan, a month devoted to fasting; and the canonical festivals of ʿĪd al-Fiṭr and ʿĪd al-Aḍḥā. Buddha Purnima (also known as Wesak or Vesak), commemorating the Buddha's birth, enlightenment, and death; Mahavira Jayanti, marking the birthday of the saviour Mahavira; Guru Nanak's birthday; and Christmas are important to Buddhists, Jains, Sikhs, and Christians, respectively, but are celebrated by people of all faiths. More than 2,000 fairs take place annually in the state. The largest religious festival of India, the Kumbh Mela, held at Allahabad every 12 years, attracts millions of people.

HISTORY

The history of Uttar Pradesh can be divided into five periods: (1) prehistory and mythology (up to c. 600 BCE), (2) the Buddhist-Hindu period (c. 600 BCE to c. 1200 CE), (3) the Muslim period (c. 1200 to c. 1775), (4) the British period (c. 1775 to 1947), and (5) the postindependence period (1947 to the present). Because of its position in the heart of the Indo-Gangetic Plain, it has often been the focal point in the history of all of northern India.

PREHISTORY AND MYTHOLOGY

Archaeology has shed new light on the prehistoric civilization of what is now Uttar Pradesh. The remains of several human skeletons found in the area of Partapgarh (Pratapgarh) have been dated to about 10,000 BCE. Other knowledge of the area prior to the 7th century BCE has been gained largely through Vedic literature (of the ancient Indian Vedic religion) and the two great Indian epics, the *Ramayana* and the *Mahabharata*, which describe the Gangetic Plain within Uttar Pradesh. The setting of the *Mahabharata* is the area around Hastinapur, in the western part of the present-day state, while the *Ramayana* is set in and around Ayodhya, the birthplace of Rama (an incarnation of the god Vishnu and the hero of the story). Another fountainhead of mythology in the state is the area around the holy cities of Mathura, where Krishna (another incarnation of Vishnu) was born, and nearby Vrindavan.

THE BUDDHIST-HINDU PERIOD

A systematic history of India and the area of Uttar Pradesh dates to the end of the 7th century BCE, when 16 *mahajanapadas* (great states) in northern India were contending for supremacy. Of these, seven fell entirely within the present-day boundaries of Uttar Pradesh. From the 5th century BCE to the 6th century CE, the region was mostly under the control of powers centred outside the modern boundaries of the state, first at Magadha in present-day Bihar and later at Ujjain in present-day Madhya Pradesh. Among the great kings who ruled over the region were Chandragupta (reigned *c.* 321–297 BCE) and Ashoka (3rd century BCE), both Mauryan emperors, as well as Samudra Gupta (4th century CE) and Chandra Gupta II (reigned *c.* 380–415). A later famous ruler, Harsha (reigned *c.* 606–647), was based within the state's present borders. From his capital at Kanyakubja (present-day Kannauj), he was able to control the whole of Uttar Pradesh as well as parts of what are now Bihar, Madhya Pradesh, Punjab, and Rajasthan.

Meanwhile, by the 6th century BCE, the ancient Vedic religion had largely evolved into Brahmanism, which in turn would evolve into classical Hinduism by the 2nd century BCE. According to tradition, it was during this period—likely sometime between the 6th and 4th centuries BCE—that the Buddha preached his first sermon at Sarnath, near Varanasi. The religion he founded, Buddhism, spread not only across India but also to many distant lands, such as China and Japan. The Buddha is said to have attained *parinirvana* (complete nirvana) at Kushinagara (now in Kasia, in eastern Uttar Pradesh).

At first, Buddhist and Brahmanic or Hindu culture flourished side by side.

Sculptures and architecture replete with Buddhist symbolism reached their zenith during the 3rd-century-BCE reign of Ashoka. Hindu art saw its greatest development during the period of rule by the Gupta dynasty (4th to 6th centuries CE). After the death of Harsha, about 647, there was a gradual downfall of Buddhism accompanied by a revival of Hinduism. The chief architect of this revival, the philosopher Shankara, born in southern India, visited Varanasi, traveled through the plains of Uttar Pradesh, and is thought to have established the famous temple at Badrinath (now in Uttarakhand) in the Himalayas.

THE MUSLIM PERIOD

Although Muslim incursions into the area occurred as early as 1000–30 CE, Muslim rule over northern India was not established until the last decade of the 12th century, when Mu'izz al-Dīn Muḥammad ibn Sām (Muḥammad Ghūrī) defeated the Gahadavalas (who occupied much of Uttar Pradesh) and other competing dynasties. For nearly 600 years Uttar Pradesh, like much of India, was ruled by one Muslim dynasty or another, each centred in or near Delhi.

In 1526 Bābur—a descendant of the conquerors Genghis Khan and Timur—defeated Sultan Ibrāhīm Lodī of Delhi and laid the foundation of the most successful of the Muslim dynasties, the Mughals, whose empire, centred in what is now Uttar Pradesh, dominated the subcontinent for more than 200 years. The greatest extent of the empire came under Akbar (reigned 1556–1605), who constructed a grand new capital, Fatehpur Sikri, near Agra. His grandson, Shah Jahān (reigned 1628–58), built at Agra one of the world's greatest architectural achievements, the Taj Mahal (a mausoleum constructed in memory of his favourite wife, who died in childbirth). Shah Jahān also built several other architecturally important buildings in Agra as well as in Delhi.

The Mughal Empire promoted the development of a new composite culture. Akbar, its greatest exponent, employed in his court men preeminent in architecture, literature, painting, and music, irrespective of their caste or creed. Several new sects seeking a common ground between Hinduism and Islam, as well as between the various castes of India, developed during this period. Ramananda (c. 1400–70), a Brahman (Hindu priest), founded a *bhakti* (devotional) sect that claimed that salvation was not dependent on one's sex or caste; Kabīr (1440–1518) preached the essential unity of all religions. The downfall of the Mughals in the 18th century led to the shifting of the centre of this composite culture from Delhi to Lucknow, the

The Hindu deity Vishnu reclining on the serpent Sesha; sandstone relief panel on the Vishnu temple at Deogarh, Uttar Pradesh, India, 5th century CE. P. Chandra

seat of the nawab (ruler) of Oudh (now Ayodhya), where art, literature, music, and poetry flourished in an atmosphere of communal harmony.

THE BRITISH PERIOD

The area of present-day Uttar Pradesh was gradually acquired by the East India Company (a British trading company) over a period of about 75 years, from the last quarter of the 18th century to the mid-19th century. Territories wrested from a number of powers in the northern part of the Indian subcontinent—the nawabs, the Sindhias of Gwalior (now in Madhya Pradesh), and the Gurkhas of Nepal—were first placed within the British province known as the Bengal Presidency, but in 1833 they were separated to form the North-Western Provinces (initially called the Agra Presidency). The kingdom of Oudh, annexed by the company in 1856, was united with the North-Western Provinces in 1877. The resulting administrative unit had borders almost identical to those of the future state of Uttar Pradesh. In 1902 the name was changed to the United Provinces of Agra and Oudh (later shortened to the United Provinces).

The Indian Mutiny, a widespread revolt against the East India Company in 1857–58, was centred in the United Provinces. Sparked by a mutiny of soldiers at Meerut on May 10, 1857, the revolt spread within months to more than 25 cities. In 1858, with the revolt virtually crushed, administration of the United Provinces and the rest of British India were transferred from the East India Company to the British crown.

With the rise of Indian nationalism beginning in the late 1880s, the United Provinces stood at the forefront of the movement for independence. It gave India many of the most important nationalist political leaders, such as Motilal Nehru, Pandit Madan Mohan Malaviya, Jawaharlal Nehru, and Purushottam Das Tandon. Mahatma Gandhi's noncooperation movement of 1920–22, designed to shake the foundations of the British Empire in India, spread throughout the United Provinces, but mob violence in the village of Chauri Chaura (in the eastern part of the provinces) caused Gandhi to suspend the movement. The United Provinces was also a centre of Muslim League politics.

Throughout the British period, there was extensive development of canals, railways, and other means of communication within the provinces. The British also promoted the growth of modern education, and a number of colleges and universities were established.

UTTAR PRADESH SINCE INDIAN INDEPENDENCE

In 1947 the United Provinces became one of the administrative units of the newly independent Dominion of India. Two years later the autonomous states of Tehri-Garhwal (now in Uttarakhand),

Rampur, and Varanasi, all within its borders, were incorporated into the United Provinces. With the adoption of a new Indian constitution in 1950, the United Provinces were renamed Uttar Pradesh and became a constituent state of the Republic of India.

Since independence, the state has maintained a dominant role within India. It has given the country several prime ministers, including Jawaharlal Nehru; Nehru's daughter, Indira Gandhi; and Atal Bihari Vajpayee of the Bharatiya Janata Party. Prominent leaders of national opposition (minority) parties, such as Acharya Narendra Dev, one of the founders of the Praja Socialist Party, also have hailed from Uttar Pradesh. At the state level, politics have tended to be fractious.

Soon after the formation of Uttar Pradesh, unrest developed in the Himalayan regions of the state. The people there felt that the state's very large population and physical dimensions made it impossible for the government, seated in Lucknow, to look after their interests. Widespread unemployment and poverty and an inadequate infrastructure contributed to their discontent. Their demand for a separate state gained momentum in the 1990s. Agitation was heightened by a violent incident in Muzaffarnagar on Oct. 2, 1994, when police fired at pro-statehood demonstrators; a number of people were killed. Finally, in November 2000 the new state of Uttaranchal (renamed Uttarakhand in 2007) was carved out of the northwestern part of Uttar Pradesh.

CHAPTER 10

SELECTED NORTHEASTERN INDIAN STATES

Northeastern India is marked by two distinctive topographies: the vast, densely populated alluvial lowlands of the Ganges (west) and Brahmaputra (east) river valleys and the relatively remote uplands of the far northeast. The states highlighted in this chapter are representative of those two landscapes.

ASSAM

Assam state is located in the northeastern part of India and is bounded to the north by the kingdom of Bhutan and the state of Arunachal Pradesh, to the east by the states of Nagaland and Manipur, to the south by the states of Mizoram and Tripura, and to the west by Bangladesh and the states of Meghalaya and West Bengal. The name Assam is derived from the word *asama*, meaning "peerless" in the now extinct Ahom language. The neighbouring states of Arunachal Pradesh, Nagaland, Mizoram, and Meghalaya were once part of Assam. The capital, formerly Shillong (now the capital of Meghalaya), was shifted to Dispur, a suburb of Guwahati, in 1972. Area 30,285 square miles (78,438 square km). Pop. (2008 est.) 29,929,000.

LAND

A land of plains and river valleys, Assam has three principal physical regions—the Brahmaputra River valley in the north, the Barak River (upper Surma River) valley in the south, and the hilly region between Meghalaya (to the west) and Nagaland and Manipur (to the east) in the south-central part of the state.

RELIEF AND DRAINAGE

Of these three regions, the Brahmaputra River valley is the largest. According to Hindu mythology, the Brahmaputra rises as the son of the god Brahma from a sacred pool known as the Brahmakund, in neighbouring Arunachal Pradesh. The river enters Assam near Sadiya in the extreme northeast and runs westward through the length of Assam for nearly 450 miles (725 km) before turning south to enter the plains of Bangladesh. Studded with low, isolated hills and ridges that rise abruptly from the plain, the valley is rarely more than 50 miles (80 km) wide and is surrounded on all sides, except on the west, by mountains. Numerous streams and rivulets that flow from the neighbouring hills empty into the Brahmaputra. Although only a small portion of the Barak River valley lies within Assam's borders, it nevertheless forms an extensive lowland area that is important for agriculture in the state's southern region. Geologically, the Brahmaputra and Barak valleys lie on ancient alluvial sediments, which themselves cover a variety of deposits from the Neogene and Paleogene periods (i.e., some 2.6 to 65 million years old). Among these deposits are hard sandstone, soft and loose sand, conglomerates, coal seams, shales, sandy clays, and limestone.

The south-central hills between Meghalaya, Nagaland, and Manipur include the North Cachar Hills and form part of the Meghalaya Plateau, which may have been an extension of Gondwana (an ancient landmass in the Southern Hemisphere that once grouped together South America, Africa, Australia, and part of the Indian subcontinent). Isolated from the main plateau by the embayments of the Kepili River, this upland displays a rugged topography. It generally has a northerly slope, with average elevations ranging from about 1,500 feet (450 metres) to about 3,300 feet (1,000 metres).

Roughly between the Brahmaputra valley and the south-central hill region are the northern ranges, which extend northeastward from Dabaka (east of Dispur) to Bokakhat in east-central Assam. The Rengma Hills to the south of the ridge average about 3,000 feet (900 metres). Their most prominent peak is Chenghehishon (4,460 feet [1,360 metres]).

Earthquakes are common in Assam. Among the most severe are those recorded in 1897, with the Shillong Plateau as the epicentre; in 1930, with Dhuburi as the epicentre; and in 1950, with Zayu

(Rima) in Tibet at the Arunachal Pradesh border as the epicentre. The 1950 earthquake is considered one of the most disastrous in South Asia's history. It created heavy landslides that blocked the courses of many hill streams. The floods that followed the bursting of these earthquake-generated dams caused more loss of life and property than the earthquake itself.

CLIMATE

Average temperatures in Assam range from highs in the upper 90s F (about 36 °C) in August to lows in the mid-40s F (about 7 °C) in January. The cool season generally lasts from October to February and is marked by fogs and brief showers. The state escapes the normal Indian hot, dry season. Although some rain occurs from March through May, the heaviest precipitation comes with the southwest monsoon, which arrives in June, stays through September, and often causes widespread and destructive flooding. Annual rainfall in Assam is not only the highest in the country but also ranks among the highest in the world; its annual average varies from about 70 inches (1,800 mm) in the west to more than 120 inches (3,000 mm) in the east.

PLANT AND ANIMAL LIFE

Forests, formerly extending over nearly two-fifths of the state's area, were reduced by the creation of Meghalaya and Mizoram in the early 1970s. In the early 21st century about one-third of Assam was covered with various types of woodlands, including tropical evergreen and deciduous forests, broad-leaved hill forests, pine forests, and swamp forests, as well as grasslands. Assam is home to some 75 species of trees, many of which have commercial value. Sal (*Shorea robusta*) and hollong (*Dipterocarpus rhetusus*) trees are among the most bountiful of the hardwoods. Bamboo, orchids, and ferns also are abundant.

Assam has numerous wildlife sanctuaries, the most prominent of which are two UNESCO World Heritage sites—the Kaziranga National Park (inscribed in 1985), on the bank of the Brahmaputra River, and the Manas Wildlife Sanctuary (inscribed in 1992), near the border with Bhutan. Both are refuges for the fast-disappearing Indian one-horned rhinoceros, and the sanctuary at Manas is known especially for its tigers and leopards. Among the other notable inhabitants of Assam's forests are elephants, gaurs (wild oxen), wild pigs, various species of deer, and primates, such as langurs and hoolock gibbons. Common birds include cormorants, herons, ducks, and other water birds, as well as warblers, thrushes, owls, and peacocks. Hornbills are characteristic of Assam, although they are endangered in some areas. The state also has dozens of species of reptiles, including poisonous snakes, such as kraits, cobras, and vipers; an array of lizards, skinks, and geckos; and many types of turtles.

PEOPLE

Assam has an ethnically diverse population that reflects the state's geographic position at the juncture between China, Southeast Asia, and the Indian subcontinent.

POPULATION COMPOSITION

The people of the plains of the Brahmaputra and Barak valleys are mainly of Indo-Iranian ancestry. By the time of their arrival

Shaiva temple in Sibsagar, Assam, India. Foto Features

in the region, however, the local Aryan peoples had become intermixed with Asiatic peoples. The Ahom people, who arrived in the region from mainland Southeast Asia during the 13th century, ultimately stem from Yunnan province of southern China. A significant minority of the population consists of rural indigenous peoples who fall outside the Indian caste system; as such, they are officially designated as Scheduled Tribes. The Boro constitute the largest of these groups. Most of the Scheduled Tribes live in the south-central hill region and are of Asiatic descent.

Assamese, an Indo-Aryan language, is the official and principal language of the state, and an unbroken record of Assamese literary history is traceable from the 14th century. Tibeto-Burman languages are spoken by most of the Scheduled Tribes, although the Khasi people speak an Austroasiatic tongue; some groups have adopted Assamese as their first language. The people in the Barak valley in southern Assam mostly speak Bengali (also called Bangla), which, like Assamese, is an Indo-Aryan language.

About two-thirds of the Assamese are Hindus, the majority of whom follow Vaishnavism, which venerates the deity Vishnu. Roughly one-fourth of the population practices Islam, most Muslims being settlers from Bangladesh or converts from the lower strata of Hindu society. Although many of the Scheduled Tribes have converted to Christianity, some continue to practice traditional local religions; the Mikir and Kachari peoples are mostly Hindus.

SETTLEMENT PATTERNS AND DEMOGRAPHIC TRENDS

The great majority of Assam's people live in rural areas. The distribution of population is uneven, however, reflecting the hilly terrain, the number of rivers, the forests, the small amount of cultivable land, and the lack of industrialization. The agricultural zone of the Barak River valley supports relatively dense settlement.

Since the late 20th century, population growth has been unusually rapid, mostly due to immigration into Assam of tea garden labourers, herders from Nepal, Muslims from West Bengal, and refugees from Bangladesh. Increasing population in the state's urban areas reflects not only the growth of industries and the expansion of commercial activity but also the tendency of many of the immigrants—particularly those from Bangladesh—to live near towns. In the early 21st century Guwahati had the most significant urban population.

ECONOMY

Agriculture is of basic importance to Assam, engaging about half of the total working population and generating roughly one-third of the state's gross product. Industry is much less developed than in other parts of the country.

AGRICULTURE, FORESTRY, AND FISHING

Rice accounts for more than two-thirds of the sown area. Tea and jute, widely cultivated in the Brahmaputra valley, are important foreign-exchange earners. Assam grows a large portion of the country's tea. Other crops include oilseeds, pulses (legumes, such as peas, beans, or lentils), corn (maize), sugarcane, rape (an oil-yielding plant, the leaves of which are used for fodder), mustard, potatoes, and fruits. Through improved cultivation methods, some farms yield more than one crop per year.

Livestock and dairy farming have shown moderate growth since the late 20th century, largely promoted by the government. Nevertheless, these activities remain but small contributors to the state's economy. Sericulture (raising of silk worms), on the other hand, is well established; Assam is a major producer of silk.

In the forestry sector, sal and other tropical hardwoods are highly valued. Depletion of forest resources and increased erosion, however, have led the government to impose logging bans and enact other legislation to reestablish the country's woodlands. Aside from timber, important forest products include bamboo, firewood, and lac (the source of shellac).

Aquaculture has been a major focus of agricultural development since the mid-1990s, and yields have increased. Overall yield, however, has continued to fall short of domestic demand.

RESOURCES AND POWER

Minerals exploited commercially in the state include petroleum, coal, natural gas, and limestone. Since the late 19th century, extensive oil reserves have been discovered in northeastern Assam; the refinery at Digboi, built in 1901, was the first in South Asia. Later, refineries were established in Guwahati and Nunmati. Coal—used locally by the railways, tea estates, and steamships—also is found in northeastern and south-central Assam. Liquefied natural gas is produced in the northeast, and limestone is quarried in the Mikir Hills.

Assam's energy is provided by thermal and hydroelectric plants. Less than half of the state's energy is generated locally, however. A significant portion of Assam's power is purchased from the national government, private sources, and, to a much lesser extent, other state governments.

MANUFACTURING

Development of the manufacturing sector has been inhibited by the state's isolation from the rest of India, by an underdeveloped transport system, by a small local market, and by the lack of sufficient capital. Small-scale industrial enterprises produce (or process) fertilizer, jute, paper, silk and textiles, sugar, chemicals, electronics, and cement. Sawmills and plywood and match factories make use of timber resources.

TRANSPORTATION

Historically, geography has inhibited the growth of efficient transport systems, and underdeveloped transport and communication systems have in turn hindered economic development in Assam. The Brahmaputra, for example, long has been a major barrier to integrating the transportation networks lying north and south of the river. The situation improved, however, with the opening of several rail and road bridges since the late 20th century.

With Assam's abundance of waterways, inland water transport is important. The Brahmaputra and Barak (Surma) rivers are the state's primary water channels. Numerous passenger ferries operate between various points on the Brahmaputra, and freight service is offered between Guwahati and Kolkata, West Bengal.

There is considerable air traffic between Assam and Kolkata. Among the towns with air service are Guwahati, Dibrugarh, Jorhat, Tezpur, and Silchar. The Guwahati airport offers international service.

GOVERNMENT AND SOCIETY

Like most other Indian states, Assam has a governmental structure that is defined by the national constitution of 1950.

CONSTITUTIONAL FRAMEWORK

The governor, who is the head of state, is appointed by the president of India and is assisted by a popularly elected unicameral legislature and a Council of Ministers. The state of Assam comprises about two dozen districts, each of which is administered by a deputy commissioner. Districts are subdivided at several levels, with the village as the smallest administrative unit.

The high court at Guwahati has jurisdiction not only over the state of Assam but also over the states of Nagaland, Meghalaya, Mizoram, Manipur, Tripura, and Arunachal Pradesh through outlying benches. The chief justice and all other high court justices are appointed by India's president. Permanent judges serve until they are a maximum of 62 years old. Short-term judges are appointed to help with periodic backlogs. Lower courts include district courts, sessions courts, and magistrate's courts.

EDUCATION AND WELFARE

Education, which is free up to the secondary level, is compulsory for children between the ages of 6 and 12. Government universities are located in the state's larger cities, including Guwahati, Jorhat, Dibrugarh, Tezpur, and Silchar. Assam also has specialized colleges in the arts, sciences, commerce, law, and medicine. Welfare-extension projects, operating through dozens of centres, provide recreational and cultural facilities for women and children.

CULTURAL LIFE

The cultural life of Assam is interwoven with the activities of a number of cultural institutions and religious centres, such as the *satra* (seat of a religious head known as the *satradhikar*) and *namghar* (prayer hall). *Satras* in Assam have been looking after the religious and social well-being of the Hindu population since the 15th century. The Assamese people observe all the pan-Indian religious festivals, but their most important celebrations are the three Bihu festivals. Originally agricultural festivals, these are observed with great enthusiasm irrespective of caste, creed, and religious affinity.

The Bohag Bihu, celebrated in the spring (usually mid-April), marks the commencement of the new year (first day of the Bohag or Baishakh month). Also known as Rangoli Bihu (from *rang*, meaning "merrymaking and fun"), it is accompanied by much dancing and singing. The Magh Bihu, celebrated in mid-January (in the month of Magh), is a harvest festival. Known also as Bhogali Bihu (from *bhog*, meaning "enjoyment and feasting"), it is a time of community feasts and bonfires. The third Bihu festival, the Kati Bihu (in mid-October or November), is also called the Kangali Bihu (from *kangali*, meaning "poor"), because by this time of year the house of an ordinary family is without food grains, as the stock is usually consumed before the next harvest.

Weaving is another important aspect of the cultural life of the people of Assam, particularly of the women. Nearly every Assamese household, irrespective of caste, creed, and social status, has at least one loom, and most women are expected to be skilled in producing fine silk and cotton cloths.

HISTORY

In the earliest recorded times, Assam was part of Kamarupa, a state that had its capital at Pragjyotishapura (now Guwahati). Ancient Kamarupa included roughly the Brahmaputra River valley, Bhutan, the Rangpur region (now in Bangladesh), and Koch Bihar, in West Bengal. King Narakasura and his son Bhagadatta were famous rulers of Kamarupa in the *Mahabharata* period (roughly 400 BCE to 200 CE). A Chinese traveler, Xuanzang, left a vivid account of the country and its people about 640 CE. Although information about the following centuries is meagre, clay seals and inscriptions on copper plates and stone that date from the 7th to the mid-12th century indicate that the inhabitants of the region attained considerable power and a fair degree of social, economic, and technological development. The copper plates further provide clues as to the locations of important ancient settlements and the routes connecting them.

Assam was ruled by various dynasties—the Pala, Koch, Kachari, and Chutiya—and there was constant warfare among the princes until the coming of the Ahom people in the 13th century. The Ahom crossed the Patkai Range from Myanmar (Burma) and conquered the local chieftains of the upper Assam plain. In the 15th century the Ahom, who gave their name to the region, were the dominant power in upper Assam. Two centuries later they defeated the Koch, Kachari, and other local rulers to gain control of lower Assam up to Goalpara. Ahom power and prosperity reached a zenith during the rule of King Rudra Singh (reigned 1696–1714), before the kingdom was occupied by warriors from Myanmar in the late 18th century.

Conflict among the princes gradually weakened the central administration until 1786, when the ruling prince, Gaurinath Singh, sought aid from Calcutta (Kolkata), which by that time had become the capital of British India. A British army officer, sent by the British governor-general in India, restored peace and subsequently was recalled, in spite of the protests of the Ahom king. Internal strife then caused one crisis after another until, in 1817, forces from Myanmar entered Assam in response to the appeal of a rebellious governor and ravaged the area.

The British, whose interests were threatened by these developments, ultimately drove out the invaders, and, after the Treaty of Yandabo was concluded with Myanmar in 1826, Assam became a part of British India. A British agent, representing the governor-general, was appointed to administer Assam, and in 1838 the area was incorporated into British-administered Bengal. By 1842 the whole of the Brahmaputra valley of Assam had come under British rule. A separate province of Assam (administered by a chief commissioner) was created in 1874 with its capital at Shillong. In 1905 Bengal was partitioned, and Assam was amalgamated with eastern Bengal; this created such resentment, however, that in 1912 Bengal was reunited, and Assam was once more made a separate province. During World War II, Assam was a major supply route for Allied forces operating in Burma. Several battles fought in the area in 1944 (e.g., at Bishenpur in Manipur and Kohima in Nagaland) were decisive in halting the Japanese advance into India.

With the partition and independence of India in 1947, the district of Sylhet (excluding the Karimganj subdivision) was ceded to Pakistan (the eastern portion of which later became Bangladesh). Assam became a constituent state of India in 1950. In 1961 and 1962 Chinese armed forces, disputing the McMahon Line as the boundary between India and Tibet, occupied part of the North East Frontier Agency (now Arunachal Pradesh but then part of Assam). In December 1962, however, they voluntarily withdrew to Tibet.

Since the early 1960s Assam has lost much territory to new states emerging from within its borders. In 1963 the Naga Hills district became the 16th state of India under the name of Nagaland. Part of Tuensang, a former territory of the North East Frontier Agency, was also added to Nagaland. In 1970, in response to the demands of the tribal peoples of the Meghalaya Plateau, the districts embracing the Khasi Hills, Jaintia Hills, and Garo Hills were formed into an autonomous state within Assam; in 1972 it became a separate state under the name of Meghalaya. Also in 1972 Arunachal Pradesh (the North East Frontier Agency) and Mizoram (from the Mizo Hills in the south) were separated from Assam as union territories; both became states in 1986.

Despite the separation of these ethnic-based states, communal tensions and violence have remained a problem in Assam. In the early 1980s, resentment among the Assamese against "foreigners," mostly immigrants from Bangladesh, led to widespread violence and considerable loss of life. Subsequently, disaffected Boro tribesmen (in Assam and Meghalaya) agitated for an autonomous state. The militant United Liberation Front of Assam waged a vigorous guerrilla campaign for the outright secession of Assam from India throughout the 1990s and into the 21st century.

BIHAR

Bihar state, in eastern India, is bounded by Nepal to the north and by the Indian states of West Bengal to the northeast and Uttar Pradesh to the west. In November 2000 the new state of Jharkhand was created from Bihar's southern provinces and now forms the state's southern and southeastern borders. The capital of Bihar is Patna.

Bihar occupied an important position in the early history of India; for centuries it was the principal seat of imperial powers and the main focus of Indian culture and civilization. The derivation of the name Bihar from the Sanskrit *vihara* (Buddhist monastery) reflects the prominence of such communities in the region in ancient times. Area 38,301 square miles (99,200 square km). Pop. (2008 est.) 93,823,000.

LAND

The state is naturally divided by the Ganges (Ganga) River into two regions—the North Bihar Plains and the South Bihar Plains. Together these two regions form part of the middle Gangetic Plain.

RELIEF, DRAINAGE, AND SOILS

Except for the foothills of the Himalayas in the extreme northwest, the North Bihar Plain is a flat alluvial region, less than 250 feet (75 metres) above sea level and prone to flooding. The Ghaghara, the Gandak, the Baghmati, the Kosi, the Mahananda, and other rivers flow down from the Himalayas of Nepal and make their way to the Ganges in frequently changing channels. Depressions and lakes mark the abandoned courses of streams. The Kosi River, long known as the "Sorrow of Bihar" for its tendency to cause destructive floods, has been confined within artificial embankments. The soil of the northern plain consists mostly of new alluvium—chalky and light-textured (mostly sandy loam) west of the Burhi (Old) Gandak River and nonchalky and heavy-textured (clay and clay loam) to the east. Another natural hazard—seismic activity—also affects this area, which lies within the Himalayan earthquake zone. The earthquakes of 1934 and 1988 were especially severe and caused widespread devastation and loss of life.

The land of the South Bihar Plain is more varied than that of its northern counterpart, with many hills rising from the level alluvium. The southern rivers, with the exception of the Son, are all small; their water is diverted into irrigation channels. The soil consists mainly of older alluvium, composed of a darkish clay or yellowish loam, with poor, sandy soils predominating toward the south of this region. In the southwest, beyond the Son River valley, lies the Kaimur Plateau, with horizontal sandstone strata over a limestone base.

CLIMATE

There are three well-defined seasons: the hot-weather season, lasting from March to mid-June; the season of southwest monsoon rains, from mid-June to October; and the cold-weather season, from November to February. May is the hottest month, with temperatures regularly exceeding 90 °F (32 °C), except in the extreme north. The coolest month is January, with temperatures typically rising into the low 70s F (about 22 °C). The normal annual rainfall varies from about 40 inches (1,000 mm) in the west-central part of the state to more than 60 inches (1,500 mm) in the extreme north. Nearly all the rain falls between June and October, with July and August being the wettest months. The cold-weather season is the most pleasant part of the year.

PLANT AND ANIMAL LIFE

The natural vegetation of Bihar is deciduous forest, but only a small portion of the total area is forested. Most forests occur in the Himalayan foothills; those on the plain have largely been removed in order to cultivate the land. Valuable resin-yielding sal trees (*Shorea robusta*) are found in the Himalayan foothills, along with an abundance of bamboo, reeds, and grasses. Common trees of the plain include banyans (*Ficus benghalensis* or *F. indica*), Bo trees (*F. religiosa*), and palmyra palms.

The more inaccessible forest regions of Bihar are home to various species of large mammals, most notably Bengal tigers, leopards, elephants, and several types of deer. Crocodiles are most numerous along the Kosi River. In the early 21st century significant populations of the endangered adjutant stork (*Leptoptilos dubius*) were found in the Kosi and Ganges floodplains. Small mammals, birds, reptiles, and fish are common throughout the state.

PEOPLE

For the most part, the peoples of Bihar are classified according to religion, social caste and lineage, and language, rather than by specific ethnic affiliation.

POPULATION COMPOSITION

Hindus constitute the majority of the population, and Muslims are the largest minority group. Most Muslims live in northern Bihar, particularly in and around the city of Purnia in the northeast. The Hindu population comprises the elite upper castes (Brahmans, Bhumihars, Rajputs, and Kayasthas); the officially designated Backward Classes (Yadavas, Kurmis, and Banias), constituting the socially and economically disadvantaged; and the Scheduled Castes, including Chamars or Mochis, Dusadhs, and Mushars. There also are smaller groups of distinct indigenous peoples, the Scheduled Tribes, that fall outside the caste hierarchy; most are Hindus, and a few are Christians.

Indo-European languages—including Hindi, Urdu (primarily the language of Muslims), and the Bihari languages of Bhojpuri, Maithili, and Magahi—are spoken by most of the population. Bhojpuri is spoken in the western districts of Bhojpur, Rohtas (also called Sasaram, after its administrative centre), Saran, and East and West Champaran; Maithili is spoken in Darbhanga and Saharsa; and Magahi is spoken in Patna, Gaya,

and Munger. Austroasiatic languages are spoken by the Munda, Santhal, and Ho indigenous minorities, while another Scheduled Tribe, the Oraon, speak a Dravidian language.

SETTLEMENT PATTERNS AND DEMOGRAPHIC TRENDS

Bihar is one of India's most densely populated states, with well over 850 people per square mile (more than 325 per square km). In the early 21st century the state also had one of the country's highest population growth rates. The state is primarily rural, with the vast majority of the population living in compact or clustered villages in the cultivated plains. The harnessing of the Kosi River has stabilized settlement in its valley, while a highly developed system of irrigation supports a large population on the South Bihar Plain. The major cities in Bihar are Patna, Gaya, Bhagalpur, Muzaffarpur, Darbhanga, Munger, and Bihar Sharif.

ECONOMY

Agriculture engages nearly three-fourths of Bihar's population, and Bihar is one of India's top producers of vegetables and fruits. Despite significant gains in mining and manufacturing in the late 20th century, the state has continued to lag behind other Indian states in per capita income; by government standards, a large segment of the population remains below poverty level. At the turn of the 21st century the creation of the state of Jharkhand from Bihar's southern region further strained Bihar's struggling economy.

AGRICULTURE

About half of Bihar is under cultivation, but population pressure has pushed cultivation to the furthest limits, and little remains to be developed. The transitional nature of the climatic zone is reflected in the cropping pattern, which shows a mixture of wet and dry crops. Rice is everywhere the dominant crop, but wheat, corn (maize), barley, and pulses (legumes) are important supplementary crops. Sugarcane is grown in a fairly well-defined belt in the northwest. Jute, a crop of the hot, moist lowlands, is found only in the easternmost plain districts. There are three harvests in a year: *bhadai*, dominated by corn that is sown from May to June and gathered in August and September; *aghani*, consisting primarily of rice sown in mid-June and gathered in December; and *rabi*, made up largely of wheat that ripens in the plains in the spring (March to May).

Fruits and vegetables are grown extensively. Muzaffarpur and Darbhanga are particularly noted for mangoes, bananas, and litchi fruits. Vegetables are important in the vicinity of large towns. The potato-growing area near Bihar Sharif, in Patna district, produces the best variety of seed potato in India. Chilies and tobacco are important cash crops on the banks of the Ganges.

RESOURCES AND POWER

Bihar's mineral wealth was virtually depleted when the mineral-rich Chota Nagpur plateau became part of Jharkhand. Still, there are a few pockets in the state where minerals are found. Bauxite is found in Munger. The Rohtas district has dolomite, glass sand, cement mortar, and other minerals. Mica deposits are found in Gaya, Nawada, and Munger. Gaya and Munger also produce salt, as does Muzaffarpur.

Bihar's energy is provided by a small number of thermal and hydroelectric power stations, but these do not meet the needs of the entire state. Several power stations were lost with the partitioning of Jharkhand. In the early 21st century less than half of the state's villages had regular electricity.

MANUFACTURING

Bihar has been slow to develop industry. A number of agencies have been set up by the state government to boost the pace of development. Most workers in the manufacturing sector are employed in household industries; the rest are employed in steel and other metal-based and food-processing industries.

The larger industries are mainly in Dalmianagar (paper, cement, chemicals), Baruni (petrochemicals), and Patna (light manufacturing). Among the agriculturally based industries are sugar refining, tobacco processing, silk production, and jute milling. Traditional cottage industries are popular in Bihar; they most notably include sericulture (raising of silkworms and raw silk production), lac (resin used to produce shellac) and glasswork, handloom products, brassware, and pottery. Paintings of mythological stories produced on cloth in and around the town of Madhubani have become a foreign-exchange item.

TRANSPORTATION

The waterways, once important, are now of little significance. Although all-weather roads reach just over one-third of Bihar's villages, several national highways pass through the state, including the venerable Grand Trunk Road, which is one of India's oldest roadways. Road service is best around Patna, where Allied operations during World War II brought many improvements. The rail line between Kolkata (Calcutta) and Delhi, which crosses Bihar, opened in 1864. Because of the dense population, the railways carry a heavy load of traffic. They generally run parallel to the rivers because of the difficulty of constructing bridges. Consequently, travel between important towns is often long and tedious. Regularly scheduled airlines serve Patna.

GOVERNMENT AND SOCIETY

The structure of Bihar's government, as in most other Indian states, is defined by the national constitution of 1950.

CONSTITUTIONAL FRAMEWORK

The state has a bicameral legislature consisting of the upper-house Legislative Council (Vidhan Parishad) and the lower-house Legislative Assembly (Vidhan Sabha). Appointed by the president of India, the governor is the head of the state and functions on the advice of the chief minister, who is the head of the Council of Ministers. The bureaucratic hierarchy, located in the Patna secretariat, is headed by a chief secretary.

The state is parceled into several divisions, which are further divided into districts. Administration is the responsibility of a deputy commissioner at the district level. Below the district, each subdivision has its own administrative officer.

The police force is headed by an inspector general, assisted by superintendents at the district level. There is a high court at Patna, with a chief justice and several other judges. Below the high court are district courts, subdivisional courts, *munsifs'* (subordinate judicial officers') courts, and village councils.

HEALTH AND WELFARE

Medical facilities, though improving, are still inadequate outside the towns. Villages are served mainly by allopathic (traditional Western) and ancient Indian medical (Ayurvedic) dispensaries. Unanī (traditional Muslim) and homeopathic systems of medicine are also popular. Large and well-equipped hospitals and medical colleges are located at Patna, Darbhanga, and Bhagalpur. Respiratory diseases, dysentery, and diarrhea figure prominently among the causes of death. Cholera and malaria seldom occur, and smallpox and bubonic plague have been eradicated.

EDUCATION

Although the literacy rate has nearly tripled in the second half of the 20th century to nearly half the state's population, Bihar still ranks low in literacy among Indian states. The rate for men is significantly higher than that for women. The state's general aim is to educate all children at least up to the age of 14. In the early 21st century most of those eligible were enrolled in the primary schools. However, only a small proportion were able to continue to the secondary level, as economic necessity forced them to work. Vocational and technical schools are sponsored by government departments.

Prominent institutions of higher learning in Bihar include Patna University (1917), the oldest and most important, at Patna; Babasaheb Bhimrao Ambedkar Bihar University (formerly Bihar University; 1960), at Muzaffarpur; and Tilka Manjhi Bhagalpur University (formerly Bhagalpur University; 1960), at Bhagalpur. The latter two schools offer graduate programs and have a number of affiliated colleges.

CULTURAL LIFE

The cultural regions of Bihar show a close affinity with the linguistic regions.

Maithili is the language of old Mithila (the area of ancient Videha, now Tirhut), which is dominated by orthodoxy and the Maithil Brahman way of life. Maithili is the only Bihari language with a script of its own, called Tirhuta, and a strong literary history; one of the earliest and most celebrated writers in Maithili was Vidyapati (15th century), noted for his lyrics of love and devotion.

The Bhojpuri language has hardly any written literature but does have a considerable oral narrative tradition. Magahi too has a rich tradition of oral literature. The North and South Bihar plains also have contributed significantly to contemporary Hindi and Urdu literature.

Many villages of the Scheduled Tribes have a dancing floor, a sacred grove (*sarna*) where worship is offered by a village priest, and a bachelor's dormitory (*dhumkuria*). The weekly market, *hat*, plays an important part in the tribal economies. Tribal festivals such as Sarhul, which marks the flowering of the sal trees, and Soharai, celebrated after the rice harvest, are occasions of great festivity.

Places of religious and cultural interest abound in Bihar. Nalanda is the seat of the ancient and celebrated Nalanda Buddhist monastic centre; the nearby Rajgir Hills area, with its ancient and contemporary temples and shrines, is visited by people of many faiths; and Pawapuri is the place where Mahavira, the renowned teacher of Jainism, attained nirvana (enlightenment, or freedom from an endless cycle of reincarnation). Gaya

Hindu pilgrims bathing and washing at a ghat (stairway) on the Phalgu River in Gaya, Bihar, India. © R.A. Acharya/Dinodia Photo Library

is an important place of Hindu pilgrimage, and nearby Bodh Gaya, where the Buddha attained enlightenment, is the holiest place of Buddhism; in 2002 the Mahabodhi temple complex at Bodh Gaya was designated a UNESCO World Heritage site. Hariharkshetra, near Sonpur, north of Patna, is famous for one of the oldest and largest animal fairs in India, which is held every November. Among the numerous Hindu celebrations held in Bihar, Holi (a colourful spring fertility festival) and Chaat (a tribute to the Sun, primarily by women) are indigenous to the region.

HISTORY

In the Early Vedic period (beginning with the entrance of the Vedic religion into South Asia about 1500 BCE), several kingdoms existed in the plains of Bihar. North of the Ganges was Videha, one of the kings of which was the father of Princess Sita, the wife of Lord Rama and the heroine of the *Ramayana*, one of the two great Hindu epic poems of India. During the same period, the capital of the ancient kingdom of Magadha was Rajagriha (now Rajgir), about 45 miles (70 km) southeast of Patna; to the east was the kingdom of Anga, with its capital at Campa (near Bhagalpur). A new kingdom later arose in southern Videha, with its capital at Vaishali. By about 700 BCE, the kingdoms of Vaishali and Videha were replaced by a confederacy of the Vrijji—said to be the first republican state known in history. It was in Magadha, in the 6th century BCE, that the Buddha developed his religion and that Mahavira, who was born at Vaishali, promulgated and reformed the religion of Jainism.

About 475 BCE the capital of the Magadha empire was located at Pataliputra (modern Patna), where it remained under Ashoka (emperor of India from about 273 to 232 BCE) and the Guptas (a dynasty of emperors who ruled India in the 4th and 5th centuries CE) until the onslaught of the Hephthalites from the north in the middle and late 5th century CE. In the 6th–7th centuries the city was devastated by the migration of the Son River; the Chinese pilgrim Xuanzang recorded that in 637 the city had few inhabitants. It regained some of its glory, but it is doubtful that it ever served as the capital of the Pala empire (which lasted from about 775 to 1200). During the ensuing Muslim period (about 1200 to 1765), Bihar had little independent history. It remained a

provincial unit until 1765, when it came under British rule and—together with Chota Nagpur to the south—was merged with the state of Bengal.

Originally, Chota Nagpur was mostly forest-clad and was ruled by chiefs of various aboriginal tribes. Though British authority was only gradually established in the plains to the north during the second half of the 18th and the beginning of the 19th century, occasional revolts against the British took place in Chota Nagpur, the most important being the Ho revolt of 1820 to 1827 and the Munda uprising of 1831 to 1832. Later, Bihar was an important centre of the Indian Mutiny of 1857–58. Bihar formed a part of the Bengal Presidency under the British until 1912, when the province of Bihar and Orissa was formed; in 1936 the two became separate provinces of British-ruled India.

Bihar played an active role in the successive phases of Indian nationalism. Mohandas Karamchand (Mahatma) Gandhi, the nationalist leader who advocated nonviolent resistance, first launched the *satyagraha* ("devotion to truth") movement against the tyranny of the European indigo planters in the Champaran region of northern Bihar. Rajendra Prasad, who played a leading part in the freedom movement and was elected the first president of independent India, was born in the Saran district, northwest of Patna.

Upon India's independence in 1947, Bihar became a constituent part (becoming a state in 1950), and in 1948 the small states with capitals at Saraikela and Kharsawan were merged with it. In 1956, when the Indian states were reorganized on a linguistic basis, a territory of some 3,140 square miles (8,130 square km) was transferred from Bihar to West Bengal. In 1990, for the first time since independence, a state government was elected from a party other than that controlling the national government, and in 2000 most of the Chota Nagpur plateau in Bihar's southern region became part of the new state of Jharkhand.

SIKKIM

Sikkim is located in the northeastern part of India in the eastern Himalayas and is one of the smallest states in the country. It is bordered by the Tibet Autonomous Region of China to the north and northeast, by Bhutan to the southeast, by the Indian state of West Bengal to the south, and by Nepal to the west. The capital is Gangtok, in the southeastern part of the state. Area 2,740 square miles (7,096 square km). Pop. (2008 est.) 594,000.

LAND

Long a sovereign political entity, Sikkim became a protectorate of India in 1950 and an Indian state in 1975. Its small size notwithstanding, Sikkim is of great political and strategic importance for India because of its location along several international boundaries.

RELIEF

Sikkim is a basin surrounded on three sides by precipitous mountain walls. There is little lowland, and the variation in relief is extreme. Within a stretch of roughly 50 miles (80 km), the land rises from an elevation of about 750 feet (225 metres) in the Tista River valley to nearly 28,200 feet (8,600 metres) at Kanchenjunga, India's highest peak and the world's third highest mountain. The Singalila Range separates Sikkim from Nepal in the west, while the Dongkya Range forms the border with the Tibet Autonomous Region of China to the east. Several passes across this range afford easy access to the Chumbi valley in Tibet and, beyond the valley, to the Tibetan capital of Lhasa.

Some two-thirds of Sikkim consists of perpetually snow-covered mountains, dominated by the Kanchenjunga massif. The residents of Sikkim have traditionally viewed the mountain as both a god and the abode of gods. According to legend, the Abominable Snowman, or yeti, called Nee-gued in Sikkim, is said to roam its slopes. Other major peaks—all above 23,000 feet (7,000 metres)—include Tent, Kabru, and Pauhunri.

DRAINAGE

The Sikkim basin is drained by the Tista River and its tributaries, such as the Rangit, Lhonak, Talung, and Lachung, which have cut deep valleys into the mountains. Originating in the northeast from a glacier near the Tibetan border, the Tista River descends steeply, dropping about 15,700 feet (4,800 metres) to Rangpo (Rongphu), on the border with West Bengal, where it has cut a gorge through the Darjiling Ridge (7,000–8,000 feet [2,100–2,400 metres]) before emerging onto the Indo-Gangetic Plain.

Climate

Sikkim exhibits a variety of climatic types, from almost tropical conditions in the south to severe mountain climates in the north. In Gangtok, temperatures in January (the coldest month) drop into the low 30s F (about 0 °C); in August (the warmest month), temperatures may reach the low 80s F (about 28 °C). Depending on elevation and exposure, annual precipitation varies from 50 to 200 inches (1,270 to 5,080 mm), most occurring during the months of the southwest monsoon (May through October). The heavy rains and snows often trigger destructive landslides and avalanches.

Plant and Animal Life

More than two-fifths of Sikkim is forested. Sal (a type of hardwood), pandanus, palms, bamboos, ferns, and orchids are common in the subtropical forests found below about 5,000 feet (1,500 metres). In the temperate forests (5,000 to 13,000 feet [1,500 to 4,000 metres]), oak, laurel, maple, chestnut, magnolia, alder, birch, rhododendron, fir, hemlock, and spruce predominate. Alpine tundra replaces forest at the higher elevations.

Sikkim has a rich and varied animal life, including black bears, brown bears, red pandas, numerous species of deer, blue sheep, gorals (small goat-like mammals), and Tibetan antelope. Tigers, leopards, and lesser cats are also found. Birdlife includes pheasants, partridges, quail, eagles, barbets, Himalayan cuckoos, Tibetan black crows, and minivets. Sikkim has several national parks and a number of wildlife sanctuaries, which provide a protected environment for the state's diverse flora and fauna. Kanchenjunga National Park (established in 1977), near the peak from which it draws its name, is among the largest of India's high-elevation conservation areas.

People

Roughly three-fourths of Sikkim's residents are Nepalese in origin; most speak a Nepali (Gorkhali) dialect and are Hindu in religion and culture. About one-fifth of the population consists of Scheduled Tribes. The most prominent of these tribal groups are the Bhutia, the Lepcha, and the Limbu; they all speak Tibeto-Burman languages and practice Mahayana Buddhism as well as the indigenous Bon religion. There is a notable Christian minority in Sikkim, as well as a tiny community of Muslims. A small fraction of Sikkim's people belong to the Scheduled Castes.

Dwellings on the Himalayan slopes at Lachung, Sikkim state, India. Alice Kandell—Rapho/ Photo Researchers

The great majority of Sikkim's population is rural, living in scattered hamlets and villages. Gangtok is Sikkim's largest settlement. Other notable towns include Singtam, Rangpo, Jorethang, Naya Bazar, Mangan, Gyalshing, and Namchi.

ECONOMY

Sikkim's economy is based predominantly on agriculture, with the sector engaging more than half of the working population.

AGRICULTURE

Corn (maize), rice, buckwheat, wheat, and barley are produced in terraced fields along the valley flanks. Beans, ginger, potatoes, vegetables, fruits, and tea also are grown. Sikkim is one of the world's principal producers of cardamom. Many of Sikkim's farmers also raise livestock, including cattle, pigs, sheep, goats, and poultry. Cattle and buffalo are limited mainly to the subtropical humid belt,

Typical house in Mangan, Sikkim state, India. Alice Kandell from Rapho/Photo Researchers

while yaks and sheep are herded in the higher elevations in the north.

RESOURCES AND POWER

Copper, lead, and zinc are mined in Sikkim. The state also has deposits of other minerals, including coal, graphite, and limestone. Only a fraction of Sikkim's mineral resources are commercially exploited.

The hydroelectric potential of Sikkim's Tista River system is considerable. There are a few large hydroelectric stations and many smaller plants that provide energy to Gangtok, Rangpo, Singtam, and Mangan. Rural electrification has remained a government priority.

MANUFACTURING

Until the early 1970s, Sikkim had only cottage industries—producing handwoven textiles, carpets, and blankets—as well as traditional handicrafts, such as embroidery, scroll paintings, and wood carving. Since that time, several small-scale industries have developed. These produce, most notably, processed foods (including liquor), watches and watch jewels, and small electronics parts.

Transportation

Roads, though not extensive, are the primary mode of travel. Ropeways, which are similar to ski lifts, also have been provided at many points. The capital of Gangtok is nearly 75 miles (120 km) from the nearest airport, at Baghdogra, and 70 miles (110 km) from the railhead at Shiliguri, both in West Bengal.

Government and Society

The structure of Sikkim's government, as in most other Indian states, is defined by the national constitution of 1950.

Constitutional Framework

The constitution of Sikkim provides for a governor—appointed by the president of India—as the head of state. The governor is aided by the state Council of Ministers, which is led by a chief minister. The Legislative Assembly (Vidhan Sabha) is a unicameral elected body, with a portion of the seats allocated to the combined Lepcha and Bhutia populations. One Lepcha-Bhutia seat is reserved for the nominee of the lamas (Tibetan Buddhist religious leaders); some seats also are reserved for representatives of the Scheduled Castes. The final court in the judiciary system is the High Court at Gangtok, from which appeals may

be made to the Supreme Court of India. Lower courts include district courts, which handle both criminal and civil cases, and sessions courts, which generally handle civil cases; judicial magistrates rule on criminal offenses.

The state is divided into a handful of districts. Within each district, local headmen serve as liaisons between the people and the district administration. *Panchayats* (village councils) administer the villages and implement welfare programs.

Health

Sikkim has several hospitals and, in each district, at least one community health centre. Rural regions are served by primary health centres and subcentres. The state participates in national programs to control tuberculosis, blindness, and other diseases. Diarrheal diseases (including cholera), respiratory infections of various sorts, hepatitis, and family-planning issues remain among Sikkim's principal health concerns.

Education

Primary and secondary education in Sikkim is offered free of charge through hundreds of government schools. However, there also are many private schools operating within the state. Higher education is available at a number of institutions, including the Sikkim Manipal University of Health, Medical and Technological Sciences (1995) in

Gangtok, as well as smaller colleges offering degrees in law, engineering, teaching, religious studies, and other fields.

Cultural Life

Sikkim's cultural life, though showing strong Tibetan influences, retains a character derived from the various tribes of Sikkim and their pre-Buddhist customs. The most important festival of the year is the two-day Phanglhapsol festival in August or September, in which masked dancers perform in honour of Kanchenjunga, the presiding deity. The Namgyal Institute of Tibetology (1958), in Gangtok, has one of the largest collections of Tibetan books in the world. Many monasteries are repositories of wall paintings, *thang-kas* (religious paintings mounted on brocade), bronze images, and other artworks.

History

Little is known of Sikkim's history prior to the 17th century. The state's name is derived from the Limbu words *su him*, meaning "new house." The Lepcha were early inhabitants of the region, apparently assimilating the Naong, Chang, Mon, and other tribes. The Bhutia began entering the area from Tibet in the 14th century. When the kingdom of Sikkim was established in 1642, Phuntsog Namgyal, the first *chogyal* (temporal and spiritual king), came from the Bhutia community. The Namgyal dynasty ruled Sikkim until 1975.

Sikkim fought a series of territorial wars with both Bhutan and Nepal beginning in the mid-18th century, and Nepal subsequently came to occupy parts of western Sikkim and the submontane Tarai region to the south. It was during this period that the largest migration of Nepalese to Sikkim began. In 1816 these territories were restored to Sikkim by the British in return for its support during the Anglo-Nepalese War (1814–16), but by 1817 Sikkim had become a de facto protectorate of Britain.

The British East India Company obtained the city of Darjiling from Sikkim in 1835. Incidents between the British and Sikkim led to the annexation in 1849 of the submontane regions and the subsequent military defeat of Sikkim, culminating in the Anglo-Sikkimese Treaty of 1861. The treaty established Sikkim as a princely state under British paramountcy (though leaving the issue of sovereignty undefined), and the British were given rights of free trade and of road making through Sikkim to Tibet. In 1890 an agreement was concluded between the British and the Tibetans that defined the border between Sikkim and Tibet. Tibet also acknowledged the special relationship of British India with the kingdom of Sikkim. A British political officer was subsequently appointed to assist the *chogyal* in the administration of Sikkim's domestic and foreign affairs, in effect becoming the virtual ruler of the state.

After India attained independence in 1947, political parties began to be formed in Sikkim for the first time. Among their aims were the abolition of feudalism, the establishment of popularly elected government, and accession of Sikkim to India—all demands resisted by the *chogyal* and his supporters. The *chogyal* was unable to hold his ground, however. The bulwark of the feudal system was dismantled in 1949, with the abolition of noncultivating rent-collecting landowners. In 1950 the Indo-Sikkimese Treaty made Sikkim an Indian protectorate, with India assuming responsibility for the external relations, defense, and strategic communications of Sikkim. The terms of the treaty also included increased popular participation in government, and five general elections based on adult suffrage were held between 1952 and 1974. In the last of these elections, two rival parties merged to form the Sikkim Congress, which swept the polls. The party subsequently launched a campaign to obtain greater political liberties and rights, and the *chogyal* attempted to suppress the movement. When the situation got out of control, the *chogyal* asked the government of India to take over the administration. India prepared a constitution for Sikkim that was approved by its national assembly in 1974. In a special referendum held in 1975, more than 97 percent of the electorate voted for the merger of Sikkim with India. Sikkim became the 22nd state of India on May 15, 1975.

WEST BENGAL

The state of West Bengal is located in the northeastern part of India. It is bounded to the north by the state of Sikkim and the country of Bhutan, to the northeast by the state of Assam, to the east by the country of Bangladesh, to the south by the Bay of Bengal, to the southwest by the state of Orissa, to the west by the states of Jharkhand and Bihar, and to the northwest by the country of Nepal. Although in area West Bengal ranks as one of the smaller states of India, it is one of the largest in population. The capital is Kolkata (Calcutta). Area 34,267 square miles (88,752 square km). Pop. (2008 est.) 87,869,000.

LAND

West Bengal has a peculiar configuration; its breadth varies from 200 miles (320 km) at one point to hardly 10 miles (16 km) at another. Its roughly 1,350-mile (2,200-km) frontier with Bangladesh, neither natural nor well defined, is of strategic importance.

RELIEF AND DRAINAGE

West Bengal may be broadly divided into two natural geographic divisions—the Gangetic Plain in the south and the sub-Himalayan and Himalayan area in the north. The Gangetic Plain contains fertile alluvial soil deposited by the Ganges (Ganga) River and its tributaries and distributaries. It also features numerous marshes and shallow lakes formed out of dead river courses. Indeed, the Ganges, which now runs through the narrow middle section of the state before entering Bangladesh, has been moving steadily eastward for centuries; very little of its water now goes to the sea via the western distributaries, of which the principal one is the Hugli (Hooghly). The state capital, Kolkata, is situated on the Hugli in the southern portion of West Bengal. Another important river, the Damodar, joins the Hugli southwest of Kolkata. The elevation of the plain increases slowly toward the west; the rise is most marked near the Chota Nagpur plateau of neighbouring Jharkhand.

The sub-Himalayan tract, known as the West Bengal Duars, or Western Duars, is a part of the Tarai lowland belt between the Himalayas and the plain. Once infested with malaria, the area is now well-drained and cultivated. Some of the finest tea plantations of India are situated there. North of the Duars, the Himalayan mountain ranges rise abruptly along the northern boundary of the state. Mount Kanchenjunga, actually located in adjacent Sikkim, dominates the landscape of the area, particularly in Darjiling (Darjeeling). On a clear day, Mount Everest also can be seen in the distance.

CLIMATE

West Bengal's climate is transitional between tropical wet-dry in the southern portions and humid subtropical in the north. Throughout West Bengal there is a pronounced seasonal disparity in rainfall. For example, Kolkata averages about 64 inches (1,625 mm) per year, of which an average of 13 inches (330 mm) falls in August and less than 1 inch (25 mm) in December. The state also is subject to considerable variability from year to year. In the sub-Himalayan region, rainfall is considerably greater.

The year may be broadly divided into three marked seasons—the hot and dry season (March to early June), with dry sultry days and frequent thunderstorms; the hot and wet season (mid-June to September), when rain-bearing monsoon winds blow from the southwest; and the cold (cool) season (October to February), when days are dry and clear and stable atmospheric conditions prevail. Average high temperatures at Kolkata range from about 80 °F (27 °C) in December and January to nearly 100 °F (38 °C) in April and May.

PLANT AND ANIMAL LIFE

Forests occupy more than one-tenth of the total land area of the state, and the region as a whole has a rich and varied plant life. In the sub-Himalayan plains the principal forest trees include sal (*Shorea robusta*) and shisham, or Indian rosewood (*Dalbergia sissoo*); the forests are interspersed with reeds and tall grasses. On the Himalayan heights vegetation varies according to the altitude, with coniferous belts occurring at higher levels. The delta of the Hugli constitutes the western end of the dense coastal mangrove forest called the Sundarbans. A large portion of this unreclaimed and sparsely populated area bordering Bangladesh and the Bay of Bengal has been set aside as a national park.

The forests are inhabited by tigers, panthers, elephants, gaurs (wild cattle), and rhinoceroses, as well as by other animals of the Indian plain, large and small. Reptiles and birds include the same species as are common throughout the Indian subcontinent.

PEOPLE

The majority of West Bengal's people live in rural villages. Of those living in urban areas, more than half reside in greater Kolkata.

Of the different religions, Hinduism claims the adherence of more than three-fourths of the population. Most of the remainder is Muslim. Throughout the state, Buddhists, Christians, Jains, and Sikhs constitute small minority communities.

Bengali, the main language of the state, is spoken by much of the population. Other languages include Hindi, Santali, Urdu (primarily the language of Muslims), and Nepali (spoken largely in the area of Darjiling). A small number of people speak Kurukh, the language of the Oraon indigenous group. English, together with Bengali, is the language of administration, and English and Hindi serve as lingua francas at the national level.

ECONOMY

Agriculture dominates both the landscape and the economy of West Bengal. Its proportion of agricultural land is among the highest of all the Indian states. However, the Kolkata region is among the most industrialized areas in the country, and the state manufactures a wide range of products.

AGRICULTURE

Rice, which requires extensive irrigation, is the leading crop in nearly every area. Indeed, despite its relatively small size, West Bengal produces a significant percentage of India's rice harvest. Jute, the second leading crop, is especially prominent along the border with Bangladesh and south of the Ganges River. Mangoes, jackfruit, and bananas are widely produced in the southern and central portions of the state. Wheat and potatoes are produced as winter crops throughout the south. The northern areas around Darjiling and Jalpaiguri have long been known for their production of high-quality tea. The Darjiling region also produces oranges, apples, pineapples, ginger, and cardamom.

INDUSTRY

The state's most important industrial belt is a corridor extending for a number of miles north and south of Kolkata, along the Hugli River. Another significant industrial region is located along the Damodar River. There are steel plants at Durgapur and Burnpur and a locomotive plant at Chittaranjan. Haldia, the terminus of an oil pipeline from Assam and the site of a large oil refinery, also has a petrochemical industry. Other important manufactures include ships, automobiles, chemicals and fertilizers, wagons, electronics, paper, and cotton textiles. The state has a large number of small-scale and cottage industries as well. In the late 20th and early 21st centuries, the only mineral resources of West Bengal that sustained nationally significant exploitation were coal and clay for brickmaking.

TRANSPORTATION

Local river transportation was augmented by steam navigation in the 19th century—first introduced between Kolkata, Allahabad (Uttar Pradesh), and Guwahati (Assam). The division of Bengal in 1947 and the ongoing deterioration of river channels have disrupted river transport. Nevertheless, Kolkata and its sister port of Haldia, farther south, still handle international trade. West Bengal saw the inauguration of the railway system in eastern India in 1854, and local railway headquarters are now located in the state. Kolkata was the first Indian city to open an underground railway system. National highways link West Bengal with the rest of India, while state highways provide internal connections. There is an international airport at Kolkata as well as several smaller airfields within the state.

GOVERNMENT AND SOCIETY

The structure of the government of West Bengal, like that of most Indian states, is determined by the national constitution of 1950.

CONSTITUTIONAL FRAMEWORK

The head of state is the governor, who is appointed by the president of India. The elected Council of Ministers, with a chief minister at its head, aids and advises the governor. The chief minister is appointed by the governor, and the other ministers are appointed by the governor on the advice of the chief minister. The Council of Ministers is collectively responsible to the state legislature, which consists of a single house, the Legislative Assembly (Vidhan Sabha). The constitution provides for a High Court; its chief justice and judges are appointed by the president of India. Other judges are appointed by the governor.

The state is divided administratively into a number of districts. Each district, except that of Kolkata, is administered by a collector, who is also the district magistrate. Districts, in turn, are divided into subdivisions, each administered by a subdivisional officer. Units of police jurisdiction vary in area according to population. Most encompass several *mawzas* (villages).

With the object of developing rural self-government, *mawzas* were grouped together under elected local authorities known as *panchayats*. Established under the West Bengal Panchayat Act of 1956, *panchayats* are entrusted with sanitary and conservation services and with the supervision of the village police and the development of cottage industries. A three-tiered *panchayat* system, comprising several thousand village-level *panchayats*, several hundred intermediate-level *panchayats*, and more than a dozen district-level *panchayats*, covers the rural area.

HEALTH AND WELFARE

Medical facilities include hospitals, clinics, health centres, and dispensaries. Family-planning services are available in district bureaus, as well as in urban and rural centres. An employees' state insurance scheme provides factory workers with health, employment, safety, and maternity insurance and also provides a free medical service.

A social welfare directorate coordinates various welfare services dealing with orphans, people with mental and physical disabilities, and the underprivileged. The government's social-welfare enterprises are supplemented by private agencies, of which the most prominent are the Ramakrishna Mission, founded by the Hindu reformer and teacher Vivekananda in 1897, and the Order of the Missionaries of Charity (1948), founded by Mother Teresa, recipient of the 1979 Nobel Peace Prize.

EDUCATION

West Bengal has more than 10 degree-granting universities, as well as engineering and medical colleges and many technical institutes. The universities of Calcutta (1857), Jadavpur (1955),

and Rabindra Bharati (1962) are all located in Kolkata. The science laboratories of the University of Calcutta, the Indian Association for the Cultivation of Science, and the Bose Institute have made notable contributions to science. The Asiatic Society of Bengal, a scholarly organization founded in 1784, is headquartered in Kolkata. Vishva-Bharati University, in Shantiniketan (now part of Bolpur), is a world-famous centre for the study of Indology and international cultural relations.

The state has a central library, together with a number of district, area, and rural libraries. More than 5,000 adult education centres aid in literacy training. The state's literacy rate, which approached 70 percent in the early 21st century, is one of the highest in India, and the disparity in the rate between men and women is lower than the national average.

CULTURAL LIFE

Bengalis have long fostered art, literature, music, and drama. The visual arts have, by tradition, been based mainly on clay modeling, terra-cotta work, and decorative painting. Bengali literature dates to before the 12th century. The Caitanya movement, an intensely emotional form of Hinduism inspired by the medieval saint Caitanya (1485–1533), shaped the subsequent development of Bengali poetry until the early 19th century, when contact with the West sparked a vigorous creative synthesis. The modern period has produced, among others, the Nobel Prize–winning poet Rabindranath Tagore (1861–1941), whose contribution still dominates the Indian literary scene.

Traditional music takes the form of devotional and cultural songs. Rabindra Sangeet, songs written and composed by Tagore, draw on the pure Indian classical as well as traditional folk-music sources. They exert a powerful influence in Bengali cultural life.

The theatre is popular, and performances—amateur as well as professional—are sophisticated. *Yatras* (*jatras*), traditional open-air performances that may treat mythological and historical topics or contemporary themes, are popular both in the countryside and in urban areas. The *kavi* is an impromptu duel in musical verse between village poets. The *kathakata*, a religious recital, is another traditional form of rural entertainment, based on folklore.

The film industry is a well-established modern form of popular entertainment. Bengali films have earned national and international awards for their delicate handling of Indian themes; the works of the directors Satyajit Ray, Tapan Sinha, Mrinal Sen, and Aparna Sen are particularly notable.

History

The name of Bengal, or Bangla, is derived from the ancient kingdom of Vanga, or Banga. References to it occur in early Sanskrit literature, but its early history is obscure until the 3rd century BCE, when it formed part of the extensive Mauryan empire inherited by the emperor Ashoka. With the decline of Mauryan power, anarchy once more supervened. In the 4th century CE the region was absorbed into the Gupta empire of Samudra Gupta. Later it came under control of the Pala dynasty. From the beginning of the 13th century to the mid-18th century, when the British gained ascendancy, Bengal was under Muslim rule—at times under governors acknowledging the suzerainty of the Delhi sultanate but mainly under independent rulers.

In 1757 British forces under Robert Clive defeated those of the nawab (ruler) of Bengal, Sirāj al-Dawlah, in the Battle of Plassey. In 1765 the nominal Mughal emperor of northern India, Shah 'Ālam II, granted to the British East India Company the *dīwānī* of Bengal, Bihar, and Orissa—that is, the right to collect and administer the revenues of those areas. By the Regulating Act of 1773, Warren Hastings became the first British governor-general of Bengal. The British-controlled government, centred at Calcutta (now Kolkata), was declared to be supreme: essentially, the governor-general of Bengal was the chief executive of British India. Thus, the Bengal Presidency, as the province was known, had powers of superintendence over the other British presidencies, those of Madras (now Chennai) and Bombay (now Mumbai).

Britain was not, however, the only European presence in Bengal. The town of Hugli, north of Calcutta, was the location of a Portuguese factory (trading post) until 1632; Hugli-Chinsura (Chunchura), the next town south, was the Dutch post until 1825; the next town, Shrirampur (Serampore), was the Danish post until 1845; and Chandernagore (Chandannagar) remained in French hands until 1949.

From 1834 Bengal's governor-general bore the title "governor-general of India," but in 1854 the post was relieved of the direct administration of Bengal, which was placed under a lieutenant governor. Thenceforward, the government of British India became distinct from that of Bengal. In 1874 Assam was transferred from the charge of the lieutenant governor and placed under a separate chief commissioner. In 1905 the British determined that Bengal had become too unwieldy a charge for a single administration, and, in spite of violent Hindu protests, it was partitioned into two provinces, each under its own lieutenant governor: one comprised western Bengal, Bihar, and Orissa; the other included eastern Bengal and Assam. In 1911, because of continued opposition to partition, Bengal was reunited under one governor, Bihar and Orissa under a lieutenant governor, and Assam once more under a chief commissioner. At the same time, Delhi became the capital of India in place of Calcutta.

Under the Government of India Act (1935), Bengal was constituted an autonomous province in 1937. This remained the situation until the Indian subcontinent was partitioned into the two dominions of Pakistan and India after the British withdrawal in 1947. The eastern sector of Bengal, largely Muslim, became East Pakistan (later Bangladesh); the western sector became India's West Bengal. The partition of Bengal left West Bengal with ill-defined boundaries and a constant inflow of non-Muslim, mostly Hindu, refugees from East Pakistan. More than 7 million refugees entered the already densely populated state after 1947, and their rehabilitation placed an immense burden on the administration.

In 1950 the princely state of Cooch Behar (Koch Bihar) was integrated with West Bengal. After the linguistic and political reorganization of Indian states in 1956, West Bengal gained some 3,140 square miles (8,130 square km) from Bihar. The additional land provided a link between the previously separated northern and southern parts of the state.

CHAPTER 11

SELECTED CENTRAL INDIAN STATES

The three central Indian states highlighted in this chapter represent the two main landscapes found in this region: the lowland areas found on each coast (Gujarat) and the interior uplands of the Deccan (Madhya Pradesh and Maharashtra).

GUJARAT

The state of Gujarat is located on India's western coast, on the Arabian Sea. It is bounded primarily by Pakistan to the northwest and by the Indian states of Rajasthan to the north, Madhya Pradesh to the east, and Maharashtra to the southeast. Gujarat also shares a small segment of its southeastern border with the Indian union territory of Dadra and Nagar Haveli, and, together with the Arabian Sea, it surrounds the territory of Daman and Diu.

The state capital is Gandhinagar, on the outskirts of the north-central city of Ahmadabad (Ahmedabad)—the former capital, the largest city in the state, and one of the greatest cotton-textile centres in India. It was in Ahmadabad that Mahatma Gandhi built his Sabarmati ashram (Sanskrit: *ashrama*, "retreat," or "hermitage") as a headquarters for his campaigns.

Gujarat draws its name from the Gurjara (supposedly a subtribe of the Huns), who ruled the area during the 8th and 9th centuries CE. The state assumed its present form

Royal Palace at Jamnagar, Gujarat, India. Baldev—Shostal Assoc./EB Inc.

in 1960, when the former Bombay state was divided between Maharashtra and Gujarat on the basis of language. Area 75,685 square miles (196,024 square km). Pop. (2008 est.) 56,408,000.

LAND

Gujarat encompasses the entire Kathiawar Peninsula (Saurashtra) as well as the surrounding area on the mainland. The state's coastline is 992 miles (1,596 km) long, and no part of the state is more than 100 miles (160 km) from the sea.

RELIEF, DRAINAGE, AND SOILS

Gujarat is a land of great contrasts, stretching from the seasonal salt deserts of the Kachchh (Kutch) district in the northwest, across the generally arid and semiarid scrublands of the Kathiawar Peninsula, to the wet, fertile, coastal plains of the southeastern part of the state, north of Mumbai. The Rann of Kachchh—including both the Great Rann and its eastern appendage, the Little Rann—are best described as vast salt marshes, together covering about 9,000 square

An intermittent river in the southern Gir Range, on the Kathiawar Peninsula, Gujarat, India.
Gerald Cubitt

miles (23,300 square km). The Rann constitutes the Kachchh district on the west, north, and east, while the Gulf of Kachchh forms the district's southern boundary. During the rainy season—slight though the rains may be—the Rann floods, and the Kachchh district is converted into an island; in the dry season it is a sandy, salty plain plagued by dust storms.

To the southeast of Kachchh, lying between the Gulf of Kachchh and the Gulf of Khambhat (Cambay), is the large Kathiawar Peninsula. It is generally arid and rises from the coasts to a low, rolling area of hill land in the centre, where the state reaches its highest elevation, at 3,665 feet (1,117 metres), in the Girnar Hills. Soils in the peninsula are mostly poor, having been derived from a variety of old crystalline rocks. Rivers, except for seasonal streams, are absent from the area.

To the east of the Kathiawar Peninsula, small plains and low hills in the north merge with fertile farmlands in the south. The richness of the southern soils is attributable to their partial derivation from the basalts of the Deccan, the physiographic region that constitutes most of south India. Southeastern Gujarat is crossed from east to west by the Narmada and Tapti (Tapi) rivers, both of which empty into the Gulf of Khambhat. Toward the eastern border with Maharashtra, the terrain becomes mountainous; the region is the northern extension of the Western Ghats, the mountain range that runs parallel to the Arabian Sea on the western edge of southern India.

CLIMATE

Winter (November through February) temperatures in Gujarat usually reach a high in the mid-80s F (about 28 °C), while lows drop into the mid-50s F (about 12 °C). Summers (March through May) are quite hot, however, with temperatures typically rising well above 100 °F (38 °C) during the day and dropping only into the 90s F (low 30s C) at night.

Gujarat is drier in the north than in the south. Rainfall is lowest in the northwestern part of the state—in the Rann of Kachchh—where it may amount to less than 15 inches (380 mm) annually. In the central portion of the Kathiawar Peninsula as well as in the northeastern region, annual rainfall typically amounts to about 40 inches (1,000 mm). Southeastern Gujarat, where the southwest monsoon brings heavy rains between June and September, is the wettest area; annual rainfall usually approaches 80 inches (2,000 mm) along the coastal plain.

PLANT AND ANIMAL LIFE

Forests cover only a small portion of Gujarat, reflecting human activity as well as meagre rainfall. Scrub forest occurs in the northwestern region and across the Kathiawar Peninsula, the main species being the babul acacia, the caper, the Indian jujube, and the toothbrush bush (*Salvadora persica*). In some parts of the peninsula and northeastern Gujarat, such deciduous species as teak, catechu (cutch), axlewood, and Bengal *kino* (butea gum) are found. Deciduous forests are concentrated in the wetter southern and eastern hills. They produce valuable timbers, such as Vengai padauk (genus *Pterocarpus*; resembling mahogany), Malabar *simal*, and *haldu* (*Adina cordifolia*). The west coast of the peninsula is known for its algae, and the east coast produces the papyrus, or paper plant (*Cyperus papyrus*).

Gir National Park, in the southwestern region of the Kathiawar Peninsula, contains rare Asiatic lions (*Panthera leo persica*), and endangered Indian wild asses (*Equus hemionus khur*) are protected in a sanctuary near the Little Rann of Kachchh. The Nal Sarovar Bird Sanctuary, near Ahmadabad, attracts many species of birds migrating from the Siberian plains and elsewhere in winter. Saras cranes, Brahmini ducks, bustards, pelicans, cormorants, ibises, storks, herons, and egrets are among the most notable species. The Rann of Kachchh is the only nesting ground of the greater flamingo in India. There is excellent offshore and inland fishing in Gujarat. Catches include pomfret, salmon, *hilsa* (a type of shad), jewfish (scianid fish), prawn, Bombay duck (a food fish), and tuna.

PEOPLE

The diverse peoples constituting the Gujarati population may be categorized broadly as either Indic (northern-derived) or Dravidian (southern-derived).

POPULATION COMPOSITION

The Indic peoples include the Nagar Brahman, Bhatia, Bhadela, Rabari, and Mina castes. The Parsis, originally from Persia, represent a much later northern influx. Among the peoples of southern origin are the Bhangi, Koli, Dubla, Naikda, and Macchi-Kharwa. The rest of the population, including the aboriginal Bhil community, is of mixed heritage. Members of the Scheduled Castes and Scheduled Tribes form roughly one-fifth of the state's population. Portions of the mountainous region of southeastern Gujarat are populated almost entirely by tribal peoples.

Gujarati and Hindi are the state's official languages. Gujarati, the more widely spoken of the two, is an Indo-European language derived from Sanskrit through Prakrit, ancient Indic languages other than Sanskrit, and Apabhramsha, a language spoken in northern and western India from the 10th to the 14th century. Gujarat's contact by sea with foreign countries also led to the introduction of Persian, Arabic, Turkish, Portuguese, and English words.

Hinduism is the religion of most of the population. Adherents of Islam constitute the largest minority. However, there are also significant communities of Jains, who are more strongly established in Gujarat than in other parts of India; Zoroastrians, or Parsis, whose ancestors fled Persia sometime after the 7th century; and Christians.

SETTLEMENT PATTERNS

Roughly three-fifths of the residents of Gujarat are rural. The main concentration of population is in the eastern part of the state, in the plains surrounding the cities of Ahmadabad, Kheda, Vadodara, Surat, and Valsad; the region is both agriculturally productive and highly industrialized. Other concentrations of population occur on the Kathiawar Peninsula, particularly on the southern coast between the cities of Mangrol and Mahuva, in the interior around Rajkot, and on the Gulf of Kachchh around Jamnagar. The distribution of population gradually decreases toward the Kachchh district in the northwest and toward the hilly regions of eastern Gujarat.

Most of the major cities are found in the more fertile regions, and many of them—such as Rajkot, Junagadh, Porbandar, Bhavnagar (Bhaunagar), and Jamnagar, all on the peninsula—were once the capitals of small states. The most urbanized area of Gujarat is the Ahmadabad-Vadodara (Baroda) industrial belt in the east-central region. Since the late 20th century, this area has become just one segment of an ever-expanding urban agglomeration along the highway that links the northern and southern parts of the state.

ECONOMY

Although unfavourable climatic conditions, soil and water salinity, and rocky terrain have hampered Gujarat's agricultural activities, the sector has remained a major component of the state's economy, employing about half of the workforce. Gujarat is also rich in minerals and has a well-developed manufacturing sector.

AGRICULTURE

Wheat, millet, rice, and sorghum are the primary food crops, with rice production being concentrated in the wetter areas. Principal cash crops include cotton, oilseeds (especially peanuts [groundnuts]), tobacco, and sugarcane. Commercial dairying is also important.

RESOURCES AND POWER

Gujarat's mineral wealth includes limestone, manganese, gypsum, calcite, and bauxite. The state also has deposits of lignite, quartz sand, agate, and feldspar. The fine building stones of Porbandar, on the Kathiawar Peninsula, are among Gujarat's most valuable products, and the state's output of soda ash and salt amounts to a significant portion of the national yield. In addition, Gujarat produces petroleum and natural gas.

The state draws its electricity from a variety of sources. The bulk of Gujarat's power is supplied by coal- and gas-fueled thermal plants, followed by hydroelectric generators. There also are a number of wind farms scattered across the state.

Manufacturing and Labour

Gujarat occupies a leading place in India's manufacturing sector, especially in the production of chemicals, pharmaceuticals, and polyester textiles. The state's major industrial belt exists in its southern sector. There is a large oil refinery at Koyali (near Vadodara), which supports a nearby petrochemical industry. Pharmaceutical production is concentrated at Vadodara, Ahmadabad, and Valsad. Small-scale, largely agriculture-based manufacturing is located in the Kathiawar Peninsula. Vegetable oil, cotton textiles, and cement are among the products of these industries.

Favourable investments, the availability of resources and power, solid management, and labour efficiency have been the basis of the state's industrial development. Moreover, the Gandhian approach to labour problems—strict reliance on the truth, nonviolence, settlement by arbitration, minimal demands, and the use of the strike only as a last resort—has had a great impact in the field of industrial relations in Gujarat, which has remained relatively free from labour unrest.

Transportation

Gujarat's towns and cities are well connected—to each other and to the rest of India—by road and rail. Coastal shipping routes link the state's many ports. Kandla is a major international shipping terminal. There is air service both within the state and to major Indian cities outside Gujarat.

Government and Society

The governmental structure of Gujarat, like that of most Indian states, is defined by the national constitution of 1950.

Constitutional Framework

The governor is the chief executive and is appointed by the president of India. The Council of Ministers, led by the chief minister, aids and advises the governor. Gujarat's Legislative Assembly (Vidhan Sabha) is an elected unicameral body. The High Court is the highest judicial authority in the state. Various lower courts—including the city courts, the courts of district and sessions judges, and the courts of civil judges—operate within each administrative district.

The state is divided into more than two dozen administrative districts. The revenue and general administration of each district is overseen by the district collector, who also functions as the district magistrate for the maintenance of law and order. With a view toward involving the people in local government, elected governing councils (panchayats) were introduced at the village level in 1963.

Health and Welfare

Health and medical services in Gujarat include programs to control malaria, tuberculosis, HIV/AIDS, and other communicable diseases; to prevent blindness; and to eradicate leprosy and polio. Other services focus on reproductive and family health and on health education. Primary health centres offer medical services throughout the state. Public and private hospitals as well as medical colleges offer more specialized services, primarily in the larger urban areas. Various state institutions address the welfare needs of children, women, people with disabilities, and senior citizens. Special programs also are available to assist those who belong to communities that, by tradition, have been socially, economically, and educationally disadvantaged.

EDUCATION

Primary schooling for all children between the ages of 7 and 11 is available in most villages with 500 or more inhabitants. Special schools serve children in the rural tribal regions. Secondary schools are spread throughout the state in larger villages, towns, and urban areas.

Gujarat has a number of important institutions of higher education. Among the state's most notable universities are Maharaja Sayajirao University of Baroda (1949) in Vadodara and Gujarat University (1949) in Ahmadabad. Major research institutions include the Physical Research Laboratory (1947; a unit of the national Department of Space) in Ahmadabad, the Ahmadabad Textile Industry's Research Association (1949), the Central Salt and Marine Chemicals Research Institute

(1959) at Bhavnagar, and the National Institute of Design (1961) and the Sardar Patel Institute of Economic and Social Research (1965), both in Ahmadabad. In addition to its universities and research centres, Gujarat has numerous smaller tertiary institutions (e.g., engineering colleges and technical schools) with specialized curricula.

CULTURAL LIFE

Much of the culture of Gujarat reflects the mythology surrounding the Hindu deity Krishna (an incarnation of the god Vishnu), as transmitted in the Puranas, a class of Hindu sacred literature. The older *rasnritya* and *raslila* dance traditions honouring Krishna find their contemporary manifestation in the popular dance called *garaba* (also spelled *garba*). This dance is performed primarily at the *navaratra* festival, which honours the goddess Durga; female dancers move in a circle, singing and keeping time by clapping their hands or clashing together sticks called *danda*. Also commonly performed at *navaratra* is *bhavai*, a type of popular, rural, comic drama that depicts various aspects of rural life. All of the roles in *bhavai*—both male and female— are played by men.

Shaivism (Shivaism), the cult of the Hindu god Shiva, has long flourished in Gujarat; so too has Vaishnavism (the worship of the god Vishnu), from which have emerged not only the cult of *bhakti* (devotion) but also a rich repertoire of verse and song. Notable Vaishnava saints, poets, and musicians include Narasimha, who composed *padas* (verses) in the 15th century; Mira Bai, a 16th-century Rajput princess who renounced her royal home and composed *bhajans* (devotional songs); Premanand, an 18th-century poet and writer; and Dayaram, an 18th-century composer of songs who popularized the *bhakti* cult.

In the Jain tradition, writings of the prolific 12th-century author Hemacandra continue to be held in high regard. Hemacandra produced numerous textbooks on various aspects of Indian philosophy, as well as grammatical analyses of Sanskrit and Prakrit. He also wrote an epic history of the world from a Jain perspective as well as a number of poems.

Mahatma Gandhi is also recognized as one of the state's most prodigious authors. Noted for their vigour and simplicity, Ghandi's writings in Gujarati have exerted a strong influence on modern Gujarati prose.

The ancient architectural style of Gujarat, known for its luxuriousness and intricacy, is preserved in monuments and temples such as those in Somnath and Dwarka in the southwestern part of the state; Modhera in the north; and Than, Ghumli (near Porbandar), the Girnar Hills, and Palitana in the Kathiawar Peninsula. Under Muslim rule, a distinctive architectural style that blended Muslim and Hindu elements developed. This style is exemplified by many of the 15th- and 16th-century mosques and tombs of Ahmadabad.

Detail of a bandhani-*work sari from Gujarat, 19th century; in the Chhatrapati Shivaji Maharaj Vastu Sangrahalaya, Mumbai, India.* P. Chandra

In addition to its architecture, Gujarat is widely recognized for its highly skilled craftwork. Notable products include the *jari* (gold and silver embroidery) of Surat, the *bandhani*-work (using a tie-dyeing technique) fabrics of Jamnagar, and the *patola* silk saris (garments worn by Indian women) of Patan, in northern Gujarat. Also from the northern region, the toys of Idar, the perfumes of Palanpur, and the hand-loomed products of Kanodar are well known. Ahmadabad and Surat are renowned for their decorative woodwork depicting miniature temples and mythological figures.

Among the most durable and effective of the state's cultural institutions are the trade and craft guilds known as the *mahajans*. Often coterminous with castes—and largely autonomous—the guilds have in the past solved disputes, acted as channels of philanthropy, and encouraged arts and other cultural activities.

HISTORY

Early human settlement in Gujarat traces back hundreds of thousands of years—to the Stone Age—in the valleys of the Sabarmati and Mahi rivers in the eastern part of the state. The emergence of a historical record is linked with the spread of the Indus (Harappan) civilization, which flourished in the 3rd and 2nd millennia BCE. Centres of this civilization have been found at Lothal, Rangpur, Amri, Lakhabaval, and Rozdi (mostly in the Kathiawar Peninsula).

The known history of Gujarat begins with the Mauryan dynasty, which had extended its rule over the area by the 3rd century BCE, as indicated by the edicts of the emperor Ashoka (c. 250 BCE), which are carved on a rock in the Girnar Hills of the Kathiawar Peninsula. After the fall of the Mauryan empire, Gujarat came under the rule of the Shakas (Scythians), or western Kshatrapas (130–390 CE). The greatest of the Shaka

leaders, Mahakshatrapa Rudradaman, established his sway over Saurashtra (a region roughly corresponding to the Kathiawar Peninsula) and Kachchh, as well as over the neighbouring province of Malwa and other areas in what are now the states of Madhya Pradesh Rajasthan.

From the late 4th to the late 5th century, Gujarat formed a part of the Gupta empire until the Guptas were succeeded by the Maitraka dynasty of the kingdom of Valabhi, which ruled over Gujarat and Malwa for three centuries. The capital, Valabhipura (near the eastern coast of the Kathiawar Peninsula), was a great centre of Buddhist, Vedic, and Jaina learning. The Maitraka dynasty was succeeded by the Gurjara-Pratiharas (the imperial Gurjaras of Kannauj), who ruled during the 8th and 9th centuries; they, in turn, were followed shortly afterward by the Solanki dynasty. The boundaries of Gujarat reached their farthest limits during the reign of the Solankis, when remarkable progress was made in the economic and cultural fields. Siddharaja Jayasimha and Kumarapala are the best-known Solanki kings. Karnadeva Vaghela, of the subsequent Vaghela dynasty, was defeated in about 1299 by 'Alā' al-Dīn Khaljī, sultan of Delhi; Gujarat then came under Muslim rule. It was Aḥmad Shah, the first independent sultan of Gujarat, who founded Ahmadabad (1411). By the end of the 16th century, Gujarat was ruled by the Mughals; this lasted until the mid-18th century, when the Marathas overran the state.

Gujarat came under the administration of the British East India Company in 1818. After the Indian Mutiny of 1857–59, the area became a province of the British crown and was divided into Gujarat province, with an area of about 10,000 square miles (26,000 square km), and numerous native states (including Saurashtra and Kachchh). With Indian independence in 1947, the province of Gujarat was included in Bombay state; in 1956 the province was enlarged to include Kachchh and Saurashtra. On May 1, 1960, India's Bombay state was split into present-day Gujarat and Maharashtra.

In April 1965, fighting broke out between India and Pakistan in the Rann of Kachchh, an area that had long been in dispute between the two countries. A cease-fire came into force on July 1, and the dispute was submitted to arbitration by an international tribunal. The tribunal's award, published in 1968, gave nine-tenths of the territory to India and one-tenth to Pakistan. Gujarat was again gripped by violence in 1985; triggered by proposed changes in the concessions reserved for the Scheduled Castes, the disturbances soon escalated into Muslim-Hindu riots and continued for five months. In January 2001 the state was rocked by a devastating earthquake, which had its epicentre at Bhuj in the Kachchh district. About a year later, in February 2002, Gujarat experienced a resurgence of large-scale rioting and Muslim-Hindu communal violence.

MADHYA PRADESH

Madhya Pradesh, as its name implies—*madhya* means "central" and *pradesh* means "region" or "state"—is situated in the heart of India. The state has no coastline and no international frontier. It is bounded by the states of Uttar Pradesh to the northeast, Chhattisgarh to the southeast, Maharashtra to the south, Gujarat to the southwest, and Rajasthan to the northwest. The capital is Bhopal, in the west-central part of the state. Area 119,016 square miles (308,252 square km). Pop. (2008 est.) 69,279,000.

LAND

Madhya Pradesh lies over a transitional area between the Indo-Gangetic Plain in the north and the Deccan plateau in the south. Its physiography is characterized by low hills, extensive plateaus, and river valleys.

RELIEF

The elevation of Madhya Pradesh ranges from 300 to 3,900 feet (90 to 1,200 metres). In the northern part of the state the land rises generally from south to north, while in the southern part it increases in elevation toward the west. Important ranges of hills are the Vindhya Range, in the west, and its northern branch, the Kaimur Hills, both of which reach elevations of 1,500 feet (460 metres), and the Satpura, Mahadeo, and Maikala ranges, in the south, which have elevations of more than 3,000 feet (900 metres). The Dhupgarh Peak (4,429 feet [1,350 metres]), near Pachmarhi in south-central Madhya Pradesh, is the state's highest point. Northwest of the Vindhya Range is the Malwa Plateau (1,650 to 2,000 feet [500 to 600 metres]). Other features include the Rewa Plateau, in the rugged eastern region of the Vindhya Range, the Bundelkhand Upland, north of the Vindhyas, the Madhya Bharat Plateau, in the extreme northwest, and the Baghelkhand Plateau, in the northeast.

DRAINAGE AND SOILS

Madhya Pradesh contains the source of some of the most important rivers in the Indian peninsula: the Narmada, the Tapti (Tapi), the Mahanadi, and the Wainganga (a tributary of the Godavari). The Chambal forms the state's northern border with Rajasthan and Uttar Pradesh. Other rivers include tributaries of the Yamuna and the Son (itself a tributary of the Ganges [Ganga]).

Soils in Madhya Pradesh can be classified into two major groups. Fertile black soils are found in the Malwa Plateau, the Narmada valley, and parts of the Satpura Range. Less-fertile red-to-yellow soils are spread over much of eastern Madhya Pradesh.

CLIMATE

The climate in Madhya Pradesh is governed by a monsoon weather pattern. The distinct seasons are summer (March through May), winter (November through February), and the intervening rainy months of the southwest monsoon (June through September). The summer is hot, dry, and windy; in Bhopal, low temperatures average in the upper 70s F (about 25 °C), while high temperatures typically reach the low 100s F (about 40 °C). Winters are usually pleasant and dry, with daily temperatures normally rising from about 50° (about 10 °C) into the upper 70s F (about 25 °C). Temperatures during the monsoon season usually range from the low 70s F (low 20s C) to the upper 80s F (low 30s C).

The average annual rainfall is about 44 inches (1,100 mm). In general, precipitation decreases westward and northward, from 60 inches (1,500 mm) or more in the east to about 32 inches (800 mm) in the west. The Chambal valley in the north averages less than 30 inches (750 mm) of rainfall per year. Most parts of Madhya Pradesh receive almost all of their precipitation in the monsoon months; however, there is considerable rainfall over the northern part of the state in December and January.

PLANT AND ANIMAL LIFE

In the early 21st century, official statistics indicated that nearly one-third of the state's total area was forested, but satellite imagery revealed the proportion to be closer to one-fifth. An even smaller percentage of Madhya Pradesh consists of permanent pasture or other grazing land. The main forested areas include the Vindhya Range, the Kaimur Hills, the Satpura and Maikala ranges, and the Baghelkhand Plateau. Among the state's most notable trees are teak and sal (*Shorea robusta*), both of which are valuable hardwoods; bamboo; salai (*Boswellia serrata*), which yields a resin used for incense and medicine; and *tendu*, the leaves of which are used for rolling *bidis* (Indian cigarettes).

The forests abound in large mammals, such as tigers, panthers, bears, gaurs (wild cattle), and many types of deer, including chital (spotted deer), sambar, blackbucks, and the rare barasingha (swamp deer). The woodlands also are home to many species of birds. Madhya Pradesh has a number of national parks and many wildlife sanctuaries, of which the best known are Kanha National Park, in the southeastern part of the state, for the barasingha; Bandhavgarh National Park, in the east, for the endangered white tiger; and Shivpuri (Madhav) National Park, in the north, where there is a bird sanctuary. The Kanha National Park has a sanctuary for tigers, and the National Chambal Sanctuary (administered jointly with Rajasthan and Uttar Pradesh), in the northwest, has been established for the conservation of (freshwater) Ganges river dolphins (*Platanista gangetica*), as well as crocodiles, gavials (crocodile-like reptiles), and various large terrestrial animals.

PEOPLE

About one-fifth of the people in Madhya Pradesh are officially classified as members of Scheduled Tribes

POPULATION COMPOSITION

Among the most prominent of these tribes are the Bhil, Baiga, Gond, Korku, Kol, Kamar, and Maria. Non-Scheduled peoples, who hold a higher status within the Indian social system, make up most of the remaining four-fifths of the state's population.

Hindi, the official state language, is also the language most widely spoken in Madhya Pradesh. Eastern Hindi dialects, represented by Bagheli and Awadhi, are spoken in the southern and eastern parts of the state and in the upper Narmada River valley. Bundeli, a Western Hindi dialect, is spoken in the central and northwestern districts of Madhya Pradesh; Malvi, recognized by some as a Western Hindi dialect as well, is the speech of western Madhya Pradesh.

The second most important language in terms of the number of speakers is Marathi. Urdu, Oriya, Gujarati, and Punjabi are each spoken by sizable numbers. Also spoken are Telugu, Bengali, Tamil, and Malayalam. The Bhil speak Bhili, and the Gond speak Gondi.

Most of the people are Hindus. There are, however, significant minorities of Muslims, Jains, Christians, and Buddhists. There is also a small Sikh population.

SETTLEMENT PATTERNS

Roughly three-fourths of the population of Madhya Pradesh is rural, but the distribution of this population is very uneven. Densely populated rural regions are confined largely to the river valleys—the upper Wainganga, the lower Chambal, and the Narmada—and to scattered patches on the Malwa Plateau in western Madhya Pradesh. The largest urban areas are Bhopal, in west-central Madhya Pradesh; Indore, in the west; and Jabalpur (Jubbulpore), in the east-central region. Other major cities include Gwalior, in the north, Ujjain, in the west, and Sagar (Saugor), in the central part of the state.

ECONOMY

Agriculture is the basis of Madhya Pradesh's economy. Less than half of the land area is cultivable, however, and its distribution is quite uneven because of variations in topography, rainfall, and soils. Although Madhya Pradesh is rich in minerals, these resources have yet to be fully exploited. Likewise, Madhya Pradesh has remained an industrially underdeveloped state.

AGRICULTURE

The main cultivated areas are found in the Chambal River valley and on the Malwa and Rewa plateaus. The Narmada valley, covered with river-borne alluvium, is another fertile region.

Agriculture in Madhya Pradesh is characterized by low productivity and the use of nonmechanized methods of cultivation. Because only a portion of the sown area is irrigated, the state's agriculture has remained heavily dependent on rainfall; some regions often suffer from drought. Irrigation in Madhya Pradesh is carried out primarily by means of canals, wells, and tanks (village lakes or ponds).

The most important crops are wheat, sorghum, corn (maize), rice, and pulses. Rice is grown principally in the east, where there is more rainfall, while in central and western Madhya Pradesh wheat and sorghum are more important. The state is one of the largest producers of soybeans in India. Other crops include linseed, sesame, sugarcane, and cotton, as well as various millets, which are grown in hilly areas.

Livestock and poultry farming also are prominent in Madhya Pradesh. The state contains a significant portion of the country's livestock—cows, buffaloes, goats, sheep, and pigs. In addition, the state's many rivers, canals, ponds, and reservoirs support a fisheries industry.

RESOURCES AND POWER

There are large reserves of coal and important deposits of iron ore, manganese ore, bauxite, limestone, dolomite, copper, fireclay, and kaolin (china clay). At Panna, in the northeast, there are diamond reserves.

The state is well endowed with hydroelectric power potential, and a number of hydroelectric projects have been developed jointly with neighbouring states. Madhya Pradesh also draws a portion of its power from several thermal stations located within the state. Most of these thermal plants are coal-fired.

MANUFACTURING

Despite the overall lack of industry in the state, there are several centres of large- and medium-scale manufacturing, most notably in Indore, Gwalior, Bhopal, and Jabalpur, where industrial estates have been established as part of planned development. The principal government-sponsored industries include paper milling, cement production, and the manufacture of heavy electrical items, microelectronics, and optical fibres. Cement works and paper mills also have been established in the private sector, as have facilities for the production of sugar, textiles (cotton, wool, silk, and jute), lumber, flour, and various seed and vegetable oils. Other products of Madhya Pradesh include fertilizer, synthetic fibres, and chemicals.

Of the state's small-scale enterprises, the hand-loom industry has flourished, with saris (garments worn by Indian women) made in Chanderi, gold and silver thread embroidery produced in Bhopal, and carpets woven in Gwalior. The artisans of Gwalior also produce handmade pottery. Jabalpur and Sagar are well-known centres for the manufacture of bidis (hand-rolled cigarettes).

TRANSPORTATION

In comparison with most other Indian states, Madhya Pradesh has a somewhat less developed infrastructure and communication network. Although served by several national highways, the state has a low density of roads, especially in remote rural areas. However, the construction of bridges across the Narmada and other rivers has greatly helped the development of all-weather traffic routes. The main railroads that pass through the state were originally laid down to connect the ports of Chennai (Madras), Mumbai (Bombay), and Kolkata (Calcutta) with their hinterlands. Important railway junctions include Bhopal, Ratlam, Khandwa, and Katni. Airports at Bhopal, Gwalior, Indore, Jabalpur, and Khajuraho offer domestic service.

GOVERNMENT AND SOCIETY

The structure of the government of Madhya Pradesh, like that of most other states of India, is determined by the national constitution of 1950.

CONSTITUTIONAL FRAMEWORK

The head of state is the governor, who is appointed by the president of India. The governor is aided and advised by the Council of Ministers, which is headed by a chief minister and is responsible to the elected, unicameral Legislative Assembly (Vidhan Sabha). Madhya Pradesh has High Court benches at Indore, Gwalior, and Jabalpur, from which appeals can be made to the Supreme Court of India. Lower courts include district courts and family courts.

At the local level, the state is divided administratively into a number of divisions, which in turn are subdivided into numerous districts. Each division is headed by a commissioner and each district by a collector. The collector exercises both executive and magisterial power. Since 1962 the lowest level of local administration has been entrusted to village *panchayat*s (village councils). In addition, official grievance-redress committees help to solve local problems.

HEALTH AND WELFARE

Every district in Madhya Pradesh has at least one hospital, typically in an urban centre, and hundreds of community and primary health centres and subcentres spread across the rural areas. The state also has several eye hospitals, mental hospitals, and other specialized facilities for the prevention and treatment of tuberculosis, venereal disease, and rabies, which, along with filariasis and leprosy, have remained major health concerns. Gwalior has a cancer research centre. Malaria, which was formerly endemic throughout Madhya Pradesh, has been virtually eradicated.

The government has implemented several social welfare programs, including adult literacy classes and various schemes directed toward the special problems of rural youths, the Scheduled Tribes, and members of other traditionally marginalized communities. There are also a number of programs for women and girls, which include informal social service clubs called *mahila mandal*s, schemes for helping rural women with problems of motherhood, and programs that make education available to girls from economically disadvantaged families. Grants-in-aid are given to social welfare and physical welfare institutions, while the government operates leprosy clinics, as well as homes for the impoverished or otherwise needy citizens.

EDUCATION

Roughly two-thirds of the state's population is literate. There are schools for primary, middle, and high-school education, as well as specialized schools for polytechnics, industrial arts, and crafts. Madhya Pradesh has a number of state universities; among these, the Dr. Harisingh Gour University (1946; formerly University of Saugar), located at Sagar, and Vikram University (1957), in Ujjain, are the oldest and best known, while the music school at Khairagarh is one of the finest in India. Jabalpur has an agricultural university, and there is an institute of journalism and public relations in Bhopal.

CULTURAL LIFE

Ancient temples, fortresses, and cave works reflect the rich history of Madhya Pradesh. In addition, the state's tribal

Produce merchants in front of the Jāmi' Mosque, Mandu, Madhya Pradesh. © Hubertus Kanus/SuperStock

peoples have maintained a remarkable oral tradition.

THE ARTS

Some of the most remarkable ancient artwork of Madhya Pradesh is found in caves. The Bagh caves, near the western town of Mhow, are adorned with paintings on Buddhist topics that date roughly to the 5th century CE. Stemming from about the same period (4th to 7th century) are the Udayagiri caves (Brahmanical and Jaina monasteries), near Vidisha, which exhibit artwork and rock-cut architecture similar to those of the well-known Udayagiri caves in the neighbouring state of Orissa.

In the foothills of the Vindhya Range, prehistoric paintings dating from roughly 10,000 BCE adorn the walls of the Bhimbetka rock shelters (designated a UNESCO World Heritage site in 2003). In west-central Madhya Pradesh, one of the state's oldest historical monuments is the stupa (Buddhist mound forming a memorial shrine) at Sanchi, near Vidisha. Originally constructed by Ashoka, emperor of India from about 265 to 238 BCE, the stupa was expanded by the Shunga kings, who ruled the area during the 2nd and 1st centuries BCE. The remains of another stupa, dating to about 175 BCE, were excavated in Bharhut, near Satna, and are now housed in the Indian Museum at Kolkata; the distinctive narrative style of decoration found on this stupa is known as Bharhut sculpture.

The Khajuraho temples, in northern Madhya Pradesh, are widely recognized for their erotic art; they were built by the Chandela kings, who ruled in the region roughly from the early 9th to the mid-11th century. The 14th- and 15th-century palaces and mosque at Mandu, near the western town of Dhar, and the Gwalior fort—perhaps the most impressive of the residences of the former princes of Madhya Pradesh—also constitute notable architectural achievements.

Many traditions of the tribal peoples of Madhya Pradesh have remained strong, and a great deal of indigenous mythology and folklore has been preserved. The *pardhan* (bards of the Gond community) continue to sing of the legendary deeds of Lingo-pen, the mythical originator of the Gond people. The *Pandwani* is the Gond equivalent of the *Mahabharata* (one of the two great Hindu epics), while the *Lachmanjati* legend is the Gond equivalent of the *Ramayana* (the other great Hindu epic). All tribes have myths and legends regarding their origin. Some songs are associated with the celebration of particular life events, such as birth and marriage, while other songs accompany various styles of dance. Folk literature, riddles, and proverbs are other components of the state's rich oral-traditional heritage.

CULTURAL INSTITUTIONS

The state has several well-known annual cultural events, such as Kalidas Samaroh (for the visual and performing arts) in Ujjain, Tansen Samaroh (classical music) in Gwalior, and a dance festival in Khajuraho, where artists from all over India participate. In Bhopal there is a unique multifaceted cultural complex, the Bharat Bhavan, which functions as a meeting ground for artists from various fields; the sprawling complex houses a museum, a library, an open-air theatre, and a number of conference halls. The state has important yearly religious *melas* (gatherings) in Mandsaur (Mandasor) and Ujjain, both in the Malwa region of western Madhya Pradesh.

HISTORY

Rock paintings and stone and metal implements found in the rivers, valleys, and other areas of Madhya Pradesh indicate that the area has been inhabited since prehistoric times. One of the earliest kingdoms known to have existed in the region was Avanti, with its capital at Ujjain. Located in the western part of present-day Madhya Pradesh, this state was part of the Mauryan empire (4th–3rd century BCE) and was later known as Malwa. Attracted by the region's fertile black soils, settlers from different parts of India migrated to Malwa via three important migratory routes—from the western coast, from the Deccan plateau, and from the ancient city of Shravasti and its surrounding territory in the north.

DYNASTIC RULE

Among the various dynasties that ruled part or all of Madhya Pradesh between the 2nd century BCE and the end of the 10th

century CE were the Shungas (*c.* 185–*c.* 73 BCE), who ruled in eastern Malwa, the Satavahanas (1st or 3rd century BCE–3rd century CE), the Shakas (2nd–4th century CE), and the Nagas (2nd–4th century CE). The whole of Madhya Pradesh lying north of the Narmada River formed part of the Gupta empire (4th–5th century CE) and was the scene of a power struggle against the nomadic Hephthalites (Hunas) and the Kalachuris, the latter of whom occupied part of Malwa but only for a brief period. Yashodharman was the Malwan king who defeated the Hephthalites in the 6th century. During the first part of the 7th century, Malwa was annexed by the emperor of northern India, Harsha (Harahavardhana).

By the 10th century the Kalachuris had risen again to occupy eastern Madhya Pradesh, including the Narmada valley; their contemporaries were the Paramaras of Dhar in what is now the western region, the Kachwahas of Gwalior in the north, and the Chandelas of Khajuraho, about 100 miles (160 km) southeast of Jhansi. Later the Tomaras ruled at Gwalior, and the tribal Gonds ruled over several districts.

MUSLIM AND BRITISH RULE

Muslim invasion of the area began in the 11th century. The Hindu domains of Gwalior were incorporated into the Delhi sultanate in 1231 by the sultan Iltutmish. Later, in the early 14th century, the Khaljī sultans of Delhi overran Malwa, which was subsequently annexed into the Mughal

Empire by Akbar (ruled 1556–1605), the greatest of the Mughal emperors. Maratha power extended into Malwa at the beginning of the 18th century, and a large part of what is now Madhya Pradesh had come under the control of an alliance of Maratha rulers—the Maratha confederacy—by 1760. With the defeat of the *peshwas* (hereditary Maratha chief ministers who centralized Maratha rule) in 1761, the Sindhia dynasty of Marathas was established at Gwalior in the north and the Holkar dynasty, also Maratha, at Indore in the southwest.

In the early 19th century the area became increasingly agitated as Pindari robber bands, composed of horsemen formerly attached to armies of Maratha chiefs, began to raid towns and villages from their hideouts in central India. The Pindaris, who received the tacit protection of the Sindhia and Holkar dynasties, had formed these autonomous bands beginning in the late 18th century, when the Maratha confederacy was weakening from internal dissension and from the growing military presence of the British. By 1818 British armies were able to suppress not only the Pindaris but also the various Maratha dynasties. That year the Nerbudda (now Narmada) River and Saugor (now Sagar) territories, containing much of northern Madhya Pradesh (including Gwalior and Indore of the Sindhia and Holkar dynasties), were ceded to the emerging British Empire.

During the next 40 years the British consolidated their control over the area. In the early 1830s British armies were

required to suppress the thugs (Hindi: *thag*), a fraternity of assassins and plunderers (dating from at least the 14th century) who were roaming across central India. By 1854 all of Madhya Pradesh had fallen under British control. The present borders began to take shape in 1861, when the Sagar and Narmada territories and the Nagpur plain to the south were merged to create the Central Provinces. In 1903, with the addition of the Muslim territory of Berar, the area was renamed the Central Provinces and Berar. This administrative unit, however, did not include those parts of the north and west of the present state (Malwa, Bundelkhand, and Baghelkhand) that from 1854 formed sections of the Central India Agency. The Muslim state of Bhopal, situated between the Central India Agency and the Central Provinces and Berar, remained a protectorate of the British.

MADHYA PRADESH SINCE INDIAN INDEPENDENCE

When India became independent in 1947, the new states of Madhya Bharat and Vindhya Pradesh were carved out of the old Central India Agency. Three years later, in 1950, the Central Provinces and Berar was renamed Madhya Pradesh. With the States Reorganization Act of 1956, Madhya Pradesh was redistributed along linguistic lines. The act transferred the southern Marathi-speaking districts of Madhya Pradesh to the Bombay state (now in Maharashtra) and merged several Hindi-speaking areas—the states of

Bhopal and Vindhya Pradesh, as well as most of Madhya Bharat—with Madhya Pradesh. In 2000 its eastern provinces became the state of Chhattisgarh.

MAHARASHTRA

The Indian state of Maharashtra occupies a substantial portion of the Deccan plateau in the western peninsular part of the subcontinent. It is bounded by the Indian states of Gujarat to the northwest, Madhya Pradesh to the north, Chhattisgarh to the east, Andhra Pradesh to the southeast, Karnataka to the south, and Goa to the southwest and by the union territory of Dadra and Nagar Haveli and the Arabian Sea to the west.

Maharashtra's capital, Mumbai (formerly Bombay), is an island city on the western coast, connected to the mainland by roads and railways. Aptly called the gateway of India, Maharashtra is one of India's biggest commercial and industrial centres, and it has played a significant role in the country's social and political life.

Maharashtra is a leader among Indian states in terms of agricultural and industrial production, trade and transport, and education. Its ancient culture, at one stage considerably obscured by British dominance, survives largely through the medium of a strong literary heritage. A common literature in Marathi, the predominant language of the state, has in fact played an important role in nurturing a sense of unity among the Maharashtrians.

Area 118,800 square miles (307,690 square km). Pop. (2008 est.) 106,894,000.

LAND

Maharashtra's shape roughly resembles a triangle, with the 450-mile (725-km) western coastline forming the base and its interior narrowing to a blunt apex some 500 miles (800 km) to the east.

RELIEF, DRAINAGE, AND SOILS

The state presents an interesting range of physical diversity. To the west is the narrow Konkan coastal lowland, which reaches its widest extent near Mumbai. Numerous minor hills dominate the relief. There are many small, swift, west-flowing streams, most of them less than 50 miles (80 km) long. The biggest, Ulhas, rising in the Bhor Ghat, joins the sea after an 80-mile (130-km) course.

The Western Ghats (a mountain range at the western edge of the Deccan plateau; *ghat* means "pass" in Marathi) run almost continuously for 400 miles (640 km) north-south, with the foothills reaching to within 4 miles (6.4 km) of the Arabian Sea. Elevations increase northward to peaks of some 4,720 feet (1,440 metres). There are a few passes through which roads and railroads link the coast with the interior. The eastern slopes of the Ghats descend gently to the Deccan plateau and are sculptured by the wide mature valleys of the Krishna, Bhima, and Godavari rivers.

Lava trap formations near Satara, Maharashtra, India. © Satish Parashar/Dinodia Photo Library

Between the Narmada valley in the north, the Krishna basin in the south, and the western coast to as far east as the city of Nagpur, the Ghats and the triangular plateau inland are covered with extensive lava outpourings called traps. They reach a maximum thickness of 10,000 feet (3,000 metres) near Mumbai. The differential erosion of lava has resulted in characteristic steppelike slopes, uniform crest lines, and a table-top appearance of many hills in Maharashtra.

Around Nagpur, the Deccan trap gives way to undulating uplands (about 890 to 1,080 feet [270 to 330 metres] high) underlain by ancient crystalline rocks. The Wardha-Wainganga valley, part of the larger Godavari basin, trends southward and has many lakes.

A major part of Maharashtra is covered in black soils derived from decomposed lava rocks that are commonly called "black cotton soils" (because cotton often is grown in them). Drifts along the slopes have eroded into medium brown and light-coloured sandy soils. Saline soils in the river valleys are the results of impeded soil drainage followed by intense evaporation.

CLIMATE

The climate is characteristically monsoonal (i.e., wet-dry), with local variations. India's southwest monsoonal rains break on the Mumbai coast usually in the first week of June and last until September, during which period they account for about four-fifths of the annual rainfall. Four seasons are normal: March–May (hot and dry); June–September (hot and wet); October–November (warm and dry); and December–February (cool and dry).

The Western Ghats and the ranges on the northern borders greatly influence the climate and separate the wet Konkan Coast from the dry interior upland, an area called the Desh. Rainfall is extremely heavy in Konkan, averaging about 100 inches (2,540 mm), with some of the wettest spots receiving up to 250 inches (6,350 mm) but rapidly diminishing to one-fifth of that amount east of the Ghats. Rainfall increases again in the eastern areas, reaching about 40 to 80 inches (1,000 to 2,000 mm) in the extreme east.

The coastal regions enjoy equable temperatures; monthly averages at Mumbai are in the low 80s F (about 27–28 °C). A change of more than about 13 °F (7 °C) between day and night temperatures is unusual. Pune (Poona), higher up on the plateau, benefits from cooler temperatures throughout the year. In the interior, average summer temperatures reach into the low 100s F (about 38–41 °C), and winter temperatures average in the low 70s F (about 21–23 °C).

PLANT AND ANIMAL LIFE

Forests cover less than one-fifth of the state and are confined to the Western Ghats, mainly their transverse ranges, the Satpura Range in the north, and the Chandrapur region in the east. On the coast and adjoining slopes, plant forms are rich with lofty trees, variegated shrubs, and mango and coconut trees. The forests yield teak, bamboo, myrobalan (for dyeing), and other woods.

Thorny savanna-like vegetation occurs in areas of lesser rainfall, notably in upland Maharashtra. Subtropical vegetation is found on higher plateaus that receive heavy rain and have milder temperatures. Bamboo, chestnut, and magnolia are common. In the semiarid tracts, wild dates are found. Mangrove vegetation occurs in marshes and estuaries along the coast.

Wild animals include tigers, leopards, bison, and several species of antelope. The striped hyena, wild hog, and sloth bear are common. Monkeys and snakes occur in great variety, as do ducks and other game birds. The peacock is indigenous. Many of these animals can be viewed at the state's national parks at Tadoba, Chikhaldara, and Borivli. The state's abundant marine life in the waters off the western coast remains largely unexploited.

PEOPLE

Maharashtrians are ethnically heterogeneous. Marathas and Kunbis (descendants of settlers who arrived from the north about the beginning of the 1st century CE) make up the majority of the remainder of the state population. The Bhil, Warli, Gond, Korku, Govari, and other tribal communities live on the slopes of the Western Ghats and the Satpura Range.

Marathi, the official state language, is spoken by more than four-fifths of the population. Other languages spoken in the state are Gujarati, Hindi, Telugu, Kannada, Sindhi, Urdu, Bengali, Malayalam, and English. There are also many local languages, including Konkani on the west coast and Gondi, Varhadi, and Mundari in the eastern and northern forests.

Maharashtra's religious diversity reflects that of India as a whole. Hindus predominate, followed by Muslims and Buddhists. There are many Christians in the metropolitan areas. Jewish and Parsi (a religious minority adhering to Zoroastrianism) groups have settled mostly in urban areas; Parsis live mainly in Mumbai and its environs. Other religious minorities include Jains and Sikhs, whose small communities are widespread.

About two-thirds of the population is rural and lives in villages. Mumbai, the largest city in the state, is also the most populous metropolis in India. Nagpur, Pune, and Solapur are other major cities. Of particular historical interest is the Mughal city of Aurangabad in the northwest-central part of the state, which contains several monuments and other historic buildings.

ECONOMY

The national and state governments have promoted both improved agricultural techniques and increased industrialization of the economy. As a result, Maharashtra has become one of the most developed and prosperous Indian states. Mumbai, India's best-equipped port, handles an enormous foreign trade. It is a hub of manufacturing, finance, and administration but also a national centre for motion-picture production. Pune has developed many industries because of its proximity to Mumbai. Nagpur and Solapur have textile and other agriculturally based industries.

AGRICULTURE

Insufficient rainfall in much of Maharashtra constitutes the main obstacle to agriculture in the state. Measures to combat food deficits have included the electrification of irrigation pumps, the use of hybrid seeds, more efficient cultivation, and incentives offered to farmers. Maharashtra is the largest producer of sugarcane in India. Grain sorghum, millet, and pulses dominate the cropped area. Rice grows where rainfall exceeds 40 inches (1,000 mm), and wheat is a winter crop in fields that retain moisture. Cotton, tobacco, and peanuts (groundnuts) are major crops in areas with heavy rainfall. Mangoes, cashew nuts, bananas, and oranges are popular orchard crops.

Millet field near Satara, Maharashtra, India. B. Bhansali/Shostal Associates

RESOURCES AND POWER

Most of Maharashtra's known mineral resources—including manganese, coal, iron ore, limestone, copper, bauxite, silica sand, and common salt—occur in the eastern districts, with some deposits in the west. The Bhandara, Nagpur, and Chandrapur regions are particularly rich in bituminous coal. Undersea oil deposits were discovered near Mumbai in the 1970s and have since been exploited, enhancing the city's economic importance nationally. The mountainous areas of the state possess significant timber reserves.

Hydroelectric and thermal stations provide most of the state's power. Large thermal power plants, which burn coal, are located near Nagpur and Chandrapur. The nuclear power facility at Tarapur, 70 miles (113 km) north of Mumbai, was India's first nuclear power plant.

MANUFACTURING

The manufacture of cotton textiles is the oldest and largest industry in

Maharashtra. Mumbai, Nagpur, Solapur, Akola, and Amravati are the main factory centres; woolen goods are produced especially in and around Nagpur and Solapur. Other hubs of traditional agriculturally based industry include Jalgaon and Dhule (edible oils processing) and Kolhapur, Ahmadnagar, and the Sangli-Miraj industrial complex (sugar refining). Fruit canning and preservation are important in Nagpur, Bhusawal, Ratnagiri, and Mumbai. Manufactured forest products include timber, bamboo, sandalwood, and *tendu* leaves—the latter used for rolling *bidi* (Indian cigarettes). Small-scale agroprocessing of food grains and other crops is virtually ubiquitous in the state.

The Mumbai-Pune complex boasts the state's greatest concentration of heavy industry and high technology. The petrochemical industry has developed rapidly since the installation of India's first offshore oil wells near Mumbai in 1976. Oil refining and the manufacture of agricultural implements, transport equipment, rubber products, electric and oil pumps, lathes, compressors, sugar-mill machinery, typewriters, refrigerators, electronic equipment, and television and radio sets are important. Automobiles are also assembled there.

The eastern area around Nagpur, Chandrapur, and Bhandara supports major coal-based industries, along with plants that process ferroalloys, manganese and iron ores, and cement. Aurangabad and Thane are also important industrial hubs.

TRANSPORTATION

The state's rail network is vital to Maharashtra's transport system. The Konkan Railway links Mumbai with settlements in the coastal plain. Wardha and Nagpur are important junctions on the rail routes.

National highways connect the state with Delhi, Kolkata (Calcutta), Allahabad, Hyderabad, and Bangalore (Bengaluru).

Daily air services connect Mumbai with Pune, Nagpur, Aurangabad, and Nashik. The international airport at Mumbai is one of India's busiest and largest hubs, and Nagpur is the centre of India's domestic air service. Inland water transport plays a limited role in Maharashtra, and other than Mumbai there are only minor ports on the western coast.

GOVERNMENT AND SOCIETY

The structure of the government of Maharashtra, like that of most other states of India, is determined by the national constitution of 1950.

CONSTITUTIONAL FRAMEWORK

The head of state is the governor, who is appointed by the president of India. The governor is aided and advised by the Council of Ministers (led by a chief minister) and is responsible to the legislature, which consists of two houses: the Vidhan Parishad (Legislative Council) and the Vidhan Sabha (Legislative

Assembly). Both bodies meet for regular sessions in Mumbai and once annually in Nagpur. Seats are reserved for members of Scheduled Castes and Scheduled Tribes and for women. Maharashtra is represented in the Lok Sabha and the Rajya Sabha (which are, respectively, the lower and upper houses of the Indian Parliament).

Executive authority in the state is exercised by the cabinet in the name of the governor. The district collector and chief executive officer—responsible for the collection of land revenue and special taxes and for coordinating the work of other departments—are the key figures within the local administrative areas.

The judiciary, a High Court headed by the chief justice and a panel of judges, is based in Mumbai. There are branches of this court at Nagpur and at Aurangabad.

Maharashtra comprises three conventional regions: western Maharashtra, Vidarbha, and Marathwada. Each is divided administratively into districts, which are further divided into *talukas* (townships). Local administrations consist of *zilla parishads* (district councils), *panchayat samiti* (township councils), and *gram panchayats* (village councils). Cities and towns have corporations and municipal councils as elected bodies.

The Public Service Commission and a State Selection Board select candidates for appointment to all state services. This process is carried out largely by means of competitive examinations.

HEALTH AND WELFARE

Scores of hospitals and clinics, including general hospitals, women's hospitals, and mental health institutes, are in Maharashtra. Medical personnel mainly consist of allopathic (traditional Western) and Ayurvedic (ancient Indian) practitioners. Unanī (traditional Muslim) and homeopathic systems of medicine are also popular. The state is a leader in the prevention and control of malaria and parasites such as guinea worms and the nematodes that cause filariasis, in the immunization of children and expectant mothers, and in the treatment of tuberculosis, goitre, leprosy, cancer, and HIV/AIDS. Regional blood banks are in Mumbai, Pune, Aurangabad, and Nagpur, and emergency centres are found in all districts. The state has repeatedly received national recognition for its family-planning program. In Mumbai the Haffkine Institute, a leading bacteriologic research centre specializing in tropical diseases, and the Indian Cancer Research Centre (located in the Tata Memorial Hospital) are well known.

EDUCATION

At the beginning of the 21st century, Maharashtra's literacy rate was one of the highest of all the Indian states, with about three-fourths of the population aged 15 and over able to read and write. The state provides free compulsory education for children between ages 6 and 14. Vocational and multipurpose high schools also have grown in importance.

Larger institutions for higher education include the University of Mumbai (1857) and Shreemati Nathibai Damodar Thackersey Women's University (1916) in Mumbai, Rashtrasant Tukadoji Mahara Nagpur University (1923) in Nagpur, the University of Pune (1949) in Pune, Shivaji University (1962) in Kolhapur, and Yashwantrao Chavan Maharashtra University (1989) in Nashik. There are other universities in Aurangabad, Ahmadnagar, Akola, Amravati, Jalgaon, and Kolhapur. Some prominent institutions in the state include the Central Institute of Fisheries Education, the Indira Gandhi Institute of Development Research, the International Institute for Population Sciences, and the Tata Institute of Social Sciences in Mumbai and the Deccan College Postgraduate and Research Institute and the Gokhale Institute of Politics and Economics in Pune.

Several medical, dental, and Ayurvedic colleges are in Mumbai, Nagpur, and Pune. Most district hospitals maintain nursing schools. Technical education is provided by engineering colleges and polytechnic and industrial institutes. Almost every *taluka* (township) has a technical school.

An important adjunct to education in the state is training courses run by the country's security establishment. The National Defence Academy near Pune is a premier institution that provides cadet training for India's defense forces.

The College of Military Engineering at Pune is run by the Indian Army Corps of Engineers. Sainik schools (competitive secondary schools that prepare students to serve in the National Defence Academy) and the voluntary National Cadet Corps provide military training. There are also institutes in Maharashtra for research and development in explosives, armament technology, vehicle research, and naval, chemical, and metallurgical laboratories.

CULTURAL LIFE

Maharashtra is a distinct cultural region. Its long artistic tradition is manifested in the ancient cave paintings found at Ajanta and Ellora just north of Aurangabad, both which were designated UNESCO World Heritage sites in 1983, in a number of medieval architectural masterpieces, in its classical and devotional music, and in its theatre. Pune, where numerous organizations sustain these great traditions, is the state's undisputed cultural capital.

THE ARTS

Music in Maharashtra, like Marathi literature, has an ancient tradition. It became allied with Hindustani music about the 14th century. In more recent times Vishnu Digambar Paluskar and Vishnu Narayana Bhatkhande greatly influenced Indian classical music. Contemporary vocalists include Bhimsen Joshi and Lata Mangeshkar.

In rural Maharashtra the foremost diversion is *tamasha*, a performance form that combined music, drama, and dance. The typical *tamasha* troupe comprises seven artists, including a female dancer for featured roles and a bawdy clown.

The theatre and the cinema are popular in urban areas of Maharashtra. Leading playwrights V. Khadilkar and Vijay Tendulkar and actor Bal Gandharva raised the status of the Marathi drama as an art form. The Indian movie industry, known as Bollywood, began in Mumbai in the 1930s, and by the early 21st century its films had gained popularity among international audiences. Prabhat Film Company in Pune is one of the country's leaders in cinema; some of its best-known productions are *Sant Tukaram* (1936) and *Sant Dnyaneshwar* (1940). Maharashtrian film pioneers are Dadasaheb Phalke and Baburao Painter, and artists of Hindi cinema include Nana Patekar and Madhuri Dixit.

RECREATION

Many festivals are held throughout the year in Maharashtra. Holi and Ranga Panchami are spring festivals. The Dassera (Dashahara) is an autumn event that commemorates the day on which Maratha warriors traditionally started on their military campaigns. During Pola in August, farmers bathe, decorate, and parade their bulls through the streets, signifying the start of the sowing season. The Ganesha festival, celebrating the birth of Hindu deity Ganesha, is held during the rainy season and is by far the most popular in Maharashtra. Its public celebration was first sponsored by the nationalist political leader Bal Gangadhar Tilak in 1893. Clay idols of Ganesha are sold throughout the state. Unique to Maharashtra is the Hurda party, in which a farmer invites neighbouring villagers to partake of fresh ears of grain sorghum. 'Āshūrā', observed on the 10th day of Muḥarram (the first month of the Islamic calendar), honours the martyrs of Islam, although Hindus also participate. Folk songs and traditional dances accompany all these celebrations.

HISTORY

The name Maharashtra, denoting the western upland of the Deccan plateau, first appeared in a 7th-century inscription and in the account of Xuanzang, a Chinese traveler at that time. According to one interpretation, the name derives from the word *maharathi* (great chariot driver), which refers to a skillful northern fighting force that migrated southward into the area. The group's language, intermingled with the speech of the earlier Naga settlers, became Maharastri, which by the 8th century had developed into Marathi. There was also a continuous influx of people from remote Greece and Central Asia.

During this early period the territory constituting the modern state of Maharashtra was divided between several Hindu kingdoms: Satavahana, Vakataka,

Kalacuri, Rashtrakuta, Chalukya, and Yadava. After 1307 there was a succession of Muslim dynasties. Persian, the court language of the Muslims, had a far-reaching effect on Marathi. By the middle of the 16th century, Maharashtra was again fragmented between several independent Muslim rulers, who fought each other endlessly. It was in the midst of this chaos that a great leader, Shivaji, was born in 1627. Shivaji showed astonishing prowess by founding a large Maratha empire that shook Delhi-based Mughal rule to its foundations.

During the 18th century almost all of western and central India, as well as large segments of the north and east, was brought under Maratha suzerainty. It was this empire that succumbed to the British from the early 19th century onward. When India became independent in 1947, the province, long known as the Bombay Presidency, became Bombay state. The following year a number of former princely states (notably Baroda [now Vadodara]) were merged into the new state, and on Nov. 1, 1956, a major linguistic and political reorganization of the states of peninsular India resulted in the addition of large parts of Madhya Pradesh and the erstwhile Hyderabad to Bombay state. The outcome of this reorganization was a state in which most of the Gujarati-speaking peoples lived in the north and most of the Marathi-speaking peoples lived in the south. As a result of the demands of the two language groups, the state was divided into two parts on May 1, 1960, thus creating Gujarat in the north and Maharashtra in the south. Bombay, remaining part of Maharashtra, became the new state's capital. The city's name was changed to Mumbai in the mid-1990s.

CHAPTER 12

SELECTED SOUTHERN INDIAN STATES

S outhern India is marked by its ethnic diversity. In many of the region's states one ethnolinguistic group predominates, as in three of the states profiled in this chapter—the Andhras of Andhra Pradesh, the Malayalis of Kerala, and the Tamils of Tamil Nadu. Goa, the other state discussed (and the second one listed below), was a Portuguese colony for some four and a half centuries before becoming part of India and has its own unique identity.

ANDHRA PRADESH

The southeastern Indian state of Andhra Pradesh is bounded by the Indian states of Tamil Nadu (formerly Madras) to the south, Karnataka (Mysore) to the west, Maharashtra to the northwest and north, and Chhattisgarh and Orissa to the northeast; the eastern boundary is a 600-mile (970-km) coastline along the Bay of Bengal. The capital is Hyderabad.

The state draws its name from the Andhra people, who have inhabited the area since antiquity and who have developed their own language, Telugu. Andhra Pradesh came into existence in its present form in 1956 as a result of the demand of the Andhras for a separate state. Although it is primarily agricultural, the state has some mining activity and a significant amount of industry. Area 106,204 square miles (275,068 square km). Pop. (2008 est.) 82,180,000.

LAND

The state has three main physiographic regions: the coastal plain to the east, extending from the Bay of Bengal to the mountain ranges; the mountain ranges themselves, the Eastern Ghats, which form the western flank of the coastal plain; and the plateau to the west of the Ghats.

RELIEF, DRAINAGE, AND SOILS

The coastal plain, also known as the Andhra region, runs almost the entire length of the state and is watered by several rivers, flowing from west to east through the hills into the bay. The deltas formed by the most important of these rivers—the Godavari and the Krishna—make up the central part of the plains, an area of fertile alluvial soil.

The Eastern Ghats are part of a larger mountain system extending from central India to the far south and running parallel to the east coast. Interrupted by the great river valleys, these mountains do not form a continuous range. They have highly porous soils on their flanks.

The plateau to the west of the ranges—part of the Deccan—is composed of gneissic rock (gneiss being a foliated rock formed within the Earth's interior under conditions of heat and pressure); it has an average elevation of about 1,600 feet (500 metres). The southern

portion of the plateau is commonly called Rayalaseema, and the northern portion is called Telangana. As the result of erosion, the plateau is a region of graded valleys, with red, sandy soil and isolated hills. Black soil is also found in certain parts of the area.

CLIMATE

A summer that lasts from March to June, a season of tropical rains that runs from July to September, and a winter that lasts from October to February constitute the three seasons of Andhra Pradesh. Throughout much of the state, annual maximum temperatures range from the mid-70s to the low 80s F (the mid-20s C), while minimum temperatures usually read in the low 50s F (about 10 to 12 °C). On the coastal plain, however, summers are extraordinarily warm, with temperatures often exceeding 100 °F (38 °C) in some places. Conversely, summers are cooler and winters colder on the central plateau. Annual rainfall, which derives largely from the southwest monsoon, varies widely across the state. Some coastal areas may receive as much as 55 inches (1,400 mm) of rain, while the northern and western parts of the plateau may receive as little as 20 inches (500 mm).

PLANT AND ANIMAL LIFE

Mangrove swamps and palm trees fringe the coastal plain of Andhra Pradesh, while thorny vegetation covers the scattered hills of the plateau. Of the state's total area, about one-fourth is forest-covered, with dense woodlands occurring primarily in the north along the Godavari River and in the south in the Eastern Ghats. The forests consist of both moist deciduous and dry savanna vegetation; teak, rosewood, wild fruit trees, and bamboo are plentiful. Elsewhere in the state, neem (which produces an aromatic oil), banyan, mango, and the pipal (or Bo; *Ficus religiosa*) are among the common trees. Andhra Pradesh also has an array of flowering vegetation, including jasmine, rose, and a number of endemic species—particularly in the hilly region of the Eastern Ghats.

Animal life, apart from common domestic types (dogs, cats, and cattle), includes tigers, blackbucks, hyenas, sloth bears, gaurs, and chitals, which abound in the hills and forest areas. There also are dozens of species of birds, including flamingos and pelicans, as well as some rare varieties, such as the Jerdon's courser (*Rhinoptilus bitorquatus*), which is found in the thorny or scrub-covered areas surrounding the Eastern Ghats. The eastern coast is a nesting ground for sea turtles.

PEOPLE

The population of Andhra Pradesh, like that of the other states of India, is highly diverse. In general, the state's various communities are identified more readily by a combination of language, religion, and social class or caste than they are by specific ethnic affiliation. Telugu is the official and most widely spoken

language in the state; a small minority speaks Urdu, a language primarily of northern India and Pakistan. Most of the remaining groups speak border-area languages, including Hindi, Tamil, Kannada, Marathi, and Oriya. Lambadi (Banjari) and a number of other languages are spoken by the state's Scheduled Tribes.

The great majority of the residents of Andhra Pradesh practice Hinduism. Smaller segments of the population follow Islam or Christianity. Christians live mostly in the urban centres and coastal areas, while Muslims are concentrated in the Telangana and Rayalaseema regions.

More than one-fourth of the population lives in urban areas. Of the urban dwellers, over a third inhabit the industrial and manufacturing areas around the three main cities—Hyderabad, Vishakhapatnam, and Vijayawada. With increasing industrial development, these cities began to merge with neighbouring towns, forming urban agglomerations.

ECONOMY

Dominated by the production of food grains, agriculture is the primary sector of the state's economy. However, mining (notably of coal) and manufacturing are significant components as well.

AGRICULTURE, FORESTRY, AND FISHING

Andhra Pradesh is one of the leading rice-growing states in the country and is a major producer of India's tobacco. The state's rivers, particularly the Godavari and the Krishna, account for its agricultural importance; for a long time their benefits were restricted to the coastal districts of the Andhra region, which had the best irrigation facilities. Since the mid-20th century, however, great efforts have been made to tap the waters of these and other rivers for the benefit of the dry interior; indeed, a significant portion of the state's total investment for development is allotted to agricultural irrigation.

Canal irrigation in the Telangana and Rayalaseema regions of the plateau has given rise to agro-industrial complexes rivaling those of coastal Andhra Pradesh. The Nagarjuna Sagar multipurpose project, diverting the waters of the Krishna for irrigation, has increased substantially the production of rice and sugarcane. Rice flour, rice-bran oil, paints and varnishes, soaps and detergents, cardboard and other packaging materials, and cattle feed are all produced from local paddy rice. Other agricultural commodities now grown statewide include chili peppers, sorghum, pulses (peas, beans, and lentils), castor beans, peanuts (groundnuts), and cotton—all of which are processed locally as well—and grapes, mangoes, bananas, and oranges. This economic development in Telangana and Rayalaseema—further stimulated by improved agricultural technology, use of chemical fertilizers and pesticides, and upgrades in transport, marketing, and credit systems—has helped to reduce the political tensions that formerly existed between interior and coastal Andhra Pradesh.

The woodlands of Andhra Pradesh annually yield high-quality timber, such as teak and eucalyptus. Nontimber forest produce—including sal seeds (from which an edible oil is extracted), tendu leaves (for rolling local cigarettes), gum karaya (a type of emulsifier), and bamboo—is also important.

With its long coastline and many rivers, the state has a significant and expanding fishing industry. Much of the yield is drawn from freshwater and marine aquaculture, but open-sea fisheries are significant as well. Prawns and shrimp are among the main products of the industry.

RESOURCES AND POWER

Among the state's principal mineral resources are asbestos, mica, manganese, barite, and high-grade coal. Low-grade iron ore is found in the southern parts of the state. Andhra Pradesh produces a major share of the country's barite. It is the only state in southern India that possesses significant coal reserves. In the early 21st century, large deposits of natural gas were discovered onshore and offshore in the basins of the Godavari and Krishna rivers. The diamond mines of Golconda were once renowned worldwide for producing the Koh-i-noor diamond and other famous stones; efforts have been made to revive production in the area. Quartz, limestone, and graphite also occur. The state has established a mining and metal trading corporation to lead the exploitation of its mineral resources.

Most of Andhra Pradesh's energy is produced by thermal generators in the public sector, with hydroelectric power stations providing an important secondary source of energy. In addition, the government has established several wind farms. A number of private companies operate generators powered by natural gas; they also have worked to develop wind, biomass, and other nonconventional power sources.

MANUFACTURING

Although Andhra Pradesh has since the mid-20th century become one of the most highly industrialized states in India, manufacturing continues to account for a small percentage of the state's income. Industries such as shipbuilding, aeronautics, and the manufacture of electrical equipment, machine tools, and drugs have been established in the Vishakhapatnam and Hyderabad areas. Private enterprises, many of them located in and around the urban agglomeration of Vijayawada and Guntur in the east-central region, produce chemicals, textiles, cement, fertilizers, processed foods, petroleum derivatives, and cigarettes. A number of important enterprises of moderate size, such as sugar factories, are scattered across the medium and smaller urban areas. There is a mammoth steel plant at Vishakhapatnam, where raw materials and port facilities are easily accessible; an oil refinery also is located there, as is a large shipbuilding yard. The phenomenal increase in power generated by hydroelectric and thermoelectric projects since the late 20th century has benefited industrialization and irrigation.

TRANSPORTATION

There are airports in the state at Hyderabad, Vijayawada, Tirupati, and Vishakhapatnam. An extensive road and rail system connects Andhra Pradesh with most other parts of India. Bus transportation, a large share of which is privately operated, offers facilities for express travel between various cities. The river canals in coastal areas, especially the saltwater Kommamur (Buckingham) Canal running parallel to the coast from the Krishna River to Chennai (Madras), are used for cargo transportation. Vishakhapatnam is a major international seaport.

GOVERNMENT AND SOCIETY

Andhra Pradesh is a constituent unit of the Republic of India; as such, the structure of its government, like that of most Indian states, is defined by the national constitution of 1950.

CONSTITUTIONAL FRAMEWORK

A governor, appointed by the president of India, is the executive head of the state administration, but the real power is in the hands of a chief minister and a Council of Ministers responsible to the state legislature. The state has a unicameral legislature, the Legislative Assembly

(Vidhan Sabha), which is elected by adult suffrage from territorial constituencies.

The administration is conducted by various ministries and departments, each under the direction of a minister, assisted by a staff of permanent civil servants. The State Secretariat at Hyderabad supervises the administration of the state's nearly two dozen districts. Local administration in each district is the responsibility of a district collector. Rural local government has been democratically decentralized by the introduction of a system in which local authorities operate at the village, block (a unit consisting of a group of villages), and district levels. Municipal bodies govern the urban areas.

The regional committees for Telangana and Rayalaseema are a special feature of the state government; the duty of the committees is to ensure that the views of the people of Telangana and Rayalaseema are given adequate consideration. The committees were established to protect regional interests when the regions joined Andhra Pradesh in 1956, since the areas were economically and educationally less advanced than the coastal Andhra areas. The disparities of development that existed at the regional level in Andhra Pradesh gave rise in the early 1970s to the formation of Telangana Praja Samiti (Telugu: Telangana People's Committee), a political party demanding Telangana statehood. In the following decade, organizers of another political party, Telugu Desam (Land of Telugu), advocated a reduced role for the national government in state affairs. Telugu

Desam ruled Andhra Pradesh for much of the late 20th and early 21st centuries.

The state judiciary is headed by a High Court, located in Hyderabad; the High Court has original jurisdiction in some cases and exercises appellate and administrative control over the district and lower level courts. The High Court is itself subject to the appellate authority of the Supreme Court of India in certain matters. The Secunderabad cantonment, north of Hyderabad, comprises a number of defense establishments, and Vishakhapatnam is the headquarters of the Eastern Naval Command.

HEALTH AND WELFARE

Government-supported health facilities have expanded rapidly since the late 20th century. Under the Primary Health Centres scheme, medical help, both curative and preventive, has been brought to many rural areas. Urban public medical centres, such as the large Osmania Hospital at Hyderabad and the King George Hospital at Vishakhapatnam, have undergone expansion and upgrading; and specialized institutes, including those for treating specific diseases, have been opened. There is also a family-planning program. Medical aid is free to low-income groups, and several medical-insurance schemes cover various categories of employees.

Before the state's independence, social-welfare work was mainly undertaken by private agencies. Since the mid-20th century, however, the magnitude of need and the scarcity of resources, both organizational and financial, led the government to accept primary responsibility in this field. Public investment in social welfare accounts for a large proportion of the total amount spent on planning. There are social-welfare programs for people with disabilities, for Scheduled Castes and Scheduled Tribes, and for other groups that are not fully integrated into the social structure. Such programs include, among others, those that reserve places in educational institutions, those that provide employment, and housing and land-distribution schemes. A separate government department addresses women's concerns. There remain, nevertheless, many privately run social organizations that operate alongside those of the government; the Andhra Mahila Sabha, for instance, broadly promotes women's welfare.

EDUCATION

The state's educational system provides for 10 years of schooling followed by a two-year junior college course leading to undergraduate and postgraduate education. Primary school has been compulsory since 1961, and both primary and secondary school are provided free of charge. In the early 21st century the literacy rate was roughly 60 percent.

Andhra Pradesh has some 20 universities, a number of which provide postgraduate instruction and research facilities. The Central Institute of English and Foreign Languages, which is a nationally prominent institution, is located at Hyderabad. Since the late 20th century, technical education has received special attention in order to meet the demands of industrialization. Various industrial-training institutes offer vocational training, while the engineering colleges of the universities train advanced technical personnel. Scholarship programs are available for Scheduled Castes, Scheduled Tribes, and other disadvantaged groups in all educational institutions that receive substantial financial assistance from state and federal agencies. Privately run facilities also operate at all levels.

CULTURAL LIFE

The Andhras' contribution to India's cultural heritage is substantial. Architecture and painting have been highly developed arts in the region since ancient times. The *kuchipudi* style of dance is unique in the Indian tradition, while Carnatic (South Indian) music has derived much from Andhra roots. Many of southern India's major classical composers have been Andhras, and Telugu has been the language of most of the compositions. Telugu, one of the four literary languages of the Dravidian family, occupies a prestigious place among Indian languages, being renowned for its antiquity and admired by many for its mellifluous quality. Telugu literature was prominent in the Indian literary renaissance of the 19th and 20th centuries, as the writing resonated with a revolution in literary forms and expression, stimulated to a large degree by Western genres. Andhra Pradesh has many periodicals in English, Telugu, and Urdu. Muslim culture in the Telangana region further enriches the state's cultural diversity.

Before independence, arts and literature thrived mostly under the sponsorship of royal patrons and private organizations, many of which still function. Since independence, the state has created autonomous academies to revive, popularize, and promote fine arts, dance, drama, music, and literature.

The conscious cultivation of cultural expression is more an urban than a rural phenomenon, for cultural performances, literary meetings, and religious discussions occur mostly in towns or cities. Cultural development in different parts of the state under different historical circumstances resulted in the occurrence of recognizable variations in dialect, in caste structure, and in other traditions, all of which ultimately served to diversify the rural arts. Rural cultural media such as balladry, puppetry, and storytelling are indigenous to the area; use of these media in social and political communication is also common. The penetration of the mass media, especially of radio and television, into rural areas has helped to bring an awareness of classical traditions to the rural communities and of rural arts to the urban population. Andhra Pradesh is among the few major moviemaking states of India.

HISTORY

Although Sanskrit writings dating to about 1000 BCE contain references to a people called Andhras living south of the central Indian mountain ranges, definitive historical evidence of the Andhras dates from the times of the Mauryan dynasty, which ruled in the north from the late 4th to the early 2nd century BCE. The great Mauryan emperor Ashoka (reigned c. 265–238 BCE) sent Buddhist missions to the Andhras in the south. About the 1st century CE, the Satavahanas (or Satakarni), one of the most renowned of the Andhra dynasties, came to power. Its members ruled over almost the entire Deccan plateau and even established trade relations with Rome. They were patrons of diverse religions and also were great builders; their principal city, Amaravati, contained Buddhist monuments that inaugurated a new style of architecture. Experts ascribe parts of the famous paintings in the Ajanta caves of the Deccan to the Andhra painters of that period. Buddhism prospered under the Andhras, and in their capital flourished the great Buddhist university of antiquity, where Nagarjuna (c. 150–250), the founder of the Mahayana school of Buddhism, taught. The ruins of the university, at Nagarjunakonda, still reflect its former glory.

The Andhras continued to prosper over the next millennium, and in the 11th century the eastern Chalukya dynasty unified most of the Andhra area. Under

Dream of Maha Maya presaging the Buddha's birth, marble relief from Nagarjunakonda, Andhra Pradesh state, India, Amaravati style, c. 3rd century CE; in the Indian Museum, Kolkata (Calcutta). P. Chandra

the Chalukyas, Hinduism emerged as the dominant religion, and the first of the Telugu poets, Nannaya, began translating the Sanskrit epic, the *Mahabharata*, into Telugu, marking the birth of Telugu as a literary medium. During the 12th and 13th centuries the dynasty of the Kakatiyas of Warangal extended Andhra power militarily and culturally; during their regime the commercial expansion of the Andhras toward Southeast Asia reached its peak.

By this time, however, followers of Islam had established themselves in the north, and their invasion of the south led to the fall of Warangal in 1323. But the rise of the kingdom of Vijayanagar, to the southwest of Warangal, arrested further expansion of the Muslim power for some time. Widely acclaimed not only as the greatest kingdom in Andhra history but also as one of the greatest in Indian history, Vijayanagar, under the rule of its preeminent king Krishna Deva Raya (reigned 1509–29), became synonymous with military glory, economic prosperity, good administration, and artistic splendour. Telugu literature, for instance, flourished during this period. The formation of an alliance between the various neighbouring Muslim principalities ultimately led to the fall of Vijayanagar in 1565, leaving the Muslims in control of the Andhra areas.

In the 17th century, European traders began to involve themselves in Indian politics, as successive nizams (rulers) of Hyderabad, seeking to consolidate their kingdom against rivals, obtained first French and later British support.

In exchange for their help, the British acquired from the nizam the coastal Andhra districts lying to the north of the city of Madras (now Chennai) and later the hinterland districts. Thus, the major part of the Andhra country came under British rule. Part of the Telugu-speaking areas, known as the Telangana region, remained under the nizam's dominion, and the French acquired a few towns.

Indian nationalism arose during the 19th century, and the Andhras took a place at the forefront of the movement. Leaders such as Kandukuri Veerasalingam were pioneers in social reform. In the struggle against British rule, Andhra leaders played decisive roles. Pride in their historical and linguistic achievements led them to demand a separate province. Simultaneously, a movement was organized to unite the Telugu-speaking peoples living under British rule with those under the nizam's administration. Once India gained independence, the Andhras' demand for separate statehood became so insistent that, when the central government refused to comply, a local leader, Potti Sreeramulu, fasted to death in 1952 to dramatize the issue. The government finally acceded to the people's request by creating on Oct. 1, 1953, the Andhra state, which included the Telugu-speaking districts of the former Madras state to the south, thus paving the way for the formation of linguistic states throughout India in 1957. The erstwhile state of Hyderabad, which had joined independent India in 1949, was split up, and its nine Telugu-speaking districts (constituting Telangana) were joined to the Andhra state on Nov. 1, 1956, to form the new state of Andhra Pradesh.

GOA

The state of Goa, comprising a mainland district on the country's southwestern coast and an offshore island; it is located about 250 miles (400 km) south of Mumbai (Bombay). It is bounded by the states of Maharashtra on the north and Karnataka on the east and south and by the Arabian Sea on the west. The capital is Panaji (Panjim), on the north-central coast of the mainland district. Formerly a Portuguese possession, it became a part of India in 1962 and attained statehood in 1987. Area 1,429 square miles (3,702 square km). Pop. (2008 est.) 1,628,000.

LAND

Sandy beaches, estuaries, and promontories characterize the 65-mile (105-km) coastline of mainland Goa. In the interior region, low, forested plateaus merge with the wooded slopes of the Western Ghats, which rise to nearly 4,000 feet (1,220 metres) on the eastern edge of the state. The two largest rivers are the Mandavi and the Zuvari, between the mouths of which lies the island of Goa (Ilhas). The island is triangular, the apex (called the cape) being a rocky headland separating the harbour of Goa into two anchorages.

Goa's climate is equable, with high temperatures generally in the 80s F (30s C) and low temperatures in the 70s F (20s C) throughout the year. A southwest monsoon blows between June and September. The state receives about 115 inches (3,000 mm) of rainfall annually, most occurring during the monsoon season.

PEOPLE

The Portuguese colonial heritage and the diverse local population of Goa have cultivated a unique cultural landscape.

POPULATION COMPOSITION

The population is primarily a mixture of Christians and Hindus: the western coastland and estuaries are dotted with wayside crosses and Roman Catholic churches, while the hilly east is scattered with Hindu temples and shrines. There is also a notable Muslim population in Goa, as well as smaller communities of Jains, Sikhs, and practitioners of local religions. Portuguese was once the language of the administration and the elite, and as part of that legacy, many Goans bear Portuguese personal names and surnames. Today, however, most Goans tend to speak Konkani, Marathi, or English.

SETTLEMENT PATTERNS AND DEMOGRAPHIC TRENDS

Old Goa, on the island of Goa, was once the hub of the region, but the city was decimated by war and disease in the 18th century; for the most part, only its ruins remain. Since the mid-20th century, however, efforts have been made to preserve Old Goa. Among the city's most notable landmarks are the Basilica of Bom Jesus, which enshrines the tomb of St. Francis Xavier, and the Se Cathedral, dedicated to St. Catherine of Alexandria. Both were built in the 16th century, and, with several other churches of Goa, they were designated a UNESCO World Heritage site in 1986.

There are three principal cities in contemporary Goa: Panaji (Panjim), Marmagao (Mormugão), and Madgaon (Margão). Panaji was originally a suburb of Old Goa. Like its parent city, Panaji was built on the left bank of the Mandavi estuary. Now a busy port city, it contains the archbishop's palace, the government house, and many markets. Marmagao, sheltered by a promontory and outfitted with a breakwater and quay, is one of the major ports between Mumbai and Kozhikode (Calicut; in the state of Kerala). It specializes in the shipment of iron ore and manganese. As Marmagao developed, so too did nearby Madgaon, with its industrial estate, cold-storage facilities, and large produce market.

The Roman Catholic Basilica of Bom Jesus, 16th century, Goa, India. Frederick M. Asher

Over the course of Goa's history, Portuguese rule and fluctuating economic conditions caused emigration on a large scale. Many Goans have moved not only to other parts of India but also to the former Portuguese colonies on the eastern coast of Africa.

ECONOMY

Agriculture remains a mainstay of Goa's economy, although the exploitation of minerals and manufacturing have grown in importance. Services (especially those associated with tourism) also have grown in significance.

AGRICULTURE, FORESTRY, AND FISHING

Rice, fruits (such as mangoes), coconuts, pulses (legumes), cashews, betel (areca nut), and sugarcane are among the leading crops. Principal forest products include teak and bamboo. The state has an active fisheries industry along its coast, although sustainability has been a growing concern in the 21st century. The state exports a number of its agricultural commodities.

RESOURCES

Goa is rich in minerals. Mining began in the mid-20th century, and over the next few decades it emerged as a central component of the state's economy. Iron ore, manganese, and bauxite are among the primary products of the industry. Especially since the late 20th century, however, the adverse environmental impact of opencast mining has prompted heated controversy and intermittent government-mandated moratoria on production. Although new environmental regulations were put into place in the early 21st century, mining remains a sensitive issue.

MANUFACTURING

Since the late 20th century, government policies and concessions have promoted Goa's rapid industrialization, particularly through the development of many industrial estates. Fertilizer, chemicals, pharmaceuticals, iron products, and processed sugar are among the leading large-scale industries. There also are medium- and small-scale industries, including traditional handicrafts. Goa's manufactures are distributed both domestically and abroad.

SERVICES

The service sector of Goa's economy has increased in importance since the late 20th century. This is attributable largely to the rapid growth of tourism. By the early 21st century, tourism constituted a significant segment of Goa's economy, as the state's long, sandy beaches, coastal vegetation, coconut palms, and unique hotels attracted large numbers of international and domestic visitors. The expansion of tourism, however, has raised concerns about preservation of the natural environment.

Transportation

Goa is well connected to the rest of India—and the world—by road, rail, sea, and air. In Panaji there is a large bus terminal that adjoins the station on the Konkan railway. Completed in 1998, the Konkan railway runs along India's western coast from west-central Maharashtra to southern Karnataka, where it links with the country's southern railway. Another rail line connects the state's primary port at Marmagao (via Madgaon) with the country's southwestern rail system by way of Castle Rock (in Karnataka) in the Western Ghats. There is an international airport at Dabolim, near Panaji.

Government and Society

The structure of Goa's government, like that of most other Indian states, is defined by the national constitution of 1950.

Constitutional Framework

The state's governor is appointed by the president of India for a five-year term. In addition to governing Goa, the governor administers the union territories of Dadra and Nagar Haveli and Daman and Diu. Assisting the governor is the Council of Ministers, which is headed by a chief minister and is responsible to the elected Legislative Assembly (Vidhan Sabha).

Education

Educational and training institutes range from primary schools to technical and collegiate institutions. Goa University (1985), one of India's premier postsecondary institutions, is located at Bambolim, near Panaji. The National Institute of Oceanography (1966), which is famous for its oceanographic research and for its expeditions to Antarctica, is located at Dona Paula, on the far western tip of Goa Island.

History

The ancient Hindu city of Goa, hardly a fragment of which survives, was built at the southernmost point of the island of Goa. The city was famous in early Hindu legend and history; in the *Puranas* and various inscriptions, its name appears as Gove, Govapuri, and Gomant. The medieval Arabian geographers knew it as Sindabur, or Sandābūr, and the Portuguese called it Velha Goa. It was ruled by the Kadamba dynasty from the 2nd century CE to 1312 and by Muslim invaders of the Deccan from 1312 to 1367. The city was then annexed by the Hindu kingdom of Vijayanagar and was later conquered by the Bahmanī sultanate, which founded Old Goa on the island in 1440.

With the subdivision of the Bahmanī kingdom after 1482, Goa passed into the power of Yūsuf 'Ādil Khan, the Muslim king of Bijapur, who was its ruler when seafarers from Portugal first reached

India. The city was attacked in March 1510 by the Portuguese under Afonso de Albuquerque. The city surrendered without a struggle, and Albuquerque entered it in triumph.

Three months later Yūsuf 'Ādil Khan returned with 60,000 troops, forced the passage of the ford, and blockaded the Portuguese in their ships from May to August, when the end of the monsoon season enabled them to put to sea. In November, Albuquerque returned with a larger force and, after overcoming a desperate resistance, recaptured the city, killed all the Muslims, and appointed a Hindu, Timoja, governor of Goa.

Goa was the first territorial possession of the Portuguese in Asia. Albuquerque and his successors left almost untouched the customs and constitutions of the 30 village communities on the island, abolishing only the rite of suttee (sati; the immolation of widows on the funeral pyres of their husbands).

Goa became the capital of the whole Portuguese empire in Asia. It was granted the same civic privileges as Lisbon, reaching the climax of its prosperity between 1575 and 1600. The appearance of the Dutch in Indian waters precipitated the decline of Goa. In 1603 and 1639 the city was blockaded by Dutch fleets, though never captured, and in 1635 it was ravaged by an epidemic. In 1683 a Mughal army saved it from capture by Maratha raiders, and in 1739 the whole territory was again attacked by the Marathas and was saved only by the unexpected arrival of a new Portuguese viceroy with a fleet.

The seat of the government was moved to Mormugão (now Marmagao) and in 1759 to Panjim (or New Goa; now Panaji). Cholera epidemics were one of the chief reasons for the migration of the inhabitants from Old Goa to Panjim. Between 1695 and 1775 the population of Old Goa dwindled from 20,000 to 1,600; in 1835 the city was inhabited by only a few priests, monks, and nuns.

During the 19th century, major events affecting the settlement were its temporary occupation by the British in 1809 as a result of the invasion of Portugal by Napoleon I; the governorship (1855–64) of Count de Torres Novas, who inaugurated a great number of improvements; and the military revolts of the second half of the century. The most notable of the revolts was that of Sept. 3, 1895, which necessitated the dispatch of an expeditionary force from Portugal. The infante (Portuguese prince) Affonso Henriques, duque de Oporto, accompanied this expedition and exercised governor's powers from March to May 1896.

After India achieved independence in 1947, it made claims on Goa in 1948 and 1949, and Portugal came under increasing pressure to cede Goa and its other possessions in the subcontinent to India. In mid-1954, Goan nationalists seized the Portuguese enclaves of Dadra and Nagar Haveli and established a pro-Indian administration. Another crisis occurred in 1955 when *satyagrahis* (nonviolent resisters) from India attempted to penetrate the territory of Goa. At first the *satyagrahis* were deported, but later, when large numbers attempted to cross the borders, the Portuguese authorities resorted to force, which resulted in many casualties. This led to the severance of diplomatic relations between Portugal and India on Aug. 18, 1955. Tension between the two countries came to a head on Dec. 18, 1961, when Indian troops supported by naval and air forces invaded and occupied Goa, Daman, and Diu. All three territories subsequently became part of India. Goa became a state in 1987.

KERALA

The small southwestern Indian coastal state of Kerala is bordered by the states of Karnataka (formerly Mysore) to the north and Tamil Nadu to the east and by the Arabian Sea to the south and west; it also surrounds Mahe, a segment of the union territory of Puducherry, on the northwestern coast. The capital is Thiruvananthapuram (Trivandrum).

Although isolated from the Indian interior by the mountainous belt of the Western Ghats, Kerala has been exposed to many foreign influences via its long coastline; consequently, the state has developed a unique culture within the subcontinent, not only with a diverse religious tradition but also with its own language, Malayalam. Also notable is the high social status that continues to be accorded to women of Kerala, owing to the former strength of a matrilineal kinship system. Area 15,005 square miles (38,863 square km). Pop. (2008 est.) 34,232,000.

LAND

Kerala is a small state, constituting only about 1 percent of the total area of the country. It stretches for about 360 miles (580 km) along the Malabar Coast, varying in width from roughly 20 to 75 miles (30 to 120 km).

RELIEF AND DRAINAGE

Kerala is a region of great natural beauty. In the eastern part of the state, Anai Peak (8,842 feet [2,695 metres]), the highest peak of peninsular India, crowns the Western Ghats. Descending from the rocky highlands westward toward the coastal plain is a stretch of farmlands, with different crops cultivated at different elevations. Along the coast, a linked chain of lagoons and backwaters form the so-called Venice of India. Among the more important rivers that flow to the Arabian Sea are the Ponnani (Bharatapuzha), Periyar, Chalakudi, and Pamba.

CLIMATE

The climate of Kerala is equable and varies little from season to season. Throughout the year, daily temperatures usually rise from the low 70s F (low 20s C) into the 80s F (27 to 32 °C). The state is directly exposed to the southwest monsoon, which prevails from July through September, but it also receives rain from the reverse (northeast) monsoon, which blows in October and November.

Precipitation averages about 115 inches (3,000 mm) annually statewide, with some slopes receiving more than 200 inches (5,000 mm).

PLANT AND ANIMAL LIFE

The watery coastal zones of Kerala are interspersed with coconut palm groves, while much of the Western Ghats and riverine areas are covered with rainforests and monsoon forests (tropical deciduous forests). Rolling grasslands are typical of the upland region. This diverse natural environment is home to an extraordinary array of wildlife. Mammals include sambar deer, gaurs (wild cattle), Nilgiri tahrs (wild goatlike animals; *Hemitragus hylocrius*), elephants, leopards, tigers, bonnet monkeys, rare lion-tailed macaques (*Macaca silenus*), and Hanuman and Nilgiri langurs (*Semnopithecus entellus* and *Trachypithecus johnii*, respectively). King cobras (*Ophiophagus hannah*) are among the notable reptiles, while peacocks and hornbills are common birds. The state has several national parks and wildlife sanctuaries, among which the Periyar National Park and Tiger Reserve is the largest.

PEOPLE

The Malayalis are a group of people of mixed ethnic heritage who speak Malayalam, a Dravidian language; they constitute the majority of the population of Kerala.

POPULATION COMPOSITION

Most Malayalis are descendants of the early inhabitants of India, the so-called Dravidians (speakers of Dravidian languages), who were driven southward between about 2000 and 1500 BCE when the Aryans (speakers of Indo-Aryan languages) descended into the Indian subcontinent. Over the millennia, there has been much exchange between the two groups. Elements of Indo-Aryan ancestry remain strongest among the Nambudiri, a prominent caste of orthodox Hindus. Also living in Kerala is a significant minority of Tamils, a neighbouring people of Dravidian ancestry.

More than half of Kerala's residents, including most of the Malayalis, follow Hinduism. About one-fourth of the population practices Islam, with the Moplah (Mapilla) people of the Malabar Coast constituting the state's largest Muslim community. Christians, who account for nearly one-fifth of the population, belong broadly to the Syrian Orthodox and Roman Catholic churches as well as to various Protestant denominations. Kerala also has tiny Jain, Sikh, Buddhist, and Jewish communities; there is an ancient synagogue in Kochi.

SETTLEMENT PATTERNS AND DEMOGRAPHIC TRENDS

Kerala is one of the most densely populated states in India. While only about one-fourth of the population was reported as urban in the early 21st century, such statistics are deceptive because of the close proximity of rural houses, especially in the coastal plain. Indeed, in parts of the state there are densely populated rural equivalents of urban megalopolises. The major urban centres and industrial complexes include Kochi, Thiruvananthapuram, Kozhikode, Kollam (Quilon), Alappuzha (Alleppey), Thrissur (Trichur), and Thalassery (Tellicherry).

ECONOMY

Agriculture is the state's main economic activity. Although mineral exploitation is of little consequence, manufacturing and service activities are also important contributors to Kerala's economy.

AGRICULTURE, FORESTRY, AND FISHING

Commercial plantings on less than half of the total land under cultivation earn a sizable amount of foreign exchange but have necessitated the importation of food for local consumption. Kerala's principal cash crops are rubber, coffee, and tea, which are cultivated in plantations on the slopes of the foothills, as well as areca nut, cardamom, cashew nut, coconut, ginger, and pepper. The major food crops are rice, pulses, sorghum, and tapioca. Commercial poultry farming is well developed.

The forests yield valuable timbers such as ebony, rosewood, and teak. In addition, Kerala's woodlands supply industrial raw materials such as bamboo (used in the paper and rayon industries), wood pulp, charcoal, gums, and resins. The state is also a national leader in fish production. Sardines, tunas, mackerels, and prawns are among the principal products of the industry.

RESOURCES AND POWER

Kerala lacks major reserves of fossil fuels. However, there are moderate deposits of ilmenite (the principal ore of titanium), rutile (titanium dioxide), and monazite (a mineral consisting of cerium and thorium phosphates), all of which are found in beach sands. Other minerals include limestone, iron ores, and bauxite (the principal ore of aluminum). The state is especially known for its high-quality kaolin (china clay), which is used to make porcelain.

Kerala has great hydroelectric potential, with some two dozen hydroelectric stations operating within the state. Several thermal plants supply additional energy, and in the late 20th century the state began to establish wind farms. Despite its wealth of renewable resources for power generation, Kerala has continued to import some of its electricity from elsewhere in India.

MANUFACTURING, SERVICES, AND LABOUR

Traditional cottage industries, such as weaving, the production of coconut fibre, and cashew processing, employ many

Boat traffic on the coastal waterways of Kerala. Gerald Cubitt

workers in the manufacturing sector. Of the medium- and large-scale industries, food processing is the principal employer. Other major manufactures include fertilizers, chemicals, electrical equipment, titanium, aluminum, plywood, ceramics, and synthetic fabrics. Banking, finance, and other components of the services sector also employ a significant segment of the state's workforce. However, unemployment has remained acute, with the state's high level of education among the jobless exacerbating the problem.

TRANSPORTATION

Kerala has well-developed road and railway systems. It is connected with the states of Tamil Nadu and Karnataka by national highways. A railway coming from the east through the Palghat Gap in the Western Ghats meets with a railway running from north to south through the state and on to Kanniyakumari, the southernmost town of India. There is a major port at Kochi and intermediate ports at Kozhikode, Alappuzha, and Neendakara (near Thiruvananthapuram); all handle coastal and foreign traffic. Kochi also has major shipyard and oil refining facilities and serves as a district headquarters for the Indian coast guard and as a regional headquarters for the navy. More than 1,000 miles (1,600 km) of inland waterways form the main arteries for carrying bulk freight to and from the ports. Thiruvananthapuram and Kozhikode have international airports; an airport in Kochi offers domestic service.

GOVERNMENT AND SOCIETY

The structure of the government of Kerala, like that of most other states of India, is determined by the national constitution of 1950.

CONSTITUTIONAL FRAMEWORK

Kerala's governor, appointed by the president of India, is the head of the state and functions on the advice of the chief minister, who is the head of the Council of Ministers. The state has an elected unicameral Legislative Assembly (Vidhan Sabha). The High Court in Ernakulam (near Kochi) is headed by a chief justice; appeals from the High Court may go to the Supreme Court of India. Below the High Court are district courts, subdivisional courts, munsifs' (subordinate judicial officers') courts, and munsif-magistrate courts. In addition, there are family courts and other courts that handle particular types of cases.

At the local level, the state is divided into districts, which in turn are subdivided for revenue purposes into *taluka*s (subdivisions) and villages. Since the mid-20th century, Kerala's political experience has largely been one of instability, with a proliferation of political parties and coalition governments.

HEALTH AND WELFARE

The state maintains a relatively high standard of health service. A comprehensive health insurance plan is available for workers in a number of professions, and free medical treatment is offered in many hospitals, health centres, and dispensaries. Among the top priorities of government health schemes have been the establishment of health care facilities in rural areas, the promotion of family planning, prevention of blindness, and control of communicable diseases such as leprosy, tuberculosis, and malaria.

EDUCATION

Kerala has one of the most advanced educational systems and highest levels of literacy in India. Elementary education is compulsory between the ages of 6 and 11. There are primary, middle, and secondary schools, as well as polytechnical and industrial training institutes, arts and science colleges, and professional colleges. Kerala also has several universities, including the University of Kerala (1937) in Thiruvananthapuram, the University of Calicut (1968) in Kozhikode, Cochin University of Science and Technology (1971) in Kochi, and Kerala Agricultural University (1971) in Thrissur.

CULTURAL LIFE

The cultural heritage of Kerala reflects extensive interaction with diverse communities from antiquity to the present. With an array of ancient Hindu temples with copper-clad roofs, later mosques with "Malabar gables" (triangular projections at the rooftops), and Baroque churches from the Portuguese colonial era, the state's architecture offers a chronicle of the social, spiritual, and political history of the area. Other characteristically Keralan art forms include intricate paintings on wood, thematic murals, and a remarkable variety of indoor and outdoor lamps (from which the state has earned the sobriquet "Land of Lamps").

Literature and learning, in both Tamil and Sanskrit, have flourished since the 2nd century CE; meanwhile, the Malayalam language, though an offshoot of Tamil, has absorbed much from Sanskrit and also has a prolific literature. Notable names in Malayalam poetry are Tunchattu Eluttaccan and Kuncan Nampiyar among classical poets and Kumaran Asan and Vallathol in the 20th century. In 1889 Chandu Menon wrote *Indulekha*, the first outstanding novel in Malayalam, for which he received a certificate from Queen Victoria. Thakazhi Sivasankara Pillai, who produced hundreds of works before his death in 1999, has remained among the most widely read Malayali novelists.

Most traditional dances of Kerala pertain to the great Indian epics—the *Mahabharata* and the *Ramayana*—or to the honouring of specific Hindu deities. In *kathakali*, the classical martial dance-drama of Kerala, male performers portray both male and female characters. By contrast, the *bharata natyam* dancing, dating to early Tamil times, is practiced exclusively by females.

HISTORY

Kerala is first mentioned (as Keralaputra) in a 3rd-century-BCE rock inscription left by the Mauryan emperor Ashoka. In the last centuries BCE this region became famous among the Greeks and Romans for its spices (especially pepper). During the first five centuries CE the region was a part of Tamilakam—the territory of the Tamils—and thus was sometimes partially controlled by the eastern Pandya and Chola dynasties, as well as by the Cheras. In the 1st century Jewish immigrants arrived, and, according to Syrian Orthodox Christians, St. Thomas the Apostle visited Kerala in the same century.

Much of Kerala's history from the 6th to the 8th century is obscure, but it is known that Arab traders introduced Islam later in the period. Under the Kulashekhara dynasty (c. 800–1102), Malayalam emerged as a distinct language, and Hinduism became prominent.

The Cholas often controlled Kerala during the 11th and 12th centuries. By the beginning of the 14th century, Ravi Varma Kulashekhara of the Venad kingdom established a short-lived supremacy over southern India. After his death, Kerala became a conglomeration of warring chieftaincies, among which the most important were Calicut (now Kozhikode) in the north and Venad in the south.

The era of foreign intervention began in 1498, when Vasco da Gama landed near Calicut. In the 16th century the Portuguese superseded the Arab traders and dominated the commerce of the Malabar Coast. Their attempt to establish sovereignty was thwarted by the *zamorin* (hereditary ruler) of Calicut. The Dutch ousted the Portuguese in the 17th century. Marthanda Varma ascended the Venad throne in 1729 and crushed Dutch expansionist designs at the Battle of Kolachel 12 years later. Marthanda Varma then adopted a European mode of martial discipline and expanded the Venad domain to encompass what became the southern state of Travancore. His alliance in 1757 with the raja of the central state of Cochin (Kochi), against the *zamorin*, enabled Cochin to survive. By 1806, however, Cochin and Travancore, as well as the Malabar Coast in the north, had become subject states under the British Madras Presidency.

Two years after India's independence was achieved in 1947, Cochin and Travancore were united as Travancore-Cochin state. The present state of Kerala was constituted on a linguistic basis in 1956 when the Malabar Coast and the Kasargod *taluka* (administrative subdivision) of South Kanara were added to Travancore-Cochin. The southern portion of the former Travancore-Cochin state was attached to Tamil Nadu.

TAMIL NADU

The Indian state of Tamil Nadu, located in the extreme south of the subcontinent, is bounded by the Indian Ocean to the east and south and by the states of Kerala to the west, Karnataka to the northwest, and Andhra Pradesh to the north. Enclosed by Tamil Nadu along the north-central coast are the enclaves of Puducherry and Karaikal, both of which are part of Puducherry union territory. The capital is Chennai (Madras), on the coast in the northeastern portion of the state.

Tamil Nadu represents the Tamil-speaking area of what was formerly the Madras Presidency of British India. The Tamils are especially proud of their Dravidian language and culture, and they have notably resisted attempts by the central government to make Hindi (an Indo-Aryan language) the sole national language. While it has an industrial core in Chennai, the state is essentially agricultural. Area 50,216 square miles (130,058 square km). Pop. (2008 est.) 66,396,000.

LAND

Tamil Nadu is divided naturally between the flat country along the eastern coast and the hilly regions in the north and west.

RELIEF, DRAINAGE, AND SOILS

The broadest part of the eastern plains is the fertile Kaveri (Cauvery) River delta; farther south are the arid flatlands surrounding the cities of Ramanathapuram and Madurai (Madura). The high peaks of the Western Ghats run along the state's western border. Various segments of this mountain range—including the Nilgiri, Anaimalai, and Palni hills—have peaks exceeding 8,000 feet (2,400 metres) in elevation. Anai Peak, at 8,842 feet (2,695 metres) in the Anaimalai Hills, is the highest mountain in peninsular India. The lower peaks of the Eastern Ghats and their outliers—locally called the Javadi, Kalrayan, and Shevaroy hills—run through the centre of the region. Tamil Nadu's major rivers—the Kaveri, the Ponnaiyar, the Palar, the Vaigai, and the Tambraparni—flow eastward from the inland hills.

Apart from the rich alluvial soil of the river deltas, the predominant soils of the state are clays, loams, sands, and red laterites (soils with a high content of iron oxides and aluminum hydroxide). The black cotton-growing soil known as regur is found in parts of the central, west-central, and southeastern regions of Tamil Nadu.

CLIMATE

The climate of Tamil Nadu is essentially tropical. In May and June, the hottest months, maximum daily temperatures in Chennai average about 100 °F (38 °C), while minimum temperatures average in the low 80s F (upper 20s C). In December and January, the coolest months, temperatures usually rise from about 70 °F (21 °C) into the mid-80s F (about 30 °C) daily. The average annual precipitation, falling mainly between October and December, depends on the southwest and northeast monsoons and ranges between 25 and 75 inches (630 and 1,900 mm) a year. The

An oasis on the sandy plain near Mahabalipuram, southeast of Chingleput, Tamil Nadu, India. B.S. Oza/Tom Stack & Associates

mountainous and hilly areas, especially in the extreme western part of the state, receive the most precipitation, while the lower-lying southern and southeastern regions receive the least rainfall.

PLANT AND ANIMAL LIFE

Forests cover roughly 15 percent of the state. At the highest elevations in the Western Ghats, the mountains support subalpine vegetation. Along the eastern side of the Western Ghats and in the hills of the northern and central districts, the plant life is a mixture of evergreen and deciduous species, some of which are markedly adapted to arid conditions.

Tamil Nadu has several national parks and more than a dozen wildlife and bird sanctuaries. Among the most notable of these protected areas are the Mudlumbai Wildlife Sanctuary and National Park in the Nilgiri Hills and the large Indira Gandhi Wildlife Sanctuary and National

Pillar Rock in the Palni Hills at Kodaikanal, Tamil Nadu, India. Foto Features

Park at the southern tip of the Western Ghats. These sanctuaries provide a safe habitat for a broad spectrum of fauna, including elephants, gaurs (wild cattle), Nilgiri tahrs (goatlike mammals), wild boars, sloth bears, and various species of deer. Tigers, leopards, and an assortment of primates, including macaques, langurs, and lorises, also inhabit these areas. Venomous king cobras are among the many species of reptiles that make their home in Tamil Nadu. Woodpeckers and flycatchers are common woodland birds; aquatic birds find a haven at the Vedantangal sanctuary in the south-central part of the state.

PEOPLE

The area's population evidently has changed little over the centuries.

POPULATION COMPOSITION

As speakers of a Dravidian language, the Tamils, who constitute the majority of the population, are understood to be descendants of the early inhabitants of India (the so-called Dravidians), who were driven southward between about 2000 and 1500 BCE when the Aryans (speakers of Indo-Aryan languages) descended into the Indian subcontinent. In addition to the Tamils, the population includes various indigenous communities, who live primarily in the hill regions; these people also speak Dravidian languages. In Tamil Nadu, as in the rest of the country, the caste system is strong, even though discrimination has been banned by the constitution of India. Members of Scheduled Castes account for about one-fifth of the population. Scheduled Tribes form just a small fraction of Tamil Nadu's residents.

Tamil, the official state language, is spoken by most of the people. Other Dravidian languages used within the state include Telugu, which is spoken by roughly one-tenth of the population, as well as Kannada and Malayalam, which are spoken by much smaller numbers. In the western region—near the convergence of the borders of Tamil Nadu, Karnataka, and Kerala—Kannada (and its dialect Badaga) and Malayalam are stronger. There also is a community of Urdu (an Indo-Aryan language) speakers. English is used as a subsidiary language.

The overwhelming majority of Tamil Nadu's residents practice Hinduism. There are, however, notable minorities of Christians and Muslims, with a large concentration of Christians in the far southern segment of the state. A small community of Jains is found in northern Tamil Nadu, in and around the cities of Arcot and Chennai.

SETTLEMENT PATTERNS

Although Tamil Nadu is one of the most urbanized states of India, more than half the population in the early 21st century continued to live in rural areas. The Chennai metropolitan region, covering

Village in the Anaimalai Hills, Western Ghats, Tamil Nadu, India. Gerald Cubitt

the industrial areas, townships, and villages surrounding Chennai city, has the largest population. Other important urban agglomerations include Coimbatore in western Tamil Nadu, Madurai in the south-central region, and Tiruchchirappalli in the central part of the state.

ECONOMY

Agriculture is the mainstay of life for about half the working population of Tamil Nadu. Nonetheless, it is one of the most industrialized of the Indian states, and the manufacturing sector accounts for more than one-third of the state's gross product.

AGRICULTURE, FISHING, AND FORESTRY

Since very early times, Tamil farmers have skillfully conserved scarce rainwater in small and large irrigation reservoirs, or "tanks." Government canals, tube wells, and ordinary wells also form part of the irrigation system. Because several of the river valley projects depend for water on rain brought by the erratic northeast monsoon, the government also taps subsoil water sources.

Agricultural practices have shown radical improvement since the mid-20th century through multiple cropping, the use of stronger and more productive strains of staple crops, and the application of chemical fertilizers; since the late 1960s the state has been self-sufficient in the production of food grains. The principal crops for domestic consumption are rice, millet, and other cereals, as well as peanuts (groundnuts) and pulses (such as chickpeas); sugarcane, cotton, cashews, and chilies are important cash crops. Many farmers in Tamil Nadu also raise livestock, primarily cows (especially for the dairy industry), poultry, goats, and sheep.

Tamil Nadu is one of India's top fish producers, with most of the yield coming from marine operations, although there also are many inland fisheries. In addition, the state has an active forestry sector, with pulpwood, babul (a type of acacia that yields valuable tannin), firewood, bamboo, and teak among the primary products. Rubber, grown largely in plantations, is important as well.

RESOURCES AND POWER

The major minerals mined in Tamil Nadu are limestone, bauxite, gypsum, lignite (brown coal), magnesite, and iron ore. The opencast lignite mine at Neyveli, in the north-central part of the state, is among the largest in India, and its products are used to fuel a thermal-power plant that provides much of the state's electricity. The bulk of Tamil Nadu's energy comes from thermal stations, but hydroelectric plants—especially along the Kaveri River and its tributaries—provide an important secondary source of energy. The state also is a leader in wind-power generation.

Manufacturing

Production of heavy vehicles—such as automobiles, agricultural equipment, military vehicles, and railway cars—is among the state's major industries; the railway-coach factory at Perambur (near Chennai) is one of the largest in Asia. There is an oil refinery and petrochemical plant in Chennai. Other prominent manufacturing activities include textile milling, food processing, and the production of pharmaceuticals, chemicals, and electronic parts and equipment. Tamil Nadu also is rich in handicrafts, most notably brass, bronze, and copper ware, leather work, handloomed silk, *kalamkari* (hand-painted fabric, using natural dyes), and articles fashioned from carved wood, palm leaf, and cane.

Services

The services sector has grown especially rapidly since the late 20th century, and by the early 21st century it had become the largest contributor to Tamil Nadu's economy. Expansion of the information-technology industry has been a priority of the state's economic development policies. Tourism also has been an area of emphasis, with ongoing improvements in infrastructure, accommodations, restaurants, and cultural and recreational attractions.

Transportation

The transport system of the southern Indian states converges on Chennai. A well-developed road network makes express bus service available to all major towns and places of interest. Many railways also run through the state.

Two of India's major seaports are located in Tamil Nadu—in the north at Chennai and in the south at Tuticorin. The international airport at Meenambakkam, near Chennai, is one of the largest airports in India. Domestic flights are available from a number of other cities, including Madurai, Coimbatore, and Tuticorin; the airport at Tiruchchirappalli offers domestic and limited international service.

Government and Society

The structure of the government of Tamil Nadu, like that of most other states of India, is determined by the national constitution of 1950.

Constitutional Framework

The head of state is the governor, who is appointed by the president of India. The governor is aided and advised by the Council of Ministers, which is led by a chief minister and is responsible to the elected unicameral Legislative Assembly (Vidhan Sabha). Most of the ministries are housed in the 17th-century Fort St. George in Chennai. The state's judiciary is headed by the High Court in Chennai (Madras High Court), which has original jurisdiction for the city and appellate jurisdiction for the state; the High Court also may hear original cases of an extraordinary nature from other parts of Tamil Nadu. A bench of the High Court is located in Madurai. Lower courts include district and sessions courts, magistrates' courts, and *munsifs'* (subordinate judicial officers') courts.

The state is divided into more than two dozen administrative districts, each administered by a district collector. Lower administrative and revenue units are called *talukas, firkas,* and villages. *Panchayats* (village councils) are responsible for local self-government and rural development.

HEALTH

The medical needs of Tamil Nadu's population are served by a large number of public and private hospitals, dispensaries, and primary health centres. Allopathic (Western), Ayurvedic and Siddha (traditional Indian), Unanī (a Muslim system using prescribed herbs and shrubs), and homeopathic medical treatments are all recognized and supported by the government and are available throughout the state. Among Tamil Nadu's primary health concerns are cholera, malaria, filariasis (disease caused by infestation of the blood and tissues by parasitic worms), and HIV/AIDS infection. The state has largely brought leprosy under control, although thousands of cases are still treated annually.

Various government agencies sponsor programs to improve the housing, education, and economic status of the Scheduled Castes and other traditionally disadvantaged groups. The state also provides assistance to women, children, and people with disabilities. A special insurance program is available for those with autism, cerebral palsy, and other developmental disabilities.

EDUCATION

Tens of thousands of public and private primary, middle, and high schools are scattered across the state of Tamil Nadu. In addition, there are numerous arts and science colleges, medical colleges, engineering colleges, polytechnic institutes, and industrial training institutes. Among the most prominent of Tamil Nadu's universities are the University of Madras (1857) and Tamil Nadu Veterinary and Animal Sciences University (1989), both in Chennai, Annamalai University (1929) in Chidambaram; Tamil Nadu Agricultural University (1971) in Coimbatore; and Madurai Kamaraj University (1966) in Madurai. The Dakshina Bharat Hindi Prachar Sabha (1918) in Chennai and the Gandhigram Rural University (1956) in Gandhigram, in southwest-central Tamil Nadu, are the two institutes of national importance that are engaged in popularizing the Hindi language and Mahatma Gandhi's concept of rural higher education, respectively. Tamil University (1981) near Thanjavur (Tanjore), in the eastern part of the state, focuses on the study of Tamil language, literature, and culture.

Cultural Life

Hinduism lies at the core of the culture of Tamil Nadu, and the state is the centre of traditional Hindu practices.

Cultural Milieu

Among the most famous of the state's temples, which number in the tens of thousands, are the 7th- and 8th-century structures at Mamallapura, which were designated a UNESCO World Heritage Site in 1984. The *gopurams*, or gateway towers, of such temples are dominant in most towns, particularly Chidambaram, Kanchipuram, Thanjavur, Madurai, and the Srirangam pilgrimage centre in Tiruchchirappalli. The Hindu Religious and Charitable Endowments Administration Department is responsible for the administration of the state's temples and sanctuaries.

The cycle of temple festivals attracts large congregations of devotees. Noteworthy also are the car festivals, during which large chariots decorated with religious icons are taken in procession around the temple. In addition, Tamil Nadu is scattered with sectarian monastic institutions, or *mathas*—of which the most important are the Shankara Matha at Kumbakonam and the Vaishnava compound at Srirangam—which hold various activities; Hindu families typically owe allegiance to a number of such institutions.

The Arts

Bharata natyam, one of India's major classical dance forms, and Carnatic music (South Indian classical music) are both widely practiced. Painting and sculpture are less prominent, although there are schools that teach the art of sculpture in stone and bronze. Tamil literature rapidly adopted the Western literary forms of the novel and the short story. The poet Subrahmanya Bharati (1882–1921) was one of the first to modify traditional Tamil poetry by blending popular and scholastic literary styles. Motion pictures are the most prevalent form of mass entertainment. There are both touring and permanent movie theatres, and sentimental and spectacular films, often featuring music and dancing, are produced by the film studios situated largely around Chennai.

Media and Publishing

Hundreds of periodicals are published in Tamil, most of them daily newspapers. The *Dina Thanthi* is the leading paper. Among English newspapers, *The Hindu* of Chennai is widely read and is respected for its high standard of journalism.

History

The history of Tamil Nadu begins with the establishment of a trinity of Tamil powers in the region—namely, the Chera, Chola, and Pandya kingdoms—all of which are of unknown antiquity. These

Carved figures on a tower gate of the Minaksi-Sundareshvara Temple in Madurai, Tamil Nadu, India. Picturepoint, London

kingdoms enjoyed diplomatic and trade relations with distant lands. The Pandyas were mentioned in Greek literature dating to the 4th century BCE, and in the 4th century CE, the Roman emperor Julian welcomed a Pandyan embassy. Meanwhile, the Chera dynasty cultivated a flourishing trade with western Asia.

From the mid-6th century until the 9th century, the Chalukyas of Badami, the Pallavas of Kanchi (now Kanchipuram), and the Pandyas of Madurai fought a long series of wars in the region. The period, nonetheless, was marked by a revival of Hinduism and the advance of the fine arts. From about 850, Tamil Nadu was dominated by the Cholas, of whom Rajendrachola Deva I (reigned 1014–44) was the most distinguished ruler. In the mid-14th century, the Hindu kingdom of Vijayanagar, which included all of Tamil Nadu, came into prominence. During the 300 years of Vijayanagar rule, Telugu-speaking governors and officials were introduced in the administration.

In 1640 the East India Company of England opened a trading post at the fishing village of Madraspatnam (now Chennai) with the permission of the local ruler. The history of Tamil Nadu from the mid-17th century to 1946 is the story of the British-controlled Madras Presidency in relationship to the rise and fall of British power in India. After Indian independence in 1947, the Madras Presidency became Madras state. The state's Telugu-speaking areas were separated to form part of the new state of Andhra Pradesh in 1953. In 1956 Madras was divided further, with some areas going to the new state of Kerala and other areas becoming part of Mysore (now Karnataka). What remained of Madras state was renamed Tamil Nadu in 1968.

CHAPTER 13

INDIA'S UNION TERRITORIES

In addition to its 28 states, India has six union territories that are under the direct administration of the national government. These include several small enclaves on the Indian coast that were former Portuguese (Dadra and Nagar Haveli, Daman and Diu) and French (Puducherry) colonies, two groups of islands (Andaman and Nicobar Islands, Lakshadweep), and Chandigarh—a planned city that serves as the capital of the states of Haryana and Punjab.

ANDAMAN AND NICOBAR ISLANDS

The Indian union territory of the Andaman and Nicobar Islands consists of two groups of islands at the southeastern edge of the Bay of Bengal. The peaks of a submerged mountain range, the Andaman Islands and their neighbours to the south, the Nicobar Islands, form an arc stretching southward for some 620 miles (1,000 km) between Myanmar (Burma) and the island of Sumatra, Indonesia; the arc constitutes the boundary between the Bay of Bengal to the west and the Andaman Sea to the east.

The Andamans, situated on the ancient trade route between India and Myanmar, were visited by the navy of the English East India Company in 1789, and in 1872 they were linked administratively by the British to the Nicobar Islands. The two sets of islands became a union territory of

Andaman redwood trees in the Cinque Islands, south of Rutland Island, in the southern Andamans, Andaman and Nicobar Islands, India. © Ashvin Mehta/Dinodia Photo Library

the Republic of India in 1956. Port Blair (on South Andaman Island) is the territorial capital.

The territory has for more than a century been recognized for its indigenous communities, which have ardently avoided extensive interaction with ethnic outsiders. In 2004 the islands drew global attention when they were severely damaged by a large tsunami that had been triggered by an earthquake in the Indian Ocean near Indonesia. Area 3,185 square miles (8,249 square km). Pop. (2008 est.) 411,000.

LAND

The Andamans comprise more than 300 islands. North, Middle, and South Andaman, known collectively as Great Andaman, are the main islands; others include Landfall Island, Interview Island, the Sentinel Islands, Ritchie's Archipelago, and Rutland Island. Little Andaman in the south is separated from the Nicobar Islands by the Ten Degree Channel, which is about 90 miles (145 km) wide.

The Nicobars consist of 19 islands. Among the most prominent are Car

Nicobar in the north; Camorta, Katchall, and Nancowry in the centre of the chain; and Great Nicobar in the south. About 90 miles to the southwest of Great Nicobar lies the northwestern tip of Sumatra, Indonesia.

RELIEF AND DRAINAGE

Both the Andaman and Nicobar groups are part of a great island arc, formed by the above-sea extensions of submarine ridges of the Rakhine Mountains and the Patkai Range to the north and the Mentawai Ridge (the peaks of which form the Mentawai Islands of Indonesia) to the south. The highest elevation is 2,418 feet (737 metres) at Saddle Peak on North Andaman, followed by Mount Thullier at 2,106 feet (642 metres) on Great Nicobar and Mount Harriet at 1,197 feet (365 metres) on South Andaman. In the late 20th and early 21st centuries, there were volcanic eruptions on Barren Island in the northern Andamans.

Formed of sandstone, limestone, and shale of Cenozoic age (i.e., formed during the past 65 million years), the terrain of the Andamans is rough, with hills enclosing narrow longitudinal valleys. Flat land is scarce and is confined to a few valleys, such as the Betapur on Middle Andaman and Diglipur on North Andaman. Perennial rivers are few. The coral-fringed coasts of the islands are deeply indented, forming safe harbours and tidal creeks.

The terrain of the Nicobars is more diverse than that of the Andamans.

Some of the Nicobar Islands, such as Car Nicobar, have flat coral-covered surfaces with offshore coral formations that prevent most ships from anchoring. Other islands, such as Great Nicobar, are hilly and contain numerous fast-flowing streams. Great Nicobar is the only island in the territory with a significant amount of fresh surface water.

CLIMATE

The climate of the Andaman and Nicobar Islands is tropical but is moderated by sea breezes. Temperatures typically rise from the low 70s F (about 23 °C) into the mid-80s F (about 30 °C) daily throughout the year. The territory receives roughly 120 inches (3,000 mm) of rain annually, brought mainly by the southwest monsoon, which blows from May through September, and by the tropical cyclones that follow in October and November. In the Nicobars, Great Nicobar receives considerably more rain than the other islands. The Andamans have long provided meteorological data for shipping in the Bay of Bengal; a reporting station was in operation at Port Blair as early as 1868.

PLANT AND ANIMAL LIFE

The great majority of the area of the Andaman and Nicobar Islands is covered with dense tropical forest, which supports a broad spectrum of flora and fauna. The dominant tree species include narra (also called Andaman redwood, or padauk; *Pterocarpus dalbergioides*) and various large trees of the family Dipterocarpaceae. The harbours and tidal creeks often are surrounded by mangrove swamps. Many species of tree ferns of the family Cyatheaceae are found in the Nicobars but not in the Andamans.

The islands are inhabited by only a few dozen species of terrestrial and marine mammals, a number of which—such as the Andaman wild pig (*Sus scrofa andamanensis*)—are endemic to the region. Other common mammals include macaques, spotted deer, civets, shrews, whales, dolphins, and dugongs (*Dugong dugon*). The territory is home to more than 200 species of birds, including many endemic varieties. Numerous types of snakes and lizards inhabit the forests, and saltwater crocodiles, fish, turtles, and sea snakes are abundant in the coastal waters. Many species of flora and fauna have yet to be documented systematically.

PEOPLE

Although the Andaman and Nicobar Islands territory consists of hundreds of islands, very few of them are inhabited. Roughly two dozen of the Andaman Islands support human settlements, while only 12 of the Nicobar Islands are populated.

POPULATION COMPOSITION

The vast majority of the population of the Andamans consists of immigrants from South Asia and their descendants. Most speak Hindi or Bengali, but Tamil, Telugu, and Malayalam also are common. The indigenous inhabitants of the Andaman Islands, the Andamanese, historically comprised small isolated groups—all speaking dialects of the Andamanese language. They used the bow and the dog (introduced to the Andamans c. 1857) for hunting but knew no method of making fire. Turtles, dugongs, and fish were caught with nets or harpooned from single outrigger canoes. The remoteness of the Andamanese and their general hostility toward foreigners prevented major cultural change until the mid-20th century. Few indigenous Andamanese survive today, most groups having been decimated by disease following their encounter with Europeans, Indians, and other outsiders. In the early 21st century the only Andamanese groups that remained intact and continued to practice the ways of their ancestors included a small group of Great Andamanese on Strait Island, the Sentinelese of North Sentinel Island, the Jarawa of the interior areas of Middle and South Andaman, and the Onge of Little Andaman.

The indigenous inhabitants of the Nicobar Islands, the Nicobarese (including the related Shompen), continued to constitute the majority of the population of the Nicobars in the early 21st century. They probably descend both from the Malays of insular and peninsular Southeast Asia and from the Mon (also called the Talaing) of Myanmar. The Nicobarese speak various Nicobarese languages, which belong to the Mon-Khmer language group of the Austroasiatic language family; some also speak Hindi and English. In addition to the indigenous population, there are significant numbers of Tamils and other people from the Indian mainland living in the Nicobar Islands. Many came during the 1960s and '70s in conjunction with the Indian government's program to develop the region's agriculture.

More than two-thirds of the people of the Andaman Islands are Hindu; Christians make up about one-fifth of the population and Muslims less than one-tenth. Many Nicobarese are Christian, although some communities practice local religions or have adopted Hinduism, which is prevalent throughout the region. There is also a notable Muslim minority in the Nicobars.

SETTLEMENT PATTERNS AND DEMOGRAPHIC TRENDS

The population of the Andaman and Nicobar Islands expanded particularly rapidly in the mid-20th century as immigrants took advantage of India's postindependence development initiatives in the territory. Growth began to slow by the 1980s, and by the early 21st century it had approached a rate roughly comparable to that of the rest of India. Port Blair is the only major town; it contains more than one-fourth of the territory's residents. The remainder of the population is spread across more than 500 small villages, most of which have fewer than 500 inhabitants.

ECONOMY

Agriculture is the occupation of most of the residents of the Andaman Islands. Principal crops include rice, coconuts, betel (areca nuts), fruits, and spices (such as turmeric). Rubber, oil palms, and cashews also are important. In addition to farming there is a small forestry sector on the islands, which focuses on production of sawn wood for domestic use; surpluses are exported to the Indian mainland. Similarly, the products of the islands' fisheries are intended primarily for domestic consumption.

Neither the Andaman nor the Nicobar island groups are highly industrialized. However, a variety of manufacturing activities are undertaken on both sets of islands. Furniture and other wood products are manufactured on the Andaman Islands. Processed foods and garments are among the principal products of both island groups.

Tourism is a growing industry in the Andaman and Nicobar Islands, with dozens of hotels scattered throughout the territory. Most tourists are from the Indian mainland. Popular historical attractions include remnants of the British colonial administration, such as the Andaman Cellular Jail (completed in 1906), in Port Blair, where the Indian revolutionary Vinayak Damodar (Vir) Savarkar was detained in the first half of the 20th century. The natural environment of the territory, with its many parks, gardens, and sanctuaries, is attractive to ecotourists and trekkers.

Most of the paved roads are in South Andaman. Port Blair and Diglipur are important harbours of South Andaman and North Andaman, respectively. An interisland boat service connects Port Blair with North, Middle, South, and Little Andaman islands. Air service is available to the northern and southern Indian mainland from Port Blair.

Government and Society

The administrative structure of the Andaman and Nicobar Islands, like most other Indian states and territories, is defined by the national constitution of 1950. The territory is administered by the central government through a lieutenant governor, who is appointed by the president of India. The lieutenant governor is assisted by a Council of Ministers. The territory also has its own legislature with elected members.

Health and Welfare

Basic health care is offered free of charge to residents of the Andaman and Nicobar Islands. Services are provided by hospitals in the more densely populated areas and by community health-care centres and primary health-care facilities in the more rural regions. There also is an extensive network of health-care subcentres spread across the islands. Malaria has been a perennial problem in the territory, and the government has participated in nationally sponsored mosquito-control and malaria-prevention initiatives to combat the disease. Similarly, the Andaman and Nicobar Islands territory joined the national government's leprosy-eradication program, with the result that the incidence of that illness has dropped dramatically in the territory since the 1990s.

Education

The number of educational institutions is limited, and most schools offer only primary education. Nevertheless, more than four-fifths of the territory's population is literate, which is well above the Indian national average. There are several post-secondary institutions offering industrial, technical, and teachers' training. The first nursing school opened in 2001.

History

Located on the trade routes from India to East Asia, the Andaman and Nicobar island groups have been known from earliest times. The 7th-century Chinese Buddhist monk I-ching, the Arab travelers of the 9th century, and Marco Polo (*c.* 1254–1324) are among those who mentioned the islands. The name Andaman most likely is derived from the name of the monkey god of Hindu mythology, Hanuman. The name Nicobar probably derives from the Tamil word *nakkavaram* ("land of the naked").

The British first surveyed the Andaman Islands in 1789 in search of a place to establish a penal colony for offenders from British India. Such a colony was established in 1790 but was abandoned just a few years later. In the mid-19th century, concern over native attacks on shipwrecked crews and the need for a penal settlement after the Indian Mutiny (1857–58) led the British to return to the Andamans. In 1858 they founded a new penal colony, named Port Blair. It was during a visit to Port Blair that Lord Mayo, viceroy of India (1869–72), was murdered by a convict in 1872. Meanwhile, the Danish, who had been the claimants of the Nicobar Islands—the ownership of which had since the 17th century shifted variously between France, Denmark, Austria, and Great Britain—relinquished their rights to the territory to the British in 1868.

The population of the region, particularly of the Andamans, was greatly changed by the settlement of convicts from the mainland and, beginning in the 1950s, of numerous refugees, especially from East Pakistan (since 1971, Bangladesh). Japanese forces occupied both the Andaman and Nicobar island groups from 1942 to 1945 (during World War II); after the British recaptured the islands, the penal colony in the Andamans was abolished. Administration of the Andamans and Nicobars was passed to India when it gained independence in 1947. The Andaman Cellular Jail, where Indian political prisoners were held, was declared a national monument in 1979.

In 2004 the Andaman and Nicobar island groups were struck by a tremendous tsunami that had been generated by an earthquake in the Indian Ocean near Sumatra, Indonesia. The inundation left thousands of people dead and many more displaced. The lower-lying Nicobars were most severely affected, with significant portions of some of those islands submerged by the tidal wave.

CHANDIGARH

The Indian city and union territory of Chandigarh is located about 165 miles (265 km) north of New Delhi; the territory is bounded by the state of Haryana on the east and by the state of Punjab on all other sides. It is situated on the Indo-Gangetic Plain a few miles south of the Siwalik (Shiwalik) Range, between two seasonal hill torrents, the Sukhna Cho and the Patiali Rao. The land is a flat and fertile tract of alluvial soils, and its rural farmland produces such crops as wheat, corn (maize), and rice. In the summer months (April to June) temperatures may rise above 111 °F (about 44 °C), while in the winter months (November to February) temperatures may dip into the mid-30s F (about 2 °C), with frequent showers. The monsoon season (July to September) is hot and humid.

Lying within the territory of Chandigarh are the city of Chandigarh, several towns, and a number of adjoining villages. The chief executive, or "administrator," of the territory is the governor of Punjab, who is assisted by a senior officer appointed by the national government. Chandigarh city is the capital of the territory and of the states of Haryana and Punjab. Meaning "stronghold of the goddess Chandi," Chandigarh derives its name from Chandi Mandir, a temple dedicated to the goddess that is located near the town of Mani Majra. Area union territory, 44 square miles (114 square km). Pop. (2001) city, 808,515; (2008 est.) union territory, 1,063,000.

HISTORY

With the partition of India in 1947, the old British province of Punjab was divided into two parts. The larger western part, including the Punjabi capital of Lahore, went to Pakistan. The eastern part was granted to India, but it was without an administrative, commercial, or cultural centre. Consequently, plans to find a suitable site for the capital of the new Indian Punjab were undertaken soon after partition. The Indian government considered several options—including Amritsar, Jalandhar (Jullundur), Phillaur, Ludhiana, Shimla (Simla), Ambala, and Karnal—and selected the present site of Chandigarh in 1948. It was hoped that a magnificent new state capital, scenically located at the foot of the Himalayas, would become a symbol of modernity, would heal the wounded pride of Indian Punjabis, and would house thousands of mostly Hindu and Sikh refugees who had fled from Muslim-dominated Pakistan.

The city was planned by the Swiss-born architect Le Corbusier, assisted by Maxwell Fry, Jane Drew, and several Indian architects and town planners. Construction began in the early 1950s, and most of the city was completed in the early 1960s. The project ultimately required the relocation of some 21,000 people from 58 villages.

The Chandigarh union territory was constituted on Nov. 1, 1966, when the Indian Punjab was reorganized along linguistic lines into two new states—predominantly Hindi-speaking Haryana and Punjabi-speaking Punjab. Straddled between Haryana and Punjab, the city of Chandighar was made the shared capital of the two states and of the union territory itself. Under the terms of the 1986 Punjab Accord, the entire union territory was to become part of Punjab, while the agriculturally productive, mostly Hindi-speaking areas of Fazilka and Abohar, both in Punjab, were to be transferred to Haryana; by the early 21st century, however, this plan had yet to come to fruition.

THE CONTEMPORARY CITY AND TERRITORY

The city of Chandigarh, with its well-developed infrastructure and relatively low population density, covers more than half of the union territory. It consists of more than 50 rectangular sectors, which are separated from one another by broad streets carrying the city's fast-moving arterial traffic. The main government buildings are in the northern part of the city. In the southeast are the industrial areas, separated from the residential sectors by a greenbelt planted with mango trees. Among the city's principal industries are electronics, pharmaceuticals, ceramic plumbing fixtures, and electrical appliances.

Most of the population of the territory is concentrated in the southern sector of Chandighar city. Hindus constitute by far the predominant religious group, although Sikhs form a significant minority. There also is a sprinkling of Muslims, Christians, and Jains. Hindi and Punjabi are the most widely spoken languages in the territory.

The territory has many notable educational and cultural institutions, including Punjab University (founded 1947), the Postgraduate Institute of Medical Education and Research, the Punjab Engineering College, the Government College of Art, and the Government Medical College and Hospital. There also are several specialized arts academies. Chandigarh's local museum houses a rich collection of Gandhara sculptures and Pahari and Sikh paintings, while archaeological digs in the area have yielded ancient Indus civilization (c. 2500–1700 BCE) artifacts, particularly pottery. The city also is known for its extensive rose garden and for its unusual rock garden, which contains numerous statues created from broken objects by the self-taught artist Nek Chand.

Library building (left) *of Punjab University, Chandigarh.* © Robert Frerck/Odyssey Productions

Chandigarh has a multitude of sports and recreation facilities. In the northeast is the large, artificial Lake Sukhna, which has become the main spot in the city for promenading and evening recreation. There also are many government-supported sports complexes and community centres. These have served as the training grounds for numerous nationally and internationally competitive athletes in field hockey, cricket, rowing, and other sports.

DADRA AND NAGAR HAVELI

The Indian union territory of Dadra and Nagar Haveli is located in the western part of the country, between the states of Gujarat to the north and Maharashtra to the south. It lies some 15 miles (24 km) from the Arabian Sea and about 80 miles (130 km) north of Mumbai (Bombay). The territory consists of two sections—Dadra and Nagar Haveli—which together embrace roughly 70 villages. The capital is Silvassa. Area 190 square miles (491 square km). Pop. (2008 est.) 262,000.

GEOGRAPHY

Forests cover some two-fifths of Dadra and Nagar Haveli. The terrain is undulating and hilly, reaching elevations of 1,000 feet (300 metres) in the northeast and east near the Western Ghats. Lowland areas are limited to the central plains, which are crossed by the Daman Ganga River and its tributaries. The only navigable river in Dadra and Nagar Haveli,

the Daman Ganga rises in Maharashtra and flows northwestward through the territory toward Daman, a port once famous for its docks.

The climate is typical of the region. Summers are hot, with the mean temperatures in May typically rising into the low 90s F (mid-30s C). Annual rainfall averages about 120 inches (3,050 mm), most of it falling between June and September.

About four-fifths of the population consists of various indigenous peoples (often collectively called Adivasi), the most numerous of which are the Varli, Dhodia, and Konkan. An array of languages and dialects are spoken by these communities, sometimes in addition to Gujarati and Marathi, which also are spoken in the region. The population is predominantly Hindu, with small Christian and Muslim minorities.

Farming is the chief occupation and is largely practiced by the indigenous people, most of whom live in rural areas. Much cultivation is done on terraced land. Rice and ragi (also called finger millet) are the major food crops. Wheat and sugarcane are also grown. A dam and reservoir on the Daman Ganga River in neighbouring Gujarat has extended irrigation in the territory significantly. Timber production is mainly centred on the valuable native teak.

There is very little large-scale industry; industrial estates have been established in Mashat, Khadoli, and elsewhere for producing such items as electronics, chemicals, and fabrics. Industrial growth has resulted in an influx of labour rather than directly ben-efiting the local population.

A district collector, aided by the sec-retary to the governor of the state of Goa, oversees day-to-day affairs. An elected council serves as an advisory body.

HISTORY

The history of Dadra and Nagar Haveli before India's medieval period (roughly 11th–16th century CE) remains obscure. In 1262 CE a Rajput invader defeated the local Koli chieftains of the area and became the ruler of Ramnagar, a small state that included Nagar Haveli in its ter-ritory. The region remained under Rajput rule until the mid-18th century, when the Marathas acquired Nagar Haveli.

Dadra and Nagar Haveli came under the rule of Portugal in the late 18th cen-tury. The Marathas ceded Nagar Haveli to the Portuguese in 1783 as compensation for a Portuguese vessel that their navy had destroyed. Two years later Portugal acquired Dadra, which became a kind of fief. After India achieved independence in 1947, nationalists in Goa—the oldest Portuguese possession in India—sought to break away from Portugal; their first successes were the seizure of Dadra on the night of July 21, 1954, and their cap-ture of Nagar Haveli two weeks later. A pro-Indian administration was formed in these enclaves, and on June 1, 1961, Dadra and Nagar Haveli requested accession to the Indian union. Although the Indian government had already acknowledged the incorporation of the two areas after

their liberation from the Portuguese, their status as a single union territory was made official on Aug. 11, 1961.

DAMAN AND DIU

The union territory of Daman and Diu consists of two widely separated districts on India's western coast. Daman is an enclave on the state of Gujarat's south-ern coast, situated 100 miles (160 km) north of Mumbai (Bombay). Diu encom-passes an island off the southern coast of Gujarat's Kathiawar Peninsula, 40 miles (64 km) southeast of Veraval, as well as a small area on the mainland. The town of Daman, in the Daman district, is the capi-tal of the territory. Area 43 square miles (112 square km). Pop. (2008 est.) 188,000.

GEOGRAPHY

Daman lies on an alluvial coastal plain, although outcrops of basalt create low plateaus and promontories in the area. The Daman Ganga River flows through the territory, with Daman town situ-ated where the river enters the Arabian Sea. Mean daily maximum temperatures range from the mid-80s F (near 30 °C) in January to the low 90s F (about 34 °C) in May. Annual rainfall, received mainly between June and September, aver-ages about 80 inches (2,000 mm). The greater part of Diu is covered by sand, silt, and marsh; the island portion of the district is separated from the Kathiawar Peninsula by a narrow, swampy creek. Temperatures in Diu are similar to those

Portuguese fort on the northern coast of Diu, India. © Ashvin Mehta/Dinodia Photo Library

in Daman, though rainfall is significantly less, averaging less than 25 inches (600 mm) annually.

The people of Daman and Diu are predominantly Hindu, with small Muslim and Christian minorities. Gujarati is the main language in both districts. Less than one-tenth of the territory's population consists of Scheduled Tribes. Of these communities the Dubla, Dhodia, and Varli are the largest groups.

Agriculture and fishing dominate the economies of Daman and Diu. Rice, finger millet, and pulses are among the main crops of Daman. In Diu, crops such as pearl millet and wheat flourish in the arid climate; a smaller portion of land is cultivated in Diu than in Daman, however. Much of the industrial growth of the territory has been promoted through the efforts of the government of the neighbouring state of Goa. The largest towns of the territory—Diu and Daman—are commercial centres.

The administrative districts of Daman and Diu together constitute a centrally governed union territory. The territory is headed by an administrator, the governor of Goa, who is appointed by the central Indian government.

HISTORY

The name Daman is probably derived from the Daman Ganga River, while Diu is from the Sanskrit word *dvipa*, meaning "island." From Mauryan times (4th–2nd century BCE), both were subject to various local and regional powers ruling in western India. In the 13th century Daman formed part of the Ramnagar state, which then became a tributary of the Gujarat sultans. Similarly, numerous dynasties in Kathiawar (Saurashtra) ruled Diu until it fell to the sultan of Gujarat in the early 15th century.

The Portuguese acquired Daman and Diu as part of their grand design to control the trade of the Indian Ocean. In 1535, under a treaty with Sultan Bahādur Shah of Gujarat, the Portuguese built a fort at Diu, an important port on the flourishing commercial and pilgrimage routes between India and the Middle East. By the mid-1550s all Gujarati ships entering and leaving the Gulf of Khambhat (Cambay) ports were required to call at Diu to pay Portuguese duties. In Diu the Portuguese constructed a Jesuit college, which was converted into the majestic Cathedral of Sé Matriz about the turn of the 17th century; the cathedral remains a landmark today.

Renowned for its docks and shipbuilding yards, Daman (known in Portuguese as Damão) was conquered by the Portuguese in 1559. Both Daman and Diu were subject to the governor-general of Goa as part of the Portuguese overseas province Estado da India (State of India). They remained under Portuguese rule for more than four centuries, though the decline of the Portuguese empire in Asia greatly diminished their strategic significance. Daman and Diu survived as outposts of Portuguese overseas territory until 1961, when they became part of India.

LAKSHADWEEP

The Indian union territory of Lakshadweep (formerly, Laccadive, Minicoy, and Amindivi Islands), is a group of some three dozen islands scattered over 30,000 square miles (78,000 square km) of the Arabian Sea off the country's southwestern coast. The principal islands in the territory are Minicoy and those in the Amindivi group. The easternmost island lies about 185 miles (300 km) from the coast of the state of Kerala. Ten of the islands are inhabited. The administrative centre is Kavaratti. The name Lakshadweep means "Hundred Thousand Islands" in the Malayalam language and also in Sanskrit. Area 12 square miles (32 square km). Pop. (2008 est.) 69,000.

LAND

The islands of Lakshadweep are small, none exceeding 1 mile (1.6 km) in breadth; the Amindivis are the northernmost islands of the group, and Minicoy Island is the southernmost island. Almost

Beach on Bangaram Island, Lakshadweep, India. © Evelyn Letfuss

all the inhabited islands are coral atolls. The higher eastern sides of the islands are the most suited for human habitation, while the low-lying lagoons on the western sides protect the inhabitants from the southwest monsoon. The soils of Lakshadweep are generally sandy, derived from the coral.

Throughout the year, temperatures in Lakshadweep generally range from about 70 °F (about 20 °C) to nearly 90 °F (about 32 °C). Cyclones moving across the Arabian Sea rarely strike the islands.

However, the winds and waves associated with them can alter the land features considerably.

Aside from an abundance of coconut palms, common trees include banyans, casuarinas, pandani (screw pines), breadfruits, tamarinds, and tropical almonds (genus *Terminalia*). Betel nut and betel leaf also grow in the islands. Among the most notable marine fauna are sharks, bonitos, tunas, snappers, and flying fish. Manta rays, octopuses, crabs, turtles, and assorted gastropods are plentiful. The islands also are home to an array of water birds, such as herons, teals, and gulls.

PEOPLE

With the exception of the peoples of Minicoy (whose cultures bear some affinity with those of the Maldive Islands to the south), most people of Lakshadweep are descendants of migrants from the Malabar Coast of southwest India, who had arrived in the islands sometime before the 7th century CE. After becoming established in the islands, these migrant communities (or their offspring) converted to Islam. Although Islam is the predominant religion in contemporary Lakshadweep, vestiges of the religious and social orientation of the original Hindu migrants are evident in the existence of a matrilineal kinship system and castelike social groups.

Most of the Lakshadweep islanders speak Malayalam. Mahi (or Mahl), which is akin to old Sinhalese, is spoken on Minicoy, however. Some people also speak Hindi. The population is concentrated mostly on the islands of Andrott, Kavaratti, Minicoy, and Amini.

ECONOMY

Coconut palms are the agricultural mainstay of Lakshadweep. Copra is produced and exported to the mainland. In some places the underlying coral has been excised and the tracts fertilized with organic matter, which has allowed the cultivation of bananas, vegetables, edible root crops, and millet.

Fishing also forms a major segment of the territory's economy, with tuna as the primary catch. Many fishermen continue an ancient tradition of skilled navigation. Some still sail between the islands and the Indian mainland in distinctive craft called *odam*.

Food processing—largely fish focused—is one of Lakshadweep's chief industries. There is a tuna cannery on Minicoy, where the traditional process of drying bonito also is practiced. Among the territory's other manufacturing activities are coir (coconut fibre) production, hosiery production, weaving, and boat building.

Although the government of Lakshadweep promotes tourism, the industry is closely monitored to guard against negative environmental impact. Permits are needed to visit the territory. Government-sponsored tour packages are available.

Lakshadweep is connected to the Indian mainland by sea and by air. Kozhikode (formerly Calicut), on the coast of Kerala, is the nearest mainland seaport. Kochi, also on the coast of Kerala, is the port of departure and arrival for most passenger ships serving the islands. There is an airport on the island of Agatti, which has regular plane service to and from Kochi. Mainland and interisland helicopter services also are available. There are only a few miles of roads in Lakshadweep.

GOVERNMENT AND SOCIETY

The governmental structure of Lakshadweep, like that of most other Indian states and territories, is determined by the national constitution of 1950. The territory is led by an administrator, who is appointed by the president of India. As a very small territory, Lakshadweep consists of a single district, with four subdivisions. The territory falls under the jurisdiction of the Kerala High Court.

Education in Lakshadweep has improved immensely since the mid-20th century, with primary and secondary schools available throughout the islands. Compared with other states and territories of India, Lakshadweep has one of the highest literacy rates. A college affiliated with the University of Calicut (in Kerala) offers baccalaureate degrees in several fields.

HISTORY

The islands of present-day Lakshadweep were first mentioned by a Greek sailor in the 1st century CE as a source of tortoise shell. Muslim missionary activity in the 7th century and continued contact with Arab traders eventually led to the conversion of all the islanders to Islam. Sometime before 1100 a small Hindu kingdom on the Malabar Coast annexed the islands, and after the fall of the Kulashekhara dynasty of Kerala in 1102 they passed to the Kolathiris, another small Hindu dynasty. Later in the 12th century, after a Kolathiri princess married a Muslim convert, a separate kingdom

(including the islands that eventually formed Lakshadweep) was set up in the Kannur (Cannanore) area of Kerala in order to protect the Keralan tradition of matrilineal descent.

It is possible that the first European to visit the islands was the Italian explorer Marco Polo—if the "female island" mentioned in his 13th-century travelogues was indeed Minicoy Island, as some have speculated. In 1498 the Portuguese arrived in the islands. They subsequently built a fort to control trade, particularly in coir. Residents of the islands staged an uprising in 1545.

Successive *bibis* (female rulers) and their husbands ruled the islands until control of the northern group of islands, the Amindivis, passed to Tippu Sultan, the sultan of Mysore (now Karnataka), on the mainland, in the 1780s. When Tippu was killed in battle with the British in 1799, the Amindivis came under British control. The *bibi* and her husband were permitted to retain the other islands and receive income from them in exchange for an annual payment to the British. These payments repeatedly were in arrears, and in 1908 the *bibi* ceded to the British direct administration of these islands. Sovereignty was transferred to India upon Indian independence in 1947, and the islands were constituted a union territory in 1956.

PUDUCHERRY

The union territory of Puducherry (original name Putucceri, formerly [until 2006]

Pondicherry, also spelled Pondichéry) was formed in 1962 out of the four former colonies of French India: Pondicherry (now Puducherry) and Karaikal along India's southeastern Coromandel Coast, surrounded by Tamil Nadu state; Yanam, farther north along the eastern coast in the delta region of the Godavari River, surrounded by Andhra Pradesh state; and Mahe, lying on the western Malabar Coast, surrounded by Kerala state. The territory's capital is the city of Puducherry in the Puducherry sector, just north of Cuddalore.

The original name of the territory, Putucceri, is derived from the Tamil words *putu* ("new") and *ceri* ("village"). The French corrupted this to Pondichéry (English: Pondicherry), by which it was called until its name was officially changed to Puducherry in 2006. Area 190 square miles (492 square km). Pop. (2008 est.) 1,074,000.

GEOGRAPHY

All four areas of the territory are seaside tourist resorts. The city of Puducherry is divided into two parts by a canal, and all the main streets, running parallel to one another, lead to the open roadstead offshore. The port of Puducherry does not have a harbour, and ships are forced to lie about 1 to 2 miles (1.5 to 3 km) offshore, but its roadstead was once considered the best on the Coromandel Coast. There are a promenade, a landing place for cargo, and a pier. In and around the city are artesian wells that supply a large quantity of water for irrigation, the chief local crops

being rice, sugarcane, cotton, and peanuts (groundnuts). The main industries are food processing and the manufacture of electrical appliances, textiles, paper, and lumber. The Puducherry area has about 300 villages and hamlets.

The Karaikal sector, south of the Puducherry sector, is in the fertile Kaveri River delta, in one of the most important rice-producing areas of India. The exceptional fertility of the region is to some extent reflected in the unusually high density of its rural population. The town is on the Mayavaram-Peralam route, a branchline of the southern railway.

The Mahe sector consists of two parts: the quaint picturesque town of Mahe, with its buildings situated on the left bank of the Mahe River close to its mouth; and the isolated tract known as Naluthrara, on the right bank, comprising the four villages of Chambara, Chalakara, Palour, and Pandaquel. Rice is the chief crop grown in the sector.

Yanam is a small town on the bank of a branch of the Godavari River, about 400 miles (650 km) north of the city of Chennai (Madras), near Kakinada.

The major languages spoken in the areas are Tamil, Malayalam, and Telugu. Tamil is predominant in the southern settlements of Puducherry and Karaikal; Malayalam is predominant in Mahe; and Telugu is spoken mainly in Yanam. Other significant languages in the territory include Urdu, French, Kannada, Hindi, Gujarati, English, and Marathi.

Hindus form the majority in all four regions; Muslims are an important minority in Karaikal, Mahe, and Yanam; and Christians are numerous in Puducherry. There are also a few Sikhs, Buddhists, and Jains.

There are no heavy industries or mining in the union territory; it purchases its entire power requirement from nearby states. Puducherry is governed by a lieutenant governor who is advised by a chief minister and a Council of Ministers. The jurisdiction of the Madras High Court extends over the union territory.

Puducherry contains the Hindu ashram (religious retreat) of the philosopher Sri Aurobindo (1872–1950), as well as Auroville, the international township and study centre that was named for him. The Romain Rolland Public Library houses some rare French volumes. A medical college, a law college, an engineering college, and several other colleges for general education are affiliated with the University of Madras.

History

The French East India Company (formed by Jean-Baptiste Colbert in 1666) established a settlement in 1668 at Surat and another in 1674 at Pondicherry (now Puducherry). The company's director, François Martin, made Pondicherry the capital of the French posts. Mahe was founded in 1725, followed by Yanam in 1731 and Karaikal in 1739. French concerns multiplied in Bengal, with Chandernagore (Chandannagar) as centre, especially after 1730 under the direction of Joseph-François Dupleix, who in 1742 was appointed general director.

From 1763 the French establishments in India, which were under the authority of the king after the abolition of the company in 1769, comprised—apart from a few small posts (*loges*)—no more than five settlements of moderate size: Chandernagore in Bengal, Yanam at the mouth of the Godavara River, Pondicherry and Karaikal on the Coromandel Coast, and Mahe on the Malabar Coast. The English conquest of India lessened the commercial activity of the French settlements. They were occupied by the English in 1778 and again in 1793, but in 1816 they were returned to France. The Second Republic of France granted them local government and representation in the French parliament. Under the Second Empire of France, commercial liberalism and Anglo-French understanding gave these settlements a fleeting moment of prosperity.

In 1947 the *loges* were given back to independent India. Chandernagore was finally transferred in 1951. De facto transfer of the four remaining French possessions to the Union of India took place on Nov. 1, 1954, and de jure transfer was completed on May 28, 1956. Instruments of ratification were signed on Aug. 16, 1962, from which date Pondicherry, consisting of the four enclaves, became a union territory. The territory formally took the name Puducherry in 2006.

CHAPTER 14

THE KASHMIR REGION

Kashmir constitutes the entire northwestern portion of the Indian subcontinent. It is bounded by the Uygur Autonomous Region of Xinjiang to the northeast and the Tibet Autonomous Region to the east (both parts of China), by the Indian states of Himachal Pradesh and Punjab to the south, by Pakistan to the west, and by Afghanistan to the northwest. The region, with a total area of some 85,800 square miles (222,200 square km), has been the subject of dispute between India and Pakistan since the partition of the Indian subcontinent in 1947. The northern and western portions are administered by Pakistan and comprise two areas: Azad Kashmir and Gilgit-Baltistan. The southern and southeastern portions constitute the Indian state of Jammu and Kashmir. The Indian- and Pakistani-administered portions are divided by a "line of control" agreed to in 1972, although neither country recognizes it as an international boundary. In addition, China became active in the eastern area of Kashmir in the 1950s and since 1962 has controlled the northeastern part of Ladakh (the easternmost portion of the region).

The Kashmir region is predominantly mountainous, with deep, narrow valleys and high, barren plateaus. The relatively low-lying Jammu and Punch (Poonch) plains in the southwest are separated by the thickly forested Himalayan foothills and the Pir Panjal Range of the Lesser Himalayas from the larger, more fertile, and more heavily populated Vale

Mountains, Jammu and Kashmir state, India. Encyclopædia Britannica, Inc.

of Kashmir to the north. Jammu and the vale lie in the Indian state of Jammu and Kashmir, while the Punch lowlands are largely in Azad Kashmir.

Rising northeast of the vale is the western part of the Great Himalayas. Farther to the northeast is the high, mountainous plateau region of Ladakh, which is cut by the rugged valley of the northwestward-flowing Indus River. Extending roughly northwestward from the Himalayas are the lofty peaks of the Karakoram Range, including K2 (Mount Godwin Austen), which at 28,251 feet (8,611 metres) is the second-highest peak in the world, after Mount Everest.

The region is located along the northernmost extremity of the Indian-Australian tectonic plate. The subduction of that plate beneath the Eurasian Plate—the process that for roughly 50 million years has been creating the Himalayas—has produced heavy seismic activity in Kashmir. One especially powerful earthquake in 2005 devastated Muzaffarabad, which is the administrative centre of

The Jhelum River at Srinagar, Jammu and Kashmir state, India. Richard Abeles—Artstreet

Azad Kashmir, and adjacent areas including parts of India's Jammu and Kashmir state and Pakistan's North-West Frontier Province.

This chapter focuses on the history of the Kashmir region as a whole and then on the physical and human geography of Jammu and Kashmir state.

REGIONAL HISTORY

According to legend, an ascetic named Kashyapa reclaimed the land now comprising Kashmir from a vast lake. That land came to be known as Kashyapamar and, later, Kashmir.

KASHMIR TO 1947

Buddhism was introduced to the region by the Mauryan emperor Ashoka in the 3rd century BCE, and from the 9th to the 12th century CE the region appears to have achieved considerable prominence as a centre of Hindu culture. A succession of Hindu dynasties ruled Kashmir until 1346, when it came under Muslim rule. The Muslim period lasted nearly five centuries, ending when Kashmir was annexed to the Sikh kingdom of the Punjab in 1819 and then to the Dogra kingdom of Jammu in 1846.

Thus, the Kashmir region in its contemporary form dates from 1846, when, by the treaties of Lahore and Amritsar at the conclusion of the First Sikh War, Raja Gulab Singh, the Dogra ruler of Jammu, was created maharaja (ruling prince) of an extensive but somewhat ill-defined Himalayan kingdom "to the eastward of the River Indus and westward of the River Ravi." The creation of this princely state helped the British safeguard their northern flank in their advance to the Indus and beyond during the latter part of the 19th century. The state thus formed part of a complex political buffer zone interposed by the British between their Indian empire and the empires of Russia and China to the north. For Gulab Singh, confirmation of title to these mountain territories marked the culmination of almost a quarter century of campaigning and diplomatic negotiation among the petty hill kingdoms along the northern borderlands of the Sikh empire of the Punjab.

Some attempts were made in the 19th century to define the boundaries of the territory, but precise definition was in many cases defeated by the nature of the country and by the existence of huge tracts lacking permanent human settlement. In the far north, for example, the

maharaja's authority certainly extended to the Karakoram Range, but beyond that lay a debatable zone on the borders of the Turkistan and Xinjiang regions of Central Asia, and the boundary was never demarcated. There were similar doubts about the alignment of the frontier where this northern zone skirted the region known as Aksai Chin, to the east, and joined the better known and more precisely delineated boundary with Tibet, which had served for centuries as the eastern border of the Ladakh region. The pattern of boundaries in the northwest became clearer in the last decade of the 19th century, when Britain, in negotiations with Afghanistan and Russia, delimited boundaries in the Pamirs region. At that time Gilgit, always understood to be part of Kashmir, was for strategic reasons constituted as a special agency in 1889 under a British agent.

The Kashmir Problem

As long as the territory's existence was guaranteed by the United Kingdom, the weaknesses in its structure and along its peripheries were not of great consequence, but they became apparent after the British withdrawal from South Asia in 1947. By the terms agreed to by India and Pakistan for the partition of the Indian subcontinent, the rulers of princely states were given the right to opt for either Pakistan or India or—with certain reservations—to remain independent. Hari Singh, the maharaja of Kashmir, initially believed that by delaying his decision he could maintain the independence of Kashmir, but, caught up in a train of events that included a revolution among his Muslim subjects along the western borders of the state and the intervention of Pashtun tribesmen, he signed an Instrument of Accession to the Indian union in October 1947. This was the signal for intervention both by Pakistan, which considered the state to be a natural extension of Pakistan, and by India, which intended to confirm the act of accession. Localized warfare continued during 1948 and ended, through the intercession of the United Nations, in a cease-fire that took effect in January 1949. In July of that year, India and Pakistan defined a cease-fire line—the line of control—that divided the administration of the territory. Regarded at the time as a temporary expedient, the partition along that line still exists.

Although there was a clear Muslim majority in Kashmir before the 1947 partition, and its economic, cultural, and geographic contiguity with the Muslim-majority area of the Punjab could be convincingly demonstrated, the political developments during and after the partition resulted in a division of the region. Pakistan was left with territory that, although basically Muslim in character, was thinly populated, relatively inaccessible, and economically underdeveloped. The largest Muslim group, situated in the Vale of Kashmir and estimated to number more than half the population of the entire region, lay in Indian-administered territory, with its former outlets via the Jhelum valley route blocked.

Many proposals were subsequently made to end the dispute over Kashmir, but tensions mounted between the two countries following the Chinese incursion into Ladakh in 1962, and warfare broke out between India and Pakistan in 1965. A cease-fire was established in September, followed by an agreement signed by the two sides at Tashkent (Uzbekistan) in early January 1966, in which they resolved to try to end the dispute by peaceful means. Fighting again flared up between the two in 1971 as part of the India-Pakistan war that resulted in the creation of Bangladesh. An accord signed in the Indian city of Shimla in 1972 expressed the hope that henceforth the countries in the region would be able to live in peace with each other. It was widely believed that Zulfikar Ali Bhutto, then prime minister of Pakistan, might have tacitly accepted the line of control as the de facto border, although he later denied this. After Bhutto was arrested in 1977 and executed in 1979, the Kashmir issue once again became the leading cause of conflict between India and Pakistan.

A number of movements have variously sought a merger of Kashmir with Pakistan, independence for the region from both India and Pakistan, or the granting of Indian union territory status to Buddhist Ladakh. To contend with these movements, confront Pakistani forces along the cease-fire line, and support the administrative structure of Jammu and Kashmir state, the Indian union government has maintained a strong military presence there, especially since the end of the 1980s.

The Kargil area of western Ladakh has often been the site of border conflicts, including a serious incident in 1999. In May of that year Pakistan intensified artillery shelling of the Kargil sector. Meanwhile, the Indian army discovered that militants had infiltrated the Indian zone from the Pakistan side and had established positions within and west of the Kargil area. Intense fighting ensued between the infiltrators and the Indian army and lasted more than two months. The Indian army managed to reclaim most of the area on the India side of the line of control that had been occupied by the infiltrators. Hostilities finally ended when Prime Minister Nawaz Sharif of Pakistan gave his assurance that the infiltrators would retreat.

However, shelling across the line of control continued intermittently into the early 21st century, until a cease-fire agreement was reached in 2004. Tensions in the region subsequently diminished, and India and Pakistan sought more cordial relations in general and greater regional cooperation. Limited passenger bus service began in 2005 between Srinagar and Muzaffarabad on either side of the frontier, and, after the devastating earthquake in the region later that year, India and Pakistan allowed survivors and trucks carrying relief supplies to cross

at several points along the line of control. In addition, in 2008 both countries opened cross-border trade links through the Kashmir region for the first time since the 1947 partition; trucks carrying locally produced goods and manufactures began operating between Srinagar and Muzaffarabad and between Rawalkot, Pak., and Punch, India.

Despite these advances, tensions have continued to erupt periodically in the region. One such incident involved facilities for Hindu pilgrims at the popular Amarnath cave shrine in Jammu and Kashmir state, high in the Himalayas east of Srinagar. In June 2008 a proposal by the state government to transfer a parcel of land to the shrine administrators to improve facilities for pilgrims was met with several weeks of riots and protests until the agreement was changed to a temporary occupation of the land during the annual pilgrimage.

CHINESE INTERESTS

China had never accepted the British-negotiated boundary agreements in northeastern Kashmir. This remained the case following the communist takeover in China in 1949, although the new government did ask India—without success—to open negotiations regarding the border. After Chinese authority was established in Tibet and reasserted in Xinjiang, Chinese forces penetrated into the northeastern parts of Ladakh. This was done mainly because it allowed them to build a military road through the Aksai Chin plateau area (completed in 1956–57) to provide better communication between Xinjiang and western Tibet; it also gave the Chinese control of passes in the region between India and Tibet. India's belated discovery of this road led to border clashes between the two countries that culminated in the Sino-Indian war of October 1962. China has occupied the northeastern part of Ladakh since the conflict. India refused to negotiate with China on the alignment of the Ladakhi boundary in this area, and the incident contributed significantly to a diplomatic rift between the two countries that began to heal only in the late 1980s. In the following decades, China worked to improve its relations with India, but there has been no resolution to the disputed Ladakh frontier.

JAMMU AND KASHMIR

The state of Jammu and Kashmir occupies the northernmost part of India in the vicinity of the Karakoram and western Himalayan mountain ranges. It constitutes the larger Indian-administered portion of the Kashmir region. Formerly one of the largest princely states of India, the state is bounded to the northeast by the Uygur Autonomous Region of Xinjiang and to the east by the Tibet Autonomous Region (both parts of China) and the Chinese-administered portions of Kashmir, to the south by the Indian states of Himachal Pradesh and Punjab, to the southwest by Pakistan, and to the northwest by the Pakistani-administered portion of Kashmir. The administrative capitals are Srinagar in summer and Jammu in winter. Area 39,146 square miles (101,387 square km). Pop. (2008 est.) 12,366,000.

LAND

The vast majority of the state's territory is mountainous, and the physiography is divided into seven zones that are closely associated with the structural components of the western Himalayas. From southwest to northeast these zones consist of the plains, the foothills, the Pir Panjal Range, the Vale of Kashmir, the Great Himalayas zone, the upper Indus River valley, and the Karakoram Range. The climate varies from alpine in the northeast to subtropical in the southwest; in the alpine area, average annual precipitation is about 3 inches (75 mm), but, in the subtropical zone (around Jammu), rainfall amounts to about 45 inches (1,150 mm) per year. The entire region is prone to violent seismic activity, and light to moderate tremors are common. A strong earthquake centred in neighbouring Pakistani-administered Kashmir killed hundreds in Jammu and Kashmir state in 2005.

THE PLAINS

The narrow zone of plains country in the Jammu region is characterized by interlocking sandy alluvial fans that have been deposited by streams discharging from the foothills and by a much-dissected pediment (eroded bedrock surface) covered by loams and loess (wind-deposited silt) of Pleistocene age (about 11,700 to 2,600,000 years old). Precipitation is low, amounting to about 15 to 20 inches (380 to 500 mm) per year, and it occurs mainly in the form of heavy but infrequent rain showers during the summer monsoon (June to September). The countryside has been almost entirely denuded of trees, and thorn scrub and coarse grass are the dominant forms of vegetation.

THE FOOTHILLS

The foothills of the Himalayas, rising from about 2,000 to 7,000 feet (600 to 2,100 metres), form outer and inner zones. The outer zone consists of sandstones, clays, silts, and conglomerates, influenced by Himalayan folding movements and eroded to form long ridges and valleys called *duns*. The inner zone consists of more massive sedimentary rock, including red sandstones of Miocene age (roughly 5.3 to 23 million years old), that has been folded, fractured, and eroded to form steep spurs and plateau remnants. River valleys are deeply incised and terraced, and faulting has produced a number of alluvium-filled basins, such as those surrounding Udhampur and Punch. As precipitation increases with elevation, the lower scrubland gives way to pine forests.

THE PIR PANJAL RANGE

The Pir Panjal Range constitutes the first mountain rampart associated with the Himalayas and is the westernmost of the Lesser Himalayas. It has an average crest line of 12,500 feet (3,800 metres), with individual peaks rising to some 15,000 feet (4,600 metres). Consisting of an ancient rock core of granites, gneisses, quartz rocks, and slates, it has been subject to considerable uplift and fracturing and was heavily glaciated during the Pleistocene Epoch. The range receives heavy precipitation in the forms of winter snowfall and summer rain and has extensive areas of pasture above the tree line.

THE VALE OF KASHMIR

The Vale of Kashmir is a deep, asymmetrical basin lying between the Pir Panjal Range and the western end of the Great Himalayas at an average elevation of 5,300 feet (1,620 metres). During the Pleistocene Epoch it was occupied at times by a body of water known as Lake Karewa; it is now filled by lacustrine (still water) sediments as well as alluvium deposited by the upper Jhelum River. Soil and water conditions vary across the valley. The climate is characterized by annual precipitation of about 30 inches (750 mm), derived partially from the summer monsoon and partially from storms associated with winter low-pressure systems. Snowfall often is accompanied by rain and sleet. Temperatures vary considerably by elevation; at Srinagar the average minimum temperature is in the upper 20s F (about –2 °C) in January, and the average maximum is in the upper 80s F (about 31 °C) in July. Up to about 7,000 feet (2,100 metres), woodlands of deodar cedar, blue pine, walnut, willow, elm, and poplar occur; from 7,000 to 10,500 feet (3,200 metres), coniferous forests with fir, pine, and spruce are found; from 10,500 to 12,000 feet (3,700 metres), birch is dominant; and above 12,000 feet are meadows with rhododendrons and dwarf willows as well as honeysuckle.

THE GREAT HIMALAYAS ZONE

Geologically complex and topographically immense, the Great Himalayas contain ranges with numerous peaks reaching elevations of 20,000 feet (6,100 metres) or more, between which lie deeply entrenched, remote valleys. The region was heavily glaciated in Pleistocene times, and remnant glaciers and snowfields are still present. The zone receives some rain from the southwest monsoon in the summer months—and the lower slopes are forested—but the mountains constitute a climatic divide, representing a transition from the monsoon climate of the Indian subcontinent to the dry, continental climate of Central Asia.

THE UPPER INDUS RIVER VALLEY

The valley of the upper Indus River is a well-defined feature that follows the geologic strike (structural trend) westward from the Tibetan border to the point in the Pakistani sector of Kashmir where the river rounds the great mountainous mass of Nanga Parbat to run southward in deep gorges that cut across the strike. In its upper reaches the river is flanked by gravel terraces; each tributary builds an alluvial fan out into the main valley. The town of Leh stands on such a fan, 11,500 feet (3,500 metres) above sea level, with a climate characterized by an almost total lack of precipitation, by intense insolation (exposure to sunlight), and by great diurnal and annual ranges of temperature. Life depends on meltwater from the surrounding mountains, and vegetation is alpine (i.e., consists of species above the tree line), growing on thin soils.

THE KARAKORAM RANGE

The great granite-gneiss massifs of the Karakoram Range—which straddles the Indian and Pakistani sectors of Kashmir—contain some of the world's highest peaks, including K2 (also called Mount Godwin Austen), with an elevation of 28,251 feet (8,611 metres); at least 30 other peaks exceed 24,000 feet (7,300 metres). The range, which is still heavily glaciated, rises starkly from dry, desolate plateaus that are characterized by extremes of temperature and shattered rock debris. The Karakoram, along with other areas in and around the Himalayan region, is often called the "roof of the world."

Peaks of the Zaskar Range of the Himalayas near Sonamarg, Jammu and Kashmir state, India. Josef Muench

ANIMAL LIFE

Among the wild mammals found in the state are the Siberian ibex, the Ladakh urial (a species of wild sheep with a reddish coat), the rare *hangul* (or Kashmir stag) found in Dachigam National Park, and black and brown bears. There are many species of game birds, including vast numbers of migratory ducks.

PEOPLE

The cultural, ethnic, and linguistic composition of Jammu and Kashmir varies across the state by region. About two-thirds of the population adheres to Islam, a greater proportion than in any other Indian state; Hindus constitute most of the remaining third. There also are small minorities of Sikhs and Buddhists. Urdu is the state's official language.

THE JAMMU REGION

Jammu, winter capital of the maharajas (the former Hindu rulers of the region) and second-largest city in the state, was historically the seat of the Dogra dynasty. More than two-thirds of the region's residents are classified as Hindu. Most of Jammu's Hindus live in the southeastern portion of the region and are closely related to the Punjabi-speaking peoples in Punjab state; many speak the Dogri language. The majority of the state's Sikhs also live in the Jammu region. To the northwest, however, the proportion of Muslims increases, with Muslims making up a dominant majority in the area around the western town of Punch.

KASHMIRIS OF THE VALE AND HIGHLANDS

The Vale of Kashmir, surrounded by the highlands of the broader Kashmir region, always has had something of a unique character. The vast majority of the people are Muslims who speak Kashmiri or Urdu. Culturally and ethnically, their closest links are with peoples in the northwestern highlands of the Gilgit district of the Pakistani-administered sector of Kashmir. The Kashmiri language is influenced by Sanskrit and belongs to the Dardic branch of Indo-Aryan languages, which also are spoken by the various hill peoples of Gilgit; Kashmiri has rich folklore and literary traditions. The great majority of the population resides in the lower reaches of the vale. Srinagar, Jammu and Kashmir's largest city, is located on the Jhelum River.

LADAKH

The Great Himalayas are an ethnic and cultural, as well as physical, divide. The portion of the Ladakh area (sometimes called "Little Tibet") located in northeastern Jammu and Kashmir is thinly populated. To the east, around Leh, the inhabitants are predominantly Buddhists of Tibetan ancestry who speak a Tibeto-Burman language (Ladakhi). In the region around

Houseboats along the shore of Nangin Lake, Srinagar, Jammu and Kashmir, India.
Gerald Cubitt

Kargil to the west, however, the population is predominantly Muslim, most belonging to the Shīʿite branch of Islam.

SETTLEMENT PATTERNS

The state's physiographic diversity is matched by a considerable variety of human occupation. In the plains and foothills of the southwestern region, colonization movements from the Punjab areas over a long period of time have produced numerous agricultural settlements. In the *dun* regions and lower valleys of the foothills, where alluvial soils and the availability of water for irrigation make agriculture possible, the population is sustained by crops of wheat and barley, which are gathered in the spring (*rabi*) harvest, and of rice and corn (maize), gathered in the late summer (*kharif*) harvest; livestock also are raised. The upper sections of the valleys support a sparser population that depends on a mixed economy of corn, cattle, and forestry. Herders migrate to higher pastures each spring to give their flocks the necessary forage to produce milk and clarified butter, or ghee, for southern lowland markets. In winter the hill dwellers return to lower areas to work in government-owned forests and timber mills. Agricultural hamlets and nucleated villages predominate throughout the state; cities and towns such as Jammu and Udhampur function essentially as market centres and administrative headquarters for the rural populations and estates in the vicinity.

ECONOMY

The majority of the people of Jammu and Kashmir are engaged in subsistence agriculture of diverse kinds on terraced slopes, each crop adapted to local conditions. Mineral resources are limited, though the state has considerable hydroelectric potential. Manufacturing is characterized by a variety of handicraft industries.

AGRICULTURE

Rice, the staple crop, is planted in May and harvested in late September. Corn, millet, pulses, cotton, and tobacco are—with rice—the main summer crops, while wheat and barley are the chief spring crops. Many temperate fruits and vegetables are grown in areas adjacent to urban markets or in well-watered areas with rich organic soils. Sericulture (silk cultivation) is also widespread. Large orchards in the Vale of Kashmir produce apples, pears, peaches, walnuts, almonds, and cherries, which are among the state's major exports. In addition, the vale is the sole producer of saffron in the Indian subcontinent. Lake margins are particularly favourable for cultivation, and vegetables and flowers are grown intensively in reclaimed marshland or on artificial floating gardens. The lakes and rivers also provide fish and water chestnuts.

Cultivation in Ladakh is restricted to such main valleys as those of the Indus, Shyok, and Suru rivers, where it consists of small irrigated plots of barley, buckwheat, turnips, and mustard. Plants introduced in the 1970s by Indian researchers have given rise to orchards and vegetable fields. Pastoralism—notably yak herding—long has been a vital feature of the Ladakh economy; breeding of sheep, goats, and cattle has been encouraged. The Kashmir goat, which is raised in the region, provides cashmere for the production of fine textiles. Some Gujjar and Gaddi communities practice transhumance (seasonal migration of livestock) in the mountains. In addition to supplying pasture for the livestock, the mountains also are a source of many kinds of timber, a portion of which is exported.

RESOURCES AND POWER

The state's limited mineral and fossil fuel resources are concentrated primarily in the Jammu region. Small reserves of natural gas are found near the city of Jammu, and bauxite and gypsum deposits occur in the vicinity of Udhampur. Other minerals include limestone, coal, zinc, and copper. The pressure of population on land is apparent everywhere, and all available resources are utilized.

All the principal cities and towns, including Leh, and a majority of the villages are electrified, and hydroelectric and thermal generating plants have been constructed to provide power for industrial development based on local raw materials. Major power stations are located at Chineni and Salal and on the upper Sind and lower Jhelum rivers.

MANUFACTURING

Metalware, precision instruments, sporting goods, furniture, matches, and resin and turpentine are the major manufactures of Jammu and Kashmir, with the bulk of the state's manufacturing activity located in Srinagar. Many industries have developed from rural crafts, including handloom weaving of local silk, cotton, and wool, carpet weaving, wood carving, and leatherwork. Such industries, together with the making of silverwork, copperwork, and jewelry, were stimulated first by the presence of the royal court and later by the growth of tourism; however, they also owe something to the important position achieved by Srinagar in west Himalayan trade. In the past the city acted as an entrepôt for the products of the Punjab region on the one hand and of the high plateau region east of the Karakoram, Pamir, and Ladakh ranges on the other hand. Routes still run northwestward into Gilgit via the Raj Diangan Pass and northeastward via the Zoji Pass to Leh and beyond. Handicraft manufacture also is important in Ladakh, particularly the production of cashmere shawls, carpets, and blankets.

TOURISM

Although facilities for visitors to Jammu and Kashmir have improved considerably since the late 20th century, the state's potential in the tourist sector has remained generally untapped. Nevertheless, tourism has made a significant socioeconomic impact on Ladakh, which was largely isolated from outsiders until the 1970s. In addition to historical and religious sites, visitor destinations include the snow-sports centre at Gulmarg south of Baramula in the Pir Panjal Range, the hot mineral springs at Chumathang near Leh, and the state's many lakes and rivers. Mountain trekking is popular from July through September.

TRANSPORTATION

Transport within Jammu and Kashmir remains a problem, although the Indian central government has made a substantial investment in developing the state's infrastructure. As a result of the India-Pakistan dispute over the Kashmir region, the route through the Jhelum valley from Srinagar to Rawalpindi, Pak., was closed in the late 1940s. This made it necessary to transform a longer and more difficult cart road through Banihal Pass into an all-weather highway in order to link Jammu with the Vale of Kashmir; included was the construction of the Jawahar Tunnel, which at the time of its completion in 1959 was one of the longest in Asia. This road, however, is often made impassable by severe weather, which causes shortages of essential commodities in the vale. A road also connects Srinagar with Kargil and Leh. Jammu

is the terminus of the Northern Railway of India. In the early 21st century a rail link was completed between Jammu and Udhampur, with work well under way to extend the connection to Srinagar. Srinagar and Jammu are connected by air to New Delhi and other Indian cities, and there is air service between Srinagar, Leh, and Delhi.

GOVERNMENT AND SOCIETY

The state of Jammu and Kashmir retains a special status within the union government of India. Unlike the rest of the states, which are bound by the Indian constitution, Jammu and Kashmir follows a modified version of that constitution—as delineated in the Constitution (Application to Jammu and Kashmir) Order, 1954—which affirms the integrity of the state within the Republic of India. The union government has direct legislative powers in matters of defense, foreign policy, and communications within the state and has indirect influence in matters of citizenship, Supreme Court jurisdiction, and emergency powers.

CONSTITUTIONAL FRAMEWORK

Under the constitution of Jammu and Kashmir, the governor, who is head of state, is appointed by the president of India and is aided and advised by an elected chief minister and a council of ministers. The legislature consists of two houses: the Legislative Assembly (Vidhan Sabha), comprising several dozen members elected from single-member constituencies; and the smaller Legislative Council (Vidhan Parishad), with most members elected by various groups of politicians, local administrators, and educators and a few appointed by the governor. The state directly sends six elected representatives to the Lok Sabha (Lower House) and six members, elected by the combined Legislative Assembly and Council, to the Rajya Sabha (Upper House) of the Indian Parliament. The High Court consists of a chief justice and 11 other judges, who are appointed by the president of India.

HEALTH AND WELFARE

Medical service is provided by hospitals and dispensaries scattered throughout the state, although accessibility to health care is somewhat lower in Ladakh than in other areas. Influenza, respiratory ailments such as asthma, and dysentery remain common health problems. Cardiovascular disease, cancer, and tuberculosis have increased in the Vale of Kashmir since the late 20th century.

EDUCATION

Education is free at all levels. Literacy rates are comparable to the national average. The two major institutes of higher education are the University of Kashmir at Srinagar and the University of Jammu, both founded in 1969. In addition, agricultural schools have been established in Srinagar (1982) and Jammu (1999). A specialized institute of medical sciences was founded in Srinagar in 1982.

CONCLUSION

India is perhaps the quintessential place on Earth where physical geography is closely intertwined with human habitation. First-time visitors to the country inevitably are struck by the sheer number of people there. Indeed, India's average population density is some 1,000 per square mile (400 per square km), nearly three times greater than the density of the more populous China and more than 12 times that of the United States. No part of the country is truly uninhabited, except for the most inaccessible mountain slopes in the far north and northeast and the most inhospitable desert areas in the northwest.

The Indian subcontinent is one of the cradles of humanity, and its people have a deep, ancient, and intense relationship to this vast and varied land in which they live. This is perhaps best seen in the reverence given to the great rivers—notably the innumerable ghats (bathing stairs) located along the Ganges as it wends its way through northern India—or in the remarkable cave temples at Ajanta and elsewhere that are carved out of the living rock. And this relationship can be glimpsed in the land stewardship of hundreds of millions of farmers, who have made great strides in expanding cultivation and providing irrigation to their crops but still suffer if the life-giving monsoon rains fail.

India's people reflect the great contrasts in the country's landscape. Dozens of languages are spoken by a wide array of peoples, and this highly spiritual country has spawned numerous religious practices, including two of the world's major religions—Hinduism and Buddhism. India's rich and varied cuisine, celebrated throughout the world, also reflects the diversity of its people. Economically, the Indian people encompass those who enjoy the highest levels of wealth and luxury and others who are mired in the deepest poverty and misery—the two groups often living close to each other. And while hundreds of millions of subsistence farmers are able to eke out only the barest of livings from the land, a growing number of highly skilled technocrats are engaged in some of the world's most sophisticated research and manufacturing activities.

Although the great majority of India's population is still classified as rural, the country has more than two dozen cities with populations of one million or more and dozens more with at least a half million inhabitants. The great majority of these places have been settled for centuries, their buildings representing a fascinating juxtaposition of architectural styles ancient and new. Everywhere, it seems, there are vast crowds of people—thronging the streets and roads; packing the buses, trains, and subways; reflecting the country's intricate social hierarchy. They and their rural counterparts live in the world's most populous democracy as part of a vast social experiment that was nurtured during the colonial period and has flourished as a true representation of India's great plurality and diversity.

Appendix: Statistical Summary

Official name: Bharat (Hindi); Republic of India (English).

Form of government: multiparty federal republic with two legislative houses (Council of States: 245[1]; House of the People: 545[2]).

Chief of state: President.

Head of government: Prime Minister.

Capital: New Delhi.

Official language: Hindi; English.

Official religion: none.

Monetary unit: Indian rupee (Re, plural Rs).

Population (2009 est.): 1,198,003,000.

Density (2009 est.)[4]: persons per sq mile 979.9, persons per sq km 378.3.

Urban-rural (2008): urban 29.0%; rural 71.0%.

Sex distribution (2008): male 51.87%; female 48.13%.

Age breakdown (2008): under 15, 30.9%; 15–29, 26.9%; 30–44, 21.2%; 45–59, 13.1%; 60–74, 6.4%; 75–84, 1.3%; 85 and over, 0.2%.

Population projection: (2020) 1,367,225,000; (2030) 1,484,598,000.

Major cities (2006 est.; urban agglomerations, 2007 est.): Mumbai (Bombay) 12,880,000 (18,978,000); Delhi 11,220,000 (15,926,000); Kolkata (Calcutta) 4,640,000 (14,787,000); Chennai (Madras) 4,350,000 (7,163,000); Bangalore (Bengaluru) 5,100,000 (6,787,000); Hyderabad 3,630,000 (6,376,000); Ahmadabad 3,770,000 (4,663,533); Pune (Poona) 3,040,000 (4,672,000); Surat 3,020,000 (3,842,000); Kanpur 2,900,000 (3,162,000); Jaipur 2,820,000 (2,917,000); Lucknow 2,540,000 (2,695,000); Nagpur 2,270,000 (2,454,000); Patna 1,660,000 (2,158,000); Bhopal 1,640,000 (1,727,000); New Delhi[6] 302,363[7].

Linguistic composition (2001)[8]: Hindi 41.03%; Bengali 8.11%; Telugu 7.19%; Marathi 6.99%; Tamil 5.91%; Urdu

5.01%; Gujarati 4.48%; Kannada 3.69%; Malayalam 3.21%; Oriya 3.21%; Punjabi 2.83%; Assamese 1.28%; Maithili 1.18%; Bhili/Bhilodi 0.93%[9]; Santhali 0.63%; Kashmiri 0.54%; Nepali 0.28%; Gondi 0.26%[9]; Sindhi 0.25%; Konkani 0.24%; Dogri 0.22%; Khandeshi 0.20%[9]; Tulu 0.17%[9]; Kurukh/Oraon 0.17%[9]; Manipuri 0.14%; other 1.14%. Hindi (roughly 66%) and English (roughly 33%) are also spoken as lingua francas.

Castes/tribes (2001): number of Scheduled Castes (formerly referred to as "untouchables") 166,635,700; number of Scheduled Tribes (aboriginal peoples) 84,326,240.

Religious affiliation (2005): Hindu 72.04%; Muslim 12.26%, of which Sunni 8.06%, Shī'ī 4.20%; Christian 6.81%, of which Independent 3.23%, Protestant 1.74%, Roman Catholic 1.62%, Orthodox 0.22%; traditional beliefs 3.83%; Sikh 1.87%; Buddhist 0.67%; Jain 0.51%; Bahā'ī 0.17%; Zoroastrian (Parsi) 0.02%[10]; nonreligious 1.22%; atheist 0.17%; remainder 0.43%.

Households (2001): Total number of households 193,579,954. Average household size 5.3. Type of household: permanent 51.8%; semipermanent 30.0%; temporary 18.2%. Average number of rooms per household 2.2; 1 room 38.4%, 2 rooms 30.0%, 3 rooms 14.3%, 4 rooms 7.5%, 5 rooms 2.9%, 6 or more rooms 3.7%, unspecified number of rooms 3.2%.

DEMOGRAPHY				
STATES	CAPITALS	AREA		POPULATION
		SQ MI	SQ KM	2008 PROJECTION[3]
Andhra Pradesh	Hyderabad	106,204	275,068	82,180,000
Arunachal Pradesh	Itanagar	32,333	83,743	1,200,000
Assam	Dispur	30,285	78,438	29,929,000
Bihar	Patna	38,301	99,200	93,823,000
Chhattisgarh	Raipur	52,199	135,194	23,646,000
Goa	Panaji	1,429	3,702	1,628,000
Gujarat	Gandhinagar	75,685	196,024	56,408,000
Haryana	Chandigarh	17,070	44,212	23,772,000
Himachal Pradesh	Shimla	21,495	55,673	6,550,000
Jammu and Kashmir	Srinagar	39,146	101,387	12,366,000
Jharkhand	Ranchi	28,833	74,677	30,010,000
Karnataka	Bangalore (Bengaluru)	74,051	191,791	57,399,000

| STATES | CAPITALS | AREA | | POPULATION |
		SQ MI	SQ KM	2008 PROJECTION[3]
Kerala	Thiruvananthapuram (Trivandrum)	15,005	38,863	34,232,000
Madhya Pradesh	Bhopal	119,016	308,252	69,279,000
Maharashtra	Mumbai (Bombay)	118,800	307,690	106,894,000
Manipur	Imphal	8,621	22,327	2,627,000
Meghalaya	Shillong	8,660	22,429	2,536,000
Mizoram	Aizawl	8,139	21,081	980,000
Nagaland	Kohima	6,401	16,579	2,187,000
Orissa	Bhubaneshwar	60,119	155,707	39,899,000
Punjab	Chandigarh	19,445	50,362	26,591,000
Rajasthan	Jaipur	132,139	342,239	64,641,000
Sikkim	Gangtok	2,740	7,096	594,000
Tamil Nadu	Chennai (Madras)	50,216	130,058	66,396,000
Tripura	Agartala	4,049	10,486	3,510,000
Uttar Pradesh	Lucknow	93,933	243,286	190,891,000
Uttarakhand	Dehra Dun	19,739	51,125	9,497,000
West Bengal	Kolkata (Calcutta)	34,267	88,752	87,869,000
UNION TERRITORIES				
Andaman and Nicobar Islands	Port Blair	3,185	8,249	411,000
Chandigarh	Chandigarh	44	114	1,063,000
Dadra and Nagar Haveli	Silvassa	190	491	262,000
Daman and Diu	Daman	43	112	188,000
Lakshadweep	Kavaratti	12	32	69,000
Puducherry (Pondicherry)	Puducherry (Pondicherry)	190	492	1,074,000
NATIONAL CAPITAL TERRITORY				
Delhi	Delhi	573	1,483	17,076,000
TOTAL		1,222,559[4,5]	3,166,414[4]	1,147,677,000

VITAL STATISTICS

Birth rate per 1,000 population (2008): 22.8 (world avg. 20.3).
Death rate per 1,000 population (2008): 8.2 (world avg. 8.5).
Natural increase rate per 1,000 population (2008): 14.6 (world avg. 11.8).
Total fertility rate (avg. births per childbearing woman; 2008): 2.80.
Life expectancy at birth (2008): male 63.0 years; female 67.0 years.

NATIONAL ECONOMY

Gross national income (2008): US$1,215,485,000,000 (US$1,070 per capita).
Budget (2008–09). Revenue: Rs 9,009,530,400,000,000 (tax revenue 51.7%, of which corporate taxes 18.3%, income tax 10.0%, excise taxes 9.8%; capital revenue 37.6%; nontax revenue 10.7%). Expenditures: Rs 9,009,530,000,000 (current expenditure 89.2%, of which public debt payments 21.4%, subsidies 14.3%; defense 8.2%; capital expenditure 10.8%).
Public debt (external, outstanding; 2007): US$74,419,000,000.

FOREIGN TRADE

Imports (2007–08): US$251,654,000,000 (crude petroleum and refined petroleum 31.6%; electronics 8.2%; transportation equipment 8.0%; nonelectrical machinery and apparatus 7.9%; gold 6.6%; chemicals and chemical products 4.6%; base metals 3.5%; electronic goods [including computer software] 9.7%; precious stones [significantly diamonds] 3.2%; metal ores [significantly copper ore and concentrates] 3.1%).
Major import sources: China 10.8%; U.S. 8.4%; Saudi Arabia 7.7%; United Arab Emirates 5.4%; Iran 4.3%; Germany 3.9%; Switzerland 3.9%; Australia 3.1%; Kuwait 3.1%; Iraq 2.7%.
Exports (2007–08): US$163,132,100,000 (refined petroleum products 17.4%; gems and jewelery [significantly diamonds] 12.1%; textiles and wearing apparel 11.9%; food, beverages, and tobacco 11.3%; chemicals and chemical products 9.1%; machinery and apparatus 5.6%; fabricated metal products 4.3%; transportation equipment 4.3%; iron ore 3.6%).
Major export destinations: U.S.12.7%; United Arab Emirates 9.6%; China 6.6%; Singapore 4.5%; U.K. 4.1%; Hong Kong 3.9%; Netherlands 3.2%; Germany 3.1%; Belgium 2.6%; Italy 2.4%; Japan 2.4%.
Food (2005): daily per capita caloric intake 2,529 (vegetable products 92%, animal products 8%), 139% of FAO recommended minimum requirement; undernourished population (2002–04) 209,500,000 (20% of total population based on consumption of a minimum daily requirement of 1,820 calories).

Military

Total active duty personnel (November 2008): 1,281,000 (army 85.8%, navy 4.3%, air force 9.4%, coast guard 0.5%); paramilitary forces 1,300,700.

Military expenditure as percentage of GDP (2008): 2.3%; per capita expenditure US$21.

1   *Includes 12 members appointed by the President.*
2   *Includes 2 Anglo-Indians appointed by the President.*
3   *Populations are March 1, 2008, official projections based on the 2001 Indian census results.*
4   *Excludes 46,660 sq miles (120,849 sq km) of territory claimed by India as part of Jammu and Kashmir state but occupied by Pakistan or China; inland water constitutes 9.6% of total area of India (including all of Indian-claimed Kashmir).*
5   *Detail does not add to total given because of rounding.*
6   *Within Delhi urban agglomeration.*
7   *2001 census.*
8   *Scheduled ("officially recognized") languages of India.*
9   *Nonscheduled ("not officially recognized") language.*
10   *2000 estimate.*

GLOSSARY

alluvium Sediment, such as mud or sand, that is deposited by flowing rivers.

ashram A religious retreat (Sanskrit: ashrama, "retreat," or "hermitage").

bastis Urban settlement; a collection of huts standing on a plot of land of at least one-sixth of an acre in an urban area.

bhakti sect Devotional sect.

cantonment A military camp.

civil lines Residential areas originally built by the British for senior officers.

clastic Rocks with a fragmented appearance that are made up of pieces of older rocks or other solid material.

dacoits Violent gangs of criminals.

damascened Decorated with wavy lines.

duns Heavily cultivated flat valleys, or flat-floored basins.

doab A piece of land that is located between two rivers.

escarpment A cliff that separates two fairly level pieces of land.

factory Trading post.

gaur Indian bison.

ghat A set of stairs that rises up from a river, especially a river used for bathing.

gymkhana A sports and social club.

gotras Lineages, Brahmans.

hill stations Villages at a high elevation where privileged individuals such as government officials were stationed to avoid India's intense summer's heat.

humus Rich dark earth that is created when vegetables and animals decompose.

insolation Exposure to sunlight.

jatis Social or caste group.

lateritic soils Very hard, brick-like soils.

machans Observation posts.

mawza Village.

nawab Ruler.

pandits Learned scholars.

playa Saline lake beds, known as dhands in India.

pulses Legumes, including beans and peas.

Puranas A class of Hindu sacred literature.

Rajput A warrior of the historical region of Rajputana (now Rajasthan).

sadhus Jain holy men.

sarna Sacred grove.

satyagraha movement "Devotion to truth" movement. A nonviolence resistance movement started by Mahatma Gandhi.

Scheduled Castes Formerly "untouchables"; groups that officially occupy a low position within the traditional caste system.

Scheduled Tribes A term generally applied to indigenous peoples who fell outside the predominant Indian social hierarchy.

schist A kind of mica-rich metamorphic rock that contains somewhat parallel layers that can split into flakes.

Shaivite The cult of the Hindu God Shiva.

shikara A type of gondola-like boat that can be found in Kashmir.

sitar A stringed instrument similar to a lute.

suzerainty A dependent area that is administered by a ruler or a state.

tabla A musical instrument made up of two small drums, one of which is larger than the other.

tanks Rain-filled shallow depressions.

tehsil Political unit of division.

thugs (Hindi: thag) Groups of assassins and plunderers who once roamed across central India.

tirthas Places where Hindus go on pilgrimage.

transhumance The seasonal migration of livestock.

traps Lava outpourings.

Vaishnavism The worship of the god Vishnu.

FOR FURTHER READING

Behera, Navnita Chadha. *Demystifying Kashmir*. Washington, DC: The Brookings Institution Press, 2006.

Bindloss, Joe. *India* (Lonely Planet Country Guide). Oakland, CA: Lonely Planet, 2009.

Danielou, Alain (author), Kenneth F. Hurry (translator). *A Brief History of India*. Rochester, VT: Inner Traditions, 2003.

Editors of Time Out (authors). *Time Out Mumbai and Goa* (Time Out Guides). London: Random House, 2008.

Grover, Nirad. *100 Wonders of India*. Mumbai: Roli Books, 2008.

Habibullah, Wajahat. *My Kashmir: Conflict and the Prospects for Enduring Peace*. Washington, DC: United States Institute of Peace, 2008.

Hardy, Justine. *In the Valley of Mist: Kashmir: One Family In a Changing World*. New York, NY: Simon and Schuster, 2009.

Hollick, Julian Crandall. *Ganga: A Journey Down the Ganges River*. Washington, DC: Island Press, 2007.

Kadur, Sandesh (author) and Kamal Bawa (author), *Sahyadris: India's Western Ghats—A Vanishing Heritage*. Bangalore: Ashoka Trust for Research in Ecology and the Environment, 2005.

Koch, Ebba. *The Complete Taj Mahal*. New York, NY: Thames & Hudson; 2006.

Lobo, Lancy and Shashikant Kumar. *Land Acquisition, Displacement and Resettlement in Gujarat: 1947-2004*. New Delhi: Sage Publications India Pvt LTD, 2009.

Masselos, Jim, and Naresh Fernandes. *Bombay Then and Mumbai Now*. New Delhi: Lustre Press, 2009.

Mehta, Suketu. *Maximum City: Bombay Lost and Found*. New York, NY: Vintage Books, 2004.

Michell, George. *Temple Towns of Tamil Nadu.* Mumbai: Marg Publications, 2008.

Norton, James H.K. *Global Studies: India and South Asia.* New York, NY: McGraw-Hill/Dushkin, 2009.

O'Reilly, James (editor) and Larry Habegger (editor). *Travelers' Tales India: True Stories* (Travelers' Tales Guides). Redwood City, CA: Direct Publishers Group, 1998.

Singh, Malvika, and Rudrangshu Mukherjee. *New Delhi: Making of a Capital.* New Delhi: Lustre Press, 2009.

Tammita-Delgoda, SinhaRaja. *A Traveller's History of India* (Traveller's History). Brooklyn, NY: Interlink Books, 2002.

Thapar, Bindia, Surat Kumar Manto, and Suparna Bhalla. *Introduction to Indian Architecture.* Singapore: Periplus Editions, 2004.

Travers, Robert. *Ideology and Empire in Eighteenth-Century India: The British in Bengal* (Cambridge Studies in Indian History and Society). Cambridge, UK: Cambridge University Press, 2007.

Zaidi, Annie (author), Karuna Ezara Parikh (editor), Karam Puri (illustrator), Akshay Mahajan (illustrator), Vipul Sangoi (illustrator). *Gujarat, A Journey . . .* Gurgaon, Haryana, India: Trio Omni Media, 2008.

INDEX